Emerging English Modals

Topics in English Linguistics 32

Editors

Bernd Kortmann
Elizabeth Closs Traugott

Mouton de Gruyter
Berlin · New York

Emerging English Modals

A Corpus-Based Study of Grammaticalization

by

Manfred G. Krug

Mouton de Gruyter
Berlin · New York 2000

Mouton de Gruyter (formerly Mouton, The Hague)
is a Division of Walter de Gruyter GmbH & Co. KG, Berlin.

♾ Printed on acid-free paper which falls within the guidelines of the
ANSI to ensure permanence and durability.

Gedruckt mit Unterstützung der
Deutschen Forschungsgemeinschaft. D 25

Library of Congress Cataloging-in-Publication-Data

Krug, Manfred G., 1966−
    Emerging English modals : a corpus-based study of gram-
maticalization / Manfred G. Krug.
        p.   cm. − (Topics in English linguistics ; 32)
    Includes bibliographical references and index.
    ISBN 3-11-016654-2 (cloth : alk. paper)
    1. English language − Modality. 2. English language −
Discourse analysis. 3. English language − Grammaticalization.   I. Title.   II. Series.
PE1315.M6 K78 2000
425−dc21
                                            00-056234

Die Deutsche Bibliothek − Cataloging-in-Publication-Data

Krug, Manfred G., 1966−
Emerging English modals : a corpus-based study of grammati-
calization / Manfred G. Krug. − Berlin ; New York : Mouton
de Gruyter, 2000
   (Topics in English linguistics ; 32)
   Zugl.: Freiburg (Breisgau), Univ., Diss., 1999
   ISBN 3-11-016654-2

ut silvae foliis pronos mutantur in annos,
prima cadunt, ita verborum vetus interit aetas,
et iuvenum ritu florent modo nata vigentque. (...)

multa renascentur quae iam cecidere cadentque
quae nunc sunt in honore vocabula, si volet usus,
quem penes arbitrium est et ius et norma loquendi.

Horace, *ars poetica*, 60-72

[As the trees full of leaves change as years go by
and the earliest are falling, so an older generation of expressions falls out of use.
And new ones, just born, flourish and grow vigorous like youth itself.

Many expressions will be born again that have become obsolete, and many will
drop out of use that are now prominent – if usage wants it so.
For with usage lies the judgement and the norm and the standard of language.]

Translation by M.K.

Preface

Many people have contributed in one way or another to this book, which is a slightly revised version of my PhD thesis, submitted to the University of Freiburg in February 1999. I am particularly grateful to my supervisor Bernd Kortmann, whose support has been truly exceptional throughout this project. I would also like to extend my gratitude to Christian Mair, who took on the role of deputy supervisor. Their work and continual feedback have had a pervasive influence on this study, and without them, my interest in grammaticalization would probably never have been triggered in the first place.

There are various other members in the department whom I would also like to thank. Their support is just one indicator of the stimulating and cooperative working environment I am privileged enough to be a part of. For discussions and valuable comments on earlier drafts, I would like to thank in particular Verena Haser, Marianne Hundt and Richard Matthews. Lieselotte Anderwald's company in the office was also of great benefit. We regularly exchanged ideas, research methods and home-made biscuits. I believe I was the main beneficiary, certainly as far as the biscuits were concerned! I wish to thank Lowri Williams and Neale Laker for discussions on (and occasional distractions from) emerging modals. Thanks are further due to Susanne Wagner for her help with the index and layout and also to Allison Felmy for spotting what I hope were the last couple of typos in the manuscript.

I gratefully acknowledge a grant from the German Academic Research Council (DAAD) for a two-month research trip to the United States and heartfelt thanks go to Patricia Slatin for putting me up for several weeks in the Maybeck house on the Berkeley Hills. This research trip had a great impact on the direction of my project and enabled me to discuss my approach and several results with Douglas Biber, Joan Bybee and Elizabeth Traugott. For their interest, support and later comments on the manuscript, I am extremely grateful. Elizabeth Traugott has become the co-editor of this book, and her comments were of great use during the revisions. By granting me access to the unpublished ARCHER corpus at Flagstaff, it was Douglas Biber who made it possible for me to include quantitative long-term investigations in this study. His comments on Chapters 5 and 6 were also much appreciated.

In addition, I gratefully acknowledge a grant from the 'Friends of Freiburg University' for the trip to a symposium on 'Frequency Effects and Emergent Grammar' at Carnegie-Mellon University. Thanks go again to Joan Bybee for inviting me back and for her invaluable feedback on my paper. The discussions with Paul Hopper and other participants at the symposium proved to be most helpful for the present work too. This study has also profited from discussions at various other conferences and talks where preliminary results were presented. Thanks go to the audiences at Albuquerque, Berkeley, Göttingen, Iasi, Kassel and Växjö. I still owe Lucian Anderwald a couple of pints for scanning Peter Trudgill's map of English modern dialects onto the computer, and I thank Peter Trudgill himself for allowing me to plot my distributions of emerging modals on his original map.

Special thanks also go to three old friends. Kathrin Lüddecke's comments on a draft chapter showed me the value of a classicist's views in the field of linguistics; Armin Schüler proved to be just the expert I needed on statistical matters; and the comments from my physics expert Dirk Rudolph led me to refine my ideas relating to the analogy between gravitation theory and developments in the English auxiliary domain. In addition, I would like to thank all those, too numerous to list, who were involved in the compilation of the corpora which I used. It goes without saying that – despite the great help which I have received from so many colleagues and friends – the remaining inadequacies are entirely my own.

My dearest thanks, finally, go to Sandra, whose support and encouragement have played more than an auxiliary role in the completion of this work. In the last three years *haftas* and *gottas* perhaps too seldom gave way to *wannas*. I dedicate this book to her.

Freiburg, May 2000

Contents

List of figures

List of tables

List of maps

1   Introduction

1.1   Subject-matter and central claims

Almost two decades ago, Bolinger argued that "the system of modal auxiliaries in English [is] now undergoing a wholesale reorganization" (1980a: 6). Subsequent research, however, has focused either on general properties and typological aspects of auxiliaries (Palmer 1986; Heine 1993; Bybee et al. 1994) or on the central modals of English. Work on the English central modals in turn falls into two groups: studies of their present-day English semantics (e.g. Coates 1983; Palmer 1989; Sweetser 1990) and studies of their history (Lightfoot 1979, 1991; Plank 1984; Kytö 1991a; Warner 1993; Denison 1993, *inter alia*). Due to the focus on the central modals, Givón's more recent statement is still fairly general and thus reminiscent of Bolinger's observation from 1980:

> The history of the tense-aspect-modal system of English is far from over. New operators are still being introduced into the system; and both those and the system as a whole are in the process of being re-shaped. (1993: 187)

As similar statements by other researchers indicate (e.g. Bybee & Dahl 1989: 60; Croft 1990: 190), it has apparently become received wisdom in linguistics that change is under way in the English auxiliary domain. But despite occasional attempts to handle both central modals and semantically related constructions (Perkins 1983; Matthews 1991; Mindt 1995; Westney 1995), the 'wholesale reorganization' has not yet been adequately documented. So even in 1997, Traugott can still only state:

> the modal auxiliaries *can, could, may, might, must, shall, should, will, would*, and auxiliary *do* have held center stage in recent accounts of the history of English syntax ... and semantics ... However, the so-called quasi-modals (e.g. *be to, be going to, have to, ought to, had better, be about/able/bound to*), which are in an intermediate position between raising predicates and modal operators, have largely been relegated to the sidelines ... [A]s a class the quasi-modals have still not received the attention that they deserve. (1997: 193)

Traugott's term *quasi-modal* covers Quirk et al.'s (1985: 136-148) categories of marginal modals, modal idioms and semi-auxiliaries. Biber et al.'s (1999: Ch. 6.6) taxonomy subsumes these categories under the heading of semi-modals. It is members of these categories that the present investigation will focus on.

This work is essentially based on grammaticalization theory – a branch of linguistics which has gained prominence since the 1980s. It focuses on the interaction between diachrony and synchrony, *langue* and *parole* or, for that matter, competence and performance, I-language and E-language. It does not see these levels as distinct linguistic domains, as much structurally oriented work does. It is important for the present purposes that such an interactionist view entails that per- formance effects may over time cause new grammatical code relations. Hence the importance of statistical empirical research, which led me to adopt a predominantly corpus-based approach.[1]

Based on synchronic and diachronic analyses, I will propose that structures like BE GOING TO, HAVE GOT TO, HAVE TO and WANT TO are currently changing their categorial status. More specifically, I will claim that several quasi-modals are assuming some, but not all, features that are typical of the core members of the English modal paradigm. Let me illustrate some facets of this process: common reduced pronunciations that in writing are rendered as *gonna, gotta, hafta* and *wanna* are indicative of change in progress. The observable synchronic variation can be exploited methodologically to the extent that coexisting variants are seen as reflecting diachronic change. This perspective has become standard in lexicalization and grammaticalization studies (Aitchison 1991: Chs. 3f; Hopper & Traugott 1993: Ch. 1; McMahon 1994: Ch. 9). The following examples of univerbation (or contraction, coalescence, fusion) may help to illustrate this point:

(1)	*want to*	>	*wanta*	>	*wanna*
(2)	*is/am/are going to*	>	*'s/'m/'re going to*	>	*gonna*
(3)	*have got to*	>	*'ve got to*	>	*gotta*

I shall argue that (1) to (3) are instances of ongoing grammatical- ization – more exactly, auxili(ariz)ation – and that the above phono- logical variants represent different stages in the evolution of new auxiliaries.[2] Change, however, is by no means restricted to the phonological level. It is immediately obvious that morphology too is involved when an erstwhile autonomous morpheme (*to*) cliticizes on a verbal host as in (1) to (3). That change is not restricted to phonology comes as no surprise, though, since grammaticalization theory predicts that grammaticalizing elements undergo concomitant changes in semantics, morphology, syntax and pragmatics. Important aspects to be dealt with in the present work include therefore: syntactic reanalysis; phonological erosion; cliticization; increase in discourse frequency;

iconicity; the question of tense neutrality; the genesis of modal semantics; extension from deontic to epistemic or future meanings; semantic generalization; subjectification and other types of pragmatic inferencing.

On aggregate, the evidence will allow for generalizations as regards historical and ongoing change in the English auxiliary system. As will be seen, grammaticalization theory helps to abstract away from a number of seemingly disparate individual developments and reveals a number of striking parallels for the items under investigation. This approach facilitates their integration into a dynamic model of categorization, which supports the assumption that we are witnessing the rise of a new class of English verbs: that of emerging modals.

Positing the rise of a new taxonomical layer is, of course, the result of this study, not its starting point. It emerges essentially from a consideration of the changing linguistic characteristics observable for a subset of items which have commonly been labelled as 'quasi-modals' (e.g. Quirk 1965; Lightfoot 1979; Nagle 1989; Traugott 1997). Categorization, therefore, is here conceived as an ongoing process. In order to be able to model this process, it is necessary for the linguist to identify the major factors at work. The most salient determinants in the present case are almost certainly phonological form, morphosyntactic properties and discourse frequency of potential category members. These variables are thus included in a mathematical simulation of a model which is adapted from classical Newtonian gravitation theory (see Trudgill 1973 for an early application of gravitation in a different linguistic domain).

Perhaps the most important result produced by the model – and hence the best justification for applying it – is that it yields a prototypical internal structure for the group of emerging modals which is intuitively plausible and which is supported by linguistic correlates. If the model is correct, this category contains (at least) the items BE GOING TO, HAVE GOT TO, WANT TO, HAVE TO, NEED (TO), OUGHT (TO) and DARE (TO), where the order indicates decreasing centrality. While the entire field of items interacts in complex ways, the model furnishes evidence that it is chiefly the more central and frequent members (like BE GOING TO) which act as gravitational centres and which influence the more peripheral, less frequent ones (like OUGHT TO). A further reasonable prediction of the model appears to be that degrees of centrality are determined essentially by the number of linguistic properties that are shared among potential category members.

1.2   Emerging modals and emergent grammar

It seems necessary at this point to clarify what I understand by the term *emerging modals*. This section therefore defines the term. First of all, the boundaries between *emerging (modals)* and related concepts need to be delineated. While certainly akin to Hopper's notion of emergent grammar (1987, 1998), my conception of *emerging* is not coextensive with his conception of *emergent* (cf. Hopper 1998: 157). Hopper and this study share the assumption that flux is endemic to language. And from both perspectives, investigating variation in a given language is seen as a suitable heuristic in order to arrive at a better understanding of the flux of language. However, at least two noteworthy differences can be identified. One is that I am probably more optimistic about the existence and observability of synchronic structure, despite recognizing the general flux. It should not go unnoticed, though, that this point is at least partially acknowledged in Hopper's revised version (1998) of his 1987 paper, too.[3] The second difference is that my use of *emerging* is rather specific, hence less far-reaching, since it is applied to only one verbal category of English. I wish to stress, however, that I would expect similar states-of-affairs to obtain in other areas of English grammar and in other languages as well. In general, therefore, the two concepts share much common ground, in particular the fundamental assumption that there is "continual movement towards structure" (Hopper 1987: 142).

Moreover, I use *emerging* in a narrow and a wide sense. In the narrow sense, the term refers only to the four constructions BE GOING TO, HAVE TO, HAVE GOT TO and WANT TO (it will be remembered that the gravitation model identifies these four as the central members of the class). In these cases, the term is meant to indicate primarily that the items are recent: unlike the central modals (*shall, would* etc.), none of the aforementioned constructions is inherited from Germanic. In fact, except HAVE TO, none is attested in Old English. As will be borne out by the empirical chapters, all four constructions have become common only in the course of Modern English, indeed only in the last 150 years. In addition, as short-term and apparent-time studies will reveal, these constructions are currently – i.e. in British and American English at the turn of the millennium – becoming more widely used and, crucially, also more modalized. Therefore, *emerging* carries another implication which is aspectual in nature: that change and spread are occurring under our very eyes.

Further, if one looks at (1) to (3), it is striking that the more recent variants (rightmost column) form a more homogeneous group than their source constructions (leftmost column). That alone might suffice to suggest the rise of a new class of verbs, but such a far-reaching claim calls for substantiation from the ensuing analysis which involves more evidence. Positing a new category, finally, is the link to my second use of *emerging*. In this wider sense, the term is a label for the entire category, and thus additionally includes the items NEED (TO), OUGHT (TO) and DARE (TO). These constructions are different in two ways from the previous group. For one thing, they are older. For another, they are not spreading in present-day English. As far as their discourse frequency is concerned, they are either relatively stable or even decreasing. Nevertheless, diachronically they seem to be assuming precisely those morphosyntactic and phonological properties that are typical of the category of emerging modals, thus suggesting that we are dealing with marginal members of the same class.

1.3 Organization of the individual chapters

Chapter 2 sets out the theoretical, empirical and methodological foundations. These help determine the scope of the study. It concludes with a discussion of terminological problems and a brief review of previous research. Chapters 3 to 5 constitute the empirical body of this work. Chapters 3 and 4 detail the developments undergone by HAVE GOT TO, HAVE TO and WANT TO. Quantitative and qualitative evidence from both historical and contemporary periods of the English language will be presented. Synchronic evidence is essentially variationist in nature: intraspeaker (stylistic) and interspeaker variation (age, sex, region) and their roles in language change will be examined.

Chapter 5 is an attempt at generalization. To that end it presents a cursory look at the highly frequent construction BE GOING TO, but also at the less frequent marginal modals NEED (TO), OUGHT (TO) and DARE (TO). On the basis of this broader range of items, Chapter 5 puts the different strands together so as to identify recurrent paths in the evolution of new English auxiliaries. It is here that a dynamic approach to categorization will be proposed and explained. A model in terms of gravitation will be outlined and tested quantitatively. Chapter 5 also discusses the relevance of the findings of this study for linguistic theory. The final chapter summarizes the main results and delineates areas for potentially fruitful future research in the field of auxiliary verbs.

2 Theoretical, methodological and empirical foundations

2.1 Chapter outline

The major theoretical concepts and frameworks underlying the present study constitute a tightly interwoven network and share many assumptions. These are treated in sections 2.2 to 2.5. While sections 2.2 (Functionalism, economy, frequency) and 2.3 (Grammaticalization) deal with language-internal forces in the diffusion of linguistic change, section 2.4 discusses an important factor in change that operates both within and across languages, *viz.* contact.[1] Evidently, general theories of linguistic change are among the central pillars of this study, but no attempt at a survey of available models will be made (recent relevant monographs include Aitchison 1991; McMahon 1994; Labov 1994; Harris & Campbell 1995; Trask 1996; Lass 1997; Dixon 1997). Nor will I try to cover any of the aforementioned frameworks in depth. Instead, I will focus on how the individual frameworks and concepts bear on the study of language change in progress.

Section 2.5 is essentially methodological; it presents some issues related to corpus-based approaches. Section 2.6 defines the scope and aims of this study. While the scope falls out partly from the theoretical and methodological premises, discourse frequency, too, plays a central role in determining the subject-matter. Section 2.7 describes the synchronic and diachronic sources that will be used in the empirical body of this study and sections 2.8 to 2.10, finally, deal with definitional issues and present a synopsis of previous work.

2.2 Functionalism, economy, frequency

Functionalism, economy and frequency are closely linked and are therefore treated within a single section. There is in fact also considerable overlap between these concepts and grammaticalization theory, but for its unique motivating status grammaticalization is granted separate treatment.

Largely as a response to the rigid formalism of generative grammar and its claims pertaining to the autonomy of grammar, the late 1970s and 1980s saw the development of various branches in the **functional paradigm**.[2] Influential frameworks in this tradition include Dik's Functional Grammar (1978ff), Givónian Functionalism (1979ff), Haiman's Natural Syntax (1980ff), Hallidayan Systemic-Functional Grammar ([2]1994 [[1]1985]), Langacker's Cognitive Grammar (1987; 1991) or Foley & VanValin's Reference Grammar (1984). As an obvious result of this proliferation, functionalism is by no means a monolithic theory. Nevertheless, all functional models exhibit a pervasive influence from the Prague Linguistic Circle and they share a common set of assumptions, most of which are well supported by cross-linguistic investigations. These assumptions are conveniently summarized in Givón (1995: 9):

- language is a social-cultural activity
- structure serves cognitive or communicative function
- structure is non-arbitrary, motivated, iconic
- change and variation are ever-present
- meaning is context-dependent and non-atomic
- categories are less-than-discrete
- structure is malleable, not rigid
- grammars are emergent
- rules of grammar allow some leakage

It goes without saying that a mere list of such functionalist premises is a crude simplification. For discussion and qualification see Givón (1995; 1998), Croft (1995) or the papers in Darnell et al. (eds., 1998) and Lockwood et al. (eds., forthcoming). The histories and intricacies of individual functional approaches, however, need not concern us here.[3] Nor shall I attempt to define the exact role of economy in synchronic and diachronic linguistics. The interested reader is referred to publications by Zipf (1929ff), Hooper (1976), Haiman (1980ff), Croft (1990: Chs. 7, 9; 1995) or Krug (1998a) Here I will pinpoint the ways in which functionalism, economy and frequency interact. Further, I will sketch their relevance for the investigation of language change in general and for the study of emerging English auxiliaries in particular.

Givón's well-known cyclic wave from discourse pragmatics to zero (1979: 208f) plays a pivotal role in defining the relationship between functionalism and language change. According to his model, discourse over time gives rise to the emergence of syntactic constructions, which in turn over time become morphologized. Progressive phonological erosion and lexicalization eventually lead to the loss of overt grammatical material:

(1)   Discourse $\rightarrow$ Syntax $\rightarrow$ Morphology $\rightarrow$ Morphophonemics $\rightarrow$ Zero[4]

This observation has important implications for the evolution of new English auxiliaries (such as *gotta*) from complex constructions (such as HAVE GOT TO). In the ensuing chapters I will build on the functionalist insights mentioned above and utilize them in selecting items for and methods of investigation. Not all stages of Givón's cyclic wave will receive the same amount of attention, even though all will figure in this book. In its historical parts, the present study focuses on mechanisms observable in the early stages of grammaticalization. Here, then, most research will centre around the interface between discourse and syntax. In its variationist parts, however, it is morphology and its neighbouring levels that will take centre stage.

Among the assumptions underlying the Givónian cyclic wave is a rather unexciting-sounding tenet of all functionalist – as well as many nonfunctionalist – approaches. It is concisely expressed by Haiman (1994a: 3): "human languages change through use." Givón has proposed an explanation which aims to specify how and why languages change. He maintains that much language structure has a Darwinian aetiology: in biology, there is a limited variety of organs which perform essential living functions; on all levels of human communication, the number of strategies encountered is smaller than is logically possible. Based on this analogy, Givón (1984: 30) maintains that the driving force in the evolution of structure in language is *functional adaptation* (a term borrowed from evolutionary biology).

As Croft (1990: 253f) points out, much of this adaptation is due to processing constraints. It is here that **economy** factors come into play. Seminal to work on economy are two principles that were isolated on the basis of empirical investigations by Zipf (1929ff). First, his 'Principle of Economical Specialization' informs us that the age of a word in a given language correlates with its text frequency. Second, his 'Principle of Economical Abbreviation' states an inverse correlation between a word's text frequency and its morphological complexity. In a nutshell, frequently employed words tend to be short and old. Such synchronic facts are not without consequences for the study of language change.

In view of the present focus on multi-constituent constructions, it is important to note that Zipf's findings seem to extend beyond the level of individual words. Based on the analysis of contractions like *she's* or *they've*, I have argued elsewhere (Krug 1998a) that **discourse frequency** impacts not only on the history of single-word items. I have suggested that the frequency with which two words cooccur in a sequence can be exploited for predicting the likelihood of their coalescence. This phenomenon is called 'String Frequency Factor'. This factor posits that, other things being equal, the more frequent a given string of words is, the higher becomes the probability that the two items undergo univerbation. Bybee & Scheibman (forthcoming) have demonstrated independently that string frequency also has explanatory power for phonological erosion in longer stretches such as *I don't know*. It will be interesting to see whether this economical principle can also help to account for the grammaticalizing structures under investigation here.

What is not known is the relationship that holds between Zipf's three criteria *age*, *discourse frequency* and *morphological simplicity*. Do these three parameters develop in sync? If not, which of them is primary, which secondary, which tertiary? Further, Zipf's principles do not apply as exceptionless rules in the domain of English auxiliaries. As Biber et al. (1998: 206) note, "the length of the history for a given form does not necessarily correspond to its productivity" (productivity is used here in the sense of 'text frequency'). We would therefore like to know what kinds of constraints are at work in the erosion of constructions and the formation of new categories. The following chapters will attempt to elucidate such issues.

As is obvious from the discussion of Zipfian principles, discourse frequency is probably the most important common denominator of functionalism and economy when it comes to defining their relation to theories of language change. Witness DuBois' (1985: 363) famous dictum that "grammars code best what speakers do most." This is a central postulate of all discourse-based approaches. It makes explicit one consequence of Givón's above-mentioned cyclic wave from discourse pragmatics to zero: frequently occurring entities will be conventionalized, i.e. sedimented, as part of grammar.[5] It is also on such frequentative grounds that certain structures are singled out for investigation in section 2.6: high incidence turns a given item into a candidate which is likely to enter grammaticalization paths – or, rather, into a candidate which is likely to continue its journey along such paths (cf. Bybee et al. 1994: Ch. 1).

Since Zipf's time, frequency of occurrence has played a rather marginal role in the description of language and language change. Much early cognitive linguistics considered frequency as epiphenomenal. Hopper's (1987) work on emergent grammar is an exception. Partly due to the more wide-spread use of computers (see 2.5 below), frequentative research has progressively moved towards the centre of linguists' attention and in the cognitive sciences more generally (e.g. Bybee 1985; 1999a; Kytö 1991a; Harley 1995; Boyland 1996; Torres Cacoullos 1999; Bybee & Scheibman forthcoming; Nübling 2000; papers in Bybee & Hopper forthcoming). The overall trend is also reflected in the make-up of a new major grammar of English (Biber et al. 1999), which is broadly usage-based and hence offers a wealth of quantitative information. Within cognitive linguistics, a trend towards frequentative research can be observed too. A case in point is the 1999 symposium "Frequency Effects & Emergent Grammar" (see papers in Bybee & Hopper, eds., forthcoming). This increasing importance of frequentative matters is reflected in the focus and method of the present study. Mention of emergent grammar leads naturally to the next section on grammaticalization theory proper.

2.3   Grammaticalization

Certainly the central theoretical pillar of this study, grammaticalization merits a somewhat longer treatment.[6] Now, why is grammaticalization all-important in a study of change in progress focusing on the English modal realm? First of all, the ubiquity of grammaticalization has become a linguistic commonplace. Croft (1990: 241f) for instance stresses that in any area of linguistics ongoing grammaticalization is the norm rather than the exception (cf. also Givón's premisses of functionalism cited in the previous section). Croft also clarifies the relationship between grammaticalization and variation:

> Examples of synchronic variation based in grammaticalization patterns are pervasive in the grammars of human language. Careful examination of almost any grammatical domain in any language will reveal variant forms whose phonological structure, grammatical behavior and semantic/pragmatic range of functions differ along one or more of the parameters of grammaticalization.

It is evident that this observation applies to the domain of English auxiliaries. Just compare the layering of partially synonymous structures like HAVE GOT TO, HAVE TO, *gotta*, *must*. Their coexistence in present-day English clearly attests to the initially quoted commonplace that the entire modal system of English is currently being restructured. More significantly, the findings in the empirical chapters will allow for generalizations that have implications for some central issues in grammaticalization theory such as the claim of structural unidirectionality. The following sections briefly review the major claims and lines of development in grammaticalization theory.

2.3.1 Early proponents of grammaticalization theory

As Lehmann (1995 [1982]: Ch. 1), Heine et al. (1991: Ch. 1) and Harris & Campbell (1995: Ch. 2) point out, the origins of grammaticalization research can be traced back at least to the 18th century French philosophers de Condillac and Rousseau. Some more specific claims of modern grammaticalization theory date from the 19th century, notably from research in the tradition of evolutionary typology and agglutination theory (von Schlegel 1818; von Humboldt 1825). Nearly a century later, the neogrammarian von der Gabelentz (1891) was the first to introduce (a) the notion of an evolutionary spiral for the description of the development of grammatical categories, which is a clear predecessor of Givón's famous cyclic wave quoted above, and (b) the two forces *Bequemlichkeitstrieb* and *Deutlichkeitstrieb*, which can be seen as the precursors of Zipfian (1929) economy principles and Horn's (1984) speaker and hearer based Q- and R-principles, notions which will figure prominently in the empirical chapters.

Several pivotal insights that still enjoy currency today are found in Meillet's work from the beginning of the 20th century (1912). As far as we know, it was also he who invented the term *grammaticalization*, which he defined as the development of an erstwhile autonomous lexical word into a grammatical element:

> ['grammaticalization'] consiste dans le passage d'un mot autonome au rôle d'élément grammatical. (1912: 385)

or similarly:

> l'attribution du caractère grammatical à un mot jadis autonome (1912: 385).

While processes that fit Meillet's above definitions indubitably qualify as episodes of grammaticalization today, his emphasis on words appears too narrow now. Meillet also discusses the role of phrases in grammaticalization, but more recently attention has generally moved away from individual words. The modern definitions of grammaticalization quoted in the remainder of this section therefore employ terms like *morpheme, item, unit, element* or *entity* rather than Meillet's *word*. Compare for instance another classic definition by Kuryłowicz:

> Grammaticalization consists in the increase of the range of a morpheme advancing from a lexical to a grammatical or from a less grammatical to a more grammatical status, e.g. from a derivative formant to an inflectional one. (1975: 52 [1965])

Grammaticalization in our present understanding, then, not only encompasses but indeed focuses on more complex constructions (cf. Bybee et al. 1994: 11; Tabor & Traugott 1998; Bisang 1998; Heine 1999; Lehmann 1999; Bybee 1999a, 1999b; forthcoming; Traugott 1999). This is another tendency which is reflected in the topic of the present study.

2.3.2 The Cologne project: Lehmann, Heine and associates

Seminal to much contemporary thinking in grammaticalization is work that was carried out in the early 1980s within the framework of the Cologne Project on Universals and Typology, notably studies by Lehmann, Heine and his collaborators. Clearly, their work did not appear in a vacuum. Simultaneously, independent but related work such as Bybee (1985) or Bybee & Pagliuca (1985) was under way. Both schools owe much inspiration to previous typological studies in the Greenbergian tradition. But even though the papers in Li (1977) on mechanisms of syntactic change and Givón's work *On understanding grammar* (1979) represent modern milestones in the development of grammaticalization theory, it was not until 1982 that the emergence of a new linguistic discipline took clear shape.

In a now classic study, Lehmann (1995 [1982]) was the first to propose a coherent overall framework of grammaticalization. In it he makes rather specific claims about the interaction of six parameters. Table 2.1, to which I will take recourse at various points in the

remainder of this book, illustrates the correlation between these
parameters as grammaticalization proceeds.

Table 2.1.   Correlation of grammaticalization parameters (adapted from Lehmann
1995 [1982]: 164)

parameter	weak grammaticalization	–	process	→	strong grammaticalization
integrity	bundle of semantic features; possibly polysyllabic	–	attrition	→	few semantic features; oligo- or monosegmental
paradigmaticity	item participates loosely in semantic field	–	paradig-maticization	→	small, tightly integrated paradigm
paradigmatic variability	free choice of items according to communicative intentions	–	obligatori-fication	→	choice systematical-ly constrained, use largely obligatory
structural scope	item relates to constituent of arbitrary complexity		– condensation →		item modifies word or stem
bondedness	item is independently juxtaposed		– coalescence →		item is affix or even phonological feature of carrier
syntagmatic variability	item can be shifted around freely	–	fixation	→	item occupies fixed slot

Two years after Lehmann's pioneering work, Heine & Reh (1984)
published a study focusing not so much on historical changes and the
grammaticalization cycle (or spiral) but on the internal mechanisms
involved in the process. Despite the differences in perspective, their
results are broadly consonant with Lehmann's work.[7] Heine & Reh
(1984: 16-45; summarized and slightly revised in Heine et al. 1991: 15,
which I quote for brevity's sake) arrive at the tripartite distinction given
below. The order within and across the processes is taken typically to
reflect their chronological order:

    a) *Functional processes:* desemanticization, expansion, simplification, and
       merger;
    b) *Morphosyntactic processes:* permutation, compounding, cliticization,
       affixation, and fossilization;
    c) *Phonetic processes:* adaptation, erosion, fusion, and loss.

Heine & Reh (1984: 67; again slightly revised in Heine et al. 1991) further provide a list of characteristics which in fact explicates much of the above table taken from Lehmann (1995 [1982]). They state that the further a linguistic unit grammaticalizes,

   a) the more it loses in semantic complexity, functional significance, and/or expressive value;

   b) the more it loses in pragmatic and gains in syntactic significance;

   c) the more reduced is the number of members belonging to the same morphosyntactic paradigm;

   d) the more its syntactic variability decreases, that is, the more its position within the clause becomes fixed;

   e) the more its use becomes obligatory in certain contexts and ungrammatical in others;

   f) the more it coalesces semantically, morphosyntactically, and phonetically with other units;

   g) the more it loses in phonetic substance. (Heine et al. 1991: 15-16)

2.3.3 Recent developments

As has been pointed out, the discipline of grammaticalization has a venerable, long-standing tradition but it was not until the 1980s that it gained importance within linguistics. Indicative of this birth of a new discipline is the 1988 meeting of the Berkeley Linguistics Society, which made grammaticalization the topic of its parasession. The early 1990s, then, in addition to countless journal articles have seen a rapid succession of major works exclusively devoted to the field: three textbooks, that is, Heine, Claudi & Hünnemeyer (1991), Hopper & Traugott (1993), Diewald (1997) and two highly influential collections of papers, that is, Traugott & Heine (eds., 1991, 2 vols.) and Pagliuca (ed., 1994). The first half of this decade also saw the publication of two major typologically oriented works in grammaticalization (Heine 1993; Bybee, Perkins & Pagliuca 1994), and in 1995 Lehmann's seminal study from 1982 was finally made available in print. Interestingly, in all the works cited in this paragraph, English auxiliaries figure prominently. A further indicator of the preeminent status of grammaticalization research in current linguistics – and the terminological profusion in the field – is the appearance of a three-volume dictionary on grammaticalization terminology (Lessau 1994). Two collections of papers that are bound to have an influence on the field have just appeared (Ramat & Hopper, eds., 1998; Joseph & Janda, eds., 1999).

Further work is in progress (Bybee & Hopper, eds.; Kemenade, ed.; Wischer & Diewald, eds.; Fischer et al., eds.).

Despite the fact that the discipline is currently thriving – or maybe indeed because of the profusion of grammaticalization studies – some central aspects still await clarification. In general, current work is aiming to define more precisely "which phenomena are appropriately dealt with under the rubric of grammaticalization" (Ramat & Hopper 1998: 1f). In other words, defining the scope of the discipline is still a major issue. Important questions, then, concern the boundaries of grammaticalization vis à vis lexicalization and reanalysis (e.g. Haspelmath 1998). Such work goes hand in hand with attempts to turn grammaticalization into a formally more adequate theory. That this is a necessary undertaking is indicated by the fact that some adherents of formal approaches to language (most notably linguists standing in a generativist tradition) entertain the view that grammaticalization does not deserve to be called a proper theory at all (e.g. Newmeyer 1998: Ch. 5; cf. also the discussion in Darnell et al., eds., 1998).

Let us briefly consider some of the reasons for the current widespread appeal and success of grammaticalization. One reason is surely that this line of research has fruitfully integrated – and continues to integrate – advances in the domains of semantics, syntax, morphology and phonology, as well as advances in the area of categorization. Therefore it is no coincidence that today grammaticalization and the theoretical frameworks outlined above are closely interrelated and mutually profit from progress in individual branches. Most of the major proponents work in more than one of these fields. Another reason for the appeal of grammaticalization is the reconciliation of two fundamental oppositions in much structuralist research of the 20th century: synchrony vs. diachrony on the one hand and *langue* vs. *parole* (or related dichotomies) on the other. As for the first alleged dichotomy, rather than favour an exclusively synchronic or an exclusively diachronic approach to language, grammaticalization adopts a panchronic view. In doing so it has elucidated the relationship between ongoing variation and historical change (see Lehmann 1985). As to the latter dichotomy, from a grammaticalization perspective *parole* is seen as impacting on *langue* (e.g. Traugott & König 1991: 189), a point which is concisely made also by Bybee (1998: 236): "language use shapes the grammar and lexicon."

To conclude, grammaticalization owes much of its appeal to its truly interdisciplinary nature. It is this bridging of previous divides in linguistics which makes grammaticalization one central component of what Croft (1990: 258f) has described as the 'dynamic paradigm':

> This ... may turn out to be a new linguistic paradigm, the **dynamic paradigm**, in which the study of all types of linguistic variation – crosslinguistic (typology), intralinguistic (sociolinguistics and language acquisition) and diachronic (historical linguistics) – are unified.

Let us return to a more modest level, which is more immediately relevant to the identification of grammaticalization episodes in the domain of English auxiliaries. Particularly relevant to the present study is Hopper's 1991 article "On some principles of grammaticization," since it focuses on early stages of grammatical change, which are less easily accessible than changes that have gone to completion. Hopper (1991: 22) identifies five principles underlying the evolution of grammatical items which will figure prominently in this work, too:

(1) *Layering:* 'Within a broad functional domain, new layers are continually emerging. As it happens, the older layers are not necessarily discarded, but may remain to coexist with and interact with the newer layers.'

(2) *Divergence:* 'When a lexical form undergoes grammaticalization to a clitic or affix, the original lexical form may remain as an autonomous element and undergo the same changes as ordinary lexical items.'

(3) *Specialization:* 'Within a functional domain, at one stage a variety of forms with different semantic nuances may be possible; as grammaticization takes place, this variety of formal choices narrows and the smaller number of forms selected assume more general grammatical meanings.'

(4) *Persistence:* 'When a form undergoes grammaticization from a lexical to a grammatical function, so long as it is grammatically viable, some traces of its original lexical meanings tend to adhere to it, and details of its lexical history may be reflected in constraints on its grammatical distribution'

(5) *De-categorialization:* 'Forms undergoing grammaticization tend to lose or neutralize the morphological markers and syntactic privileges characteristic of the full categories Noun and Verb, and to assume attributes characteristic of secondary categories such as Adjective, Participle, Preposition, etc.'

More recently, Traugott (e.g. 1995, 1997) has stressed that subjectification often accompanies grammaticalization (see Ch. 3.2.1 below for a brief discussion). There is a continuing line, though, between this newer claim and her general emphasis on pragmatic factors in grammaticalization (e.g. 1982; 1988; 1999). Current work in the field is partly attempting to formalize the theory, partly voicing caveats concerning rather strong claims made previously (cf. papers in Ramat & Hopper 1998). Many caveats centre around the claim of unidirectionality, others concern the notion of scope. Nordlinger & Traugott (1997), for instance, have offered an analysis of *ought to* which discusses whether or not scope restriction (see Table 2.1) is an adequate criterion of grammaticalization (their answer is no). Some researchers have questioned the omnipresence of reanalysis in grammaticalization (e.g. Haspelmath 1998). We will return to these issues in the empirical chapters. Bisang (1998), finally, stresses the role of contact in grammaticalization. This will be tackled from a more general perspective in the next section.

2.4   Contact-induced change and sociolinguistic dialectology

In the last decade, contact-based explanations of variation and change have received new impetus from two linguistic disciplines: typology and research into regional variation within individual languages.[8] As to the former, several members of the EUROTYP project (e.g. Kortmann 1997; van der Auwera, ed. 1998; Thieroff 1999) and studies based on the GRAMCATS database (e.g. Bybee 1997) have demonstrated that areal factors are far from insignificant in crosslinguistic research and that there is abundant empirical evidence for positing present-day convergence areas beyond the well-known Balkan *Sprachbund*.[9]

More directly relevant to the present study are recent developments in work on language-internal regional variation. First of all, a 1996 collection of essays on American English (Schneider, ed.) contains several contributions which stress the omnipresence of contact phenomena (Kretzschmar; Mufwene; Frazer; Fennel & Butters).[10] More important from a methodological point of view, Schneider (1996: 1) notes that the gap between the two most prominent research traditions in intralanguage variation – (traditional) dialect geography and Labovian sociolinguistics[11] – has narrowed immensely:

> Some thirty years ago, camp affiliations were strong – so-called 'dialect geographers' and so-called 'sociolinguists' would have held conflicting opinions on questions such as principles of informant selection [or] the nature of reliable data ... Today, boundaries between sub-fields have become blurred ...

Not only have methods and data bases become more alike, there has also been a paradigm shift as regards subject-matter in dialectology. As

Schneider has observed, "the study of **variation** and **change** of linguistic varieties has largely replaced earlier, monolithic notions of dialect."[12] A relatively new approach crosscutting subdisciplines has been labelled "sociolinguistic dialectology" (Chambers 1993). Such interdisciplinary research addresses various problems which McMahon (1994: 231) has identified in much traditional dialect research:

> They all [i.e. traditional dialect surveys carried out in Germany, France England, Scotland, Italy or the USA] involve essentially the same methods of dialect geography, using direct interviewing, questionnaires or a combination of the two, and the results are usually published in atlas form, with each map showing the particular variants of a word used in different areas of the country. These are frequently of limited interest, notably because data are often presented without analysis or attempts at explanation, and especially because of their emphasis on 'purity' – the recording of a dialect before it becomes corrupted by the young or by incomers from other areas. To obtain information on this unsullied state, early dialect surveys concentrated on only one type of informant, the NORMS ... or Non-mobile, Older, Rural Males. Speakers falling into this category were generally thought to speak a 'purer' version of the dialect than mobile individuals, who might have had their speech contaminated by other varieties; young people, who more easily incorporate innovations into their language; urban informants, who are surrounded by speakers of different varieties; and women, who ... tend to produce more standard speech than men.

As was mentioned before, in its 'synchronic' parts this study is essentially a sociolinguistic variationist study in the Labovian research tradition. In other words, by pursuing a study of language variation and change, I shall try to elucidate the roles of precisely those variables which are excluded from most traditional dialect research, *viz*. different age groups and sex. Following the aforementioned trend towards a sociolinguistic dialectology, however, I will also employ methods of dialect geography. Graphs showing regional distributions will be plotted and isoglosses identified. Wikle (1997) discusses the theoretical foundations of the cartographical techniques which underlie the method adopted here.

In one respect, however, the present study is fundamentally different from most previous work in traditional dialect geography. Rather than deal with categorial differences, I will approach diatopic (as well as diastratic) differential behaviour statistically, that is, in terms of degrees (a model is Kretzschmar 1996). This is a natural consequence of the subject-matter and changing external conditions. As for subject-matter, part of the present work aims at a research gap in dialectology. While many studies exist on phonological and lexical differences, relatively little is known about dialect syntax. Anderwald & Kortmann (forthcoming) note this general dearth of syntax studies in dialect research:

> Up to the 1980s syntax played almost no role in dialect research, and since then only few studies on variation in dialect grammar have been published. Most of these studies are confined to a single grammatical phenomenon in one dialect. What is virtually non-existent are comparative studies of a particular phenomenon in a representative selection of dialects, for instance in the dialects of England, Scotland and Ireland.[13]

In a similar vein, Fennell & Butters (1996: 285) appeal for more frequentative analyses on syntactic dialectal variation in particular:

> It is a great pity that dialectologists in past generations have so frequently overlooked syntactic variables in favor of phonological, morphological, and lexical ones. One hopes that modern dialectologists will be more scrupulous about recording actual occurrences of syntactic variables, so that future researchers who wish to work panchronically may be more comfortable with their conclusions.

Their appeal for statistical approaches is particularly relevant to the present study. Since grammatical(izing) structures are by definition frequent in all varieties, it is trivially true that approaches in terms of presence or absence of a grammatical unit are pointless. Further, relatively clear-cut isoglosses (of the type that may still hold for nouns like *bonnet*) seem less likely today than in previous times, even in the lexicon. This is chiefly because of changing external conditions: modern communication networks and socioeconomic developments result in the erosion of traditional dialects (Chambers 1993). Such developments, then, call for variationist approaches in *all* areas of research. Further, researchers widely agree that British dialects are currently converging.[14] Convergence affects predominantly morpho-syntax, and only to a lesser extent the sound system or the lexicon (McMahon 1994: 213). Since morphosyntax is the focus of the present study, statistical analyses seem indispensable.

In sum, different worlds and different subject-matters seem to require different methods. Consequently modern dialectologists, especially those working on morphosyntactic variation, have to resort to methods involving large and if possible representative machine-readable databases as well as to statistical methods in order to test their hypotheses. Corpus-based methods are the topic of the next section.

2.5   A corpus-based approach

Corpus-based research is one of the fastest-growing areas in linguistics. Indicative of this development is the publication of a vast body of recent corpus-based studies and the emergence of a series (*Language and Computers: Studies in Practical Linguistics*). A new journal that is explicitly devoted to the field (*International Journal of Corpus Linguistics*) was recently published for the first time. Also, over the last few years as many as five textbooks have appeared (Stubbs 1996; McEnery & Wilson 1996; Barnbrook 1996; Biber et al. 1998; Kennedy 1998).

I will not enter the rather futile discussion whether corpus linguistics constitutes a linguistic branch in its own right or just a method. Below I list the most important characteristics of contemporary corpus-based analysis, which, taken together, "result in a scope and reliability not otherwise possible" (Biber et al. 1998: 4, from where the following points are adapted):

- it is empirical, analyzing the actual patterns of use in natural texts;
- it utilizes a large and principled collection of natural texts ... as the basis for analysis;
- it makes extensive use of computers for analysis, using both automatic and interactive techniques;
- it depends on both quantitative and qualitative analytical techniques.

Even though fruitful corpus work in roughly the above sense was carried out long before the advent of computer (e.g. Käding 1897; Zipf 1929ff), the introduction of machine-readable databases with sophisticated search programmes has immensely facilitated the quantification of processes that were difficult to investigate before. A case in point is the observation of a diachronic increase in discourse frequency, which is now established as a central criterion of grammaticalization (cf. Bybee et al. 1994: 8; Lehmann 1995: 127-30). Coates (1983: 3) and Palmer (1989: x) make a strong case for corpus-based research into English modal verbs. The present functionalist-frequentative approach to the study of emerging modals in fact necessitates modern corpus-related methods of investigation.

English has profited disproportionately from the general trend towards compiling corpora. It is doubtless the language for which the greatest variety of corpora is currently available. Some of the largest databases of present-day English owe their existence at least partly to the interest, and funding, of dictionary compilers (e.g. the Bank of English Corpus; the British National Corpus). But there is also a considerable number of projects – both completed and in progress – whose main objective is to improve existing descriptions of the relevant periods and varieties of the English language. These include the Lancaster-Oslo-Bergen Corpus and the Brown Corpus (both with texts from 1961); their Freiburg analogues from 1991/92; the Historical Part of the Helsinki Corpus (comprising Old, Middle and Early Modern English); and A Representative Corpus of Historical English Registers (texts from 1650 to the present).[15] Many of these projects have been completed very recently or will shortly be released. This puts the present researcher in a very fortunate situation and explains why this study could not be carried out before.

2.6   Scope and aims

2.6.1   Scope

Here is not the proper place for defining auxiliarihood (see the discussion in 2.8). Quite on the contrary, definitional premises seem counterproductive at this early stage, because they might narrow the focus of the present study in arbitrary ways. Heine (1993: 70) provides a typological definition of auxiliarihood: "An auxiliary is a linguistic item covering some range of uses along the Verb-to-TAM-chain."[16] TAM, that is "tense, aspect, modality etc." (Heine 1993: 53), can in no way be handled within a single study. For feasibility I therefore exclude bound morphemes. A loose working definition of the present scope, then, involves three criteria:

> The present study will investigate **verbs** and **verbal complexes** (not bound morphemes) which take a **verbal complement** and contribute to making **grammatical distinctions** in the domains of tense, mood, aspect, modality, voice and *Aktionsarten*.[17]

Hence, at the outset the term *auxiliary* is taken in a literal, rather broad sense. It denotes a 'helping' construction which involves a verb that has syntactic and/or semantic scope over another verb. The remainder of this section will limit the scope of this study on the basis of four additional criteria:

(i)   the theoretical foundations outlined in the preceding sections

(ii) the state of the art in the domain of auxiliary verbs and verbal complexes

(iii) feasibility restrictions and practical considerations

(iv) empirical facts: actual discourse frequency will be exploited as an indicator of functional importance

While factors (i) to (iii) are fairly conventional in scope considerations, the empirical factor (iv) may appear rather radical at first sight. Making discourse frequency an overt, central criterion is probably novel; in essence, however, it is far from revolutionary. First, any study dealing with grammar advocates, if implicitly, frequency as an underlying criterion because there is a correlation between grammatical status and high frequency.[18] Second, as has been pointed out above, empirical research ties in closely with functionalist theory. Horace was one of the first writers to stress the primacy of spoken discourse. His famous functionalist dictum (the motto of this work) considers usage to be the prime factor in language change (*ars poetica* vv. 60-72). Proceeding from this assumption, I take spontaneous speech to be the most appropriate data base for establishing frequency rankings that hold explanatory potential for ongoing developments.[19] There are at least two reasons for taking this view. First, it is spontaneous private speech that we can expect to be least subject to monitoring. Thus we exclude two factors which have often been claimed to be inhibiting linguistic change, *viz.* prescriptivism and formality considerations. Second, it is face-to-face interaction that constitutes the primary and most natural communicative contact situation (in its most general sense, that is understood as the encounter of idiolects in social networks). According to established linguistic theory (e.g. Milroy & Milroy 1978, 1991; Croft 1995; Chambers & Trudgill 1998; Mufwene forthcoming), this type of language-internal contact facilitates adaptation, accommodation and thus the propagation of innovative features.

Let us begin by considering some empirical facts. Figure 2.1 and Appendix 1 survey the discourse frequency of the most common lexical verbs,[20] all modal verbs and the marginal modals NEED (TO), OUGHT (TO), DARE (TO) and USED TO. A total of 130 verbs was investigated. We can therefore rather confidently assume that Figure 2.1 and Appendix 1 (the continuation of the top 30 verbs given here), include the top eighty verbs of English spontaneous speech.[21]

Notice that the discourse frequencies of the individual verbs as found in the spontaneous speech of the BNC are remarkably congruent with those obtained by Biber et al. (1999: Chs. 5f). This consonance suggests that given a sufficiently large spoken corpus, frequency distributions of very common verbs will be recurrent, irrespective of the sampled individual discourse topics and text types. This in turn seems to permit the interpretation of frequency patterns in terms of general cognitive and functional importance.

It seems worthwhile to briefly discuss the import of Figure 2.1 and Appendix 1 for the relationship between discourse frequency and grammatical status. For the sake of convenience and simplicity, I consider as *grammatical* all those items which according to Quirk et al. (1985: 120-146) have at least a loose connection to the English auxiliary complex. In their classification (see Table 2.7 below), these include the central modals, primary verbs, marginal modals, semi-auxiliaries and modal idioms.[22] For illustration, it is best to set out the proportions of auxiliary verbs in tabular form:

Table 2.2.   Proportions of auxiliary verbs among the 80 most frequent verbs in spontaneous spoken British English

High-frequency verbs	1-10	11-20	21-30	31-40	41-50	51-60	61-70	71-80
Proportion of auxiliary verbs	50%	40%	40%	20%	20%	0%	0%	10%

It is striking that the proportion of auxiliary verbs (when measured in groups of ten) progressively decreases from the first ten verbs to the next ten, and so on. The proportion drops sharply after the top thirty verbs from 40% to 20%. This is the ratio for the fourth and fifth groups. After these 50 most frequent English verbs, grammatical items crop up rather sporadically (less than one in ten on average). In other words, there is a tantalizing correlation between high frequency and auxiliary status: among the top thirty verbs almost half enjoy auxiliary status, and at 20% the correlation between auxiliary status and the 31st to 50th verb is still significant.

On frequentative grounds, therefore, the first 30 verbs of English conversation represent an attractive frequency-based cut-off point for the scope of this study. But it is not only the proportion of auxiliary verbs that drops sharply for the next group, it is also essentially the top 30 verbs that exceed an incidence of one occurrence per thousand words (which is the same as 1,000 per million) in the spontaneous speech of the BNC. To render such figures in more accessible relations: on standard estimates (e.g. Biber et al. 1999: Ch. 5) one per thousand words translates roughly into one occurrence in ten minutes. According to the same estimator, BE would occur on average some 6 times per minute, GET roughly once per minute, and GOING TO once in three minutes. These figures refer to the average number of words produced in natural conversation. Notice though that this is a low estimate. If we carry out a calculation in terms of speech production (roughly 6 syllables or 3 words per second are a standard measure, cf. Aitchison 1994: 7), the incidence would be roughly twice as high. It is further noteworthy that the 50th most frequent verb (at approximately 500 occurrences per million words) is very nearly half as frequent as the 30th. This incidence will figure prominently below in the discussion of historical material, when I shall try to identify initial stages of grammaticalization of certain constructions.

Let us now turn to a brief discussion of the corpus findings. Among the top 30 verbs, modal verbs form the largest group: *can, will, would, could, should* (plus their clitic forms *'ll, 'd*). The most frequent ones are the primary verbs (BE, DO, HAVE). GET, the next most frequent item, is arguably a member of this class, too, as will shortly be explained. Only a few lexical verbs are found among the top 30 verbs of English spontaneous speech. These fall into the following natural semantic classes:

(i) cognitively important verbs pertaining to the world of reasoning and/or perception such as KNOW, SEE, THINK, MEAN, LOOK

(ii) verbs of saying, feeling and reporting (overlapping with the preceding group): MEAN, SAY, TELL, THINK

(iii) verbs that are commonly used in equative (copular) patterns: GET, LOOK

(iv) highly generalized verbs of motion: COME, GO

(v) generalized dynamic verbs for expressing thematic roles such as benefactive, patient or agent: GIVE, MAKE, PUT, TAKE

(vi) volitional verbs : LIKE, WANT (+ NP)

Figure 2.1 and Appendix 1 offer a fruitful ground for functional considerations on cognitively important verbs, but such a discussion extends beyond the scope of the present study. The above groups of highly frequent verbs, then, are outside the scope of this work because they do not qualify as auxiliaries according to the working definition outlined at the beginning of this section.

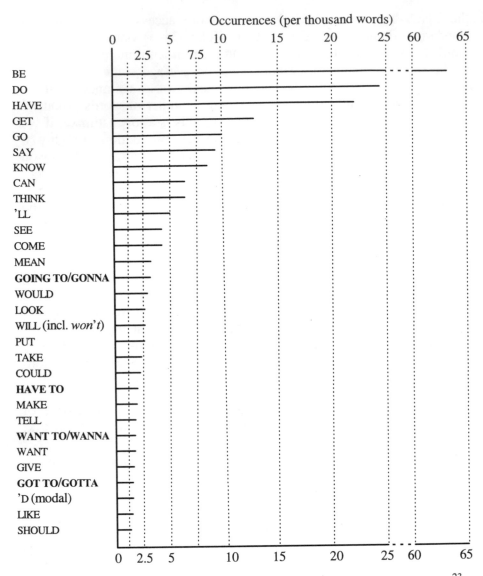

Occurrences (per thousand words)

Figure 2.1.   The 30 most frequent verbs in spontaneous speech in the BNC[23]

Further, we know rather a lot about the primary verbs BE, DO and HAVE. These can function as either auxiliary or main verbs.[24] It is hardly surprising, therefore, that they top the list of the most frequent English verbs. Clearly, this is in part due to their auxiliary status in a number of grammatical constructions (perfect, passive, negation, questions). On frequentative grounds alone, GET deserves to be classified with BE, DO and HAVE. But there are also two formal criteria which justify this classification among the group of primary verbs. First, GET is commonly employed as an auxiliary in passive constructions (as in *He got beaten*), an option leaning towards the informal pole when compared to the BE passive. Second, like BE, GET is highly frequent as a main verb in equative structures, where, different from BE, it has an inchoative meaning component (cf. *It gets* 'becomes' *interesting*). Yet even though GET qualifies as an auxiliary in a vast number of uses, it will not be the subject of the present study since it has been dealt with in some detail in a number of recent studies (such as Hübler 1998: Ch. 7; Hundt forthcoming), some of them corpus-based (e.g. Johansson & Oksefjell 1996). In sum, for reasons of feasibility and because the primary verbs have been widely discussed, I will not investigate these four most frequent auxiliary verbs of present-day English. On similar grounds this study will not be concerned with the group of central modal verbs.

The four verbal complexes which fit all the criteria for inclusion in the present study are, then, (BE) GOING TO, HAVE TO, WANT TO and (HAVE) GOT TO. First, they easily qualify as auxiliary constructions on the basis of the above definition: they contain verbal nuclei and are semantically related to the central modals (formal criteria will be discussed in the empirical chapters). Second, their fundamental cognitive and functional importance emerges very clearly from the above chart. All three rank among the 30 most frequent verbs in English conversation and are well ahead of a number of central modals and of all marginal modal verbs. In fact, the positions of (BE) GOING TO etc. can be assumed to be even higher. The verbal status of such items as MEAN, SEE and KNOW, for instance, is often debatable because they are prominent in discourse markers and highly generalized constructions.[25] Third, the four items singled out all take infinitival *to* complements. Syntactically, therefore, they form a rather homogeneous group which lends itself well to a corpus-based investigation. Fourth and perhaps most important, despite their high discourse frequency, they have largely been neglected in the linguistic literature. This statement applies least to BE GOING TO. It is probably no coincidence that the most frequent item has received the most attention in the literature, if only in recent years. BE GOING TO has in fact become the paradigm case of grammaticalization (e.g. Hopper & Traugott 1993: Chs. 1, 3; Traugott 1994; Danchev & Kytö 1994; Mair 1997; Berglund 1999; Nicolle 1998; Poplack & Tagliamonte forthcoming; or, from a creolist perspective, Mufwene 1996b). Thus, in the present study BE GOING TO will be discussed less exhaustively than the remaining three constructions.

2.6.2 Aims

The main goal of the present study is to integrate synchronic and diachronic variation into an overall framework of grammaticalization. In other words, I attempt to present what might be termed an 'integrative study of synchronic and diachronic variation'. My more specific aims, then, are twofold. On the one hand I will investigate the domain of modality in English; on the other, I try to present a general account of the diffusion of linguistic change. Both aims address a research gap in the area of English auxiliarihood: even though GOING TO (frequently) and WANT TO (occasionally) do receive mention in seminal works on grammaticalization (e.g. Hopper & Traugott 1993; Traugott 1994; Bybee et al. 1994), no integrative study of either BE GOING TO, HAVE GOT TO, WANT TO or HAVE TO is available so far. More important than integrative studies for each individual item is a discussion within a single volume that attempts to identify and explain parallels between them. In order for such a study to render descriptively adequate results, it must not omit – as most previous studies have done – important variants such as *wanna, gonna* and *gotta*. Only by including such variants can one expect to gain a better understanding of the commonly stated reorganization in the realm of English modality. Among the modal-specific questions that the present study will address are the following:

I.   Diachronic development
   - How have these structures evolved so as to occupy their prominent position in present-day English?
   - What are the motivations for their rise?
   - Which mechanisms of change (such as metaphor, context-induced inferencing, drastic increase in discourse frequency and generalization) occur at which stage of the grammaticalization process?

II.   Synchronic description
   - How do the items interact with other items from the same semantic domains?
   - What are their syntactic and stylistic constraints?
   - How do they pattern regionally?
   - How are they distributed along social parameters of variation such as age, sex or education?

Since this is a study on grammaticalization, it goes without saying that we also want to elucidate how the two levels of description relate to one another. In which ways do synchrony and diachrony interact in the field of developing modals? And it is here that we touch on the interface between the narrow confines of modality and a more general dynamic model of categorization and linguistic change. Due to pivotal theoretical and typological studies such as Hopper & Traugott (1993), Bybee et al. (1991; 1994) and Heine et al. (1991) we now know a lot about the general processes involved in grammaticalization, the forces at work as well as the resulting crosslinguistic paths of development. But we still know relatively little about the intricacies of grammaticalization.[26] It is only from a wealth of empirical studies that we can identify these intricacies. The present study aims to be a modest contribution to the missing evidence. And since it is, *inter alia*, a study of change in progress, the identification of synchronic patterns of distribution (variation according to style, region, sex, age) can perhaps sometimes be more than (merely) a descriptively adequate account. Ideally, that is, when recurrent, such synchronic patterns can be interpreted as pathways in the diffusion of linguistic change. In sum, it is hoped that the approach to the study of synchronic and diachronic variation offered here will not only lead to new insights into developments in the domains of English modality but also represent a first step towards a unified account of variation as envisaged by Croft (1990, 1995).

2.7   The sources of the present study

This section introduces the corpora that will be used in the present study and briefly outlines the motivation behind their use. Thus it relates the empirical sources to the methodological foundations outlined in the preceding sections. Two fundamentally different approaches to the study of change are available. The real-time approach investigates the usage of certain phenomena across different stages of a given language, for instance a development from Old English via Middle and Early Modern English to present-day English. It is truly diachronic in that language users or records of their usage from different periods are consulted. This approach is realized here by the combined use of historical and present-day English corpora. A study in apparent time, by contrast, investigates usage patterns of language users from one period only, usually the period contemporary to that of the researcher.

McMahon (1994: 242) summarizes the expected distribution of older and newer variants in a given speech community where change is under way:

> A variant being introduced by linguistic change will occur much more frequently in the speech of younger people... However, a variant being lost... [will be encountered] with many more occurrences in older informants.

A further approach to language change can either focus on individual synchronic stages, or it can combine diachrony and synchrony. It compares different styles and genres in order to identify which language varieties tend to be conservative, which progressive. If such a study is conducted exclusively on the basis of current material, this may help isolate recurrent pathways of change which in turn allows one to make predictions about future developments while a change is still in progress.[27] Comparing different genres and styles is not a new approach, but it has recently been refined methodologically by Biber (e.g. 1988, 1995), Sigley (1997) or Hundt & Mair (forthcoming). Its strong point is that it can be fruitfully combined with the real time approach (e.g. Biber & Finegan 1997; Biber 1998), which adds a further variationist dimension. In the present study this third approach is reflected in the investigation of

   (i) different types of variation in the British National Corpus (informal spoken, formal spoken, written),

   (ii) press and fictional language in four British and American one-million-word corpora from 1961 and the 1990s,

   (iii) drama and fictional language in ARCHER.

These corpora are described in more detail in the next sections.

2.7.1 Historical corpora

In order to carry out real time studies and to trace the origin of the structures under investigation, two historical corpora are used: the diachronic component of the Helsinki Corpus and the ARCHER Corpus (A Representative Corpus of Historical English Registers).

2.7.1.1 *The diachronic components of the Helsinki Corpus*

Denison (1993: 3) notes that much historical work had to rely on previously sampled "great repositories of information" such as the *Oxford English Dictionary* (1933; [2]1989; OED) or Jespersen's (1909ff) and Visser's (1963ff) multi-volume grammars of English.[28] He goes on to point out the usefulness of the Helsinki Corpus for studies such as the present one:

> In future the materials collected for the Helsinki Corpus of English Texts should provide a useful controlled sample, especially for comparing usage in different periods, genres, registers, and so on.

The diachronic components of the Helsinki Corpus comprise the periods from Old English to Early Modern British English. Table 2.3 (adapted from Kytö 1991b: 2) presents an overview of how the material is spread across individual subperiods.

Table 2.3.   Diachronic components of the Helsinki Corpus

Sub-period		Words	Percentage
OLD ENGLISH			
I	-850	2 190	0.5
II	850-950	92 050	22.3
III	950-1050	251 630	60.9
IV	1050-1150	67 380	16.3
Total OE		413 250	100.0
MIDDLE ENGLISH			
I	1150-1250	113 010	18.6
II	1250-1350	97 480	16.0
III	1350-1420	184 230	30.3
IV	1420-1500	213 850	35.1
Total ME		608 570	100.0
EARLY MODERN BRITISH ENGLISH			
I	1500-1570	190 160	34.5
II	1570-1640	189 800	34.5
III	1640-1710	171 040	31.0
Total EMODE		551 000	100.0
Grand Total (all periods)		**1 572 820**	

2.7.1.2 ARCHER

ARCHER (A Representative Corpus of Historical English Registers) covers seven subperiods of 50 years, in all spanning the time between 1650 and 1990. It is a highly valuable source for the present study since, as far as the items under investigation are concerned, the most dramatic changes have occurred precisely during that period. ARCHER data are drawn from both written and speech-based registers. Each 50-year subcorpus includes roughly 20,000 words per register (some are larger), typically containing ten texts of approximately 2,000 words each. The entire corpus totals some 1.7m words, roughly two thirds of which are British English, while the remaining third is American English (for details see Biber et al. 1994b). Table 2.4 and Table 2.5 (both reproduced from Biber et al. 1994a) present the corpus design in terms of geographical and chronological coverage as well as distribution across different registers:

Table 2.4.   Chronological and geographical coverage of ARCHER

British	American
1. 1650-1699	
2. 1700-1749	
3. 1750-1799	4. 1750-1799
5. 1800-1849	
6. 1850-1899	7. 1850-1899
8. 1900-1949	
9. 1950-1990	10. 1950-1990

Table 2.5.   The registers of ARCHER

Written	Speech-Based
Journals-Diaries	
Letters	
Fiction	Fictional conversation
News	**Drama**
Legal opinion (1750-; USA only)	Sermons-Homilies
Medicine (excluding 18th cent. USA)	
Science (British only)	

In keeping with the Horatian motto of this study, here too I will observe the primacy of spoken language. The component of fictional conversation (i.e. conversational passages of the fiction subcorpus) is too small to allow for quantitative analysis of the items under investigation. Therefore, the drama subcorpus (c.0.23m words) will be the most important historical source for the present study. Among the registers included, it is certainly the best (though clearly not a perfect) approximation of natural spoken English. In order to avoid spurious findings, hypotheses will be checked against the fiction subcorpus (c.0.47m words). A pilot study of 18th century registers by Biber (1998) seems to warrant the concentration on these two registers. It ranks drama way ahead of all remaining registers on a dimension which comes closest to a spoken-written cline. On this dimension, fiction comes second. These are the only registers which have positive values for the conversational dimension in Biber's study.

2.7.2   Corpora of contemporary English

2.7.2.1   *Four one million word corpora of written English: Brown, LOB, Frown and FLOB*

The archetype corpus (Brown) consists of written American English texts from 1961. It contains 500 samples of approximately 2,000 words each, giving a grand total of c.1 million words of running text (for the distribution across different genres, see Table 2.6 below). The British Lancaster/Oslo-Bergen Corpus was modelled on this corpus. At the University of Freiburg two analogues have recently been completed, called Frown and FLOB (short for Freiburg versions of Brown and LOB). They match their predecessors as closely as possible except that the texts are from 1992 and 1991, respectively.[29]

Table 2.6.   1m word corpora of written PDE (Brown, LOB, Frown, FLOB)

Categories		American Brown (1961) Frown (1992)	British LOB (1961) FLOB (1991)
A	Press: Reportage	44	44
B	Press: Editorial	27	27
C	Press: Reviews	17	17
D	Religion	17	17
E	Skills and Hobbies	36	38
F	Popular Lore	48	44
G	Belles Lettres	75	77
H	Miscellaneous	30	30
J	Learned	80	80
K	General Fiction	29	29
L	Mystery & Detective Fiction	24	24
M	Science Fiction	6	6
N	Adventures & Western	29	29
P	Romance and Love Story	29	29
R	Humour	9	9
Total	(approx. 1 million words)	500	500

Consulting these four corpora of present-day British and American English is doing research at the interface between synchronic and diachronic linguistics. First, brachychronic real-time studies spanning 30 years (that is, one generation) are possible for each side of the Atlantic divide. Second, comparisons of the developments in either variety add a regional dimension of change. This, then, allows statements regarding progressiveness and conservativeness of these two varieties of written English. In other words, based on the above four corpora, we can spot change as well as determine and compare speeds of change in British and American English.

As was the case with ARCHER, there are more and less adequate subcorpora for the present purposes. Obviously, there is no genuinely speech-based register in Brown or its analogues. A study by Hundt & Mair (forthcoming), however, suggests that the text types given in Table 2.6 can be organized on a continuum in terms of their susceptibility to change, yielding slow, conservative or 'uptight' genres on the one hand and progressive or 'agile' ones on the other. This continuum largely corresponds to a cline of formality, where the ones leaning towards the formal end appear rather stable, whereas the genres leaning towards the informal end appear prone to change from below. The overall result is hardly surprising, but it should not go unnoticed that such a cline lends full support to a functional approach to language change. It suggests strongly that much natural change is ultimately triggered by the conventions of informal (that is, prototypically, spontaneous spoken) language.[30] The subcorpora primarily consulted in the present work are therefore 'agile' genres of Table 2.6: press language (categories A to C; c.0.18m words) and fictional writing (categories K to R; c.0.26m words).

2.7.2.2 The British National Corpus

The British National Corpus (hereafter BNC) was released in 1995. The complete corpus totals some 100m running words of text, of which 90m words are written and 10m words are spoken British English.[31] For the present purposes the spoken part is its most important component. Size apart, the second major asset of the BNC is that it aims at being a representative sample of present-day British English. Compare the following statements made by people involved in the compilation process:

> The BNC aims to build a corpus that can be taken to be representative of modern British English. (Clear 1993: 167)

Two years later Burnard (ed., 1995: 19) makes a representativeness claim at least for the subcorpus of spontaneous speech:

> The approach adopted uses demographic parameters to sample the population of British English speakers in the United Kingdom. Established random location sampling procedures were used to select individual members of the population by personal interview from across the country taking into account age, gender, and social group.

Another three years later in the *BNC Handbook*, a representativeness claim is couched in more cautious terms (Aston & Burnard 1998: 31-36). Despite various provisos (see 2.7.3 below), however, the spoken BNC is a valuable source. It is currently the only corpus available that allows large-scale quantitative research along different parameters of variation. Studies in apparent time or studies of social and regional variation on a similarly broad data basis are simply not otherwise possible at the turn of the millennium. As section 2.7.3 will explain, not all results produced by the corpus can be taken at face value. Rather they have to be interpreted against the backdrop of previous empirical research and linguistic theory.

As for the text types used in the present study, the written component will not figure prominently. Suffice it here to say that it contains almost exclusively post-1975 texts from various domains labelled 'imaginative', 'arts', 'leisure', 'science' or 'world affairs'. The spoken component falls into two subcorpora of roughly equal size, *viz.* spontaneous and more formal language:

- a *demographic* component of informal encounters recorded by a socially-stratified sample of respondents, selected by age group, sex, social class and geographic region;

- a *context-governed* component of more formal encounters (meetings, debates, lectures, seminars, radio programmes and the like), categorized by topic and type of interaction. (Aston & Burnard 1998: 31)

2.7.2.3 Newspapers on CD-ROM and literary texts

Occasionally, data will be provided from the British up-market daily newspaper *The Guardian* (1990-1997) on CD-ROM. It is a far larger database than the 176,000 word press subcorpora from Brown and its analogues, but it is not representative.

The complete works of Shakespeare (approximately 0.9m words from c.1600) are a valuable source of additional historical material. For qualitative research, supplementary data from modern British fictional texts will occasionally be collected. These include works by Oscar Wilde (turn of the last century), Daniel Defoe (early 18th century), Jane Austen and Charles Dickens (early 19th century). These works are meant to enlarge the database for the period in which the items under investigation underwent major changes.

For convenience, let me conclude this chapter with a chart sketching the most important databases that will be used in the present study. The focus on British English emerges very clearly from Figure 2.2. Further, there is a cluster of corpora in the second half of the 20th century, which in turn throws into relief the emphasis on contemporary English.

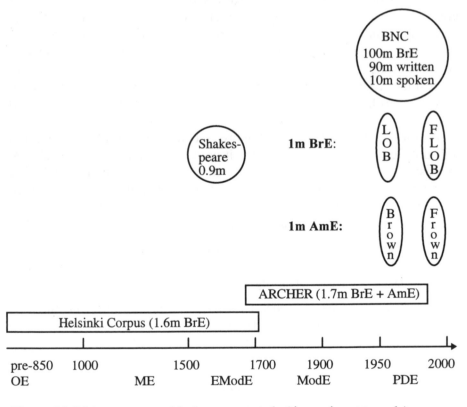

Figure 2.2. Main sources used in the present study (time axis not to scale)

2.7.3 Methodological caveats

This is the place to voice a number of methodological notes of caution. Most of them concern the nature of the corpora. The ARCHER design is ingenious for its mix of different genres and historical periods. The consequence of its richness in historical and register stratification, though, is that each fifty-year subcorpus is rather small for a given genre (on average 20,000 words). This drawback is partly remedied by the representativeness of the corpus, but sometimes it will be necessary to collapse two subcorpora (hence double both size and time span) in order to even out statistical outliers. In a weaker form this argument holds for the four one-million-word corpora (LOB, FLOB, Brown, Frown). But here the sizes of the fictional and press subcorpora is considerably greater (c.0.26 and c.0.18m words, respectively). On the historical dimension, time depth is a greater problem for the four one-million-word corpora, which span some 30 years. From these corpora alone, conclusions as regards historical change have therefore to be drawn very carefully. Additional information from longer-term trends (ARCHER and the Helsinki Corpus) will improve the judgements.

In order to avoid spurious findings, statistical tests will generally be provided. In accordance with much of the linguistic literature (e.g. Hofland & Johansson 1982: 13; Woods et al. 1986: Chs. 8f) chi-squared tests at the 5% level (i.e. $p < 0.05$) will be considered statistically significant. It should be noted, however, that statistics do not represent a safeguard against foolish conclusions; they may indeed sometimes facilitate them. Due to the size of the corpora, not all findings will be statistically significant. This applies in particular to the smaller corpora. On the other hand, equally due to its size, not all findings that are statistically significant in the large British National Corpus will be linguistically significant (see Woods et al. 1986 on the influence of sample size on statistical tests). It will therefore always be the accumulation of findings which leads to safer conclusions.

With its spoken component of 10m words the BNC is the largest spoken source of English currently available. This asset in size brings in its train a drawback regarding accuracy of transcription. As Gleason (1965: 368) observes, transcription of spoken language "always involves editing to some extent." Some twenty-five years later, despite the development of more refined techniques to investigate articulatory phenomena, such as electropalatography or electromyography, Nolan & Kerswill (1990: 308) still consider the execution, as well as interpretation, of transcriptions "highly problematic." The situation is unchanged today. While not written as a comment on the spoken BNC, Chafe's (1998: 93) statement points to some fundamental provisos that attach to the 'enhanced orthographic' transcription method which was used for its spoken component:

> visual representations of language always leave out much that is present in actual speech; when we speak of 'reducing' language to writing, the implications of the word 'reducing' are cogent.

The kind of sophisticated methods which Nolan & Kerswill find highly problematic were obviously not employed for transcribing the BNC. Crowdy (1995) describes the transcription method.[32] It is important for the present purposes that the 'enhanced orthographic' transcription scheme includes a distinction between full and contracted variants of some items under investigation here. *Wanna, gonna* and *gotta* were on a list of 'non-orthographic words' which was used by the transcribers. With the high number of transcribers and a limited number of cross-checks (20%), absolute consistency cannot be ensured. It is therefore important that the items under investigation are high-frequency constructions. On statistical grounds (high-frequency items combined with a great number of transcribers), deviations from the prescribed transcription process will be levelled rather than aggravated.

The greatest caveats attach probably to the interpretation of regional data, because the only speakers who are reliably tagged are the informants who carried the tape recorders. These assigned their interactants to regions without necessarily knowing where they came from.[33] One may assume that most speakers should have known those interlocutors who they tagged for region, but this must remain speculation so long as the tapes are inaccessible. Two further complicating factors relevant to geographical tagging are of course regional mobility of speakers and accommodation phenomena.

To conclude, individual results have to be interpreted with a great deal of caution due to the limitations of the resources. I will not point to the tentative nature of each and every finding in the empirical chapters, though. Caveats are understood throughout this study. It should also be stressed, however, that the variety of sources that the present researcher is able to use exceeds by far most previous empirical studies on English auxiliaries. Hence, while individual findings must always be seen as preliminary, one can be more confident when different sources point in the same direction (Labov 1970: 57). In addition, the plausibility of the present findings is also strengthened when they are consonant with typological studies. Fortunately, with Bybee et al. (1994) a thoroughly empirical crosslinguistic study for the field of auxiliaries is available. This provides a convenient reference point and a source of testable hypotheses for the present study. In sum, not every individual result can be taken at face value and many results will be preliminary. It is only from the overall picture, which arises from the accumulation of a host of independent data, that conclusions can be drawn.

2.8   Defining modality and auxiliarihood

2.8.1   Definitional issues

An enormous body of literature has been written on defining auxiliari-hood and modality (see e.g. Palmer 1986; Nagle 1989; Heine 1993; Hengeveld forthcoming). Unfortunately, agreement is largely confined to acknowledging the difficulty of this undertaking. As for the wider notion of auxiliary, witness for instance Heine (1993: 16, emphasis added):

> Many authors tend to employ the term *auxiliary* for elements marking such functions as **tense, aspect, or modality that are not affixes or inflections**. There is, however, considerable disagreement with regard to the exact range of notional domains that are associated with the use of auxiliaries.

The concentration on elements which are not realized as bound morphemes is adopted here too (see 2.6.1). Heine (1993) offers a lucid overview of the different approaches. There is no need to discuss them here because definition is not the central concern of the present study. As for the more narrow confines of modality, the situation is not much better. Compare for instance Palmer's (1986: 4) somewhat defeatist statement:

> The first task is to identify the relevant area of meaning; this is not easy in the case of modality. ... To begin with, the definitions are, in practice, vague and difficult to apply with any degree of precision, and do not lead to clearly distinct categories. The real problem with modality, moreover, is not just that there is great variation in meaning across languages, but that there is no clear basic feature. ... Where precise criteria are given, moreover, the precision may be more apparent than real, and may involve special pleading or a degree of circularity.

In a similar vein, Bybee et al. (1994: 176, emphasis original) note:

Mood and **modality** are not so easily defined as tense and aspect. A definition often proposed is that modality is the grammaticization of speakers' (subjective) attitudes and opinions ... Recent cross-linguistic works on mood and modality, ... however, show that modality notions range far beyond what is included in this definition. In fact, it may be impossible to come up with a succinct characterization of the notional domain of modality and the part of it that is expressed grammatically.

Palmer (1986: 4f) points further to the existence of different degrees of grammaticalization for modal markers, a problem which is immediately relevant to the present study:

Even at the formal grammatical level, grammaticalization is a matter of degree, of 'more or less' rather than 'yes or no'. Inflectional mood is a very clear example of grammatical marking, but the markers of modality may be modal verbs, clitics or particles. Whether these are grammatical or not can only be decided in terms of the degree to which they have syntactic restrictions and the extent to which they can be defined as a limited rather than open-ended system of items. ... [A] modal system (or any other grammatical system) will develop gradually over time, and at any one point in time will have reached a particular stage of development and so show a particular degree of grammaticalization.

The highly distinctive morphosyntax of the English central modals, which as modal verbs (e.g. *may*) or clitics (e.g. *'ll*) enjoy a rather advanced grammaticalized status, has attracted the attention of many researchers. Other modality markers in English, however, have been largely neglected (cf. Traugott 1997). What Palmer does not mention are modal *constructions*, which figure more prominently in current work. As was made clear in section 2.6, it is the central goal of the present study to investigate the properties and pathways of change of English verbal constructions which fall into the notional domain of modality. Also, the present study will not focus exclusively on syntactic restrictions, whose importance is emphasized in the above quotation by Palmer. Semantic, pragmatic and phonological aspects will enter the discussion crucially. Such an analysis can be expected to reveal different degrees of grammaticalization for the respective items.

This study will not add a further lengthy taxonomical discussion to the burgeoning literature on auxiliarihood and modality. Interested readers are referred to Heine (1993), Matthews (1993: 113-137) or van der Auwera & Plungian (1998). These accounts complement each other in providing a synopsis of how the relevant terms have been defined in previous work. It is important that despite definitional problems it emerges very clearly from language comparison that *auxiliary* and *modal* are indeed helpful labels crosslinguistically (e.g. Heine 1993: Chs. 1f; Bybee et al. 1994: *passim*). Van der Auwera & Plungian (1998: 80) take a pragmatic stance regarding definitional issues:

> Modality and its types can be defined and named in various ways. There is no one correct way. The only requirement is that one makes clear how one uses one's terms.

This will be done in the following paragraphs. Traditionally, the major distinction is between *deontic* and *epistemic modality* (e.g. Lyons 1977; Palmer 1986; 1994; Sweetser 1990; Traugott 1997; Hengeveld forthcoming).[34] Both terms were first used in modal logic (von Wright 1951: 1f) and are derived from classical Greek. *Deontic* is immediately derived from the deverbal noun δεον 'that which is needed', but goes back ultimately to the verb δεω 'bind', 'need'. Deontic modality, then, is concerned with 'obligation' and 'permission'. Examples include:

(2)   I *must* go home now. (Mum says so.)
(3)   You *may* go home now. (School is over.)

Epistemic modality (from Greek επιστημη 'knowledge'), on the other hand, commits the speaker to statements about the truth of a proposition. The semantic domains that are generally referred to as epistemic are thus 'probability', (logical) 'necessity' and 'possibility'. Examples include:

(4)   He *should* be at home. (The Super Bowl is on tonight and he wouldn't miss it.)
(5)   They *might* be in the cinema. (They talked about going this afternoon.)

A minor issue is that not all analysts agree as to whether or not 'volition' (also called 'desire') should be included within the semantic domain of modality. This study will follow a long-standing tradition including Jespersen (1924: 320) and the majority of researchers discussed by van der Auwera & Plungian (1998) who subsume 'volition' under deontic modality. Scholars adopting the same stance include Givón (1984), Palmer (1986) and Hengeveld (forthcoming). Tradition apart, there is some justification inherent in the term *deontic* that warrants the inclusion of volitional modality: the middle form of Greek δεω, i.e. δεομαι, has actually a 'desire' reading.

More recently, Joan Bybee (1985: Chs. 8) and her collaborators (Bybee & Pagliuca 1985; Bybee et al. 1991; 1994) have suggested a somewhat different classification based on typological work. In Bybee et al. (1991: 23), they distinguish between the following types of modality:

i.   *agent-oriented* (desire, obligation, ability, root possibility, permission)
ii. *epistemic* (possibility, probability)
iii. *speaker-oriented* (imperative, hortative, optative)

This categorization grid is further refined and slightly revised in Bybee et al. (1994: Ch. 6, App. B). As is immediately obvious, Bybee et al.'s classification is not fundamentally different from traditional approaches. The difference that is relevant to the present study is their introduction of 'agent-oriented' modality. Across languages, Bybee et al. maintain, this category better captures synchronic polysemy patterns on the one hand and diachronic paths of development on the other. It should be noted though that the concept of agent-oriented modality overlaps to a great extent with the concept of deontic modality. In addition to 'permission' and 'obligation', which are traditionally associated with deontic modality, they include 'desire', which is still a mainstream approach (see previous paragraphs). Two further important notions that Bybee et al.'s (1994) most recent definition of agent-oriented modality also encompasses are 'ability' and 'intention'. Significantly, they do not dismiss deontic modality as a useless concept. They exclude it from their taxonomy because "it cuts across the modality domain in a way that is not cross-linguistically valid" (1991: 23).

Since in the present study I will usually employ unambiguous subtypes of modality such as 'obligation' or 'intention', taxonomical issues will rarely be of importance. Nevertheless, where broader semantic notions are required, I will generally use the somewhat narrower traditional term *deontic modality*, primarily because it is more specific and because it will be more familiar to most potential readers. This is not a dogmatic decision, though. Where necessary, the wider term *agent-oriented modality* will be used as well.

The inclusion of 'intention' under agent-oriented modality by Bybee et al. (1994) leads me to the last point regarding taxonomy. Due to the "general fluidity of so-called categories" (Hopper & Traugott 1993: 7), 'volition', 'intention', 'prediction' and futural readings shade into one another synchronically.[35] Significantly for the present purposes, they also develop out of one another diachronically (see, for instance,

Traugott 1972 on semantic changes in the history of the English modals since Old English; relevant crosslinguistic work is reported in Chung & Timberlake 1985; Bybee et al. 1991; Bybee et al. 1994: 240). Further, due to overlaps, it is simply not feasible to disambiguate these senses. Take for instance intentional readings of BE GOING TO and futural examples: both notions certainly qualify as auxiliary uses; all, except (perhaps) future, qualify as modal uses. In the present study, futural uses are covered by *modality*, too. For English, this is by no means a novel approach. It has been adopted by the major reference works on English grammar in general (Quirk et al. 1985: 120-137; Biber et al. 1999) and on English modality in particular (Leech 1971 [²1987]; Lyons 1977; Palmer 1986; 1989; Coates 1983).

2.8.2 Properties of English auxiliaries and modals

Many criteria have been advanced in previous research for defining auxiliarihood in different languages. Heine (1993: 22-24) is an excellent summary. As far as the English auxiliaries are concerned, probably the best – and certainly the best known – syntactic description to date is that by Quirk et al. (1985: 120-148).[36] Related in perspective, but with a focus on quantitative data, is Biber et al. (1999). Below I provide Quirk et al.'s (1985: 137) synchronic continuum of auxiliary verbs and their list of criteria. Both will prove helpful reference points in the remainder of this study.

Table 2.7. The auxiliary verb - main verb scale (Quirk et al. 1985: 137)

	Class of verbs	Examples
(one verb phrase) ▲	(a) CENTRAL MODALS	*can, could, may, might, shall, should, will/'ll, would/'d, must*
	(b) MARGINAL MODALS	*dare, need, ought to, used to*
	(c) MODAL IDIOMS	*had better, would rather/sooner,* BE *to,* HAVE *got to,* etc
	(d) SEMI-AUXILIARIES	HAVE *to,* BE *about to,* BE *able to,* BE *bound to,* BE *going to,* BE *obliged to,* BE *supposed to,* BE *willing to,* etc
	(e) CATENATIVES	APPEAR *to,* HAPPEN *to,* SEEM *to,* GET + *-ed* participle, KEEP + *-ing* participle, etc
(two verb phrases) ▼	(f) MAIN VERB + nonfinite clause	HOPE + *to*-infinitive, BEGIN + *-ing* participle, etc

Table 2.8.   Criteria for auxiliary verbs (adapted from Quirk et al. 1985: 137)

AUXILIARY CRITERIA (Op = operator)	AUXILIARY	MAIN VERB
(a) Op in negation	He *cannot* go.	**He *hopes not* to go. (*cf* Note)
(b) Negative contraction	*can't*	**hopen't*
(c) Op in inversion	*Can* we go?	**Hope we to go?*
(d) Emphatic positive	**Yes, I DÒ can* come.	Yes, I DÒ *hope* to come.
(e) Op in reduced clause	I can come if you *can*.	**I hope to come if you hope.*
(f) Position of adverb	We *can always* go early.	We *always hope* to go early.
(g) Postposition of quantifier	They *can all* come. ?They *all can* come.	?They *hope all* to come. They *all hope* to come.
(h) Independence of subject	Ann can do it. ~ It can be done by Ann.	He hopes to do it. **It hopes to be done by him.
MODAL AUXILIARY CRITERIA	MODAL AUXILIARY	MAIN VERB
(a) Bare infinitive	I *can go*.	**I *hope go*.
(b) No nonfinite forms	**to can, *canning, *canned*	*to hope, hoping, hoped*
(c) No -*s* form	**She *cans* come.	She *hopes* to come.
(d) Abnormal time reference	You *could* leave this evening. [not past time]	You *hoped* to leave this evening. [past time]

NOTE [original]   *He hopes not to go* is acceptable in the sense 'He hopes that he will not go'; but this is then a case of the negation of *to go*, not of *hopes*.

2.9   The relevance of the history of English central modals to the study of emerging modals

This study investigates ongoing grammaticalization in the English verbal system and proposes that a new class of modal constructions is currently emerging. Grammaticalization paths are recurrent both crosslinguistically and within the history of particular languages (cf. Bybee et al. 1994: *passim*). One should therefore take a brief look at the history of the modal system in English in order to better understand current developments.

It is a well-known fact that the category of present-day English central modal verbs has evolved from an inventory of Old English preterite present verbs. While this class of verbs had a highly irregular *morphology* and modal *semantics* even in pre-Old English times, in Old

English their *syntactic* behaviour was essentially that of all main verbs (but see Plank 1984; Warner 1993 for qualifications). They progressively developed criteria that became unique to their class. More specifically, they developed four morphosyntactic features that distinguish them from (a) other auxiliary verbs and (b) lexical verbs (see Table 2.8 above). This gradual focusing of their category status consisted on the one hand in retaining characteristics that were previously available to all verbs, such as NOT negation or inversion in questions. On the other hand, the central modals also developed new distinctive properties by losing their nonfinite and tensed forms, or their tensed forms lost largely their potential to refer to past time (e.g. *must, might*).

The class of present-day English central modals is not coextensive with the OE inventory of preterite present verbs. Some preterite presents were lost such as *uton* 'let's', *THURFAN 'need', WITAN 'know'. Also, the class of central modals was supplemented by one non-preterite present verb: *will*. This had modal (originally, volitional) semantics, too. And its similarly irregular morphology groups WILLAN alongside the Old English preterite presents on formal grounds as well (cf. Denison 1993: 296). In this study I shall argue that such a gradual development of modal features is not restricted to historical periods of the English language but that HAVE GOT TO, HAVE TO, WANT TO and BE GOING TO are following rather similar paths under our very eyes.

2.10   Previous research on emerging modals

While the history of the central modals has received an enormous amount of attention in the linguistic literature, there is no book-length treatment of developments in the area of modal *constructions* that covers the time since Middle English. As was indicated above, the history of BE GOING TO has recently been elucidated by e.g. Hopper & Traugott (1993), Danchev & Kytö (1994) or Mair (1997). Little research – and particularly little corpus-based research – has been carried out for other items. Brinton's unpublished paper from 1991 and Fischer's article from 1994 (both deal with HAVE TO) are exceptions. So too is Nordlinger & Traugott's (1997) article on *ought to*. Traugott (1997) has also dealt with *promise* and *threaten* and their relation to the modal domain, largely in terms of subjectification (e.g. *It promises to be interesting*). These rare historical studies will be discussed in the relevant places of the empirical chapters.

What is available is a host of synchronic analyses. Broadly, they fall into two classes. Largely functionally oriented descriptive accounts contrast with mentally oriented generativist accounts which strive to explain the presence or absence of certain surface representations. The present study is different in perspective from either of these, since it tries to integrate diachronic and synchronic evidence in a theory of grammaticalization. I begin with a summary of descriptive accounts.

2.10.1 Largely descriptive approaches

Various monographs and reference works on present-day English have treated in some detail the grammar and semantics of constructions that fall into the semantic domain of modality (like BE GOING TO, WANT TO, HAVE TO, NEED TO, HAVE GOT TO). An early treatment is Haynes (1967). Later work – like Palmer (^{2}1989 [^{1}1979]), Quirk et al. (1985), Matthews (1991), Westney (1995), Mindt (1995) and Biber et al. (1999: Ch. 6.6) – falls into essentially the same category, even though these studies vary considerably in focus. All provide detailed discussions of syntactic, morphological, semantic and pragmatic aspects as well as comparisons with the central modals, which it would be pointless to repeat here.

Two of these studies (Mindt 1995 and Biber et al. 1999) are corpus-based in a more narrow sense as outlined on page 21 above. Both provide much valuable quantitative information on semantic and syntactic properties of the investigated constructions. Mindt's study has several drawbacks, though. Unlike Biber et al., Mindt does not adequately specify the registers which were investigated, and information on what texts entered his corpora is scarce. Second, Mindt's study is radically empirical. So much so that it does without a bibliography. Even though it is claimed that "there has been no borrowing from previous grammars" (p. 6), some of its terminology seems to be partly inspired by Quirk et al. (1985) or Haynes (1967).

Let me conclude this section with a brief discussion of two publications which partly triggered the present study. The first is an article by Bolinger (1980b) which stresses the gradience of auxiliaries and which has proved rather influential in the relevant literature (see e.g. the adaptation in Heine 1993: 72). Bolinger ranks ten items according to their degree of auxiliariness. This foreshadows a grammaticalization approach both in terminology and by adducing criteria from various domains (phonological, morphological, syntactic):

Table 2.9.   The gradience of auxiliaries (adapted from Bolinger 1980b: 297)

Condition[†]	1	2	3	4	5	6	7	8	9
'Fully established auxiliary'									
should	●	●	●	●	●	●	●	●	●
ought to	·	●	●	●	●	●	●	●	●
used to		·	·	●	●	●	●	●	●
got to					●	●	●	●	●
be supposed to					●	●	●	●	●
have to				·			●	●	●
be going to					·	·	●	●	●
want to							·	·	●
try to									●
regret to									
'Not-yet-auxiliary'									

† Conditions: 1, bare infinitive complement; 2, subject inversion; 3, negative contraction; 4, tagging; 5, non-subordination to a main verb; 6, defective conjugation; 7, VP deletion; 8, epistemic, aspectual or modal meaning; 9, *to* or *have* contraction. Heavy dots mean that the condition is well satisfied (not necessarily 100%), light dots that it is slightly satisfied.

While I do not agree with all of Bolinger's individual analyses (see empirical chapters), his method of applying a multi-criteria categorization grid that allows for gradience in category membership is very convincing as such. Related to this approach – and possibly influenced by it – is Quirk et al.'s (1985: 137) scale between full verbs and auxiliaries (see Table 2.7 above). This too has proved influential in the pertaining literature. Allowing for such clines solves some of the taxonomical problems in the domain of modal verbs and modal constructions (but not all). Both accounts are broadly compatible with grammaticalization theory.

2.10.2 The contraction debate

An account of developing auxiliaries would be incomplete without mentioning the famous contraction debate. Horn made an observation of a 'minimal pair' which was first mentioned in Lakoff (1970: 632):

(6)   Teddy is the man I want to succeed.
(7)   Teddy is the man I wanna succeed.

While (6) is ambiguous between

(6)'   'I want to succeed Teddy' and
(6)"   'I want Teddy to succeed',

(7) can only receive the first of these interpretations.

A related claim followed which stated that in most dialects of English, sentences with coreferential subjects like (8) allow *wanna* contraction, while those without subject identity like (9) do not:

(8)   Who do you wanna succeed?
(9)   *Who do you wanna succeed the president?

A review of the debate that ensued would merit a study in its own right. As Pullum & Zwicky (1988: 271) note, a "bewildering profusion of analytical proposals" has been put forward. Essentially they centre around the question of whether traces account adequately for the alleged blocking of contraction in sentences like (9). Postal & Pullum (1982) provide an excellent overview of the first decade, Pullum (1997) reports more recent contributions. Both summaries are not impartial, though. Barss (1995), Baltin (1995) and Radford (1997: 269f; 318f), present the alternative view, *viz.* that (generative) syntactic constraints can account for the presence or absence of contractibility. Further verbs figured in the discussion but WANT has remained by far the most prominent item. Bolinger (1981: 189) considered it "the single most written-about verb in recent discussions of English syntax." This was some two decades ago and many publications followed. Too many for the editor of the *Linguistic Inquiry*, who in 1986 (editor's note, p. 95) took the unprecedented step of declaring a moratorium on the topic.[37] In any case, the debate provides ample evidence of a statement made by McCloskey (1988: 18) on the style of dispute in the field of syntax:

> The study of syntax, for reasons that have never been clear ... has always been a more acrimonious business than the pursuit of sister-disciplines in formal linguistics. Phonologists, morphologists, semanticists and phoneticians can all survive and cooperate in courteous disagreement, but syntacticians seem to thrive on a more robust diet of anger, polemic and personal abuse.

Consider for instance Bolinger's (1980b: 292) statement that "*wanna* has taken its place alongside *colorless green ideas* among those expressions sacred to linguistic confabulation." Or take another extended metaphor against generativism, also by Bolinger (1981: 200):

> The great error of formalism has been to exclude speaker and hearer as explanatory concepts and to treat language as an infinitely ingenious mechanical toy that runs by itself and challenges clever minds to ferret out the works. The trace is another pawl in the self-propelled mechanism that prevents the toy from falling off when it reaches the edge of the table. It requires no assistance from that deux [*sic*] ex machina, a human speaker with an intent to communicate.

Here is not the place for yet another review of the debate. For convenience, Appendix 2, a reproduction from Postal & Pullum (1982: 131), presents a list of representative examples which figured in the debate. Whenever the present study yields results that are relevant to the debate, they will be discussed. The latest noteworthy contribution to the debate is Pullum's analysis in *Language* (1997). It is noteworthy because it represents a radical step away from previous accounts. In the description of what he calls the seven 'therapy verbs' (*wanna, gonna, usta, hafta, gotta, oughta, sposta*), Pullum dismisses generativist syntactic accounts on the one hand and lexicalization accounts on the other. Instead he suggests an account in terms of derivational morphology. In essence, Pullum suggests that a "morpholexical rule suffixes /tu/ ~ /tə/ to the base lexemes to form derived lexemes such as WANNA" (1997: 79). In other words, Pullum believes that "*to* is a suffix," very much like *under-* is a prefix in words like *undergo* (p. 85).

Even though in itself coherent and capable of accommodating a wealth of facts about the verbs in question, Pullum's approach misses out a number of potentially illuminating points, most significantly perhaps the link between phonological variants, frequency of occurrence and their impact on syntactic constituent structure and categoriality. Problematic is also the way in which he precludes NEED TO from his analysis (p. 82). These issues will be taken up in later parts of the present study. Further, he fails to mention that all the verbs which he does include have close semantic (and as we shall see also morphosyntactic) affinities with modal verbs. Aspects of language change in progress and grammaticalization are not touched upon. Another problem is that Pullum provides no statistical data or at least attested examples. He works exclusively with a (largely intuition-based) tripartite distinction between grammatical, ungrammatical and marginally acceptable. This is not only his problem. Lack of authentic data is in fact characteristic of the whole debate. Unfortunately, for instance, common pronunciations are considered unlikely.[38] Further, Pullum believes that there are no semantic or syntactic differences between the phonological variants (1997: 85). As the empirical chapters will show, this claim needs qualification.

Probably due to the lack of authentic data, various examples put forward in the debate are contrived, to say the least. One has to question the centrality of some aspects which have figured prominently in discussions on *to* contraction since the 1970s (cf. Appendix 2). As Aoun & Lightfoot (1984: 466) correctly point out, various sentences discussed in the literature "do not slip smoothly over the tongue." Reminiscent of this, Pullum (1997: 90) admits the marginality of some sentences.[39] Consider for instance:

(10)   ?I want to/*wanna present themselves in my office all those students who failed the test.

(11)   ?I don't want to/*wanna do nothing to be the response of this administration.

Notice that (11) represents a major step towards natural discourse compared to its notorious predecessor:

(11)'   I don't want to/ *wanna flagellate oneself in public to become standard practice in this monastery (e.g. Postal & Pullum 1982).

Or take another example, which is similarly difficult to process when spoken (quoted from Pullum 1997: 95):

(12)   I want, to be precise, a yellow four-door De Ville convertible.

While full forms in (10), (11) and (12) may be grammatical, such sentences are hardly ever produced in natural language, probably due to the constraints of online processing.[40] Beyond questioning a few individual example sentences of a linguistic debate, the above discussion suggests strongly that an adequate account of language should not so much focus on creativity and potentially well-formed sentences – fascinating though this may be – but take natural language as the basis of investigation. The fundamental role of discourse effects for all levels of grammar is still somewhat underestimated in current mainstream linguistics. Perhaps, however, the increasing importance of functionalist and grammaticalization studies as well as the recent tendency towards corpus-analytic approaches can be interpreted as initial signs of a paradigm shift in contemporary linguistics.

Finally, Pullum's statement that *wanna* (together with other items to be discussed) "is not modal" (1997: 82) needs qualification. He dismisses modal status on the basis of one single morphological criterion, *viz.* the existence of 3SG present suffix. As will be recalled from the preceding sections, there are more criteria for deciding on category membership in the English modal realm. Quirk et al.'s (1985: 137) list quoted above contains as many as twelve criteria; Heine's (1993) list even exceeds that figure.

In sum, I believe that morphology is not the proper locus for a discussion of Pullum's 'therapy verbs'. Nor is autonomous syntax the proper locus. The fact that word-internal assimilation processes are observable for what in writing usually appears as a sequence of autonomous words (like *have to*) is not primarily an indicator of word-formation (as Pullum believes). Rather this is an indicator of increased bonding between two formerly independent items. The framework that is best suited to the nature of this type of variation is grammaticalization theory. What Pullum fails to acknowledge is that there are degrees of membership. As Bolinger argued nearly two decades ago, categories can have more central and more marginal members. Only prototype and related nondiscrete approaches to categorization à la Heine (1993) seem capable of accommodating the often cited 'major restructuring' currently affecting the English auxiliary domain. Heine summarizes the shortcomings of purely synchronic approaches, thus suggesting that an integrated, panchronic approach to English auxiliarihood is needed:

> Any explanatory model that does not take the dynamics of linguistic evolution into consideration is likely to miss important insights into the nature of auxiliaries. (1993: 129)

To conclude the first part of this study, the main value of the contraction debate lies perhaps in pointing to the unease felt by many researchers with traditional classifications of infinitival *to* and the verbs that precede it. I now turn to investigating in some detail the items HAVE GOT TO, HAVE TO, WANT TO and BE GOING TO – on the basis of language in use. While these four items form the focus of the ensuing analysis, I shall conclude this study by integrating the less frequent items DARE TO, OUGHT TO and NEED TO into a more general discussion of ongoing change in the domain of emerging English modals.

3   HAVE GOT TO/GOTTA and HAVE TO/HAFTA

3.1   Chapter outline

This chapter details the grammaticalization of HAVE TO and HAVE GOT
TO. Since HAVE TO is a much-cited example of grammaticalization, the
established theory of its evolution is surveyed initially. Based on
authentic corpus data, the histories of both constructions are
subsequently sketched, which results in a reconsideration of some
claims made previously regarding (a) the periods of their
grammaticalization and (b) the mechanisms of change involved (e.g.
metonymy, metaphor, generalization). An additional discourse-based
factor – the early preponderance of a semi-idiomatized string *I have
(got) to say* – will be proposed as being seminal to the generalization of
both constructions. Discussions of syntactic, semantic, stylistic and
regional aspects and their role in language change ensue.

Before entering the analysis proper, let me clarify the conventions
which I adhere to in the remainder of this study: I will generally
distinguish between spellings like <hafta>, word forms such as *has*,
paradigms such as HAVE (all its word forms, i.e. *have, has, had, having,
's, 'd*). The paradigm HAVE GOT TO, then, covers all word forms of HAVE
(including HAVE deletion) followed by *got to*, plus the form *gotta*.
Phonological transcriptions like /'gɒtə/ and, where necessary, phonetic
transcriptions like ['gɑɾə] are given according to the guidelines of the
International Phonetic Association.

3.2   History and grammatical (re-)analysis

3.2.1   HAVE TO

Deontic HAVE TO entered English around a millennium before deontic
HAVE GOT TO. This is certainly one of the reasons why only the former
has received a considerable amount of attention in the linguistic
literature. Arguing for auxiliary status of HAVE TO, Visser (1969: 1478)
describes its semantics and its historical development:

> In this type [*sc. I had to write a letter*] the verb *have* is void of any idea of
> possession, and the object in it is no longer an object to *have* but to the

infinitive. *To have* is therefore here ... merely a function word, or 'auxiliary of predication' expressing nothing but duty, obligation, compulsion, necessity, etc. The development of this construction from the older constructions A [*sc.* with a stronger possession reading such as *He that hath lyttle to spende, hath not much to lose*] and B [*sc.* possession alongside obligation such as in *He has a large family to keep*] was very slow, and it is not possible to ascertain when exactly the idiom appeared for the first time on paper.

He then goes on to argue as follows:

But since the verb *to have* came to function as an auxiliary, it tended to have its place immediately before the infinitive just as the other auxiliaries, so that the word order gradually became HAVE – infinitive – object. If this word order is used as a criterion, it will be found that there are no examples before about 1200 ..., that the usage was fairly rare in Middle English and that it became firmly established in Modern English.

Just how it became firmly established since Early Modern English is the topic of section 3.3. As for the long-term history of HAVE TO, van der Gaaf (1931: 180-188) seems to have been the first to describe the rise of deontic HAVE TO as a transition through several stages. Visser (1969: 1474-1487) follows his account. Gauging from the more recent adaptations in Fleischman (1982: 58f.) and Heine (1993: 41f), van der Gaaf's analysis has become a linguistic commonplace.[1] In an unpublished paper, Brinton (1991) offers a detailed grammaticalization study, including discussion of numerous examples from the Helsinki Corpus and from previous research. She substantially refines but in essence confirms the traditional account. The interested reader may be referred to Fischer's (1994: 139-145) summary of Brinton, which is rather biased, though (a brief synopsis is also provided in Brinton & Stein 1993: 43f). It has to be stressed, for instance, that parts of Fischer's analysis do not depart as radically from either the traditional view or Brinton's account as Fischer's phrasing sometimes seems to indicate. Both accounts share with the traditional analysis the perhaps most important conclusion that the critical period in the grammaticalization of HAVE TO is Early Modern English.[2] On the basis of ARCHER data I will offer a more precise dating for the period of rapid grammaticalization, but let us first consider the traditional analysis. The most recent adaptation of it is found in Heine (1993); it assumes the following five steps in the evolution of deontic HAVE TO:

Table 3.1.   The development of deontic HAVE TO (adapted from Heine 1993: 41f)

Stage	I	I have a letter	[Possession Schema]
	II	I have a letter to mail	[Purpose Schema: Possession Schema + purpose/goal adjunct]
	III	I have a letter to write	[the possessive meaning of *have* has been bleached out]
	IV	I have to write a letter	[*have to* now functions as a unit lexeme expressing the modal notion of obligation]
	V	I have to write	[the object complement can now be deleted]

While the exact timing of each individual stage has been a matter of considerable dispute (see Brinton 1991 or Fischer 1994), it is generally agreed that the stages above square with the chronological order of attested construction types (cf. OED 1989: *s.v. have* no. 7; the accounts quoted in the previous paragraph; or Table 3.6, p. 74 below;). I will now briefly illustrate this genesis of the obligative semantics of HAVE TO by sketching some of the cognitive and syntactic processes involved, a method which has become standard practice in grammaticalization research. To begin with, Bybee et al. (1994: 184) maintain that the obligation sense "derives in part from the sense imparted by the infinitival verb forms" which follow the construction, giving a "projected sense." Since, however, HAVE is a source for obligation and futurity crosslinguistically, a considerable contribution to the obligative semantics can also be assumed to lie in the specific semantics of HAVE – or HAVE GOT for that matter. It seems plausible to assume that object movement and syntactic reanalysis (in its narrow sense, also called boundary shift or restructuring) of the kind sketched below have taken place. For the sake of convenience, Fleischman's canonical example adapted from Visser (1969: 1479, 1482) will be discussed while, for clarity's sake, I shall stick to the stages identified by Heine.

Stage (I) is a simple clause indicating possession,[3] while stage (II) is a complex sentence including a purposive subordinate clause (words in round brackets are understood):[4]

(I)   [I have a letter]

(II)   [I have a letter] [to (I) mail (a letter)]

(III)   [I have a letter] [to (I) write (a letter)]

At stage (III), too, a main clause indicating possession is followed by a subordinate clause.[5] Notice, however, that the standard classification of the subordinate clause as purposive seems somewhat problematic. One might prefer to label it postmodifying, but this is not fully satisfactory either (cf. also Note 10), as the degree of clause fusion seems rather high even at stage (III). Furthermore, as Heine (1993: 42) rightly points out, "the possessive meaning of *have* has been bleached out" at stage (III) since the letter is not yet written and hence cannot be in the possession of the speaker. In (II) and (III) both the subjects and the objects of the two clauses are coreferential. Consequently, in the subordinate clause they do not surface as overt arguments.

As is well known, clause boundaries in English are notoriously blurred due to frequent cases of clause fusion and the deletion of constituents (see for instance Hawkins 1986 or Mair 1990). Therefore, constituents are readily moved across potential clause boundaries, which licenses:

>   (IV)   [I have Ø] [to write a letter]

Here one must probably assume that the object is moved from the main into the subordinate clause since moving *to* + infinitive into the main clause appears to be no more than a theoretical option. In any case, the clause boundaries in (IV) are debatable; the alternative would be to rebracket it into a single clause:

>   (IVa)   [I have to write a letter]

What is important to note here is Heine's observation (1993: 42) that "*have to* now functions as a unit lexeme." This suggests a high degree of bondedness between its two constituents, which will be recalled as one of Lehmann's criteria for grammaticalization (Table 2.1). The transition from discontinuous HAVE TO (stage III) to contiguous HAVE TO (stage IV) is commonly agreed to be the most important step in the grammaticalization of the construction (Fischer 1994). Witness Bolinger's (1980b: 297) much cited observation that "the moment a verb is given an infinitive complement, that verb starts down the road of auxiliariness." Brinton (1991) and Fischer (1994) have already detailed the differences between contiguous (or adjacent, uninterrupted) and discontinuous (or non-adjacent) HAVE TO; in what follows I therefore concentrate on the contiguous construction.

For present-day English the tight bonding between HAVE and *to* is supported by the existence of the spellings <hafta> and <hasta>. The first mention of the connection between the assimilation processes and grammatical change in (American) English which I have been able to find is by Francis (1958: 258):

> such forms as /hæstə, hæftə ... /, prevalent in American speech on all social levels, indicate that the *to* which is customarily considered a part of the infinitive is often a part of the auxiliary instead. A grammatical change seems to be taking place here which will have to be dealt with in the grammars of the future.[6]

Bondedness is further evidenced by the fact that adverb interpolation between HAVE and *to* is highly dispreferred if not ungrammatical. Compare the following data from the spoken component of the BNC (10m words):

Table 3.2. Adverb interpolation (*actually*) with HAVE TO in the spoken BNC

		have	*had*	*has*	*having*	HAVE (SUM)
1	*actually* VERB FORM *to*	47	12	1	4	64
2	VERB FORM *to actually*	15	8	1	2	26
3	VERB FORM *actually to*	0	0	0	0	0

Table 3.3. Adverb interpolation (*really*) with HAVE TO in the spoken BNC

		have	*had*	*has*	*having*	HAVE (SUM)
1	*really* VERB FORM *to*	45	14	8	2	69
2	VERB FORM *to really*	16	5	1	1	23
3	VERB FORM *really to*	0	0	0	0	0

To begin with, it is surprising just how similar the figures for both adverbs are, not only in terms of tendencies and proportions but even in terms of actual occurrences. Intriguingly, a bondedness hierarchy emerges from the data. The two investigated adverbs have different stylistic connotations, with *actually* correlating more strongly with overt prestige (Krug 1998e),[7] so the following cline can be taken to apply generally in English. The hierarchy holds for each individual word form of HAVE and, naturally therefore, for the HAVE TO paradigm in general (from more to less tightly bonded):

(1)   HAVE + *to*   <   *to* + infinitive   <   subject + HAVE[8]

This hierarchy indicates that HAVE and *to* resist adverb interpolation most strongly and perhaps do not permit it at all (rows 3 in the above tables). By contrast, the adverb immediately preceding HAVE *to* (i.e. placement between subject and verb) is the commonest option. Adverb interpolation between HAVE *to* and the infinitive (rows 2) is in an intermediate position. This bondedness hierarchy is another piece of evidence indicating that a single-clause analysis is superior to a biclausal analysis. Interpolation resistance for HAVE and TO was noted as early as 1978 by Chomsky & Lasnik. Pullum capitalizes on this point:

> For many people (especially **older generation**, and **more British than American** speakers) ... 12 [*viz.* the sentence *We have obviously to be careful*] is grammatical, but for speakers who reject interpolation it is not; ... the speakers might have some **remnant expressions** like *If you need anything, you have only to ask,* ... (Pullum 1997: 91, emphasis added)

All this is undisputed but Pullum fails to draw the obvious conclusion that change in progress accounts for intuition-based grammaticality judgements. Increased bonding can be held responsible for the fact that it is conservative speakers (i.e. older rather than younger, British rather than American) who accept interpolation more readily than more progressive speakers.

To return to the discussion of the development of HAVE TO: for the transition from stage (IV) to (V), Fleischman (1982: 59) and Heine (1993: 42) claim deletion of *a letter*. Alternatively, one might assume that the construction is generalized further so as to embrace intransitive verbs – certainly the only feasible analysis of (Va):

(V)   [I have to write]

(Va)   [I have to go]

This stage demonstrates full reanalysis of the originally biclausal structure, since multiple analyses typical of the intermediate actualization stage – here stage IV – are no longer possible.[9] Since there is no object to either *write* or *go* at stage V, the order *have to* is fixed. Both this and the bondedness hierarchy instantiate a further criterion of grammaticalization quoted in Chapter 2: "The freedom to manipulate the element decreases" (Lehmann 1991: 493).

In Shakespeare, attestations of contiguous HAVE TO followed by the infinitive are still relatively rare (0.6 occurrences per 10,000 words; in a similar vein, Mustanoja 1960: 531). They are of a different nature, though, than the examples cited in Fleischman (1982) or Heine (1993). In Shakespeare, due to clause fusion HAVE is best analysed as apokoinou (Greek από κοινοῦ). This is a common term in the description of the classical languages, which Bußmann (1996) defines as a

> syntactic construction in which two sentences share a common element that can be either in the second sentence or on the border between the two sentences. Apokoinou refers to both sentences grammatically ...[10]

In the case at hand, HAVE must be interpreted as the main verb indicating possession of a previously mentioned object, while at the same time inviting inferences for a deontic reading. Notice that this comes in degrees: while in (2) a possession reading is rather evident, examples (3) to (7) are increasingly equivocal – especially since punctuation in Shakespeare is notoriously a matter of debate:

(2)   There is your money that I had to keep. (*The Comedy of Errors*, I, ii, 8)

(3)   Fair maid, send forth thine eye. This youthful parcel/ Of noble bachelors stand at my bestowing,/ O'er whom both sovereign power and father's voice I have to use. (*All's Well That Ends Well*, II, iii, 50-54)

(4)   ...; this doth infer the zeal I had to see him. (*Second Part of King Henry IV*, V, v, 14f)

(5)   Tranio, since for the great desire I had/ To see fair Padua, nursery of arts,/ I am arriv'd for fruitful Lombardy, ... (*The Taming of the Shrew*, I, i, 1-3)

(6)   Come, let me see what task I have to do. (*Titus Andronicus*, III, i, 276)

(7)   Ay, that's the first thing that we have to do;/ To free King Henry from imprisonment, ... (*Third Part of King Henry VI*, IV, iii, 62f)

The two most common verbal complements of HAVE TO in Shakespeare are *say* and *do*, which gives rise to advancing a discourse-based motivation in the genesis of HAVE TO (to be discussed in 3.4.1).

In a discussion of the cognitive processes involved in the evolution of obligative HAVE TO, it seems necessary to invoke the notion of subjectification (as conceptualized by Traugott).[11] As Traugott remarks, the concept of subjectification is closely connected with metonymy: "It can perhaps best be regarded as a specific type of metonymy" (1996: 5). Two of the three tendencies identified in her earlier work (1989: 34f) on this topic further clarify the concept and are at the same time helpful in accounting for the rise of the deontic modality of HAVE TO:

> Tendency I: Meanings based in the external described situation > meanings based in the internal (evaluative/perceptual/cognitive) described situation.

> Tendency III: Meanings tend to become increasingly based in the speaker's subjective belief state/attitude toward the proposition.

Consider also a more recent definition (Traugott 1996: 5):

> subjectification is a phenomenon affecting large domains of the lexicon. If the meaning of a lexical item or construction is grounded in the world of reference, it is likely that over time speakers will develop polysemies grounded in their world, whether reasoning, belief, or metatextual attitude to the discourse. In other words, subjectification is a semasiological development of meanings associated with a meaning-form pair such that the latter comes to mark subjectivity explicitly.

Building on Lyons (1977), Coates (1983) and others, Traugott (1989) has amply demonstrated that Tendency III accounts successfully for the development of epistemic from deontic meanings in the central modals. In her 1988 paper, Traugott explicitly mentions the rise of epistemic HAVE TO:

> In the case of the development of the epistemics from volitionals or deontics, there is strengthening of the subjective element, and of focus on belief and knowledge: if I say *You had to go* in the obligation sense, I invite the inference that I believe you did go. Therefore, in *You had to have gone*, derived from *You had to go*, the inference of the speaker's belief in the truth of the complement is strengthened. (1988: 411)[12]

As is immediately obvious, subjectification is also applicable to the rise of obligative HAVE TO. 'Possession' (the earlier, source meaning) typically relates to a material item in the external world. It is objectively observable. 'Obligation', by contrast, is an abstract concept and grounded in the world of reasoning. It is imposed by or on the speaker/ conceptualizer, and typically it cannot be asserted by reference to the material world (Palmer 1986: 7-11). The rise of obligative from possessive semantics, then, follows precisely the path outlined by Traugott's 'Tendency I' quoted earlier.

It is interesting that subjectification is not limited to the well-known development from one modal notion (deonticity) to another modal notion (epistemicity), but that it also encompasses the actual genesis of modal meaning. Notice, however, that this finding is by no means new. Subjectification has been invoked to account for (a) the rise of the futurity sense (treated by various analysts as modal) of BE GOING TO (Langacker 1990: 19; Traugott 1995: 34-36) and (b) the rise of epistemicity of PROMISE and THREATEN (Traugott 1997). Since it is argued here that subjectification operates in the evolution of obligative HAVE TO, and since it will also be invoked to account for the rise of 'volition' from 'lack' semantics in the case of WANT TO (Ch. 4), one can perhaps generalize and go so far as to claim that subjectification is a process that is typically involved in the evolution of modal from nonmodal semantics.

3.2.2   HAVE GOT TO

According to Webster (1996: *s.v. have*), possessive HAVE GOT followed by a noun phrase entered the English language in the 16th century (for a slightly later dating, i.e. early 17th century, see Gronemeyer 1999: 25). The obligation reading of the construction HAVE GOT TO followed by the infinitive came into the English language in the 19th century (OED *s.v. get*, no. 24; Visser 1969: 1479). One can antedate the *termini ante quos* of 1860 and 1865 given in Visser and the OED, respectively, by at least a generation. The construction is current in Dickens' *Oliver Twist* (1837/38, emphasis added throughout):

(8)   'Never did, sir!' ejaculated the beadle. 'No, nor nobody never did; but now she's dead, we've got to bury her; ...' (V, 80)

(9)   'I've got to be in London to-night; and I know a 'spectable old gentlemen as lives there, wot'll give you lodgings for nothink, and never ask for the change – that is, if any genelman he knows interduces you. And don't he know me?' (VIII, 102)

The fact that it is relatively frequent in Dickens' work suggests that HAVE GOT TO must have existed in spoken English for some time by then.[13] From the above two passages, which are replete with nonstandard phonological and grammatical features, it is apparent that the earliest uses are intended to characterize nonstandard speech. That the OED in 1989 considers it as colloquial is probably grounded in its origin in nonstandard speech and is in fact defensible today (cf. Palmer 1989: 114 and section 3.5 below), but a characterization as vulgar seems to be an inappropriate leftover from the first edition (1933). In a similar vein, the comments on HAVE GOT TO in style books have always been negative (Webster 1996 *s.v. have got*). This is not an uncommon genesis of language innovations. Confinement to nonstandard speech, however, does not seem to have lingered very long as the far less marked examples given in Visser (1969: 1479) and the OED (1989: *s.v. get*) indicate:

(10)   ... he always remembers when I've got to take my doctor's stuff. (1860, George Eliot *Mill on the Floss* I, IX, 80; taken from Visser)

(11)   The first thing I've got to do is to grow to my right size again. (1865, Lewis Carroll *Alice in Wonderland* IV, 54; taken from the OED)

(12)   I'd nearly forgotten that I've got to grow up again. (*Ibid.* 57; taken from the OED)

Another generation later, we find HAVE GOT TO in the sophisticated speech of upper class members in Oscar Wilde's comedies of manners. Rather than being nonstandard, the two examples from the excerpt below attach a higher degree of expressivity to the statement. Witness, for instance, John (Ernest) Worthing addressing his friend in *The Importance of Being Earnest* (1895, II, 353):

(13)   You are certainly not staying with me for a whole week as a
        guest or anything else. You have got to leave ... by the four-five
        train. [...] Your vanity is ridiculous, your conduct an outrage,
        and your presence in my garden utterly absurd. However, you
        have got to catch the four-five, and I hope you will have a
        pleasant journey back to town.

Present-day English grammars usually consider deontic HAVE GOT TO as
common but informal. Spoken data of contemporary British English
show that 'common' is a slight understatement: some 150 years after
entering the language, HAVE GOT TO is one and a half times as frequent
as *must,* which has been around since Old English.[14] If this doesn't
qualify as a success story, what would?

   We will shortly deal with the diachronic increase in text frequency in
more detail. Before, however, let us briefly return to the question
whether HAVE GOT TO has undergone precisely the same development as
HAVE TO. In essence, I will argue that while the HAVE TO account
presented in the previous section is cognitively plausible for HAVE GOT
TO, too, textual evidence seems to suggest otherwise.[15] My account will
emphasize the import of frequency effects and processing constraints
for explanations of linguistic change.

   To begin with, an important case in point is that even in the earliest
attested occurrences of HAVE GOT TO, word forms of HAVE are fairly
consistently used in their enclitic form.[16] Notice further that these
enclitics all follow personal pronouns. This holds for Dickens' work as
well as for the above examples (10) to (12) cited from Carroll and Eliot.
Compare some further attestations from Dickens' *Oliver Twist*
(1837/38), all of which are fictionalized oral utterances:

(14)   'Now, you know what you've got to expect, master, so ...'
        (XVI, 159)

(15)   'Let it be,' said Sikes, thrusting his hand before her. 'There's
        enough light for wot I've got to do.' (XLVII, 422)

(16)   'For business,' replied Sikes; 'so say what you've got to say.'
        (XIX, 188)

By contrast, the full form *have* correlates with

    (a) more formal environments as in the reported example (18),

    (b) preceding nonpersonal pronouns as in (17) or (19),

    (c) tensed forms of HAVE as in (18) and

    (d) less clearly deontic semantics as in all three examples below:

(17)   'Now, man, what have you got to say?' (XI, 123)

(18)   ...remarking, that he had better say what he had got to say, under cover: (XXVI, 242)

(19)   'Well, what have you got to say to me?' (XV, 154)

Let us try to elucidate the two discourse factors which I claim have played a crucial role in the evolution of HAVE GOT TO. Elsewhere (Krug 1998a) I have argued that the (string) frequency with which two adjacent linguistic items co-occur has an impact on the likelihood of their coalescence. As is intuitively plausible, high string frequency is conducive to coalescence. In that study, the bulk of the empirical evidence comes precisely from HAVE encliticization to pronouns (such as *you've, they've, where've*). Now, since the personal pronouns and HAVE even in the earliest obligation readings of HAVE GOT TO are contracted (*I've got to, we've got to* etc.), it is not unlikely that by semantic analogy to (i.e. on the model of) the older HAVE TO construction HAVE GOT extended its range of complements from nominal complements (as in *I've got a house*) to infinitival ones (as in *I've got to go*).[17] Why then, one may ask, insert *got* in the first place? Apart from the well-known factor of expressivity in language change (for a recent detailed treatment, see Hübler 1998), one may assume that processing constraints and chunking are two major conflicting forces in this instance of change. These are treated in turn in the following paragraphs.

    Due to string frequency, reduced forms of HAVE tend to cliticize on pronominal hosts – in face-to-face interaction doubtless more systematically so than in the writings of the time. This is tantamount to chunking as a consequence of repetition (Haiman 1994a, c).[18] On the other hand, deontic readings of HAVE (TO) carry much more semantic weight than auxiliary uses. Also, deontic meanings are very distinct from possession readings. Information processing reasons therefore suggest themselves as counterforces to phonological reduction.[19] The high currency of personal pronoun and following HAVE, however, almost automatically triggers their coalescence (cf. Bybee & Scheibman forthcoming). This, then, may at least partially explain why *got* comes to be inserted as a reinforcer in those cases where HAVE is reduced.

Further support for the hypothesis that conflicting discourse-based factors are at work in the evolution of deontic HAVE GOT TO is provided by the fact that certain logically possible constructions and phonological realizations are attested, while others are rare or nonexistent. Three particular points are worth remarking. First of all, even today HAVE is very rarely cliticized and never deleted when it is part of deontic HAVE TO. Compare:

(20)   ?I've [v] to go.[20]

(21)   ??He's [z] a large family to keep.

(22)   *I to go.

This shows that automatic fusion of high-frequency sequences does not work in an uninhibited way. I would attribute such facts partly to processing constraints and the semantic weight of modal HAVE TO, and partly to the phonological tendency for the English verb phrase to contain a stressed element.

The second point is an argument *ex silentio* against reanalysis in the evolution of HAVE GOT TO: while many discontinuous structures for HAVE TO (such as *He has a large family to keep*) are attested with a deontic reading as one possible or exclusive interpretation, such examples seem rare to the point of nonexistence for HAVE GOT TO, certainly up to the 19th century. There are some rare structures where *got* (though not always HAVE GOT) is followed by infinitival *to* complements in discontinuous structures that predate the earliest contiguous HAVE GOT TO strings from 1837 quoted above. However, it seems impossible to postulate deontic semantics for them. For one thing, syntactically, each of them is a purpose clause or a nonfinite noun complementation. For another, in all of the examples GET still has the lexical verb semantics of 'receive', 'manage to obtain'. Consider some examples from Shakespeare:

(23)   I then mov'd you,/ My Lord of Canterbury, and got your leave/ To make this present summons. (*King Henry VIII*, II, iv, 218f)

(24)   Ay, marry,/ There will be woe indeed, lords: the sly whoresons/
        Have got a speeding trick to lay down ladies. (*King Henry VIII,*
        I, iii, 38-40)

(25)   Have you got leave to go to shrift to-day? (*Romeo and Juliet,* II,
        v, 66)

Similarly, Defoe in *The farther adventures of Robinson Crusoe*
(1719/20: XIII):

(26)   ...; for we got leave to travel in the retinue of one of their
        mandarins, ...

A third point is that we can find intransitive verbs after a matrix
construction *got to* even in the earliest attestations. Recall two examples
invoked earlier:

(9)   I've got to be in London to-night; (Dickens 1837/38)

(12)   I'd nearly forgotten that I've got to grow up again. (Carroll
        1865)

The extant material, then, does not justify the assumption that extension
from transitive to intransitive verbal complements – i.e. the transition
from stage (IV) to (V) – has occurred with HAVE GOT TO. Let us
continue to analyse the clausal structure of these early HAVE GOT TO
examples against the stages identified for HAVE TO. Only a one-verb
phrase, hence single-clause, analysis is feasible for a sentence like (9).
In syntactic terms, therefore, HAVE GOT TO enters the language as late as
stage (V) of the stages identified for HAVE TO (p. 55 above). This yields
a structure where *got* and *to* are no longer separated by a clause
boundary and thus are closely bonded. In other words, HAVE GOT TO
appears to have entered the English language in constructions that
according to Heine's (1993) account of the evolution of HAVE TO should
be the final step in a sequence of developments. We can conclude, then,
that one often cited parameter of grammaticalization, 'expansion or
restriction of scope', seems to have played no role in the genesis of
deontic HAVE GOT TO.

    As in the case of HAVE TO, data from adverb interpolation lend
further support to a single-clause analysis. An elicitation test
demonstrated that educated British and American speakers find

sentences of the type *I've got to actually/really pretend* ... fully or at
least marginally acceptable, while nine out of ten subjects rejected *?I've
got actually/really to pretend* ... Hence, it seems certain that *got* and *to*
enjoy a much higher degree of bonding than *to* and the following
infinitive – perhaps up to the point of a strict-adjacency constraint.[21]
The elicitation test receives full support from, and is further refined by,
BNC data:

Table 3.4. Adverb interpolation (*actually*) with HAVE GOT TO in the spoken BNC

	have	*'ve*	*has*	*'s*	*had*	*'d*	∅	HAVE (SUM)
1 *actually* VERB FORM *got to*	0	0	0	0	0	0	0[22]	0
2 *actually* VERB FORM *gotta*	0	0	0	0	0	0	0	0
3 VERB FORM *got to actually*	1	6	0	0	0	0	3	10
4 VERB FORM *gotta actually*	0	3	0	0	0	0	0	3
5 VERB FORM *actually got to*	1	17	1	2	0	0	2	23
6 VERB FORM *actually gotta*	0	1	0	0	0	0	1	2
7 VERB FORM *got actually to*	0	0	0	0	0	0	0	0

Table 3.5. Adverb interpolation (*really*) with HAVE GOT TO in the spoken BNC

	have	*'ve*	*has*	*'s*	*had*	*'d*	∅	HAVE (SUM)
1 *really* VERB FORM *got to*	4	0	0	0	0	0	0	4
2 *really* VERB FORM *gotta*	0	0	0	0	0	0	0	0
3 VERB FORM *got to really*	0	6	0	0	0	2	0	8
4 VERB FORM *gotta really*	0	4	0	0	0	0	0	4
5 VERB FORM *really got to*	1	27	0	2	0	0	5	35
6 VERB FORM *really gotta*	0	5	0	0	0	0	0	5
7 VERB FORM *got really to*	0	0	0	0	0	0	0	0

The above tables clearly confirm that *got* and *to* show the tightest
bonding: interruptability for deontic GOT TO indeed tends towards zero.
This proves that the spelling <gotta> is not an *ad hoc* formation but
explainable on cognitive grounds. A similarly heavy interpolation
between *got* and *to* as, for instance, in (27) is hardly conceivable:

(27)   ... you've got to somehow or other get the blood back up to the
heart. (BNC F8D 316)

As with HAVE TO, a bondedness hierarchy for the Subject-Verb group
falls out from the data and again the two adverbs yield identical
hierarchies (from more to less closely bonded):

(28)   *got* + *to* < subject + HAVE < *to* + infinitive < HAVE + *got*

It is striking that the adverbs *actually* and *really* rarely intervene
between the subject and the finite verb. The hierarchy suggests,
therefore, that the bonding between subject and HAVE is tighter than that
holding between some constituents within the verb phrase [HAVE GOT TO
+ infinitive]. That the infinitive is less closely bonded to the remainder
of the verb phrase is hardly surprising, since one would intuitively
group HAVE GOT TO as a multi-constituent lexeme which enjoys matrix
verb status. However, that the bonding between HAVE and *got* ranks
lowest on the hierarchy calls for an explanation. I will argue here that
the key to these phenomena lies in chunking (see Haiman 1994a), which
in turn is motivated by string frequency.

On frequentative grounds, HAVE is subject to conflicting loyalties: it
collocates frequently with preceding subjects (largely personal
pronouns) as well as with following *got*. Since the former are even more
frequent,[23] HAVE tends to lean on the subject, naturally (over two thirds
of the time in the spoken BNC) in its reduced form. A typical instance
of adverb interpolation is therefore (29):

(29)   When we want urgent work done we've really got to turn the
screws tight. (BNC FUL 1913)

By contrast, the rare full form correlates with heavier NPs (as distinct
from personal pronouns), formal environments and emphasis on the
deontic meaning, which is additionally stressed by *really* in the
following example:

(30)   I think as a Group Captain er explained y'know ... the
operational staff have really got to complete their study into
what kind of tactical reconnaissance capability they want in the
next century. (BNC JNN 294)

Similarly, the fact that enclitics do not follow *actually* or *really* (rows 1 and 2 in the above two tables) – or other adverbs for that matter - may be equally attributable to low string frequency.

As a consequence of the above, the bonding between the (pronominal) subject and HAVE ranks higher on the hierarchy than some verb phrase internal sequences. This lends unequivocal support to the claim that frequency impacts on constituency (Bybee & Fleischman forthcoming) to the extent that enclitic HAVE becomes closely attached to the subject. Two fundamentally different analyses are conceivable. One is generative, the other functional. Their strong and weak points are highlighted in what follows.

To my knowledge no generative account treats HAVE GOT TO in its own right. Within these frameworks, therefore, the typically reduced form *'ve* functions as an auxiliary in forming the perfect. In formal models, infinitival *to* is standardly analysed as an auxiliary-like constituent too (on the categorial status of *to* see Chomsky 1981: 18; Pullum 1982; Radford 1997: 49-54). Let us for the sake of the argument sketch a syntactic analysis of example (9) within the broad framework of the minimalist approach as outlined in Chomsky (1995) or Radford (1997):

(31)

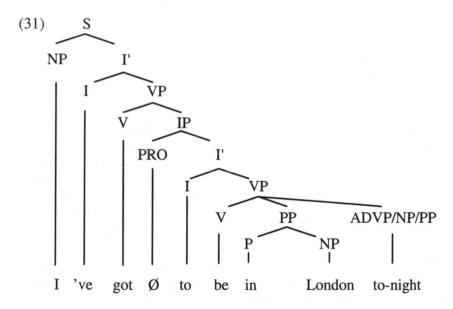

Attractive as the structure of the sentence S (or, more recently: IP; cf. Chomsky 1995: 134) may appear at first sight, the theory's major drawback is that it is not capable of accommodating ongoing developments. Notice first of all that *to-night* (this is the orthography of Dickens' original, (9) above) is correctly analysed in three ways, depending on which historical stage and theoretical stance one adopts: as a prepositional phrase (historically), a noun phrase or an adverbial phrase (currently). But this is not the major challenge at issue here.[24] The more severe problem is the separation of *got* and *to*, which is additionally aggravated by the intervening empty category PRO standing for the coreferential null subject. Irrespective of whether or not one adheres to such theory-internal principles as empty categories and traces (strong claims against them are voiced in Postal & Pullum 1982; Inkelas & Zec 1993; Pullum 1997) and even though the present type of empty category (PRO) is not taken to block contraction (Radford 1997: Ch. 8), it seems flawed from the start that phrase structure diagrams or bracketed clauses for contracted forms like *gotta* are generally avoided in the pertaining literature. Thus analysts evade the problems of their categorization. Furthermore, analysing HAVE GOT TO as perfect tense is debatable if not plainly wrong (see section 3.4.1.3 below). In sum, the analysis offered in (31) seems less than ideal. Within the generative paradigm, the best – if rather radical – solution might be to give up a spelling-based classification, recognize (HAVE) GOT TO as a single-unit item and assign it to the class I(nflection) alongside the modals. This would be tantamount to positing the reanalysis of an allegedly biclausal structure as a single clause as sketched above for HAVE TO, but it would cause other problems for the theory.[25]

By contrast, a radical analysis in the tradition of grammaticalization takes into account the gradual nature of the process. In what follows I adopt Lehmann's (1995: 13f) terminology: grammaticalization is capable of accommodating the change at hand since it can assume demorphemicization and indeed loss of HAVE. Consequently, *'ve* [v] can be analysed as mere phonetic substance. HAVE, then, is reduced to the status of a phone. On a general level, such a point has been made by Givón (1979: 208f); related is Hopper & Traugott's (1993: 10-13) discussion of the progressive loss of morpheme status of clitic *'s < us* in *let's*.

The latter analysis seems also superior for HAVE GOT TO because then the clitic does not govern (or c-command) the following verb phrase. Only under such assumptions does it make sense that the VP should take on a life of its own: this is manifest in a further decreasing bonding between *got* and HAVE (see the bondedness hierarchy given in (28) above). At the same time we witness the strengthening of the bonded-ness between [v] < *have* and the preceding NP, of which [v] can arguably be taken to be a meaningless constituent prone to deletion. Bybee & Scheibman (forthcoming) propose a similar line of argument for the constituent analysis of such phrases as *I don't know/think/want*. They outline the effect of usage on constituent structure as follows:

> While a generalized constituent structure may be an emergent property arising from many analogous utterances, specific combinations that are frequently used may diverge from the general pattern because frequency conditions autonomy in storage and renders internal analysis unnecessary ... This phenomenon reveals the essential role of repetition in creating constituent structure: while semantic and pragmatic factors determine what occurs together in discourse, the actual repetition of stretches of talk is the mechanism that binds them into constituents.

An important argument in favour of the functional analysis is that the deletion of the supposed auxiliary in (HAVE) GOT TO is fairly common: it is found around 20% of the time in formal, 30% in informal British English speech (see section 3.5). Under a grammaticalization analysis such deletion poses no problems. On the contrary, it is predicted because loss of semantically empty phonetic bulk is expected (cf. Lehmann 1995: 13).[26] Rigorous analyses in the tradition of autonomous syntax would have to assume different underlying structures and tenses for *I got to go* and *I've got to go*. Such analyses are doubtful and miss out the evolutionary path of the construction. By the same token, grammaticalization would not have to dismiss the following examples as performance errors but could accommodate them by simply analysing the reduced auxiliaries as meaningless phonetic bulk that derives from a grammatical morpheme:[27]

(32)   I'm wanna use that water to heat the plates! (BNC KD5 1186)

(33)   He said no I'm wanna call it Where's the Wally! (BNC KD0 465)

(34)   I put an agenda in my head you know? What I'm gotta do first and ... (BNC KB4 85)

(35)   I'm gonna save some money right, I'm gotta finance industry so we mechanize so you collectivize and ... (BNC KM6 253)

(36)   I'm gotta get ... my trousers ... back on. (BNC KP8 492)

(37)   I'm have to take some time over this, so I think ... (BNC JSC 313)

Let us now integrate the above observations into the monoclausal analysis of (HAVE) GOT TO. Different from HAVE TO, HAVE GOT TO has proceeded further on its path towards a modal verb (cf. sections 3.4f). The most common current form in present-day British English is cliticization of HAVE:

As was pointed out above, further phonological reduction ensued. From (VI) it is a small step to deleting the semantically vacuous enclitic form as in:

Finally or concomitant with (VI) and (VII) we witness the cliticization of the infinitival marker – or, under Pullum's (1997) analysis, a morpholexical derivation:

In the OED (1989 *s.v. gotta*), stage VIII is first attested in 1924. Not surprisingly, it occurs in a fictionalized oral utterance:

(38)   He ...went forward as if to take her arm. 'You gotta come along,' I heard. (J. Buchan *Three Hostages* XVIII, 263)

Notice that the developments sketched above for HAVE TO and HAVE GOT TO are by no means exceptional. They are but two examples of von der Gabelentz's (1891: 251) spiral model for the constant renewal of the grammatical inventory of any given language, part of which is paraphrased by Hopper & Traugott (1993: 8) as follows: "One [diachronic tendency] is for periphrastic constructions to coalesce over time and become morphological ones." *Gotta* has so far gone half the way in this process of morphologization and in its grammatical behaviour it has become more similar to the true modals than HAVE TO (see also section 3.4 below).

   Central to my grammaticalization claim is that while the different phonological and syntactic variants of the construction are all still perfectly acceptable in present-day English, it is precisely the historically older variants that are relatively rare in current spoken English; the more recent variants, by contrast, are frequent (see Appendix 3). More important still, there is clear indication that the most innovative and most modal variant, *gotta*, is on the increase (see Table 3.16, p. 110).

As was noted in 3.2.2, HAVE GOT ('possess' as in *I have got a cart*) entered the English language probably in the 16th or early 17th century. The extension from nominal complements to infinitival ones in the 19th century demonstrates the loss of the meaning component 'possession'. Together with the reduction stages (VI) to (VIII) this proves that yet another criterion listed by Lehmann (1991: 493) applies to the modalization of *gotta*: "The element loses substance both on the phonological and the semantic sides."[28] One might object that the erosion (stages VI to VIII) observed for *gotta* is not particularly noteworthy, but just a common phonological reduction typical of allegro speech and probably not reliably transcribed in the BNC. Regarding a refutation of the former argument, Pullum (1997: 82) emphasizes that "it is an important fact about the data treated here [*viz.* the seven so-called 'therapy verbs' *wanna, gonna, usta, hafta/hasta, gotta, oughta* and *sposta*] that they do NOT represent a phenomenon linked to rapid, casual, slovenly, or uneducated speech." As to the latter potential criticism, even though consistency in the transcription process cannot be guaranteed, it can still be demonstrated that a distinction between the different full and reduced forms was made by many transcribers (cf. also Appendix 3). This is not very surprising since *gotta* is part of the list of so-called 'non-orthographic words' (Burnard, ed., 1995: 96ff) that was used by the transcribers.[29] Numerous examples of the following kind could be invoked:

(39)   So I've got to sort of I've gotta record a ... (BNC KP4 992)

(40)   Yeah, we've gotta do a transcription on Friday haven't we? – Yeah. We have got to. (BNC KP5 1941)

To conclude the discussion of the early history of HAVE GOT TO and its syntactic analysis: there is compelling evidence that contiguous HAVE GOT TO with a deontic sense entered the language directly. That is to say, no previous biclausal structures need to be posited in which a possessive main clause precedes a purposive subordinate *to* clause. If this analysis is true, speakers used enclitic HAVE followed by *got to* from the start synonymously with modal HAVE TO, the most important difference probably being increased expressivity alongside associations with informal styles. In sum, none of the previous steps found in the development of deontic HAVE TO seem to obtain for the development of modal HAVE GOT TO.

The preceding section has focused on early occurrences of HAVE TO and HAVE GOT TO. Mainly qualitative analyses were presented. The existence of a construction is certainly a necessary but, I believe, not a sufficient criterion of grammatical status. Table 3.6 presents an overview of the above considerations. It includes some information on their frequency on which more detail will be offered in the next sections.

Table 3.6.   A rough sketch of the rise of HAVE TO and HAVE GOT TO

		HAVE TO + infinitive	HAVE GOT TO + infinitive
OE		Discontinuous construction, biclausal: [possession] [purposive/obligative] Subjectification and reanalysis lead to:	--
ME	c.1200	First attestations of contiguous construction	--
E M o d E	c.1600 (Shakesp.)	Contiguous construction still rare; HAVE generally apokoinou; typical complements: *say, do*	(First attestations of possessive construction HAVE GOT + NP)
M o d E	c.1800	Slow, gradual increase (see next section for details)	
	19th c.	Rapid growth (next section)	First attestations, directly contiguous and mono-clausal; no reanalysis
PDE	20th c.	Rapid growth (next section)	Rapid growth (next section)

3.3   Increase in discourse frequency

High frequency is typical of grammatical items, whereas open-class items generally enjoy much lower discourse frequencies. Characteristic of ongoing grammaticalization is therefore an increase in textual frequency. The interrelatedness between increased use on the one hand and semantic and formal changes on the other is made explicit as early as in the work of Frei (1929: 233):

> Examiné du point de vue de l'évolution, le langage présente un passage incessant du signe expressif au signe arbitraire. C'est ce qu'on pourrait appeler la loi de l'usure: plus le signe est employé fréquemment, plus les impressions qui se rattachent à sa forme et à sa signification s'émoussent. Du point de vue statique et fonctionnel, cette évolution est contre-balancée par un passage en sens inverse: plus le signe s'use, plus le besoin d'expressivité cherche à le renouveler, sémantiquement et formellement.

> (Seen from the point of view of evolution, language presents an incessant transformation from the expressive sign to the arbitrary sign. This is what one could call the law of wear and tear: the more often a sign is used, the more the notions associated with its form or its meaning become obtuse. From a static and functional point of view, this evolution is counterbalanced by a transformation in the reverse direction: the more the sign becomes worn, the more the need for expressivity looks for ways to renew it, semantically and formally.)

The present section deals with frequentative matters. Formal changes were discussed in the preceding section and will figure prominently again alongside semantic changes in section 3.4. Before we embark on the quantitative analysis, however, it is important to point out the close connection between frequency and bondedness in the context of emerging modals. Bybee & Scheibman (forthcoming) note that "bondedness within and between constructions depends on how frequently two contiguous elements occur together." This finding can be exploited for the investigation of historical change. In Krug (1998a) I demonstrated that the more often two words occur adjacent in spoken discourse synchronically, the higher is their likelihood of coalescence, which is consonant with Bybee & Scheibman's statement.[30] Furthermore, I noted that coalescence of personal pronouns with verbs like BE and HAVE has become more frequent over the last 30 years in both spoken and written English, presumably due to increased string frequency. The immediate consequences for the diachronic investigation of contiguous constructions are obvious: increases through time, then, are tantamount to tightened bondedness between adjacent items and thus extend beyond merely proving the obvious, *viz.* that a construction has become more common. On a more general level, it would seem to follow that both parameters, frequency gains and bonding, are criterial to the grammaticalization of contiguous multi-constituent constructions.[31]

3.3.1 Long-term trends: ARCHER

Here I extend a short-term investigation (Krug 1998c) for present-day English to historical stages. Since the date of this investigation, Biber et al. (1998) has appeared dealing with the entire semantic domain of obligation/necessity. Their study demonstrates the increase of what they call 'semimodals' (e.g. HAVE TO, NEED TO, BE SUPPOSED TO) in general and the specific increase in the use of some particular items (1998: 207f). However, they note (p. 209) that research in this tradition "could be carried out in much more detail," which is what I attempt in this section. With Myhill (1995), a rather detailed diachronic quantitative study of several modals and semimodals (including HAVE TO and GOT TO) is available. Despite the valuable trends he identifies, his study is not sufficient for the present purposes for four reasons:

- It is confined to American English, whereas I shall focus on British English and cross-Atlantic trends.[32]
- It is restricted to the period between 1824 and 1947,[33] while ARCHER covers a longer stretch of time (1650 to the 1990s).
- Unlike ARCHER, Myhill's corpus of nine plays is not representative.
- Understandably, given the immediate goals of his study, Myhill presents relative frequencies in semantic fields and offers no figures for the incidence of his items (e.g. occurrences per million words).

Incidence will be the focus of attention here since only from this can an increase in text frequency be derived. In fact, incidence is a central and perhaps the most easily accessible quantitative measure for determining degrees of grammaticalization. As the data will show, both HAVE TO and HAVE GOT TO reached a highly grammaticalized status only in the last 100 or so years. This is consistent with Visser's (1969: 1478) remark invoked earlier, stating for contiguous HAVE TO that "there are no examples before about 1200 ..., that the usage was fairly rare in Middle English and that it became firmly established in Modern English."[34] Hence, while earlier examples are attested (e.g. OED 1989: *s.v. have* no.7), quantitative research makes sense only from Early Modern English onwards, i.e. beginning with ARCHER.

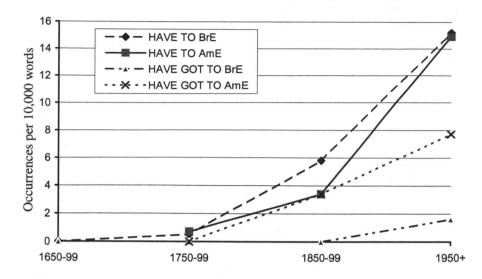

Figure 3.1.   HAVE TO and HAVE GOT TO across the centuries: Occurrences per 10,000 words in ARCHER drama

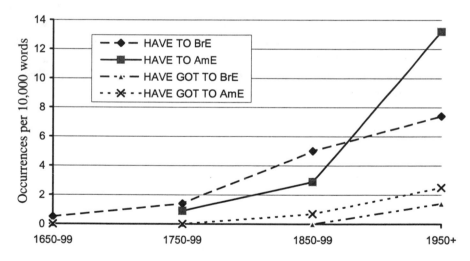

Figure 3.2.   HAVE TO and HAVE GOT TO across the centuries: Occurrences per 10,000 words in ARCHER fiction

Figure 3.1 and Figure 3.2, for dramatic and fictional writing respectively, are remarkably similar as regards overall trends. They strongly suggest that both HAVE TO and HAVE GOT TO are innovations which took a considerable step forward on their grammaticalization paths in the 19th century. The charts allow no firm conclusions as to where the constructions originated since in the 18th century their textual frequencies are almost identical in British and American English for both text types. However, given that change diffuses gradually, Figure 3.1 tentatively suggests American origin of HAVE GOT TO, which certainly gained currency more quickly here and continues to do so.

In any case, both charts suggest that American English is generally in the vanguard of change as far as these innovations are concerned: three out of four times in fiction and drama, the two constructions enjoy a higher frequency in the US today. In none of the cases is British English currently leading the spread, but once the two varieties are on a par, *viz.* for HAVE TO in late 20th century drama. Still, we need not and should not invoke cross-Atlantic influence for the increase in either construction since the cultural and political circumstances of the 18th and 19th centuries make it difficult to advocate American influence on British use.[35] Rather, I believe that these are natural changes (cf. the notion of layering and the discussion on p. 72) which the American speech community, perhaps in particular for its sociological set-up, has proved more adaptive to incorporate into its grammatical inventory.

Long-term trends for HAVE TO and HAVE GOT TO therefore are not fully consonant with the short-term developments in present-day written English identified by Hundt (1997; 1998), in whose text samples the rise of HAVE (GOT) TO seems to be led by British English. Let us now take a closer look at the development of both constructions in British English for which 50-year intervals can be plotted:

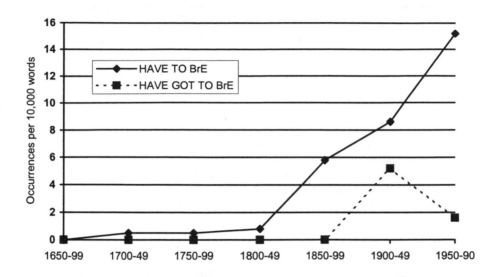

Figure 3.3.   HAVE TO and HAVE GOT TO in BrE: Occurrences per 10,000 words
in ARCHER drama (50-year intervals)

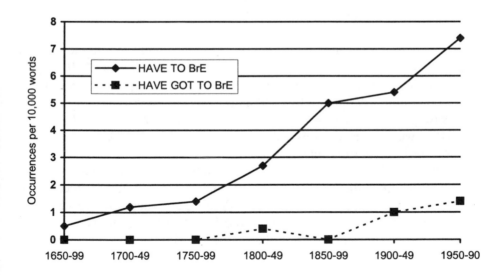

Figure 3.4.   HAVE TO and HAVE GOT TO in BrE: Occurrences per 10,000 words
in ARCHER fiction (50-year intervals)

In both text types, after an initial slow rise HAVE TO vacillated around 1 occurrence per 10,000 words until roughly 1800. If we believe Visser, this situation had lingered since Early Middle English – or even Old English if we accept modal status for discontinuous HAVE TO. Most studies on HAVE TO agree that Early Modern English is the central stage in the development of the modal construction. Witness for instance Fischer (1994: 154):

> This new position [of the object after the infinitive, rendering HAVE TO contiguous] set the scene for a grammaticalization process in which *have* developed from a full verb, but already semantically bleached ..., to a semi-auxiliary dependent on the infinitive. This took place gradually, like most grammaticalization processes, beginning in the early Modern English period.

On the basis of the ARCHER data, one would want to stress *beginning* in Early Modern English, since the major rise occurred only in the middle of the 19th century. Such a finding demonstrates very clearly the necessity of frequentative studies since probably no linguist in 1800 would have considered such an infrequent construction type as belonging to the core grammatical inventory of the English language. Visser's mention of it even for Old English can only be explained against the backdrop of his intuitions for present-day English.[36] For HAVE TO, then, we can assign a leap in grammaticalization rather precisely to the second half of the 19th century, where the incidence rose almost sixfold in drama compared to the previous 50 years.[37] It is quite remarkable that in both text categories the frequency that was isolated for contemporary spoken English as constituting a critical mark, in that it strongly correlated with grammatical status for verbs (5 times per 10,000 words, see the discussion in section 2.6 above), is reached or surpassed in precisely those periods.

Further, the increase in the fiction corpus is of a linear, gradual nature, whereas the increase in the drama material is much steeper and resembles an exponential function.[38] Predictably, then, the speech-based register proves more susceptible to the innovation and suggests strongly that HAVE TO is a construction that actually originated in discourse. The bulk of the early fictional examples attest to this fact since they occur in direct speech.

We shall see below (3.3.2.2) that for HAVE TO – as different from HAVE GOT TO – contemporary rates in the British drama corpus correspond almost exactly to contemporary spoken rates from the BNC.

If we can generalize, it seems that in grammatical change a nonstigmatized item such as HAVE TO rises in a speech-based text type approximately in-sync with actual spoken discourse, while the behaviour of an item that has received critical remarks in style books throughout its existence – here HAVE GOT TO – is less adequately reflected in a speech-based written text type. Needless to say, this is a tempting, yet highly speculative, claim, so naturally some caution is required. The fact that current rates in drama correspond to actual current British speech does not entail that this has always been the situation. In fact writers seem unlikely to employ an incoming item at natural discourse rates so long as its actual discourse frequency is extremely low. Having said this, I would allow for a time lag between speech and speech-based writing of some 50 years. This is still speculative, but probably common-sensical here given the recency of the HAVE TO construction, whose notable frequentative development spans no more than 150 years. If it is correct, we can ascribe the critical grammaticalization stage for HAVE TO to the middle of the 19th century.

As for HAVE GOT TO, it is striking that its leap in grammaticalization happened only half a century after that of HAVE TO – despite a time lag of a millennium if we consider first attestations. This finding, in fact, might help settle a facet of a famous dispute in linguistics. Lightfoot (1979, 1991) has proposed that a cluster of changes at the end of the Middle English period led to a cataclysmic restructuring of the verb phrase, in which erstwhile full verbs were reanalysed as modals, i.e. as members of a new category. His account, often labelled a 'catastrophe scenario', is widely dismissed in favour of more gradual accounts by, *inter alia*, Aitchison (1980), Plank (1984), Nagle (1989, 1990), Warner (1993), Hopper & Traugott (1993) or Harris & Campbell (1995).[39]

In particular, Lightfoot links the reanalysis of the modals to the emergence of several quasi-modals, including HAVE TO. Plank (1984: 320-322) rejects Lightfoot's claim that structures like HAVE TO came into the language soon after – and because of – the alleged cataclysmic restructuring of the modals in order to fill a syntactic vacuum left by their now defective paradigms (the new modals lacked tensed and nonfinite forms).[40] Nevertheless, Plank concedes that there is "a connection between the fate of the premodals and the development of other modal expressions" (p. 321; similarly Nagle 1989: 116). He supports his claim by citing modal semantics for discontinuous HAVE TO in Old and Middle English. In a similar vein, Nagle (1989: 113) cites deontic contiguous HAVE TO in early Middle English.

While the causal relationship between the emergence of quasi-modals and the newly acquired auxiliary status by the modals indeed seems to stand on shaky ground (cf. the discussion above on the naturalness of layering, p. 72, and the more refined quantitative analysis of Table 3.11 below), the two positions can to some extent be reconciled by ARCHER data. These indicate that Lightfoot may not have been so wrong after all. It should be noted, though, that the present data support his claims only if he assumes a highly frequent and highly grammaticalized status of the construction rather than sporadic use. There is no doubt that the construction existed in Middle English, a fact already noted by Visser (1969), but it only became sufficiently frequent to be considered a highly grammaticalized structure in the 19th century. This is Modern English and in fact another two centuries after Lightfoot's dating.

Discrepancies of this kind demonstrate that researchers have to make it very clear what they understand by 'emergence' or 'entering of a construction' in order to make their results comparable. This is particularly necessary in the context of items which are highly grammaticalized in present-day English. The problem is that more often than not such labels seem to imply, and perhaps wrongly so, that the analysts assume a currency for previous stages comparable to that of their contemporary periods. It goes without saying that I do not wish to make frequency the most important, let alone sole, criterion of grammaticalization. Syntactic and morphological criteria naturally continue to be of foremost importance. But we should probably give more weight to this quantitative criterion which has only recently become available and which is amenable to testing against independent data.

Figure 3.3 seems to suggest that the frequency of HAVE GOT TO declined in the second half of the 20th century. While a complete reversal of the trend appears unlikely for spoken English, a standstill in the second half of the present century is also attested in other spoken and written text types (see next sections). Statistical outliers of this kind seem to even out if we consider 100-year intervals (Figure 3.1). Such longer spans allow for more reliable conclusions.[41] This has consequences for short-term trends in written English such as investigated below: even statistically significant trends observed for one text type have to be treated with a great deal of caution if we want to abstract from them trends in written English or even language change in general. However, the more of the following points apply in a given instance, the more comfortable we can be with our conclusions:

a) similar trends hold for further varieties or world English in general,
b) the compared samples are representative (which the corpora used here are),
c) truly spoken (rather than only speech-based) English displays similar tendencies,
d) long-term trends point in the same direction.

3.3.2 Short-term trends

3.3.2.1 The 1960s vs. the 1990s: LOB - FLOB; Brown - Frown

Some of the data presented in this section have been discussed by Hundt (1997; 1998). Unlike her, however, I do not treat the two modal expressions HAVE TO and HAVE GOT TO as one construction. Additionally, I will present data from fictional language and provide figures for incidence, which facilitates comparison with the long-term trends identified in the previous section. Tables 3.7 and 3.8 summarize the development of the two modal constructions in British and American journalistic and fictional writings.

Table 3.7. HAVE TO and HAVE GOT TO in British journalistic and fictional writing (LOB vs. FLOB)

	LOBpress (1961)	FLOBpress (1991)	LOBfiction (1961)	FLOBfiction (1991)
HAVE TO (all word forms)	122	162	270	295
per 10,000 words	6.9	9.2	10.7	11.7
HAVE GOT TO	10	8	29	16
per 10,000 words	0.6	0.5	1.1	0.6

Table 3.8.   HAVE TO and HAVE GOT TO in American journalistic and fictional
writing (Brown vs. Frown)

	Brown-press (1961)	Frown-press (1992)	Brown-fiction (1961)	Frown-fiction (1992)
HAVE TO (all word forms)	91	129	300	261
per 10,000 words	5.2	7.4	11.8	10.3
HAVE GOT TO	4	9	38	33
per 10,000 words	0.2	0.5	1.5	1.3

While the figures for HAVE GOT TO in journalistic prose are too small to allow for any firm conclusions, the rather stable use of HAVE GOT TO in American and British fictional writing is broadly consonant with the data from ARCHER (previous section) and the BNC (following section). The apparent decrease of HAVE GOT TO in British and American fictional writing is not statistically significant.[42]

The figures for HAVE TO, by contrast, generally point to a growing use in journalistic writing in both regional varieties (statistically significant at the 5% level). Again, the differences in fictional language are not statistically significant. As far as HAVE TO is concerned, current British press language seems somewhat more progressive than its American counterpart: in the latter subcorpus both the incidence is lower and the increase is less pronounced. The fact that neither regional nor diachronic differences in fictional prose are statistically significant allows several alternative interpretations. Of course, these are restricted to fictional language and the construction at hand, notably the more frequent HAVE TO:

a) No change is in progress.

b) Change is ongoing but too slow for a time span of 30 years to yield significant results.

c) The database is too small.

d) British and American fictional language do not differ with respect to HAVE TO and HAVE GOT TO.

Let us consider these scenarios in turn. While I do subscribe to the last interpretation, I would tend to reject the second last because the smaller press subcorpora yield significant differences both regionally and diachronically. Whether change is ongoing or not is more difficult to decide and can perhaps not be answered. Especially difficult to account for is the fact that in British fictional language, HAVE TO, if anything, seems to be increasing whereas American fictional language appears to be moving in the opposite direction. But it will be recalled that the differences are not significant. So how can the oddity be explained that smaller subcorpora yield significant differences while larger ones do not? The solution is probably to be sought in differential speeds of change in different text types (Hundt & Mair forthcoming). Hundt & Mair investigate journalistic and academic prose as well as belles lettres. Witness their conclusions:

> Our findings require a model in which grammatical change is seen as mediated through genre. A new form arises, typically but not exclusively in a spoken variety, and then spreads through various genres until at a very remote point it can be said to have been established in 'the language'. ... In our material, journalistic prose and academic writing seem to be two poles on a scale of written genres differing in the degree to which they a) are open to innovations or b) are prone to retain conservative forms. What we are proposing is a cline of openness to innovation ranging from 'agile' to 'uptight' genres.

In their study, Hundt & Mair compare raw frequencies across different text types, which is justified by the fact that the corpora compared are similar in size (though not equal: they contain between 150,000 and 176,000 words, cf. Table 2.6). On the basis of the present data for HAVE TO, their model, if applied mechanically, might suggest that fiction is slower to respond to ongoing changes (thus representing a more 'uptight' written genre), whereas journalese, consistent with their own findings, leans towards the more 'agile' end. Even though this cannot ultimately be ruled out, I would prefer a somewhat different line of reasoning here. I do not wish to dispute the general validity of their model. Quite on the contrary, I believe that it is very valuable if it is refined somewhat. However, I suspect that it works best when not only the raw frequency of a certain linguistic element is compared to a later point in time but when the element is compared to one or more alternative options – as in the case of contracted vs. uncontracted sequences (e.g. *don't* vs. *do not*). Where mutually exclusive variants are not available or difficult to determine and investigate (as in the case of HAVE TO), I submit that the discriminating measure is *incidence*, that is, discourse frequency per given amounts of text.

The consequences for the interpretation of the development of HAVE TO in journalistic and fictional writing are as follows: as is indicated by the invariably higher incidence in fictional language – and more obviously so by the long-term increase in the fictional texts in ARCHER – this genre *has* already responded to the change, while press language is still in the process of adapting to the spoken mode. This entails that with regard to HAVE TO, fiction is not only *not slower* in responding to this change but the reverse is true, it is *faster* – a point that would be missed out if raw absolute frequencies were compared. This higher degree of susceptibility of fictional language to change, however, is not reflected in significant short-term differences within present-day English but can be derived from higher incidence synchronically. It is therefore not necessary to resort to historical data from ARCHER in order to recognize that this change is largely completed in fictional writing, although diachronic data are ultimately the only way of verifying such a claim.

In other words, a refined model that includes the criterion 'incidence' can capture otherwise inconclusive data to the extent that it may help explain why a change is ongoing in some genres but not in others. The best results will be obtained for functionally motivated changes from below. Since such changes typically move towards the spoken pole, a comparison with the incidence in spoken material can reveal whether a change has not (yet) been initiated in a specific text type, or whether stable behaviour is observed because the change has already come to an end. While Hundt & Mair's model implies the existence of such scenarios it cannot successfully account for them in its present shape.

This observation is relevant to the investigation of language change on a more general level: short-term changes in behaviour (e.g. since the 1960s) as well as stable behaviour can be exploited to establish progressiveness clines for different spoken and written text types. Once such rankings are available, we can rather confidently infer ongoing changes from purely synchronic variation. The same would seem to apply for regional varieties. It goes without saying that for individual changes predictions would only consist in statistical likelihood, by no means in certainty. But equally clearly, statistical likelihood increases with the number of investigated phenomena.

3.3.2.2   *Variation according to age in the BNC: Studies in apparent time*

If we compare the distribution of *gotta* and *got to* across different age groups, we carry out studies in apparent time, from which we can abstract diachronic trends (cf. the discussion in 2.7). This type of investigation can indicate whether HAVE GOT TO or one of its variants is still spreading in current British speech. The material from speakers tagged for age in the BNC constitutes a corpus of some 6 million words.

Table 3.9.   *Got to* and *gotta*: Variation according to age

	speakers aged 1-14	speakers aged 15-24	speakers aged 25-34	speakers aged 35-44	speakers aged 45-59	speakers aged 60+
1 Sum *gotta*	353	430	621	525	627	245
per million words	766	840	558	492	390	155
as % of all forms	63.1%	60.3%	46.2%	39.7%	36.8%	24.8%
2 Sum modal *got to*	206	283	722	798	1075	742
per million words	447	553	648	748	669	470
as % of all forms	36.9%	39.7%	53.8%	60.3%	63.2%	75.2%
3 Total of all forms	559	713	1343	1323	1702	987
per million words	1213	1393	1206	1240	1059	625

While the overall textual frequency of the construction (row 3) suggests that its spread – not differentiating the variants – has come to a halt for speakers under 45, the figures of Table 3.9 clearly suggest a progressive modalization across all age groups: with speakers getting younger, a perfect decline in the proportion of the older variant (*got to*) is observable. Consequently, with decreasing age, the proportion of the innovative variant (*gotta*) is strictly increasing. The incidence of the innovative variant, too, is decreasing steadily for speakers over 14. A glance at the percentages of the extreme poles – they differ by an impressive margin of nearly 40% – renders a chi-square test almost futile. Of course, then, the differences between the age groups are statistically significant (p < 0.001). Furthermore, there are two major leaps: first, speakers aged 60 and over use *gotta* markedly less often than those between 45 and 59 and, second, there is a sharp decrease in the innovative variant between speakers under 25 and the next older age group.

For HAVE TO a comparable investigation between two more and less progressive variants cannot be carried out since the BNC does not distinguish between more or less closely bonded or more or less reduced variants, even though closer transcription with orthographic variants such as <hafta> or <hasta> would suggest itself for prototypical reduced variants. Just consider the untypical progressive assimilation in ['hæstə] or ['hæftə], the latter being reflected in the spelling <hafta>, a connected-speech phenomenon which would be highly marked in word sequences such as *live to* or *leave to*, not to mention such rare sequences as *leave town*.[43] A study in apparent time can therefore only compare textual frequencies of the paradigm across different age groups:

Table 3.10.   HAVE TO: Variation according to age

	speakers aged 1-14	speakers aged 15-24	speakers aged 25-34	speakers aged 35-44	speakers aged 45-59	speakers aged 60+
1 Actual occurrences	797	881	1890	1705	2867	2107
2 per million words	1730	1721	1697	1598	1785	1334

All age groups under 60 behave rather uniformly as regards the text frequency of HAVE TO. Interestingly, for HAVE GOT TO this saturation phase, as it were, is reached one age group later (Table 3.9), which ties in with the previous finding that the grammaticalization proper for HAVE TO set in approximately 50 years before that of HAVE GOT TO (Figure 3.3). It appears then that some 30 years ago the increase in HAVE TO came to a halt in spoken British English and led to a stable distribution, consolidated on a high level of roughly 1,700 occurrences per million words. This is only slightly higher than the incidence found in contemporary British drama (approximately 1,500, see Figure 3.3) and roughly twice the incidence found in contemporary fictional writings (some 750, see Figure 3.4). The surprising congruence of the drama data with actual spoken data shows that the corpus is a good approximation of the spoken facts − certainly as far as HAVE TO is concerned while for the more recent HAVE GOT TO both text types lag well behind the spoken mode. Further, the observable increase in written registers (fiction, drama, press language) seems to be the closing of a gap between spoken and written language and thus demonstrates the pressures which discourse exerts on the written medium. More specifically, while the textual increase of both constructions seems to have come to a grind in spoken English in the second half of the 20th century, written text types, in particular those leaning towards the conceptually written (i.e. formal, conservative) pole of the cline, still seem to be narrowing the gap between it and the spoken code. To conclude, the preceding section has invoked a host of independent data that unequivocally demonstrate a surge in the discourse frequency and, by concomitance, an increase in grammaticalization. The late 19th century (for HAVE TO) and early 20th century (for HAVE GOT TO) have been identified as critical periods.

3.4 Syntax and semantics of HAVE TO and HAVE GOT TO

3.4.1 Mechanisms of grammaticalization

While the focus of the present section is on HAVE TO, I will indicate when observations extend to HAVE GOT TO. Section 3.3.1 has demonstrated a general increase in discourse frequency but this finding naturally calls for further qualitative and quantitative refinement.

Table 3.11.   The history of modal HAVE TO (ARCHER, drama)[44]

	British				American		
	17th c.	18th c.	19th c.	20th c.	1750- 1799	1850- 1899	1950+
Total	**0**	**2**	**19**	**56**	**2**	**8**	**35**
of which are deontic	0	2	19	54	2	8	35
of which are epistemic	0	0	0	2	0	0	0
animate subjects	0	2	18	54	2	8	32
inanimate subjects	0	0	1	2	0	0	3
present	0	2	5	17	2	2	14
as % of total		100%	26%	30%	100%	25%	40%
past/irrealis[45]	0	0	8	7	0	0	6
as % of total			42%	13%			17%
perfective	0	0	1	2	0	0	0
as % of total			5%	4%			
infinitival *have to*	0	0	5	30	0	6	15
as % of total			26%	54%		75%	43%
of which *will, shall, 'll (not)*			2	21		6	4
of which *would, should, 'd (not)*			2	5		0	2
of which other modals			1	0		0	1
of which *do, did (not)*			0	4		0	8

Notice that in American English HAVE TO is not less frequent but that the drama material is only half the amount of its British counterpart, giving in fact a fairly parallel incidence and development in both varieties. Even though the figures of individual cells, in particular for the early stages, are rather small and have therefore to be interpreted with some caution, we can rather confidently assume that:

- Epistemic meanings involving HAVE TO are fairly recent and even today constitute only a small proportion of all uses.
- Inanimate subjects occurring with HAVE TO are also of recent vintage and seem to be equally rare.
- Two more constructions of HAVE TO have only recently become common: interrogatives and negation by DO support.

It is trivially true that the scarcity of all three constructions does not rule out their prior existence but, equally clearly, they were not particularly frequent before. While DO support will be treated in some detail in the next section, I shall now deal in turn with inanimate subjects and the mechanisms of change involved in the evolution of epistemic semantics.

Inanimate subjects

The earliest occurrences of HAVE TO with inanimate subjects in the drama and fiction subcorpora of ARCHER date from the very end of the 19th century. Both instances are passive constructions:

(41)   (She pulls the letter out of the machine so crossly that it tears.) There! now I've spoiled this letter! have to be done all over again! (G.B. Shaw, ARCHER D6, BrE, 1895).

(42)   I was conscious that all my, let us say, imaginative and diplomatic powers would have to be exerted. (Arthur Machen, ARCHER F6, BrE, 1895)

Inanimate subjects in the main clause actualize the decategorialization and desemanticization of HAVE since inanimate NPs cannot possess anything. Such loosening selection restrictions on the subject result in unambiguously modal meaning of the predicate action. It is therefore no coincidence that 'independence of the subject' is listed as one synchronic criterion of auxiliarihood in Quirk et al. (1985: 137).

Epistemic and future readings

As has been widely documented in the works by Sweetser (1990), Kytö (1991a), Bybee et al. (1994) and Heine (1993), the extension from agent-oriented (or, more specifically, deontic) to epistemic modality is a well-trodden path in the history of the English modals as well as crosslinguistically. In many instances of change, however, it is not clear whether metaphorical transfer (argued in Sweetser 1988; 1990) or the conventionalization of context-induced inferences (generally favoured by Bybee 1988; Brinton 1988; Traugott 1989; Traugott & König 1991) is the mechanism that captures best the developments at hand. More recent work such as Bybee et al. (1994: Chs. 1, 8) or Traugott (1996) tends to acknowledge that both processes are fundamental mechanisms in semantic change and grammaticalization, but favours more strongly metonymy-driven accounts, including subjectification (see also the discussion in section 3.2.1 or the papers in Barcelona 2000).

Let us consider some textual evidence of HAVE TO against this background. The first epistemic readings in the corpus are even more recent than the first inanimate subjects and they still contain traces of deontic modality as in (43), where nonetheless the apodosis is also a logical conclusion of the protasis:

(43)   If the accused is not here, the hearing will have to go on without him. (1961, ARCHER D9, BrE)

In this context it is important to note that epistemic modality to a certain degree correlates with inanimate subjects: not only are such subjects incompatible with a possession reading (the older, lexical meaning of HAVE); it is also difficult for inanimate subjects to be obliged to complete a predicate action, that is, to co-occur with deontic HAVE TO (the earlier root modal meaning).[46]

In grammaticalization, obligation serves not only as a source domain for epistemic modality but also for the future (Fleischman 1982; Bybee et al. 1994). Even though futurity is certainly not (yet) a focal sense of HAVE (GOT) TO, it is not inconceivable that this semantics too will evolve. It was pointed out before that obligation often points to the future because the predicate action is typically not actualized. Hence examples containing an obligation reading with explicit mention of future time reference come as no surprise. Witness some examples:

(44)   So next time we have to stay at her house again? (BNC KBW
        1454)

(45)   ... twelve thousand next year then we have to er erm there has to
        be further offers from provinces. (BNC KB0 1964)

(46)   Next Thursday I've got to take a cheque into a, well a deposit
        into ... (BNC KD8 7473)

(47)   A   Is it Thursday today?
        B   No Friday.
        A   ... I can't believe I've gotta get up at flipping ten o'clock
                on Sunday!
        B   Oh! My God! (BNC KPG 393)

(48)   You got to go this Sunday? (BNC KBE 716)

The above examples are all compatible with a deontic meaning, and the
inference to a future reading is by no means conventionalized at the
present stage (recall that all of these examples contain a future temporal
adverbial). If, however, futurity actually evolves as a proper meaning of
HAVE (GOT) TO, then context-induced metonymical change seems the
more likely evolutionary path than metaphorical transfer, because future
and obligation are very much related (contiguous) domains.
        Today, for both HAVE TO and HAVE GOT TO, the older, deontic
meaning is the most frequent one (cf. Table 3.11; or Mindt 1995: 155-
162). This is not very surprising considering that both constructions are
relatively recent. Deontic modality, then, currently still constitutes their
focal sense. Let us cite one example from the BNC of both HAVE TO and
HAVE GOT TO for each modality. While (49) names explicitly the
external authority (*mum*) imposing the obligation upon the speaker, (50)
documents the deontic sense since here *gotta* is preceded by various
other items denoting obligation:

(49)   ... me mum says I have to wait. (BNC KSS 3961)

(50)   I can't, need wear them all the time, gotta. I never take them
        [i.e. speaker's glasses] off now. (BNC KCX 8448)

In the debate over whether the development from deontic to epistemic
meanings is best accounted for by metaphorical leap or by the gradual

conventionalization of inferences, Bybee et al. (1994: Ch. 6) side with Traugott (1989) in being rather sceptical of metaphor. However, they do accept metaphorical transfer for the development of epistemic *must* since "the contexts in which *must* has an obligation sense ... and the contexts in which it has an inferred certainty sense ... are largely mutually exclusive" (1994: 200f). While they allow for "a restricted set of cases [in which] the reading of *must* can be ambiguous between an epistemic and an obligation reading" (*ibid.*), they assume a basic distinction between exclusively obligative readings for future contexts on the one hand and present and past sentences with exclusively inferred certainty readings on the other (examples taken from *ibid.*):

(51)   The letter must arrive sometime next week.

(52)   The letter must be in the mail.

(53)   The letter must have been in the mail.

It appears that this position might still be too strong since although the default interpretation in (51) is indeed obligation, it is not difficult to conceive of an epistemic context such as:

(51a)   The letter must arrive sometime next week. I mailed it yesterday and it normally takes only three or four days to get there.[47]

Unlike *must*, HAVE TO does not even display a tendency for past environments to co-occur with epistemic modality. *Had to* has typically only an obligation reading:

(54)   Each category had to be put into a container and taken to a collection centre. (BNC D90 136)

As for clear instances of epistemic meanings, in the following prenatal situation inferred (near) certainty for HAVE GOT TO is in evidence given a context replete with epistemic modals and various instances of an epistemic matrix clause *I think*:

(55)   A   I think they have got a point, I think it might, it might, ...
        B   Yeah, yeah.
        A   ... have the same effect on the baby.
        B   Well it's got to I think we've, look what it's doing to
             yourself.
        A   Yeah, I think it must have some effect there ...
        B   And seeing you've got another life inside you, it must be
             doing something to them, mustn't it? (BNC KC5 1251)

There are various strategies that can trigger unambiguous epistemic
modality of HAVE (GOT) TO, for example an infinitival *to* clause
functioning as conditional protasis (56) or a probability adverb
alongside an epistemic matrix verb (57):

(56)   ... and in his exact words he said you've got to be really stupid
        to tell anyone anything in this place and I said ... (BNC KP6
        2298)

(57)   ..., and I think probably it's got to be her. (BNC KDW 1189)

Another way to epistemic modality is by implicature (58), here
strengthened by *so*. To make the context clear, in (58) a group of
youngsters is deciding which film they are going to see:

(58)   S1   A, Mash, B, Out of Africa or C, The Last Tango in
              Paris?
        S2   C
        S3   Ooh
        S4   Paris, so it's gotta be dirty innit? (BNC KCU 9339)

S4 exploits a stereotype: Paris is the city of love, therefore a film
situated in Paris has to be titillating (needless to say, the connotations of
Tango fit into this context too).[48] From both a pragmatic and a syntactic
point of view, it is noteworthy that S4 in (58) employs the invariant tag
innit, not the standard *hasn't it*, which incidentally would not sound
very natural in this context.[49] This attests on the one hand to the opacity
of the reduced auxiliary, so much so that one might argue yet again
mere phonemic status for the clitic. At the same time the use of *innit*
indicates that *gotta* is not a full-fledged central modal syntactically,
which would have to be the operator in the tag (**gottan't it?*). Parallel
examples are legion in the BNC. Compare:

(59)   S1   Well that gotta be weeks now innit?
        S2   Oh yeah!   (BNC, KE0 2845)

(60)   S1   It's got to be innit?
        S2   Mm. (BNC, KE6 1361)

(61)   S1   Gotta use the old packet of mince innit?
        S2   Yeah. Have you packed that?   (BNC, KE6 6044)

3.4.1.1   The origin of HAVE (GOT) TO revisited

The data presented in Table 3.11 (p. 89) are not without consequences for the genesis of modal HAVE TO, and they also have an impact on the gradualness vs. leap issue (i.e. whether inferencing or metaphor better accounts for semantic changes in the modal domain). It is important to recall that the increase in the construction started independently of an increase in inanimate subjects and independently of metaphor-induced epistemic meanings. It will be remembered that both uses account for rather marginal proportions of HAVE TO even today (see Table 3.11). Thus, we can hardly attribute the observed leaps in discourse frequency to such processes as loosening of subject selection restrictions or metaphor (on the latter see Heine et al. 1991: Chs. 2f; or Sweetser 1990: Ch. 3).

In progressive and futural contexts as well as in the vast majority of past contexts, invariant *must* and HAVE TO are not in competition.[50] In the simple present tense, however, the two are interchangeable. Myhill (1995) has labelled this facultative use 'nonsyntactic' HAVE TO. As Table 3.11 shows, the proportion of the nonsyntactic HAVE TO has remained relatively stable (at around 30%) in both varieties since the early 19th century, even though a slight rise seems to be in evidence, in particular for American English. This is to say that both the incidence of syntactic HAVE TO (where no near synonyms are available) and nonsyntactic HAVE TO (where such alternative items exist) has risen. This finding indeed attests to the generally accepted position that the spread of the quasi-modals is connected with the failure of the central modals to occur in certain contexts. At the same time such data make it difficult to argue that the defective paradigm of the central modals (i.e. a syntactic gap) is the prime or even sole motivation for the emergence of HAVE TO (with Plank 1984; contra Lightfoot 1979). The fact that present tense forms are among the first attested uses of modal HAVE TO musters further evidence against a causal link between the genesis of the construction and the defective paradigm of the central modal verbs, because it is precisely such present environments where the modals have always been available. Nevertheless, as grammaticalization takes off with progressive generalization to all verbs in the 19th century (which is manifest in soaring discourse frequencies), syntactic HAVE TO does constitute the majority of all uses (roughly two thirds).

To conclude, it appears that a whole gamut of interrelated developments – many of which had started or were even completed in Middle English – has proved conducive to the growing use of modal HAVE TO. Many of these factors are connected to the well-known fact that English progressively lost its inflectional endings in Old and Middle English:[51]

- the absence of nonfinite forms of MOT (*must*) and SHALL since Old English
- the trend towards the periphrastic subjunctive (*should, would, 'd*; witness the increase in Table 3.11) requiring an increasing number of infinitival forms[52]
- a growing obligatoriness of the *will* future, increasing the demand for nonfinite forms, where previously tense-neutral present forms were common (cf. the high proportion of *will* in Table 3.11)[53]
- the progressive opacity of the preterite meaning of *must*, that is, past tense form without past time reference, since Middle English (despite the few obsolescent uses reported in Jacobsson 1994)
- the gradual rise of the DO periphrasis for questions and negation since late ME (cf. Ellegård 1953; Kroch 1989; Stein 1990; Denison 1993: Ch. 10; Garrett 1998), which apparently had an impact on HAVE TO only fairly recently, though.[54]

In sum, infinitival and tensed forms of HAVE TO have indeed partially filled a syntactic gap, but this was not seminal to the rise of the construction as such. Also, the data prove that interrelated syntactic changes may, and typically do, take centuries. As was pointed out before, layering and subsequent replacement of older grammatical morphemes by periphrastic expressions is the norm rather than the exception across languages. In fact, both layering and expressivity as one of its potential cognitive triggers seem such natural principles in language change that probably no syntactic trigger is needed in the initial grammaticalization stages of a new construction.

Nevertheless, there seems to be a conducive syntactic environment for the new constructions. Almost all early contiguous HAVE GOT TO constructions (examples (10) to (19), pp. 62-64) – and almost all contiguous HAVE TO constructions in Shakespeare; cf. examples (2) to (7), p. 59 above and (64) to (70) below – occur in extracted environments like relative clauses or questions. Recall three relevant examples invoked earlier:

(6)   Come, let me see what task I have to do. (Shakespeare, *Titus Andronicus*, I, i, 276)

(16)   'For business,' replied Sikes; 'so say what you've got to say.'

(19)   'Well, what have you got to say to me?' (both from Dickens' *Oliver Twist*, p. 188 and p. 154, respectively)

Questions and relative clauses, therefore, seem to represent favourable structural environments for the incoming constructions, perhaps because syntactic boundaries between main and subordinate clauses are blurred or indeed nonexistent since one constituent is part of either clause (recall the discussion of apokoinou, p. 59 above). In any case, under extraction, i.e. in a sentence like *Tell me about the letter I have (got) to write*, the difference between the crucial grammaticalization stages III (*I have (got) a letter to write*) and IV (*I have (got) to write a letter*) appears to be neutralized.[55] The next section will introduce an additional discourse-based factor.

3.4.1.2   *A discourse-based factor in the evolution of HAVE (GOT) TO*

This section argues that the idiomatic expression HAVE TO *say/tell* has played a central role in the modalization of HAVE TO. The expression is attested as early as in Old English loan translations of Latin Bible texts, if only in discontinuous form (the following two examples are taken from Visser 1969: 1475-1486 and OED *s.v. have* no. 7, respectively):

(62)   ... ic hæbbe eow fela   to secganne ... (OE Gosp., John 16, 12)
        I have you much to say   ('I have much to say to you')

(63)   Ic hæbbe ðe to secʒenne sumðing. (c.1000 *Ags. Gosp.* Luke vii, 40)
        I have you to say   something ('I have something to say to you')

It was mentioned earlier that in Shakespearean usage, that is, around half a millennium later, contiguous HAVE TO followed by the infinitive of the verb is still relatively rare at 0.6 occurrences per 10,000 words. To compare this with current spontaneous usage, this is less than a fifth of the incidence of modern lexical verbs like WALK or SEND (cf. Appendix 1). Interestingly, though, initial idiomatization is in evidence even in Early Modern English since two verbal complements stand out in Shakespeare's dramas. These are *say* and *do*. As is characteristic of Shakespearean and even of present-day usage, such constructions do not necessarily express deontic modality and typically contain a direct object preceding HAVE:

(64)   I would fain know what you have to say. (*Much Ado about Nothing*, III, v, 28)

(65)   Sister, it is not little I have to say of what most nearly appertains to us both. (*King Lear*, I, i, 283f)

(66)   The news I have to tell your Majesty/ Is that by sudden floods and fall of waters/ Buckingham's army is dispers'd and scatter'd;/ ... (*King Richard III*, IV, iv, 511-513)

(67)   How much I had to do to calm his rage! (*Hamlet*, IV, vii, 193)

(68)   I know vat [*sic*] I have to do; adieu. (*The Merry Wives of Windsor*, V, iii, 5)

(69)   Cousins, you know what you have to do. (*Much Ado about Nothing*, I, ii, 22)

(70)   I will not have to do with you. (*Much Ado about Nothing*, v, i, 77; *Love's Labour's Lost*, V, ii, 428)[56]

Both constructions have survived to this day and instantiate early traces of grammaticalization: in sentences (64) to (70) the possession meaning of HAVE is bleached. Further, deontic meaning aspects are present or at least traceable. In the case of *do* complements (unless they are followed by *with* sb.) deontic meaning is rather the default interpretation. With verbs of saying, on the other hand, a deontic meaning component is less focal, but speakers can be compelled to say something by either an outer force (as in the case of messages, be the force imposed by the sender or the addressee) or by an internal force (such as the speaker's conscience). In fact, a related argument holds for HAVE GOT TO, where a verbal complement *say* also predates unambiguously obligative readings which are characteristic for other verbs (cf. examples (17) to (19), p. 64 above). Witness for instance an example from Jane Austen's *Pride and Prejudice* (XVII, 128, BrE 1813):

(71)   'Very true, indeed; – and now, my dear Jane, what have you got to say in behalf of the interested people who have probably been concerned ...'[57]

While HAVE TO *do* (*with*) might be conjectured to have played a role in the grammaticalization of HAVE TO,[58] this is not strongly supported by the ARCHER data. HAVE TO *say*, however, almost certainly has been a major force in the development of the modal construction. Crucially, contiguous HAVE TO *say* gained currency not until the period immediately preceding the rapid growth of deontic HAVE TO. Inspection of textual evidence from ARCHER reveals that three out of the four earliest instances of HAVE TO in the drama corpus (that is, up to 1800) are followed by a verb of saying; the fourth, not surprisingly and also reminiscent of Shakespearean usage, is *do*:[59]

(72)   But I shall have time enough to make you hear every thing I have to say to you. (BrE, John Vanbrugh *The Provok'd Wife*, 1730, II)

(73)   ...; doleful tidings I have to tell ... Then worse I have to tell, ... (AmE, John Leakock *The Fall of British Tyranny*, 1776, III, xi)

(74)   And now, Sir, all we have to do is to prevent ... (BrE, Thomas Francklin *The Contract*, 1776, II)

This finding is not confined to drama. Verbs of saying are also the earliest complements in the fictional component of ARCHER, where such structures are actually attested earlier. However, for the earliest two examples modal usage can doubtless be ruled out, while deontic and (less obviously) possessive meaning aspects are present in the slightly later example (77), where the speaker does not voluntarily break the bad news:

(75)   ..., what cause can I have to complain of that ... (John Bulteel:
        The History of Merame, ARCHER F1, BrE 1664)

(76)   ..., which I had a more eager desire to grant, then [*sic*] she could
        have to beg for: ... (*ibid.*, BrE 1664)

(77)   ...; but the News I have to tell you, will even surpass your Fears.
        (John Campbell, *The Polite Correspondence: or Rational
        Amusement*, ARCHER, F2; BrE 1740)

It is important to comment on the discourse-based genesis of HAVE TO.
First a construction – here contiguous HAVE TO – comes to be used in
arguably modal meanings such as (64)ff. In fact, weakly possessive
meanings and contexts with verbs of saying continue to predominate
until roughly 1850. By this time, the construction HAVE TO + verb of
saying, probably due to repetition, enjoys idiomatic status and is
frequent enough to qualify as marginally grammatical or, in this specific
instance, lexicalized. At this point it seems helpful to invoke Bybee's
(1985: 117) thesis that every mention of a word leaves a trace in the
mental lexicon:

> If we metaphorically suppose that a word can be written into the [mental]
> lexicon, then each time a word in processing is mapped onto its lexical
> representation it is as though the representation was traced over again,
> etching it with deeper and darker lines each time. Each time a word is heard
> and produced it leaves a slight trace on the lexicon, it increases its lexical
> strength.

Elsewhere (Krug 1998a) I have argued that this effect applies to word
sequences. Here I claim that it is a fundamental factor in the genesis of
grammatical constructions too, since only after having gained this
idiomatic status does it become possible for the construction to enter
into the next stage of the grammaticalization path. This is the
generalization stage, during which drastic frequency gains can be
observed (see Figures 3.3 and 3.4).

This additional force which I propose in the development of the
agent-oriented construction has implications for a consideration of the
mechanisms involved in grammaticalization. Metaphorical transfer, an
abrupt shift between domains (generally from more concrete to more
abstract, grammatical ones) was ruled out to account for the substantial
increase in the construction because of its low textual frequency and

relatively late occurrence (p. 95). Rather, pragmatically motivated inferences seem to hold responsible for what we witness in the case of HAVE TO *say/tell*. These gradually lead to an expansion of the contexts in which HAVE TO is used, which in turn brings about the gradual conventionalization of the modal meaning.

Let us elaborate on the reasons for this hypothesis. As Heine et al. (1991: 113) point out, inferencing "leads to the emergence of overlapping senses" and this most adequately explains the development of HAVE TO *say*. As has been pointed out above, the possession meaning of HAVE is bleached out, for what is said cannot normally be possessed, at least not physically. One might argue, though, that HAVE TO *say* denotes an abstract type of possession, i.e. 'being in possession of, for instance, news or ideas' (cf. also (71) above for a related example of HAVE GOT TO *say*). This, then, could be seen as a logical intermediate step in the progression from a possessive to a deontic reading.

What is crucial for the phrase HAVE TO *say* is that an agent-oriented reading is generated by pragmatic inferences: since the standard possession meaning is inadequate in the context, the hearer will look for a more informative, more newsworthy interpretation. This is here: 'some internal or external force obliges the speaker to say something.'[60] This context-induced reinterpretation on the part of the hearer leads to the coexistence of a (weakly or abstract) possessive and a (more focal) deontic reading of the proposition – as for example in (77). While unambiguously deontic constructions sporadically occur at earlier stages, it is only after this stage that large-scale generalization to verbs other than verbs of saying proceeds.[61] This in turn is actualized by the increase of structures with verbs where a deontic reading is the only possible interpretation such as in:

(78)   I have to be ever on my guard, and I have often been sensible
        that unless I watched every step.... (Arthur Machen, ARCHER
        F6 180, BrE, 1895)

It is at this stage that the rise in textual frequency gains momentum: the conventionalization of the inference is well under way and subsequently results in the lexicalization of the modal meaning.

To sum up, in the emergence of agent-oriented HAVE TO the mechanism of context-induced inferencing (from possession to deontic meaning) accompanied by the related mechanism of subjectification (see 3.2.1) seems to be followed by the mechanism of generalization from verbs of saying to all verbs. The mechanism of metaphor, however, appears to play no more than a complementary role.[62] In conclusion, while metaphor is a cognitively appealing concept that has rightly become an important explanatory principle in mainstream linguistics and the cognitive sciences in general, it does not seem to be the prime factor in the development of epistemic meanings of modal verbs and modal constructions. It can almost certainly be ruled out as seminal for epistemic HAVE TO and HAVE GOT TO, and even one of the classic examples, *viz.* the development of epistemic *must*, is perhaps not the clear case of metaphorical transfer it once seemed (cf. p. 93).

3.4.1.3   Gotta – *a preterite present verb?*

Based solely on an apparent parallel between HAVE GOT TO and the central modal verbs of English, the present section is essentially a suggestion for further research. Closer inspection of both historical and contemporary textual evidence is required in order to understand the details involved in what seems to be a recurrent process in the evolution of modal verbs and constructions. The parallel is established as follows: historically, *gotta* is derived from HAVE GOT TO, a perfective form. If, however, we analyse *got to* synchronically in isolation – rather than regard it as an instance of auxiliary omission – then *gotta* could be immediately derived from a simple past form. It is interesting in this context that the development of present semantics is more transparent for the older construction HAVE GOT 'have received', hence 'possess'.[63] Certainly *gotta* has lost all formal signs and semantic notions of preteriteness (if it ever had any).

In this respect, then, *gotta* seems rather similar to the central modals, which, except *will*, are all preterite present verbs. And even *will* had an irregular morphology akin to that of the preterite presents (see e.g. Campbell 1959: 343-347; Nagle 1989: 56-61; Denison 1993: 296). It will be remembered that the class of preterite present verbs had already lost their reference to past events in pre-OE times. Their new weak past tense forms then again largely lost their potential to refer to the past: *should, could, might* and *must* rarely indicate past tense today but usually counterfactuality or other modal notions. The same now seems to hold for *gotta* and, as we shall see in Chapter 4, for *wanted* in some contexts. Hence there seems to be a tendency for English verbs with modal semantics to attach non-past meanings to their preterite or perfective forms. Just how this mechanism encroached on verbal constructions like (HAVE) GOT TO and WANT TO needs to be looked at more closely in future work.

3.4.2   Present-day properties

The previous sections on diachronic trends naturally overlaps to some extent with this one on present-day syntactic and semantic properties of HAVE TO and HAVE GOT TO. Quirk et al. (1985: 141-146), Bauer (1989), Johansson & Oksefjell (1996: 66f) and Hundt (1997: 143-145; 1998: 53-55) have investigated the behaviour of the two constructions. They unanimously agree on two points. First, under negation and in questions HAVE TO occurs predominantly with DO support. Second, HAVE GOT TO is not found at all (Johansson & Oksefjell 1996) or very rarely (Hundt 1998) in negation and interrogatives. Since their data are drawn from spoken material of the 1950s to 1970s (Johansson & Oksefjell 1996) or written material (Hundt 1997, 1998), it will be interesting to test their findings against current spoken material from the BNC.

3.4.2.1   *HAVE TO*

In order to understand the current behaviour of HAVE TO under negation, we have to take a brief glance at the longer-term trends. As will be recalled from the discussion in section 2.8, for many analysts negation by NOT is a defining property of auxiliaries (e.g. *cannot, isn't*). Since HAVE can function as an auxiliary, NOT negation is theoretically an option for HAVE TO. It has, however, apparently always been rare for both HAVE TO and HAVE GOT TO. The only attested instances in either the fictional or drama subcorpora of ARCHER are British English from 1796 and 1955:

(79)   However, if you have the courage to send such a message, I have not to deliver it: ... (Frances Burney, ARCHER F3; BrE 1796)[64]

(80)   You haven't to think twice to see the pickle we'd be in then. (O'Casey, BrE 1955, ARCHER D9, 278)[65]

The dates are interesting on two counts. First, they suggest that NOT negation was used rather early (if rarely) – certainly earlier than negation by supportive DO, which only gained currency in the 20th century (see Table 3.11). The latest attestation from 1955 is interesting because while we find two instances of auxiliary negation in the LOB material from 1961 (full version), no such structure is attested in either its contemporary American English counterpart or the more recent corpora FLOB and Frown:

(81)   I was determined that as soon as I could I was going to go somewhere where she hadn't to keep me. (LOB fiction, P16, 179)

(82)   And she hadn't to doubt his sincerity any more ... (LOB fiction, P06, 57)

The virtual absence of NOT negation in present-day written English points to a diachronic development from rather unproductive auxiliary negation to DO negation. This argument is strongly supported by evidence from current spoken British English, where NOT negation occurs extremely seldom:

Table 3.12.   Negation of HAVE TO in the spoken BNC[66]

	NOT negation	DO negation
Past	7 (*hadn't to; had not to*)	136 (*didn't/ did not have to*)
Present	5 (*hasn't/haven't to; has/have not to*)	818 (*do(es)n't/ do(e)s not have to*)
Sum	12	954
Other auxiliaries	133 (notably *wouldn't, won't, shouldn't*)	

Significantly, where NOT negation is found, it occurs in the language of older speakers who apparently exhibit the retention of an obsolescent structure. Witness the only five syntactically transparent NOT negations of present tense modal HAVE TO in 10m words:

(83)   But, I haven't to tell anyone. (BNC KB8, 3764)

(84)   She said I can't tell you, I haven't to tell you! (BNC KB8, 5178)

(85)   What have I, well I haven't to, I've got to fit the erm cord symbols, you know, (BNC KC2, 272)

(86)   ... cos I know she smokes, so what does she do that we haven't to know, so I says oh I says this bed isn't gonna keep being here ... (BNC KSS, 3595)

(87)   ... he hasn't to go in, he's not bad enough (BNC KB2 2435)

The speakers of the above examples are 53 (twice), 63, 72 and 77 years of age. NOT negation in past and optative or counterfactual contexts is equally restricted to older speakers:[67]

(88)   I hadn't to put me head out, I hadn't to be seen ... (BNC KCS 1800; 63 years old)

(89)   Oh I wish I hadn't to go out tonight. (BNC KRO 416; 50 years old)

(90)   Well I mean she she hadn't to have one part of the house. It wasn't hers. ... we hadn't to go. We hadn't to go even.(BNC KSS 1183ff; 53 years old)

A regional factor, too, seems relevant since most speakers come from northern areas (see Map 3.1, p. 112, for the demarcation of regions in the BNC): of a total of eleven examples tagged for age, three each are attributed to speakers from the central North, Lancashire and the north-west Midlands; one each to a speaker from the north-east Midlands and London. Furthermore, an interesting semantic facet emerges from the above examples. They show that *haven't/hadn't to* is usually used to express prohibition synonymously with deontic *mustn't*. The written example (81) from 1961 is an exception. Intriguingly, the one spoken example which does not express prohibition (89) is uttered by the most southern (i.e. London) speaker. Generally, therefore, this renders the two negation strategies semantically distinct: DO negation 'not be obliged' contrasts with obsolescent HAVE NOT TO 'not be allowed'. That NOT negation (as well as auxiliary syntax of HAVE TO in questions) is rare for HAVE TO has been noted before by Quirk et al. (1985: 146), presumably going back to Johansson (1979):

Studies in BrE usage show that over 85 per cent of instances of *have to* in negative and interrogative clauses are constructed with DO. Elicitation tests have further indicated that negative constructions without DO (of the kind *I hadn't to walk more than a mile*) are less acceptable than interrogative constructions without DO (such as *Has he to answer the letter this week?*).

While Quirk et al.'s position is undisputed, the age of speakers using NOT negation in the BNC evidences an almost complete change and thus suggests an even stronger formulation plus a historical explanation: the fact that it is rare and only marginally acceptable is precisely due to its being obsolescent.

As Table 3.12 demonstrates, DO negation is excessively frequent (702 occurrences of *don't have to* alone in the spoken BNC), at least when compared to NOT negation. In fact, DO negation dominates the entire negation paradigm of HAVE TO since it also by far outnumbers other negated auxiliaries like *wouldn't* and *won't*. Apparently, then, we witness a development from auxiliary to main verb syntax. Suffice it here to mention two factors that help account for this development. The first is again discourse-based: for its low productivity NOT negation had not yet become highly conventionalized for HAVE TO and hence remained susceptible to change.[68] The second is one of Lehmann's parameters of grammaticalization (1995, quoted in Chapter 2), *viz.* the increased bonding between the constituents HAVE and TO. NOT negation is tantamount to separating the two constituents HAVE and TO, but interruptability has certainly decreased if we look at the history of this erstwhile discontinuous construction. Chapter 5 will discuss the implications of the apparent movement towards main verb syntax for the unidirectionality claim in grammaticalization.

3.4.2.2   *HAVE GOT TO*

As far as of HAVE GOT TO is concerned, previous analysts have not interpreted their findings in the light of ongoing grammaticalization or modalization. Let us therefore compare the syntax of the construction and its variants with the criteria for modal auxiliaries. For convenience, Tables 3.13 and 3.15 provide a summary of modal and some further auxiliary properties of HAVE GOT TO, respectively.

Table 3.13.   Modal properties of HAVE GOT TO

Modal property	Example
a) absence of non-finite forms	*I'm having got to go. (no single progressive form in the full BNC) *in order to have got to *gotting/*gottaed/*to gotta
b) cannot be preceded by other auxiliaries	*I will have got to/ gotta leave.
c) absence of inflections	
• no third person singular *-s*	*He gottas. But: She gotta open a separate bank account of her own. (BNC KC5 2591)
• no productive past tense form	*They gottaed; ??They had gotta leave at six. Cf. preference for *had to*
d) absence of imperative	*Have got to go now! *Gotta go now!
e) cannot undergo passivization	*She is gottaed.
f) negation avoided	very rare in the spoken BNC; cf. the preference for HAVE TO (see Table 3.14)

As Table 3.13 demonstrates, *gotta* has a highly defective paradigm, and it is evident that far more modal criteria apply to *gotta* than to its parent structure HAVE GOT TO – or even to the related construction HAVE TO.[69] First of all, the infinitival marker *to* is obscured so that *gotta* governs the plain infinitive. It will be recalled that this is a crucial criterion of modal verbs (cf. Krug, in press, on *wanna;* Traugott 1997: 193 on *oughta, hafta;* Pullum 1997: 85 on all 'therapy verbs'). Evidence of the synchronic opacity of *gotta* is provided by the existence of *gotta* that is immediately followed by *to*:

(91)   You've gotta to do it so it's clear, concise and puts across the information that you feel is important to get across. (instructor in a business training session, BNC JND 90)[70]

Second, *gotta* lacks nonfinite forms (such as the infinitive or present and past participles) as well as inflected forms. This is to a lesser extent also true for HAVE GOT TO, as Palmer (1989: 114), Quirk et al. (1985: 141) or Johansson & Oksefjell (1996: 66) have observed. As a consequence, *gotta* cannot follow auxiliaries other than HAVE, which in addition is often deleted (see Table 3.16). Third, passivization, emphatic positive with supportive DO and 2nd person imperative do not exist.

Furthermore, constructions that can theoretically be formed but which are untypical of modals are avoided. While the central modals take NOT negation, *gotta* can't (**gottan't*). However, *gotta* hardly occurs in negative contexts such as *haven't gotta*. The past tense *had gotta* or *had got to* is similarly rare (see Appendix 3). HAVE TO is generally used instead when these forms are required and this item therefore enjoys far higher proportions of negation and preterite forms than HAVE GOT TO. We are not dealing with small margins here: the relative frequency of negation with HAVE TO is roughly five times as frequent, past tense forms some 15 times as frequent as with HAVE GOT TO:

Table 3.14.   Negation and past forms of HAVE TO and HAVE GOT TO in the spoken BNC[71]

	HAVE TO	HAVE GOT TO
Negation	1121	142
As % of all modal uses	6.6%	1.5%
Past forms	4235	156
As % of all modal uses	25.1%	1.7%

The data on negation from the spoken BNC, then, confirm the scarcity which Hundt (1997; 1998) has observed for the written mode. Equally avoided are interrogatives (Johansson & Oksefjell 1996: 66; Hundt 1998: 55), which would require that *gotta* be used as an operator in inversion (**Gotta you go?*), if it were a fully-fledged central modal. Interestingly, in some dialects *gotta* can take DO support in questions,[72] e.g. *Do you gotta go?* Even though this makes *gotta* resemble a full verb, it nevertheless shows that speakers who use DO support reanalyse *gotta* as a new, simplex verb that is quite remote from the modal idiom which would suggest interrogative *Have you got to go?* Again, the relationship between DO support and unidirectionality will be discussed together with the behaviour of further items (HAVE TO, NEED TO, WANT TO) in Chapter 5. Table 3.15 shows that HAVE GOT TO possesses further properties that are typical of all auxiliaries, not only of modal verbs:

Table 3.15.   Further auxiliary properties of HAVE GOT TO

Auxiliary property	Example
a) independence of subject	Jane has got to/ gotta do it ~ It('s) got to/ gotta be done by Jane
b) full and reduced variants	have got to, 've got to, got to, gotta (cf. will vs. 'll)
c) operator in reduced clause	Yeah I've bloody got to haven't I. (BNC KP4 288) Yeah, we've gotta do a transcription on Friday haven't we? – Yeah. We have got to. (BNC KP5 1941)
d) no emphatic positive	*Yes, I DO have got to/ gotta come.

To sum up, patently more auxiliary criteria apply to *gotta* than to its historical predecessor HAVE GOT TO. We can conclude, then, that the variants of the construction – some orthographically and orthoepically accepted ones are given in Table 3.15 and Note 29 – represent different stages in the process of grammaticalization: the more explicit ones, i.e. the less heavily reduced ones, are also less grammaticalized. This result will receive further support from the stylistic investigation.

3.5   Stylistic variation

Table 3.16 summarizes the behaviour of the variants *got to* and *gotta* in the spoken BNC in terms of overall frequency and auxiliary omission against the background of stylistic variation. As is often the case, the informal variety is in the vanguard of change. It is hardly surprising that the reduced form *gotta* is preferred in informal situations (cf. rows 5 and 6): in broadly comparable amounts of text, *gotta* enjoys a frequency three and a half times higher in spontaneous speech than in formal contexts (the incidence, in fact, is some five times higher). Further, measured proportionately against all uses of the construction, *gotta* accounts for almost half of all occurrences in informal speech, which is twice the share of *gotta* in formal speech. The whole construction HAVE GOT TO is also roughly twice as frequent in informal contexts as in formal contexts (row 7). Thus the label of informality commonly attached to it (e.g. Palmer 1989: 114) seems justified, even though its spread documented in the apparent-time study (Table 3.9) suggests that stylistic constraints may fade in the future.

For present-day English, however, the informality of HAVE GOT TO is further supported by data for other items from the same semantic field. The reverse of what was said of HAVE GOT TO holds for *must*: this is roughly half as frequent as HAVE GOT TO in spontaneous speech, almost as frequent in public speech and some 20 times more frequent in written English. Hence, *must* leans towards the formal end of the formality cline. HAVE TO, by contrast, is rather stable across different levels of formality and thus appears to be stylistically neutral. This finding for present-day English tallies with Biber et al.'s (1998: 208f) diachronic results.

Table 3.16.   Stylistic variation of modal *got to* and *gotta* in the spoken BNC[73]

		private speech (c. 4m words)	public speech (c. 6m words)
1	Sum *had/'d/has/'s/have/'ve/not/-n't got to*	2396	2097
	as % of all *got to*	76.4%	82.4%
2	elliptical *got to*[74]	740	448
	as % of all *got to*	23.6%	17.6%
3	Sum *had/'d/has/'s/have/'ve/not/-n't gotta*	1651	571
	as % of all *gotta*	60.9%	76.5%
4	elliptical *gotta*	1059	175
	as % of all *gotta*	39.1%	23.5%
5	Sum *gotta*	2710	746
	as % of all forms	46.4%	22.7%
6	Sum *got to*	3136	2545
	as % of all forms	53.6%	77.3%
7	Total of all forms	5846	3291
8	Sum elliptical *got to* and *gotta*	1799	623
	as % of all forms	30.8%	18.9%

Not surprisingly, HAVE ellipsis – which is tantamount to univerbation and modalization of *have got to* – is more frequent in informal situations than in formal contexts (rows 2, 4, 8). This means that formality goes together with greater surface complexity, which in turn confirms Rohdenburg's complexity principle:

In cases of syntactic variation the more explicit option is generally more
formal than its less explicit counterpart. (1996: 173)[75]

Notice that the relationship between Rohdenburg's principle and the
two constructions HAVE TO and HAVE GOT TO is somewhat more
complex. Even though HAVE GOT TO is demonstrably less formal, prima
facie it seems to contain more morphological and phonetic substance
and thus to be more explicit. On second thoughts, however, this is not
the case, at least not in present-day English. It is precisely the
modalization of *gotta* which reduces the phonetic complexity (in its
truly modal form it contains four phonemes, while HAVE TO typically
contains five), turns it into a more opaque item and thus makes the two
variants conform to the complexity principle. Hence, after a short period
of language-specific 'aberration', as it were, natural language change
has apparently restored the validity of a crosslinguistic cognitive
principle for a facet of the modal system of English.

In particular, *gotta* is more often used with HAVE ellipsis than *got to*
(cf. rows 2 and 4). This confirms for British speech across all age
groups the findings of Quinn's elicitation test (1995: 125) with New
Zealand teenagers. HAVE omission turns *gotta* into a more modal
variant. Again, therefore, we see that *gotta* enjoys the highest degree of
grammaticalization of the variants investigated.

3.6   Regional variation

It was noted in section 2.4 that regional comparisons for grammatical
items are virtually nonexistent. It is such a comparative study that I
attempt here for the British Isles by adducing data from the BNC. When
we compare the incidence of *gotta* in the twenty dialect areas that are
distinguished in the BNC and then represent this graphically, we arrive
at a distribution which can be reasonably accommodated within a wave
model of language change. While it is true that historically many
morphological changes spread from the north to the south (e.g. 3 Sg. -*s*),
it is equally well known that, at least phonologically, present-day
northern British dialects are generally more conservative than the
southern ones and that in the 20th century phonological innovations have
generally spread northwards (Trudgill 1990; Wells 1997).

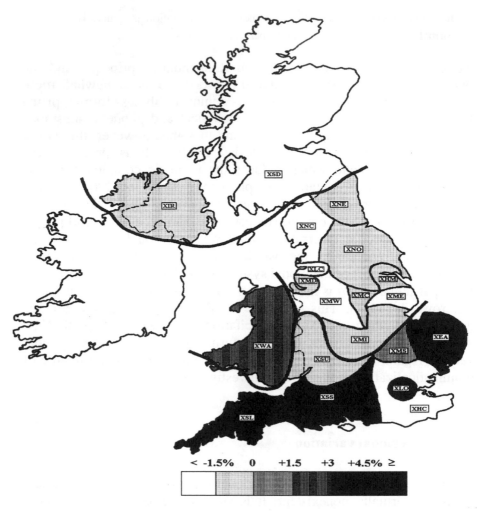

Map 3.1.   *Gotta* in the spoken BNC (divergence from mean of all regions)

DIALECT CODES AND AREAS			
XEA:	East Anglia	XMS:	South Midlands
XHC:	Home Counties	XMW:	North-west Midlands
XHM:	Humberside	XNC:	Central northern England
XIR:	Irish English	XNE:	North-east England
XLC:	Lancashire	XNO:	Northern England
XLO:	London	XSD:	Scotland
XMC:	Central Midlands	XSL:	Lower south-west England
XMD:	Merseyside	XSS:	Central south-west England
XME:	North-east Midlands	XSU:	Upper south-west England
XMI:	Midlands	XWA:	Welsh English

What we seem to identify on Map 3.1 are indeed relic areas in the far north and focal areas in the south. Note that the incidence of *gotta* is very low throughout the region north of the most important modern British dialect boundary, which Trudgill (1990: 63) has isolated on phonological grounds. Underlying the wave model is, of course, the concept of (dialect) contact. While this notion might seem outdated for present-day Britain at first sight, its value for the British Isles in particular is documented, for example, in Trudgill (1986: Ch. 2). In the specific case of *gotta*, evidence for contact comes from statistical tests: when we consider degrees of regional relatedness, chi-squared tests for adjacent regions yield on average far lower values than for non-contiguous regions.[76] Chi-squared tests are measures of strength and as such amenable to indicating differential behaviour. Contiguous regions, then, portray fewer differences as regards the use of *gotta* than nonadjacent ones. From what we know about areal spread of changes, no principle can account better for the phenomenon at hand than contact.

Given the results obtained in the previous sections on stylistic and age-related differences, the question immediately arises whether Map 3.1 is really a reflex of regional differences in speech behaviour. Might the observed regional distribution not plausibly be due to the fact that informal speech samples or younger speakers are overrepresented in what then erroneously look like focal areas? The answer is not a straightforward one. On the one hand, it has to be stressed that the proportions of the different age groups or of informal speech are not identical across the twenty regions. And, for instance, one surprising result of Map 3.1 may indeed partly be due to the overrepresentation of formal speech, which is hostile to innovations (cf. Table 3.16): the Home Counties seem to disfavour *gotta*, so that – contra Rosewarne's (1994) notion of Estuary English as today's centre for the spread of British innovations – this region apparently cannot be included among the focal areas in the present study.

The question of representativeness and the validity of studies in regional variation based on the BNC therefore is a serious one and deserves more thorough consideration. However, this is not the proper place for an exhaustive discussion of that question: the likelihood for individual maps to be skewed is obviously higher than for cumulative maps based on more innovations. The latter can be expected to be more reliable since they are likely to even out statistical outliers. Hence both arguments in favour and against the study of regional variation based on the BNC carry less weight if they make reference to just one innovation.

A fuller discussion therefore follows in section 5.3.3 below, on the basis of two cumulative maps. Suffice it, then, for the moment to give one striking example suggesting that 'region' is probably not an irrelevant variable, even though more such arguments could be produced here. The region which contains by far the largest proportion of young speakers (the two most innovative age groups, i.e. speakers aged under 25, account for 76% of the total number of words tagged for the region) and which has at the same time a very high proportion of informal speech (98%), *viz.* upper south-west England, is in the second most *conservative* group (out of six) for the present construction.[77]

To conclude this section on diatopic variation, a study in regional variation along the same lines for HAVE TO is futile because (a) unlike progressive univerbation of GOT TO, the construction HAVE TO as such is no proper innovation, as the study in apparent time has proven, and because (b) higher bonding between HAVE and *to* is not transcribed in the BNC, even though closer transcription might reveal interesting details of the grammaticalization process (see the discussion on page 88 above).

3.7   Summary

This chapter has tried to elucidate the origin and grammaticalization of HAVE TO and HAVE GOT TO. A host of independent data was put forward – including historical, regional and stylistic variationist material as well as semantic and morphosyntactic investigations. They point unambiguously to a long-standing grammaticalization process which is still ongoing for both structures. On the diachronic dimension, it was argued that HAVE TO saw a major leap towards (more) grammatical status in the second half of the 19th century, with HAVE GOT TO following suit in the first half of the 20th century. It was seen that formal syntactic accounts fail to capture the idiosyncrasies of HAVE GOT TO. Hence they were abandoned in favour of more flexible grammatical-ization accounts that can accommodate the observed developments.

As for the mechanisms of change, increase in discourse frequency and concomitant tightened bondedness were identified as fundamental parameters in the process of grammaticalization for both structures. Existing theories of the evolution of HAVE TO adequately propose syntactic reanalysis but have to be complemented by an additional discourse-based factor. It was claimed that the development of the deontic sense arose largely from context-induced implicatures (including subjectification) which were invited by the nature of early semi-idiomatized verbal complements, in particular of the type *I have to say* (something unpleasant). From here generalization to other verbs proceeded.

In the grammaticalization of HAVE GOT TO, by contrast, reanalysis is unlikely to be involved since the earliest attestations which I was able to find (of the type *I've got to be in London tonight*) cannot accommodate this mechanism. In the absence of evidence to the contrary, this observation provides counterevidence to the commonly held view that grammaticalization does not occur without reanalysis (cf. Hopper & Traugott 1993: 60f). Instead the development of HAVE GOT TO appears to suggest that change from a biclausal to a monoclausal structure is a typical but not a defining feature of modalization. This would to some extent strengthen Haspelmath's (1998) position, since he argues strongly against reanalysis in grammaticalization. There is an important caveat, though, which should prevent us from generalizing from the two individual changes investigated so far: this is the rather exceptional situation that an almost identical structure (HAVE TO) could serve as a model which in all probability *had* undergone reanalysis. More work on the first attestations of contiguous HAVE TO in early Middle English is required in order to gain a fuller picture of the role of reanalysis in modalization.

It was further argued that inferences not only played a seminal role in the evolution of root modality of both constructions, but that inferences continued to be essential in the subsequent development of epistemic meanings. Finally, implicatures are equally naturally realized when deontic meaning combines with future time reference. In sum, contrary to expectations metaphor seems to have played only a marginal role in the grammaticalization of both HAVE TO and HAVE GOT TO.

A discussion of morphological and syntactic properties of both constructions yielded the result that HAVE GOT TO has assumed more formal criteria of the core members of the English modal paradigm. In fact, HAVE TO seems to be moving towards main verb behaviour in interrogatives and negation. Finally, the general direction of change observed for the constructions in both spoken and written genres supports strongly a functionally motivated theory of language change. In the process, incidence was isolated as a central measure for determining the innovativeness of different spoken and written text types. This measure makes it possible to comment on language change in progress rather confidently on the basis of synchronic variation alone.

4   WANT TO and WANNA

4.1   Chapter outline

Volition is among those notions which Heine (1993: 30) considers
"basic to human experience and communication."[1] Not all analysts,
however, consider volitional (or: volitive, desiderative; sometimes:
bouletic, boulomaic) meaning as lying within the confines of modality
proper. Those who do, standardly treat it as a subdomain of deontic
modality (e.g. Palmer 1986: 116-19, 152f; Traugott 1989: 38;
Hengeveld forthcoming) or, more recently, agent-oriented modality
(Bybee 1985: Ch. 8; Bybee & Pagliuca 1985; Bybee et al. 1994: Ch. 6).[2]
Due to the progressive grammaticalization of the *will* future since
Middle English, no central modal has 'desire' as its central notional
domain any longer, even though some volitive traces can be found in
will and *would*. Perhaps it is only due to this facet of the English
language (which has dominated discussions of modality) that volitional
modality has received scant attention in the relevant literature.

While absent from older accounts, the verb WANT is occasionally
mentioned in more recent publications on present-day English modals
(e.g. Bybee et al. 1994: 10, 16; Bybee 1995: 506-8). A systematic
treatment of this verb and its relation to the modal paradigm, however,
has not yet been attempted. In previous work, WANT (TO) has received
various categorizations. The two most common ones are as catenative
verb (e.g. Stevens 1972: 21; Mindt 1995: 27f; Crystal 1997) or as main
verb (e.g. Quirk et al. 1985: 146; Radford 1997: 50; 154). In this chapter
I shall argue that WANT (TO) is currently assuming some semantic and
morphosyntactic features that are typical of modal auxiliaries. On my
analysis, therefore, WANT TO exhibits signs of ongoing auxiliarization
or, more exactly, modalization.

To verify my modalization claim, I will present evidence from
various linguistic levels. Historical, phonetic, syntactic, frequentative,
morphological, sociolinguistic, pragmatic and semantic aspects will
enter the discussion. In a first step the history of WANT constructions
will be described in some detail, which is important for two reasons:
first, it is relevant to the ongoing discussion in historical syntax on
impersonal verbs. Second, it is interesting on a general level to trace the
evolution of a grammaticalizing item. In fact, it will turn out that the

diachrony of WANT is an essential prerequisite for understanding the evolution of its later modal, volitional semantics. A discussion of present-day English properties and ongoing developments will ensue.

Two motivations for a modalization claim derive from language comparison and hence appear to be valid starting points for the considerations that follow. First, given its fundamental status in human communication, the text frequency of volitional meaning may be assumed to be fairly similar across languages, certainly in such closely related languages (and cultures) as English and German. Given that volition accounts for some 20% of all modal uses in German (Bouma 1973: 18),[3] it perhaps comes as no surprise that a more highly grammaticalized volitional modal verb is currently emerging in English for this frequent, hence cognitively and functionally important, notion (cf. the discussion on frequency and cognitive importance in 2.6). Second, since grammaticalization paths are recurrent, it is instructive to look at past changes and other languages in order to understand language-particular changes in progress. For a discussion of WANT it is therefore worth noting that cross-linguistically verbs of desire and volition have proved a common source for other modalities and future markers (Givón 1979: 222; Heine 1993: 27-47; Bybee et al. 1994: Chs. 6f).[4]

4.2   The rise of WANT: Increase in discourse frequency and changing patterns of complementation

The importance of frequency gains in grammaticalization was discussed above (see also Lehmann 1995: 127-30; Bybee et al. 1994: 8). In the previous chapter on HAVE TO and HAVE GOT TO, increased string frequency was identified as tantamount to increased bondedness. This would seem to apply to WANT TO as well and is probably largely responsible for the phonological erosion of the construction described in 4.4.1. Incidence will now be tested for WANT, but here I take a somewhat different perspective from that adopted in Chapter 3. Modal WANT TO followed by the infinitive did not become current until the 19th century. Nevertheless, the semantic and syntactic origins of the modal construction can be traced in the earliest uses of WANT. For that reason, I will first investigate long-term developments of the whole lexeme in the diachronic component of the Helsinki Corpus and the drama and fiction components of ARCHER. As in the previous chapter, this will be followed by a comparison of journalistic and fictional language in

Brown, LOB and their analogues from the 1990s. Finally, a study in apparent time will be carried out on the basis of the spoken component of the BNC.

To provide a broad outline of what will be detailed in the next twenty or so pages, Table 4.1 presents a purely quantitative summary of the long-term development of WANT. It shows that the lexeme has seen a remarkable expansion since Middle English. Compare the following figures from the historical Helsinki Corpus to those of the present-day English press sections in FLOB and Frown:

Table 4.1.   Increase of WANT since Old English[5]

WANT 'lack' or 'volition'	OE (up to 1150) (c.0.41 m words)	ME (1150-1500) (c.0.61 m words)	EModE (1500-1710, BrE) (c.0.55 m words)	PDE (1991/92) (c.0.18 m words)	
				BrE	AmE
occurrences	0	20	151	129	167
per 10,000 words	0	0.3	2.7	7.3	9.5

According to chi-square tests, the increase between contiguous periods (and hence also for noncontiguous ones) is statistically significant at $p \leq 0.05$. As for potential caveats regarding the selected text types, it is unlikely that the choice of press language as the present-day English variety is a contorting factor, since the finding does not appear to be text-type specific. In fictional writings (see Table 4.3), for instance, the incidence of WANT in present-day English is even higher (roughly twice that of press language).

4.2.1   Old and Middle English: From impersonal to transitive use

The Old English volitional (pre-)modal verb is WILLAN. A verb or noun WANT does not exist in this period. The first attestations in the Helsinki Corpus suggest that it entered the language in early Middle English. This is consistent with the information given in other places (e.g. Bradley & Stratmann 1891: *s.v. want*; OED 1989: *s.v. want*; Allen 1995: 224), according to which WANT is a borrowing from Old Norse. The Middle English corpus examples show that it came into the language largely functioning as a verb meaning 'lack'. Interestingly, the first attestations from the early 13th century do not yet have the now standard stem vowel grapheme <a> but <o>:[6]

(1)   ...; ne schal ham (DAT PL) neauer wontin. (HCM, SAWLES
         174:6 [c.1225, ?c.1200])

(2)   for as seinte pawel seið. alle þing turneð þen gode. to gode. ne
         mei na þing wonti þe (OBL). (HCM, HALI 131:4M; c.1225,
         ?c.1200)

(3)   ...for nawiht ne derueð ham ne nawhit ne wonteð ham (DAT PL).
         (HCM, KATHE 39:26; c.1225, ?c.1200)[7]

While (1) is impersonal and subjectless, (2) and (3) have structurally
simple pronominal subjects ('nothing'). Two remarks concerning
terminology are required here. First, while the (typically animate) dative
or oblique arguments (*ham, þe*) are termed Experiencers, what in the
above examples surface as pronominal subjects (*nawiht, na þing* –
expressing what is lacked) are standardly termed Causes. In the case of
WANT the more specific term Stimulus (e.g. Traugott 1992) seems more
appropriate and will be used in the remainder of this chapter. Further,
Denison (1993: 61-73) treats in some detail definitional issues
concerning the notion of *impersonal verb*. In order to integrate the
development of WANT I will espouse a wide view of the concept, as is
standard practice. This is conveniently summarized in Denison's (1993)
synopsis of Fischer & van der Leek's (1983) position:

> An impersonal construction is a subjectless construction in which the verb
> has 3 SG form and there is no nominative NP controlling verb concord; an
> impersonal verb is a verb which can, but need not always, occur in an
> impersonal construction (1993: 62).

Others have adopted an even wider definition (e.g. Allen 1986). And
even Denison or Fischer & van der Leek are strictly speaking outside
their confines when they discuss Jespersen's (1909-49, III) famous
hypothetical Old English LIKE construction in which a nominative plural
subject controls a plural verb (gloss and translation adapted from
Fischer 1992: 235):

(4)   þam kynge (DAT)   licodon (PL)   peran (NOM)
         to the king   liked   pears

This becomes Middle English:

         the king (SUBJ)   liked (SG)   pears (OBJ)

As Fischer (1992: 392) notes, "the impersonal construction has recently become a vigorously debated topic". Denison (1993: 61-102) provides an excellent overview of the major contributions up to that point. Later work is reported in Allen (1995; 1997) and Pocheptsov (1997). It is interesting that the syntax of (4) is exactly parallel to the most common early WANT construction (the above (1) to (3), and (7) to (9), (13) below), since it follows that many arguments put forward in the discussion apply to WANT as well. Here is not the place for a review of that debate (the reader is referred to Denison's and Allen's work and the host of studies quoted in Fischer 1992: 235-239, 392); rather we will focus on the specific development of WANT, which has received little attention in previous research. It seems obvious enough that the discussion of a single verb with no Old English attestations cannot settle a dispute that focuses on changes from Old to Middle and Modern English. It will nevertheless be possible to comment occasionally on aspects that are relevant to the history of impersonal constructions more generally.[8]

It is interesting on two counts that the earliest and also most common Middle English WANT structure is impersonal. First, this is the typical construction of its synonymous Old Norse ancestor *vanta*, even though in Old Norse both the Experiencer and the Stimulus were in the accusative case (Allen 1995: 224). Notice, however, that in very early attestations from the 12th century such as (2) and (3), the pronominal subjects can be analysed as accusative too, at least in morphological terms. Consequently (2) might be considered to be exactly parallel to the Old Norse construction in taking a double accusative. Second and more significant as regards the development of modal usage, the situation for WANT is to some extent paralleled by that of several modern English central modals such as *may, shall* and *will* which, before they became 'proper' modal verbs with all the attendant morphosyntactic criteria, had occurred with impersonal constructions since Old English times (Warner 1993: 122ff).[9]

The orthographic variants in the stem vowel point to early phonological variation, but the stem-vowel grapheme <o> in WANT was apparently soon superseded by <a>. The first two occurrences with grapheme <a> in the Helsinki Corpus (dating from around 1300) lack an Experiencer. Perhaps in its place, both contain a locative adverbial ('there(in)') akin to the modern dummy (or expletive, empty) subject, which had started to increase in frequency in Old English (Traugott 1992: 216-219; Fischer 1992: 235):

(5)   Stronge kables and ful fast,/ Ores gode an ful god seyl – / þer-
       inne wantede nouth a nayl/ þat euere he sholde þer-inne do.
       (HCM, HAVELO 24:5; c.1300)

(6)   Mete he deden plente make -/ Ne wantede þere no god mete.
       (HCM, HAVELO 38:39; c.1300)

Somewhat later case-marked human Experiencers are also attested in
the Helsinki Corpus for the <a> variant: examples (7) to (9) date from
between 1350 and 1400.[10] Some typical examples of impersonal WANT
in Middle English are given below:

(7)   And whan this wise man saugh that hym (OBJ) wanted audience,
       al shamefast he sette hym doun agayn. (HCM, CTPROS
       219.C2:25; c.1390)

(8)   Him (OBJ) wantes sight, als i said yow,... (HCM, CURSOR
       214:1; 1400, ?a.1325)

(9)   For ther nys no creature so good that hym (OBJ) ne wanteth
       somewhat (NOM/ACC) of the perfeccioun of God, that is his
       makere. (HCM, CTPROS 221.C1:1; c.1390)

Various syntacticians analyse the case of the Experiencer as dative.
While this is fully justified for Old English (Traugott 1992: 204), it
might seem less adequate for Middle English against the background of
ongoing and partly complete syncretisms in the nominal and
pronominal case systems.[11] Take for instance the masculine (the most
common gender in the examples to be discussed), which has only
objective case due to the collapse of dative and accusative north of the
Thames (Mossé 1952: §65n.1). Further, a distinction between
accusative and dative is obsolete in all areas for full NPs and second
person pronouns, as in example (13) on page 125 below.

4.2.1.1 *Problems of syntactic analysis*

It is clear from the preceding considerations that the morphological
analysis of WANT arguments is often difficult in a period of eroding
inflections. Partially due to the case syncretisms which result from
eroding inflections, the syntactic analysis of early Middle English WANT
constructions is far from trivial. This task is further complicated by
changes in constituency order, which started in Old English and

continued well into the Middle English period. The present section will deal with problems inherent in the syntactic analysis of early WANT constructions and point to some possible solutions.

To begin with, it seems worth noting that in Old English certain verbs of sensory or mental experience such as NEODIAN, BEHOFIAN 'need', LYSTAN, (GE)LUSTFULLIAN 'desire' or LONGIAN 'long' characteristically express the Stimulus by a genitive NP or, less commonly, by a prepositional phrase (Fischer & van der Leek 1983; Traugott 1992: 205, 209; Denison 1993: 63-72; Allen 1997: 5). The Old English verbs ÞOLIAN (when used in the sense 'lack, miss') and the synonymous BEÞURFAN, too, typically subcategorize a genitival Stimulus (see the entries for the respective verbs in the *Anglo-Saxon Dictionary*). In Middle English the Stimulus generally takes the form of a prepositional phrase (Denison 1993: 70). Interestingly, Denison (1993: 70) and Allen (1995: 224) cite an example of WANT which occurs in the Helsinki Corpus (1). They adopt a different punctuation from that provided in the corpus, which leads to the addition of just such a prepositional-phrase Stimulus (gloss from Denison):

(1)'   (HCM, SAWLES 174:6)
         ne   of al þet eauer wa   is ne   schal (3SG)
         nor of all that ever woeful   is not shall

         ham (OBL) neauer wontin.
         them   never lack

A second ME possibility is for two-place impersonal verbs to take two oblique arguments (10). A third possibility, attested for verbs such as LIKE since Old English, is to take a nominative Stimulus and an oblique Experiencer as in (11) and (12) (examples and glosses taken from Denison 1993: 70-72):

(10)   (c.1390, Chaucer, *Canterbury Tales*, iv. 106)
        ..., so well us (OBL) liketh yow (OBJ PL)...

(11)   (Old English, *Orosius* 84.32)
        hu   him (DAT) the sige (NOM) gelicade
        how him   the victory   pleased

(12)   (a.1395, Gower, *Confessio amantis* 1.1698)
        godd wot   how that   sche (NOM) him (OBJ) pleseth
        God knows   how (that) she   him   pleases

WANT structures like (7) to (9) have full NP Stimuli (which do not inflect for case) or a neuter pronominal Stimulus (*somewhat*, which is ambiguous between nominative and accusative in Middle English). Both can therefore be regarded as either nominative or accusative case. Under this analysis it might seem most appropriate to assume that due to eroding case distinctions the Stimulus of an erstwhile subjectless structure turns into what in our present syntactic understanding looks like the surface subject. This analysis, however, has its drawbacks: despite a less rigidly specified slot for subject placement in Old English, the typical place for the subject was never the end of its clause. On the contrary, it usually was the first constituent (Denison 1986; Kemenade 1989; Traugott 1992).[12] It seems therefore odd for the subject in the WANT construction to occur rather consistently in final position as late as the 13th and 14th centuries, when SVO is definitely largely in place. This analysis, therefore, seems less than ideal, even though it is correct on strictly morphological grounds and paralleled by various other impersonal verbs.

Closely connected with the (apparent) subject in final position is the preponderance of the Experiencer in preverbal, topicalized position. It seems instructive in this context to consider crosslinguistically attested motivations for word order and word order change. One of the best understood principles at work in organizing discourse is the tendency towards topic-comment structure (related dichotomies are theme-rheme, given-new).[13] It is entirely consistent with this principle that, whenever Experiencers are overtly expressed in WANT constructions in the ME component of the Helsinki Corpus, they are pronominal (i.e. old information). Intriguingly this holds true regardless of whether we consider impersonal or transitive structures. Thus my data seem to support the common view that maintenance of thematicity is partially responsible for the reinterpretation of Experiencers as subjects.[14] Significantly, the few exceptions equally fall out from the theme-rheme principle: the order [Stimulus – WANT – Experiencer] is found only when the Stimulus is semantically vacuous, hence a suitable theme as in (2).[15] In other words, in the impersonal WANT attestations in the corpus, case-marked pronominal Experiencers almost always precede non-vacuous, heavier nominal Stimuli. While some twenty attestations in the Helsinki Middle English component cannot be taken as the kind of hard statistical confirmation that Denison (1993: 78, 99) wants to see for the maintenance of thematicity, the observed clear tendency obtained from a carefully sampled corpus seems difficult to dismiss.[16]

A way out of the syntactic dilemma is to disregard morphological case-marking as diagnostic of objects and grant subject status to case-marked NPs, as in fact various researchers have done (e.g. Elmer 1981; von Seefranz-Montag 1983; Allen 1986; 1995). Their justification is basically that Experiencers possessed subject properties despite overt case-marking. Allen (1995: 442) cites previous research which shows

> ... that the traits associated with subjecthood are often acquired gradually, with the morphological trappings of the subject lagging behind the syntactic properties of that grammatical relation.

She goes on to argue as follows (p. 443):

> The unusual frequency of preposing for Experiencers is ... easily explained if we assume that verbs could assign their Experiencer to the syntactic role of subject but mark them lexically with a non-nominative case.

To illustrate the gradual development from impersonal to transitive WANT, let us consider some more corpus examples. It was seen that human (or divine, for that matter) case-marked Experiencers in topicalized position are likely to be interpreted as underlying subjects. From here it seems a short way towards reanalysing syntactically ambiguous WANT structures like (13) as transitive uses, which turns the (passive) Experiencer into an agentive subject, the prototypical semantic role in subjecthood. Consider for instance:

(13)   God wanteþ þee (OBJ); (HCM, CLOUD 81:34; a.1425; ?a.1400)

While *God* is not case-marked, *þee* is oblique and ambiguous between accusative and dative. Only if we supply the context does it become clear that, unlike two sentences on, *God* is not the subject of WANT but a metonymical Stimulus and *þee* not the direct object but the Experiencer:

(13)'   God woldest þou have, and synne woldest þou lacke. God wanteþ þee; and synne arte þou sekir of. Now good God help þee, for now hast þou need! (HCM, CLOUD 81:34; a.1425; ?a.1400)

It is important to note that structures like (13) seem to lead naturally to unambiguously transitive structures in which the human Experiencer becomes the uncased subject and the Stimulus a direct object. Impersonal constructions apart, such transitive uses are the second common Middle English structure, and the commonest since about

1400 (according to Mustanoja 1960: 435, citing van der Gaaf's work, the earliest attestation of personal *I want* is from c.1350):

(14)   And alle-þogh þai (PL) in helle want light,/ Yhit sal þai of alle payns haf sight,... (HCM, PRICK 253:151425 (a.1400))

(15)   And whanne þei (PL) weren (PL) mette togedre and wantedon (PL) þe child Iesu (SG), (þei wenden þat he hadde ben in feleschipe wiþ som kyn of his frendis). (HCM,WYCSER I, 356:2; c.1400)

(16)   And so no man may excusen hym fro werkys of mercy, as no man may wante werkys (GEN SG/ uncased PL) of a good wille for þat werk ys þe furste and heyȝest in man. (HCM, WYCSER I, 237:14; c.1400)[17]

In (14) to (16) transitivity is clear from the fact that a plural subject pronoun controls verb concord. Consider finally also a nonfinite transitive use:

(17)   In the begynnynge thenne of this symple exhortacyon, that I/ a chylde, wantynge the habyte of connynge, maye be dyrected by/ hym that gave to that childe Danyell... (HCM, INNOCE 3:24; 1497)

4.2.1.2 Summary

From the earliest accounts, researchers (e.g. Jespersen 1909ff, van der Gaaf 1904; Visser 1963-73 and, more recently, Lightfoot 1979; Elmer 1981; Fischer & van der Leek 1987) have argued that the loss of impersonals is closely connected with

- the loss of case distinctions
- the development of Middle English SVO word order (being the ultimate cause of)
- reanalysis (in various guises) of two-place impersonals:

    OE   dative Experiencer – verb – nominative Stimulus
as late ME   nominative subject – verb – object.

We have seen that all three factors can be reasonably accommodated in the development of transitive WANT but that none represents a sufficient explanation on its own (see also p. 143 for the proposal of an additional semantic factor). In particular reanalysis is not without critics (e.g.

McCawley 1976 or Allen 1986; 1995: Ch. 7; Denison 1990). My data for WANT both support and pose problems to reanalysis: on the one hand, reanalysis of the Stimulus subject as object was possible throughout since this was always either a full NP or a neuter pronoun, both of which do not inflect for objective case in Middle English. On the other hand, the two-place impersonal structures attested in the Helsinki Corpus – examples (7) to (9) – had a case-marked objective personal pronoun in the Experiencer position, and on morphological grounds these cannot readily be reanalysed as nominative subjects. This, then, makes it rather unlikely that the erosion of case inflections – which is relevant only for nominal topics but which does not apply to the case-marked pronominal topics of the early WANT construction – can be held responsible for the reanalysis of the Experiencer as subject.[18]

We therefore had to invoke evidence from outside morphology for the interpretation of case-marked Experiencers as underlying subjects. It was seen that discourse-pragmatic principles play a vital role in such accounts: in the data analysed the animate Experiencer, though morphologically case-marked for dative, typically occupied the topic slot, which left the comment position for the nominal Stimulus. In sum, two factors seem to have facilitated the emergence of transitive structures. The first is preferred argument structure, which led to the assignment of subjecthood to oblique pronouns. The second is that uncased Stimuli were reinterpreted as objects. It was argued that this tendency was possibly reinforced by the existence of morphosyntactically ambiguous structures such as (13), where the morphology of neither argument betrays its syntactic function.

4.2.2   Early Modern and Modern English

4.2.2.1   *Helsinki Corpus (1500-1710)*

Table 4.2 summarizes the frequency of the different attested construction types in the Early Modern English component of the Helsinki Corpus. It will be remembered that for the entire lexeme a ninefold increase in text frequency from the Middle to the Early Modern period can be observed (cf. Table 4.1 above). A comparison of the two tables shows that the nominal and verbal uses of WANT taken on their own now easily surpass the frequency of the lexeme in Middle English at large. It follows that the use of both parts-of-speech must have increased dramatically from Middle English to Early Modern English.

Table 4.2.   Construction types of WANT in Early Modern English (Helsinki Corpus)

	Verbal uses	Nominal uses	Adjectival uses	Borderline cases[19]	Total
Subtotal	78	62	5	6	151
within which	59 transitive	29 WANT *of*[20]			
within which	13 intransitive	18 *for want of*			
within which	3 WANT *of*				
within which	2 WANT *in*				
within which	1 WANT *for*				

Table 4.2 shows that verbal constructions continue to dominate. Further, the transitive pattern has ousted the impersonal construction, a situation that already prevailed in late Middle English, as was seen in the previous section. Strikingly nouns, which had been scarce in Middle English, soared during the Early Modern period: they account for nearly half of all uses and outnumber three times the occurrences of the entire lexeme in the preceding period.[21] Nouns followed by *of* plus NP became especially common. Such constructions include a large proportion of the extant idiomatic expression *for want of.*[22] Consider John Locke's useful advice to conference maniacs:

(18)   Besides he that is used to hard lodging at home will not misse his sleep (where he has most need of it) when he travells abroad for want of his soft bed and his pillars laid in order, and therefore I thinke it would not be amisse to make his bed after different fashons. (HCE, EDUC3A 45:6; 1693)

Or a late 17th century scientific treatise on electricity and magnetism:

(19)   Without therefore concluding any thing from this Experiment, save that, if the assertion I was to examin were true, the want of an Electrical faculty might be thought a Concomitant rather of the peculiar Texture of the Emrald than of its green colour, I proceeded ... (HCE, SCIE3B 36:28; 1675-76)

It is instructive to have a look at the collocates of WANT and their Z-scores.[23] In Middle English, it has no fixed complementation pattern – a phenomenon that is presumably typical of a word entering a language that is not introduced as part of a fixed expression. In Early Modern English 50 out of a total 151 occurrences of WANT are immediately followed by the preposition *of*. The two next most frequent items adjacent to *want* in Early Modern English lag far behind: they are the prepositions *for* and *in* with only six and five co-occurrences, respectively. Thus, a rather fixed collocation WANT (predominantly as NP) + *of* emerges during this period; *to*, on the other hand, which follows WANT immediately only three times in Early Modern English, has a negative Z-score. This means that its actual co-occurrence with WANT is lower than chance would have predicted. Worse news for the rise of modal WANT TO: two out of these three occurrences of contiguous WANT *to* are followed by a noun phrase, thus leaving us with only one instance (example (20) below) of infinitival rather than prepositional *to*.

A closer look at developments *within* the Early Modern English period reveals that the proportion of intransitive uses (e.g. *They are wanting*) steadily declined during that period: from half of all verbal uses between 1500 and 1570 to some five percent between 1640 and 1710. This trend has continued, as is indicated by the fact that intransitive uses today are considered archaic by the OED (1989: *s.v. want*).

Notice that so far we have sketched only the initial stages of the evolution of modal WANT by outlining the rise of a transitive verb followed by noun phrase complements. But this is a necessary precondition for the extension to infinitival complements and for volitional semantics to develop. Hence while we now better understand the rise of a new lexeme in English, we have not yet traced the immediate roots of the present-day emerging modal. It is to this task that I now turn.

Let us sum up the situation at the end of the Early Modern English period (c.1700). As far as semantics is concerned, volitional meaning aspects are certainly not yet among the focal senses of WANT in Early Modern English – despite the existence of some Middle English examples (discussed in 4.3.1 below) in which WANT bas a backgrounded volitional meaning or at least gives rise to volitional inferences. In its syntax, too, WANT during the Early Modern period is still almost always nonmodal since following infinitival *to* complements are rare to the point of nonexistence. The one instance that can be found in the Helsinki Corpus – in a letter from 1675 – is ambiguous as to its syntactic structure and clearly nonvolitional:

(20)   The King has directed me to attend him tomorrow about the matters of yr Excellencie's last letter and I shall not bee wanting to acquainte you with his Maties pleasure so soon as I know itt, and in ye meane time I desire yr Excellency will continue to mee ye happinesse of being esteemed. (HCE, OFFIC3 22:40; 1675-77)

A verbal interpretation of *wanting* in (20) would be concomitant with an analysis of the VP as a future (or modal) progressive. Given that more recent research tends towards positing a rather late date for the grammaticalization of the progressive (e.g. Strang 1982; Denison 1993), regarding *wanting* in (20) as adjectival seems preferable. Apart from (20), some examples of WANT 'lack' + NP followed by a purposive clause introduced by *to* can be found:

(21)   What wilt thou say, if a Man who hath quite lost his Sight, and hath also forgotten that ever he saw, and should think that he wants nothing to render him perfect, should we therefore judg those who retain their Sight to be blind also? (HCE, BOETH3 183:3; 1695)

(22)   I past by and went to Sterling, where I was entertained and lodged at one Master Iohn Archibalds, where all my want was that I wanted roome to containe halfe the good cheere that I might haue had there; (HCE; TRAV2A 134.C1:4; 1630)

(23)   So everything stands still for money, while we want money to pay for some of the most necessary things that we promised ready money for in the heighth of our wants – ... (HCE, DIAR3A VIII,315:7; 1666)

(24)   but Sir William, thinking the foole wanted wit to tell his griefe (though not wit to play the thiefe) had the barber depart, asking Jacke what he would eate? he sayd, nothing. What he would drinke? he sayd, nothing; which made Sir William doubt much of his health, ... (HCE, FICT2A 13:16; 1608)

All the above examples are a far cry from the modern modal construction. They are clearly biclausal and, except perhaps for (22), their two clauses do not even have coreferential subjects. In order to document the fundamental changes between 1710 and 1990, then, we definitely want to have a look at ARCHER, which covers precisely the critical period in the development of WANT TO.

4.2.2.2 ARCHER (1650-1990)

As intuitions will immediately confirm, nominal WANT has declined in frequency since Early Modern English. Verbs, by contrast, (especially those followed by the infinitive rather than by an NP complement) have increased drastically, so much so that they not only make up for the decline in nouns but lead to a statistically significant further increase in the entire lexeme (see diagrams below and Table 4.1). Such a development must be interpreted as the grammaticalization of the modal construction. On the other hand, it might also reflect a more general historical drift in English towards the maximization of verb phrases (cf. Kortmann & Meyer 1992: 163; Hundt & Mair forthcoming).

Following Bolinger's (1980b: 297) assertion that "the moment a verb is given an infinitive complement, that verb starts down the road of auxiliariness," we will henceforth concentrate on contiguous verbal WANT TO, whose share of the entire lexeme in British drama has risen from almost zero in the second half of the 17th century to roughly a third. As Figure 4.1 shows, this proportion has remained relatively stable since the second half of the 19th century.

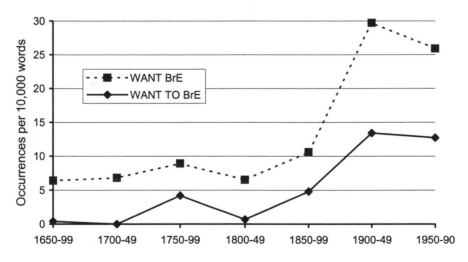

Figure 4.1. WANT and WANT TO in ARCHER drama (BrE, 50-year intervals)

Notice the S-curve shape for both the rise of the lexeme and for modal WANT TO in the drama data.[24] A saturation phase seems to have been reached for the modal construction at the incidence of around 13 occurrences per 10,000 words. Intriguingly, this is not some arbitrary discourse frequency but precisely that found for WANT TO in British contemporary conversation (BNC, see section 4.5 below). The same tendency was obtained for HAVE TO, which makes it difficult to dismiss the present finding as spurious. On the contrary, we can fairly confidently attribute the results to frequentative-functional pressures from spoken English, but it is still surprising just how good an approximation current drama data are for the items under investigation. That said, one is tempted to predict a slowing down for fictional data too, since here the graph (Figure 4.2) has reached this level with a time lag of approximately 50 years compared to drama. Such a situation suggests a slightly lower degree of susceptibility to change, maybe for this genre generally, but certainly as far as this variable is concerned.

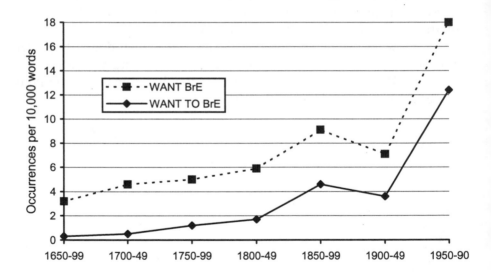

Figure 4.2.   WANT and WANT TO in ARCHER fiction (BrE, 50-year intervals)

Figure 4.2 informs us further that the proportion of the modal construction has risen continuously in British fiction, reaching as high a share as two thirds of the entire lexeme in the late 20th century. In the last fifty years, then, the increase in the lexeme has been particularly sharp and it is almost exclusively WANT TO that accounts for it.

For a regional comparison, American data are plotted alongside their parallel British components in Figure 4.3. It shows that, at least as regards WANT TO, fictional language has developed rather similarly on both sides of the Atlantic: except for the late 19th century, their graphs virtually coincide. In the drama components, by contrast, American English (with a threefold increase over the last century) has changed even more – shall we say – 'dramatically' than British English, even though the incidence here too has more than doubled during the same period.

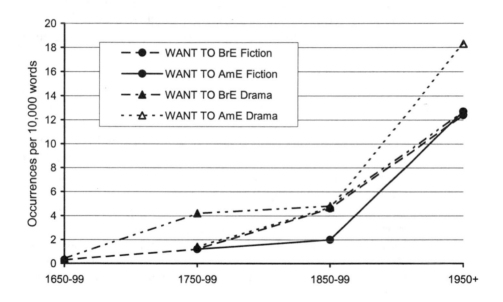

Figure 4.3. WANT TO in ARCHER drama and fiction (BrE vs. AmE)

4.2.3   Present-day English

4.2.3.1   Recent developments

As for very recent trends (summarized in Table 4.3), it is noteworthy that over the past thirty years, in both British and American English, the string frequency of modal WANT TO has increased substantially in four representative samples of press language (c.0.18m words each) and fictional language (c.0.25m words each). As rows 1 and 4 show, the increase on the American side is far more pronounced than on the British side. Also, the current ratios per given amount of text are always higher in American English, which can therefore safely be said to be more progressive with regard to the use of WANT. Another point worth making is that in British English the proportion of adjacent WANT TO measured against all instances of WANT (row 3) has increased very slightly only. By contrast, a remarkable trend towards functional streamlining in the direction of modal WANT TO is observable in American fictional and journalistic writing.

A word concerning statistical significance is in place here. While not all increases in Table 4.3 are significant at $p \leq 0.05$, it surely *is* significant that not a single pair of figures from 1961 and 1991/92 shows a slight (or even significant) decrease. Incidentally, for the verbal uses, this would contradict the claim of unidirectionality in grammaticalization. It seems appropriate in this context to quote a statement made by Labov (1970: 57), which fits the present data as well as those presented in the remaining chapters of this study:

> It is immediately obvious to the sophisticated statistician that tests of significance are irrelevant. ... It is plain that even if a particular case were below the level of significance, the convergence of so many independent events carries us to a level of confidence which is unknown in most social or psychological research.

I would not go so far as to consider statistical tests completely 'irrelevant' in the case at hand, which is why they are generally provided in this study. Nonetheless, I fully endorse Labov's view that on theoretical grounds the accumulation of data from various sources renders statistical tests superfluous, most obviously when all (or at least almost all) individual investigations point in one direction. Notice further that such considerations concern only the validity of frequentative research. The grammaticalization claims made in the present study are, of course, further strengthened by qualitative (e.g. semantic) evidence.

Table 4.3.   WANT TO in journalistic and fictional writing (LOB, FLOB, Brown, Frown)

	LOB press BrE 1961	FLOB press BrE 1991	Brown press AmE 1961	Frown press AmE 1992	LOB fiction BrE 1961	FLOB fiction BrE 1991	Brown fiction AmE 1961	Frown fiction AmE 1992
1 adjacent WANT TO	49	68	40	100	192	207	169	256
[per 10,000w]	[2.8]	[3.9]	[2.3]	[5.7]	[7.6]	[8.2]	[6.6]	[10.1]
2 all forms of WANT	95	129	86	167	365	389	342	420
[per 10,000w]	[5.4]	[7.3]	[4.9]	[9.5]	[14.4]	[15.4]	[13.5]	[16.6]
3 adjacent WANT TO as % of all WANT	51.6%	52.7%	46.5%	59.9%	52.6%	53.2%	49.4%	61.0%
4 increase in adjacent WANT TO		38.7%		150%		7.8%		88.2%

To return to the discussion of Table 4.3, it deserves mention that in 1961 the figures for American English are consistently lower than for British English. Intriguingly, thirty years later the reverse situation obtains. Due to massive increases in WANT TO (row 4), American English has consistently higher figures in the more recent corpora across the genres and for both the lexeme at large and the modal construction. This leads to the interesting fact that the use of WANT in current written American English is considerably more isomorphic (i.e. more likely to be used in the modal [V *to* VP] construction, cf. row 3) than in British English. These facts suggest strongly that while the rise of the new volitional modal probably did not originate in the US, the change obviously caught on more rapidly here than in Britain. Drama data from ARCHER (Figure 4.3) confirm this trend for the long-term development. If one can generalize, the present data seem to support the common assumption that American English is more open to change than British English. While it may be rash at this stage to make such a sweeping claim for the whole variety (which of course is by no means a homogeneous entity), it does indeed appear to be true for the rise of the new volitional modal construction in the genres investigated.

As for degrees of progressiveness of different text types, it was seen in Chapter 3, where HAVE TO and HAVE GOT TO were scrutinized, that a comparison of the increase (row 4) in two text types is not sufficient methodologically to account for degrees of progressiveness. Increase is a good indicator of the dynamics currently affecting the respective genres, while incidence is the crucial quantity for identifying progressive and conservative genres. The combined approach yields the following results: fictional language is more progressive with regard to the emerging modal WANT TO (the incidence is around twice that of press language), but at the same time fictional language is changing to a lesser extent than press language (where the increase is greater).

Let us briefly consider some potential causes for the enormous frequency gains, both long-term and short-term: rather than witnessing a recent increase in desire on both sides of the Atlantic Ocean, we are probably seeing the effects of generalization and the development of new grammatical meanings (see 4.3.2 below). One might wonder why the frequency of WANT (TO) has risen so drastically in English journalese and fictional writings in only 30 years, which is a very short period for the historical linguist.[25] A comparison of text frequencies (Table 4.4) in spoken and written present-day English helps to identify one motivation: both the entire lexeme and the modal construction are approximately three times more common in spoken English. We may therefore, again, assume that spoken performance data are influencing the written medium towards a greater use of this lexeme – a trend which has been repeatedly reported in related work (e.g. Krug 1996; Mair 1997, 1998; Hundt & Mair forthcoming). The term 'colloquialization of written norms' (coined by Mair) captures this type of development well.

Table 4.4.   Text frequency of the lexeme WANT in the BNC (spoken vs. written)

	spoken BNC (10m words)	written BNC (90m words)
occurrences of WANT	26,289	68,622
incidence per 10,000 words	26.3	7.6
occurrences of WANT TO	13,182	38,420
incidence per 10,000 words	13.2	4.3

The studies just cited are both narrower and wider in outlook from what I suggest in the following paragraphs. On the one hand they take a rather narrow view of the notion of 'colloquialization of written English', seeing it essentially as a stylistic shift towards informality. At the same time, Mair's (1997, 1998) claims are more far-reaching to the extent that they concern contemporary philosophical, psychological and social currents: he notes that the colloquialization of written norms ties in with general cultural trends to be observed in the industrialized West against formality and towards a more cooperative language use (e.g. Norbert Elias). The same position is sounded in Myhill (1995), and this much is undisputed. On purely linguistic grounds, however, one might wish to adopt a slightly different stance and define *colloquialization* as a stylistically neutral concept so as to include developments in the written language that are not marked stylistically, but which do follow the same overall tendency of narrowing the gap between the spoken and written modes. In other words, a wider notion of colloquialization is embraced here because a shift towards informality describes appropriately only the spread of overt style markers in written English like contractions (e.g. *isn't* or *wanna*). Drift towards informality applies less obviously to what one might label 'covert innovations' which enter a language furtively as it were.[26] This latter type of innovation includes items like HAVE TO and WANT TO, which are not subject to stigmatization. More adequate from a narrow linguistic perspective, then, seems the functional-frequentative explanation that spoken English is more receptive to changes than – and actually triggers changes in – the more rigidly codified written text types.

Let us now resume our discussion from the previous section, which dealt with the historical development of complementation patterns for WANT. It will be recalled that in Early Modern English the two dominant structures were transitive WANT ('lack') + NP and nominal WANT + *of*, while verbal WANT subcategorized for infinitival *to* was almost nonexistent. Between 1710 and the 1990s a complete reversal of the situation has taken place. This was demonstrated with the help of ARCHER data (Figures 4.1f). As was seen from the discussion of Table 4.3, in current British and American drama and fiction over half of all WANT occurrences are immediately followed by *to* (resulting in the modal construction), and its share of the full lexeme is increasing in both text types and both dialects. The preposition *of*, by contrast, is conspicuously absent from the list of collocates for WANT in the present-day American and British press corpora.[27] The tendencies observed in the subsections of the one-million word corpora receive full support from BNC data, spoken or written:

Table 4.5.   Word-forms of WANT in the British National Corpus[28]

	SPOKEN (10m tokens)		WRITTEN (90m tokens)	
	Occurrences	% of Σ	Occurrences	% of Σ
(1) *want* (verb)	18,218	76.2	38,202	55.8
(2) *want* (noun)	79	0.3	726	1.1
(3) *wants* (verb)	2,016	8.4	6,804	9.9
(4) *wants* (noun)	5	0.0	109	0.2
(5) *wanted* (verb)	3,176	13.3	19,630	28.7
(6) *wanted* (others)	74	0.3	653	1.0
(7) *wanting* (all)	340	1.4	2,307	3.4
Σ (1) – (7)	23,908	100	68,431	100
Sum clear cases of verbal uses	23,410	97.9	64,636	94.5

Table 4.5 demonstrates that in present-day English unambiguously verbal uses of WANT constitute well over 90% of all instances of this lexeme in both spoken and written English, with the spoken medium (98%) slightly in the lead. Second, of these verbal uses WANT TO sequences and *wanna* today account for approximately 50% (Table 4.4), a ratio which corresponds very closely to those found for contemporary British and American drama (Table 4.3).[29] In summary, a new complementation pattern, *viz.* verbal WANT + infinitival *to*, is firmly established for present-day English, while the collocability of the two elements in WANT TO is still being strengthened. Put differently, the rise of the modal usage has occurred at the expense of the remaining constructions, leaving the transitive verb (followed by a NP) in second place. Considerations concerning increased collocability lead on to the next section, which investigates degrees of bondedness in more detail.

4.2.3.2 *Bondedness and reanalysis*

Tables 4.6 and 4.7 summarize the behaviour of WANT TO with regard to adverb interpolation as found in the spoken BNC (some 10m words):

Table 4.6.   Adverb interpolation with WANT TO in the spoken BNC (*actually*)

		want	wants	wanted	wanting	Row total
1	*actually* WANT *to*	42	4	7	1	54
2	*actually wanna*	2	-	-	-	2
3	WANT *to actually*	7	1	6	0	14
4	*wanna actually*	1	-	-	-	1
5	WANT *actually to*	1	0	0	0	1
6	Column total	53	5	13	1	72

Table 4.7.   Adverb interpolation with WANT TO in the spoken BNC (*really*)

		want	wants	wanted	wanting	Row total
1	*really* WANT *to*	162	10	39	2	213
2	*really wanna*	28	-	-	-	28
3	WANT *to really*	8	0	2	0	10
4	*wanna really*	1	-	-	-	1
5	WANT *really to*	1	0	1	0	2
6	Column total	200	10	42	2	254

Roughly one fifth of all instances of contiguous *want to* in spoken British English are contracted (see Table 4.8, p. 154 below). As Tables 4.6 and 4.7 demonstrate, however, the proportion of adverb interpolation for the word form *wanna* is below one percent of all adverb interpolations found with WANT TO. This reveals that *wanna* resists interpolation more strongly than WANT TO in general and, hence, a tighter bonding in the entire Subject-Verb (SV) group can be observed for *wanna*. Overall – as well as for the individual word forms of WANT – a hierarchy serves well to indicate the degrees of bondedness within the SV group (from more to less closely bonded):

(25)   WANT + *to*   <   *to* + infinitive   <   subject + WANT

Just as in the case of HAVE TO and HAVE GOT TO, the tightest bonding between the verb and *to* proves that the univerbation manifest in the orthographic variant *wanna* is not an unmotivated *ad hoc* formation but that orthography yields to pressures from spoken discourse. Recall Bolinger's (1980b: 296) dictum that "spelling can be symptomatic." It is also significant from a syntactic point of view that WANT and *to* resist adverb interpolation most strongly, because this fact is highly suggestive of a single-clause analysis. Such an analysis is preferable to a two-clause analysis since, as Pullum (1997: 95) notes for *want*, contraction is not permitted when *to* does not introduce its infinitival complement. Consider some notorious examples from the contraction debate (see Appendix 2 for the details of their syntactic analysis) in which WANT and *to* are separated by clause boundaries and thus not contractible:

(26)   [One must want] [(in order) to become an effective overconsumer]

(27)   [I want [to be precise] an orange four-door De Ville convertible]

(28)   [I don't want anyone] [who continues to want] [to stop wanting][30]

The fact that contracted *wanna* is not only possible but indeed common in natural discourse indicates that in the vast majority of uses a monoclausal modal analysis is superior to a biclausal purposive reading (*in order*) *to*. In Quirk et al.'s (1985: 137) terminology, then, we have to do with a 'one verb phrase' rather than a 'two verb phrase'.

The question is, however, whether it is really reanalysis that has led to a monoclausal structure, as a formal account by Goodall (1991) suggests. Semantic considerations exclude a purposive reading of the *to* complements in present-day English and, significantly, for almost all examples put forward in the above discussion of the historical stages, too. Since clause fusion is relatively advanced even in the earliest examples, it would seem to follow that the data are better captured by an account which makes no reference to syntactic reanalysis at all. This stance would support Haspelmath's hypothesis that

> this notion [*sc.* reanalysis] plays a much less important role in diachronic syntax than is commonly assumed. The main mechanism of syntactic change is grammaticalization, i.e. the gradual unidirectional change that turns lexical items into grammatical items and loose structures into tight structures, subjecting frequent linguistic units to more and more grammatical restrictions and reducing their autonomy. (1998: 344)

Finally, I do not wish to invalidate Horn's famous claim (first mentioned in Lakoff 1970: 632) that sentences with coreferential subjects like (29) are more likely to allow *wanna* contraction than those without subject identity like (30). Nevertheless, it calls for an explanation that in a random sample of 500 instances of *wanna* from the spoken BNC, not a single instance of clause fusion of type (29) can be found:

(29)   Who do you wanna succeed?

(30)   *Who do you wanna succeed the president?

I suspect that sentences of type (29) are extremely rare in natural discourse because speakers anticipate the processing difficulties which such garden path constructions entail for their interlocutors. In fact, hardly any *wanna* contractions are to be found in subordinate clauses of (British) discourse at all.[31] This is probably no coincidence. To begin with, the most frequent sentence type is an affirmative monoclausal statement and hence subordination cannot be expected to account for a high proportion of WANT uses. But it should certainly be higher than almost zero per cent. Apart from processing constraints a further factor may be invoked from crosslinguistic research. As has been noted by various researchers (e.g. Traugott 1992: 273 on word order), changes start out in main clauses, while subordinate clauses often retain conservative characteristics considerably longer. Take for instance the now almost obsolete subjunctive in English *if* clauses or the obsolescent, but (especially in written English) still productive, mandative subjunctive in *that* clauses, both of which contrast with an extremely restricted set of formulaic subjunctives in main clauses such as *God save the Queen*. It may not be impossible that this general trend is reflected in the distribution of the incoming *wanna* too.

4.3   Semantic developments

4.3.1   The evolution of volitional modality

It was seen that from the earliest uses until the end of the Early Modern English period the prototypical meaning of WANT is 'lack'. The first volitional examples recorded in the OED date from the early 18th century. As Burchfield (1996: *s.v. want*) notes, "this branch of meaning, the 'wishing' branch, firmly established itself in the nineteenth century and is now the dominant sense of the verb." The meaning as such, then, seems to be rather recent. It is interesting to see, however, that we can trace the origin of what is now the most common meaning to the turn of the 14th century. Take for instance two examples from Chaucer's *Canterbury Tales* or the *Cursor Mundi* cited earlier:

(8)   Him (DAT) wantes sight, als i said yow,... (HCM, CURSOR 214:1; 1400, ?1325)

(9)   For ther nys no creature so good that hym (DAT) ne wanteth somewhat (NOM/ACC) of the perfeccioun of God, that is his makere. (HCM, CTPROS 221.C1:1; c.1390)

Someone who lacks sight is likely to desire to be able to see (8). And, according to Christian doctrine at least (9), everybody lacks the perfection of God and therefore would probably not mind having some of it. On a similar note, volitional meaning could be argued to be faintly present in other examples from that period. Recall two further examples invoked above:

(7)   And whan this wise man saugh that hym (DAT) wanted audience, al shamefast he sette hym doun agayn. (HCM, CTPROS 219.C2:25; c.1390)

(14)   And alle-þogh þai in helle want light,/ Yhit sal þai of alle payns haf sight,... (HCM, PRICK 253:15; 1425 (?1400))

In (14) the context with (in this instance erstwhile) animate subjects (*þai* 'they') suggests that these also desire to have light. Someone who lacks audience – and on realizing this refrains from speaking and sits down again – is sure to have desired an audience (7). An interesting secondary result produced by these examples is that they reveal the influence of connectives and context on the semantics of verbs: volitional traces can only be advocated if one disregards the connectives and looks at the propositions expressed in the individual clauses in isolation. In each context, however, it is in particular the connectives (*whan* 'when', *alle-þogh* 'although', *Yhit* 'yet') which turn 'lack' into the only appropriate modern gloss of *want*. While at the end of the Middle English period 'desire' can at best be considered an implicature that is sometimes realized, as was remarked above, it has become the dominant meaning in present-day English. If we now wish to determine the mechanism that best accounts for the later semantic change from 'lack' to 'desire', contiguity of these two senses seems obvious enough, because it is common for human beings to desire what they lack. Again, therefore, as in the cases of HAVE TO and HAVE GOT TO, context-induced inferencing seems to account better for the rise of the new meaning than metaphor.

Judging from the examples discussed above, in many cases 'lack' differs from 'desire' only to the extent that the speakers do not commit themselves to statements about the attitude of the Experiencer towards the proposition. In modern English the Experiencer is identical with the syntactic subject. It is worth noting, however, that assuming subject status for the dative Middle English Experiencers (i.e. assuming present-day SVO word order) and a volitional interpretation would not yield nonsensical, but indeed very much related, meanings for the four above examples. There is another instructive example where the order of arguments is different from that of the previous ones and here the morphology of Experiencer and Stimulus does not clarify the syntactic roles (cf. the discussion on p. 125):

(13)   God woldest þou have, and synne woldest þou lacke. God wanteþ þee;... (HCM, CLOUD 81:34; a.1425; ?a.1400)

On syntactic criteria, it can therefore be read as 'God wants you'. Notice that this volitional reading alongside present-day syntax is compatible with messages delivered in other places of the Bible.

The above discussion is revealing in so far as we can often replace the 'lack' meanings with 'desire' readings without major changes to the proposition conveyed. Seminal to the rise of volitional meaning, then, seems to be that the semantics of 'lack' is to a great extent reciprocal. This aspect becomes more transparent if one posits a core meaning for lack 'be absent from',[32] such that *A wants B* denotes that 'A is absent from B' and vice versa. I propose that this core meaning – alongside general cognitive principles at work in human discourse which ideally map an animate argument onto the subject in topic position (cf. Givón 1998: 54) and related syntactic factors discussed in 4.2.1.1 – is conducive to the subsequent reanalysis of a (non-agentive) Experiencer (giving the semantics of 'lack') as an agentive subject (giving the semantics of 'desire'). More gradual accounts would probably highlight the role of one specific implicature, *viz.* what is lacked by someone is also desired by him or her. On this view, which is equally plausible, the implicature was increasingly realized and thus led to the gradual conventionalization of the desiderative meaning aspect during the 18th and 19th centuries. In other words, the conventionalization of implicature would be conceived as the prime mechanism that is responsible for the genesis and spread of today's focal meaning. There is, it must be stressed, little reason to assume that the core-meaning account and the conventionalization account are incompatible with one another. On the contrary, they should be seen as complementing each other.

So far, we have accounted for the development of the desiderative semantics of WANT, but we still want an explanation for the rise of truly volitional modality, that is, the emergence of desiderative WANT that is subcategorized for the *to* infinitive. A feasible and rather elegant explanation is syntactic in nature, which reveals that (at least in the case at hand) it is impossible to isolate semantic from syntactic developments.[33] It is an account in terms of extension and would simply posit generalization of transitive WANT along the following lines: if a noun phrase can denote a desired entity, so too can an infinitive. This type of generalization is exemplified by the bracketing of the two examples below:

(31)   I want [a car]

(32)   I want [to go]

This position seems plausible, especially in view of the general increase of infinitival *to* complements since Middle English times (see Los 1998 for details).

It is no coincidence that the first unequivocally volitional examples in the OED are followed by the infinitive. Volitional semantics is closely tied to modal WANT TO. Consider two early contiguous examples from ARCHER:

(33)   And (to tell you truly) the Money, which you favour'd me with, I chiefly want [understood: the money, in order] to prosecute this design. (ARCHER D1, 1671)

(34)   This wretched State of ours I have long felt in a slighter Manner; but now perceive it so intolerable, that I have Thoughts of leaving the Kingdom, and retiring to a religious House beyong [*sic*] Sea; where Father B--- , (who now, I hear, favours you with his Company, and who wants to be rid of me,) promises I shall be admitted suitably to the imaginary Title I formerly bore; and for which he engages to procure me proper Testimonials. (ARCHER F2, 1737)

Non-volitional biclausal examples with a purposive subordinate clause such as (33) are rare. Usually – as in (34) – it is difficult to advocate the semantics of 'lack' for contiguous WANT TO. The latter, as most modern instances of WANT TO, is therefore likely to be interpreted as having volitional semantics and likely to receive a single-clause analysis. Interestingly, in (33) 'need' is a much better paraphrase for *want* than 'lack'; in fact, the 'lack' reading is logically impossible because the context makes it clear that the speaker has already been given the money. 'Necessity' is even more closely related to 'lack' than 'volition'. Moreover, 'necessity' is already within the confines of notional modality. From here it is only a minute step to unequivocally volitional semantics. One might, then, assume that there is a possible intermediate step in the evolution of desiderative meaning aspects for WANT TO. Accordingly, the path of WANT to volitional modality would be along the following contiguous domains:

(35)   LACK   →   NECESSITY   →   VOLITION

As a consequence, even though volition seems to be the focal sense in the second half of the 18th century, it comes as no surprise that various early modal WANT TO examples also have a backgrounded necessity reading. Consider especially the two instances in (36), where the speaker is obviously under strong compulsion to speak – of marriage, needless to say:

(36)   I wanted to have some chat with you, madam, in private. ... Why, madam, - I, ah -- I, ah - but let's shut the door: I was, madam, - ah! ah! Can't you guess what I want to talk about? (ARCHER D3, 1753)

(37)   Well, if I am blown up by my own mine, I shall be the only sufferer -- There's another thing I want to talk of, I am going to marry my son to Miss Moreland. (ARCHER D3, 1775)

(38)   I want to know, methinks, whether Sir Charles is very much in earnest in his favour to Lord G. with regard to Miss Grandison. I doubt not, if he be, but he has good reasons for it. (ARCHER F3, 1751)

Since infinitival *to* complements almost exclusively occur with necessity and/or volitional semantics, the fact that "the 'wishing' branch, firmly established itself in the nineteenth century" (Burchfield

1996: *s.v. want*) almost naturally coincides with the sharp rise in frequency of modal WANT TO. Drama has been shown to be most sensitive to ongoing changes. I therefore reproduce a graph from section 4.2.2.2, now focusing exclusively on modal WANT TO, which throws into relief the increase in frequency – and concomitantly in grammaticalization – in the late 18th and early 19th centuries:[34]

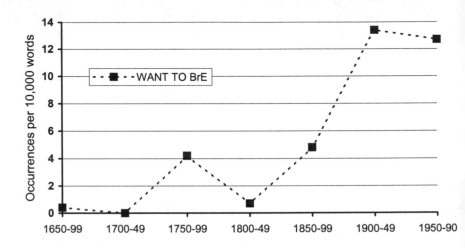

Figure 4.4.   Modal WANT TO in ARCHER drama (BrE, 50-year intervals)

Notice that, as was seen with HAVE TO and HAVE GOT TO, the steepest increase occurs at a time when the critical discourse frequency of 5 per 10,000 words is exceeded. This incidence was isolated as apparently constituting a threshold of grammaticality for verbs in contemporary spoken discourse.[35]

To conclude, it appears that a number of different explanatory factors are involved in the evolution of the modal construction, each of which on its own offers no more than a partial explanation for the emergence of volitional semantics of WANT. This may not be all that surprising since recent work on language change – such as Warner (1993), Hopper & Traugott (1993), Denison (1993) – has demonstrated that multi-factorial explanations involving clusters of individual changes from various levels of linguistic organization are generally superior to one-dimensional accounts.[36] Let us summarize the major forces identified for the rise of modal WANT TO:

- syntactic operations: generalization from NP complements to infinitival complements,

- pragmatic inferencing: enrichment from 'lack' (probably via 'necessity') to 'volition',

- semantic considerations: the reciprocal character of 'lack' giving the core meaning 'be absent from', which in turn facilitates

- syntactic reanalysis of topicalized erstwhile Experiencers as agentive subjects.[37]

4.3.2   Extension to other modal meanings

English modal verbs are typically ambiguous between several deontic and epistemic meanings (Coates 1983: Chs. 2f; Palmer 1989: *passim*). While **volitional modality** is doubtless the dominant sense today, preliminary evidence of WANT TO developing further modal meanings would tie in with an auxiliarization hypothesis. Since the new meanings are rather rare it is next to impossible to investigate them historically with the present sources, in particular on a quantitative basis given the size of currently available corpora. Even with huge corpora like the BNC it is difficult to pursue quantitative semantic analyses since more often than not new meanings depend a good deal on their co-text and context, from which they tend to arise by implicature. Moreover semantic disambiguation of corpus examples is a rather laborious task, none of my corpora is manually tagged for semantics and unfortunately the present state of automatic semantic tagging forbids using the available programmes for the fine-grained distinctions needed here. Shying away from the "chimera of intuition" (Westney 1995: 219), I will not invent examples to support the following claims; but I will cite evidence which has been gathered unsystematically. I take it, however, that most readers will be familiar with uses such as the following:

(39)   You've got tooth ache? You wanna see a dentist! (overheard in the US)

(40)   You want to take the three o'clock bus in order to catch the plane at 5 p.m. (female travel agency clerk, northern England)

(41)   You definitely wanna talk to Dr. S. from the *Auslandsamt* in order to get that money for the flight. (American lecturer)

(42)   You wanna turn right/make a left at the next corner. (common directions by Californian student in car)

(43)   The cement is the only thing that doesn't want to get put in the car-port. (English speaker from Chester unloading his car)

(44)   We want to refine those categories. Existing taxonomies don't suffice. (British lecturer at a conference)

Most current dictionaries list such an obligative meaning as being synonymous to *ought (to)*. It is generally labelled as informal, where I believe that 'informal' might be equivalent to 'incoming'.[38] Except (42), none of the above situations was particularly informal. Notice further that except (44) and, arguably, (43) all the above examples have a second person subject and therefore may be interpreted as **commands** (cf. Bybee et al. 1994: 211 on *gonna*).[39] Example (43) is interesting on a number of counts. For one thing, the voice of the clause being (GET) passive, it has an understood second person subject (*you*), too. It thus is interpretable as a (negative) command, as well. At the same time, a comparison with its corresponding active clause

(43)'   You don't want to ['must not', 'ought not to'] put the cement in the car-port

demonstrates voice neutrality, which is another typical property of modal verbs (see Ch. 2.8 above). Finally, its subject is inanimate, indicating that a syntactic constraint which does not apply to the central modal verbs (*viz.* subject selection restriction to animate subjects) is being loosened with WANT TO, as well.

Once more, the rise of a new modality seems to be motivated by implicatures. An obligative reading of WANT TO is more inferential than a straightforwardly volitional reading, which is among the most basic 'event schemas' identified by Heine (1993: 31) and therefore serves as a common source domain in auxiliarization. While in present-day English this is the default meaning, obligative readings are at least partially invited by politeness inferences: what somebody has to do in his or her own interest is what he or she is willing to do. WANT TO in such indirect speech acts, which are formally statements but which function as imperatives, is therefore synonymous to *must* or (assuming less force for the proposition) *should*, or *ought (to)*; the main difference is that WANT

TO is less face-threatening (on face-threatening acts see Brown & Levinson 1987).

It goes without saying that volition and **intention** are contiguous, indeed overlapping semantic domains (cf. Matthews 1991: 157f). Many volitional examples are compatible with an intention reading. Two examples shall suffice to demonstrate this:

(45)   Mind you, they'll probably wanna do overtime next week! (BNC, KCL 5274)

(46)   Yes. I want to go to the United States to experience a different culture. I'm doing Communication Studies which involves advertising and the media. I reckon the US is geared more towards the media. (BNC, KC5 2222)

From a cognitive point of view it is interesting to see that the present polysemy of WANT reflects to some extent the historical development of its senses. This is to say that we discover diachronic facets in a synchronic polysemy pattern.[40] Both intentional and obligative readings are more abstract and more complex than the basic cognitive notions of volition or lack. These are universally valid paths of semantic change. It fits into this context that children acquire obligative modality and intention/futurity later than volition (Stephany 1993).

The relationship between synchrony and diachrony is not quite as simple, though, because obligative readings of WANT TO are senses that are not entirely new to the lexeme WANT. The older meanings of the noun ('lack', 'need'), the adjective *wanting* ('lacking') or indeed the intransitive verb ('need'), which were discussed above, are closely related to obligative WANT TO. But as we have seen such nonmodal uses (adjective, intransitive verb, noun) appear to be on their way out, whereas the modal WANT TO is becoming ever more prominent. Two factors, then, seem to have been reinforcing one another in the rise of obligative WANT TO. The first is semantic extension from volitional to obligative modality. The second is a revival of older senses in a different syntactic environment: today obligative WANT takes *to* infinitives more often than NP complements, which were more common proportionately in earlier stages of the English language. On either interpretation, however, we are witnessing cases of polysemy rather than of homonymy.

The most surprising use of WANT TO I have come across contains an inanimate subject and expresses **epistemic** meaning:

(47)   Customer: Do you have coolers?
        Assistant: Coolers? They wanna be on one of the top
                  shelves somewhere. They only arrived this
                  morning. (Californian female shop assistant,
                  native speaker)

Does this example show us the direction where WANT TO is going? In any case, independence of subject is listed as one criterion of auxiliarihood in Quirk et al. (1985: 137). In a related fashion but on a more general level, Heine et al. (1991: 156) note:

> If two grammatical categories differ from one another only by the fact that one typically implies some human participant whereas the other implies an inanimate participant, then the latter is more grammaticalized.

For the present discussion, Heine et al.'s claim entails that epistemic WANT is more grammaticalized than volitional WANT and that the grammaticalization of WANT therefore has not come to an end, since epistemicity is obviously not conventionalized. Hence, while the use of epistemic WANT TO still seems rather odd, it may not be impossible that it will develop at some point in the future. In the preceding consideration of semantic developments, then, we have identified the following stages, which fully confirm Bybee et al.'s (1994: Ch. 6) crosslinguistic trends:

lack ($\rightarrow$ necessity) $\rightarrow$ volition $\rightarrow$ intention

                                    ↘ obligation $\rightarrow$ command

                                      ↘   (?probability)

Figure 4.5. Semantic developments of WANT (TO)[41]

To conclude, it deserves mention that the rise of volitional semantics tallies with Traugott's concept of subjectification, as did the rise of deontic modality for HAVE TO discussed in section 3.2.1 (see there for a brief outline and definition). Suffice it here to recall Traugott's Tendency III (1989: 35):

> Meanings tend to become increasingly based in the speaker's subjective belief state/attitude toward the proposition.

'Lack' is an objectively testable concept, as is expressed in the above stated core meaning of 'lack': 'A is absent from B' (p. 143). 'Volition', by contrast, pertains to the speakers' cognition: it cannot be verified through external description since only the speakers themselves have access to judgments regarding their desires. As was seen, in the 18th and 19th centuries, speakers invited inferences which led towards an enriched meaning (the implicature being: +> what is lacked is generally desired by humans). Such implicatures gave rise to the related but more internalized modal volitional semantics (probably via 'need'). Traugott (1988: 411) calls such pragmatic "strengthening of informativeness ... a type of metonymy."

As to the motivations for the observed meaning changes, we can rather confidently assume that they include two factors. One is the natural principle of layering, which owes part of its universal applicability to the continual striving of human beings for expressivity. The second is the fact that since early Middle English *will* came to function increasingly as a future marker, thus probably triggering or, rather, reinforcing the rise of a new predominantly volitional modal. To conclude the discussion of semantic developments, we have seen that Sweetser (1990: 9) is certainly right when she advocates regularity for sense developments in such domains as modality:

> Words do not randomly acquire new senses, then. And since new senses are acquired by cognitive structuring, the multiple synchronic senses of a given word will normally be related to each other in a motivated fashion.

But while Sweetser believes metaphor to be the single most important principle in motivated semantic change, we have seen that it appears to be chiefly context-driven metonymic processes that have led to the specific meaning changes of WANT (TO). This was the dominant tendency in the cases of HAVE TO and HAVE GOT TO as well.

4.4   Phonological and morphosyntactic developments within present-day English

4.4.1   Variation and concomitant obscuration of infinitival *to*

The existence of synchronic phonological variation can be an indication of ongoing morphosyntactic change (see e.g. Aitchison 1991: Chs. 3f; Bauer 1994: 12; McMahon 1994: Ch. 9). As for the sequence *want to*, there is a great deal of variation between

I   ['wɒnt̩tʰuː], ['wɒnt̩tʊ],

II   ['wɒntʊ], ['wɒntə],

III   ['wɒnə], ['wənə]

IV   [wɒn] and

V   [wɑ̃].[42]

The coalescence of *want* and *to*, quite obviously, fulfils one crucial criterion of grammaticalization, *viz.* that of phonological attrition (or erosion, decay; see Lehmann 1995: 126f). Let us now try to integrate these phonological reductions into the two well-known grammaticalization charts mentioned in Chapter 2:

i) Givón's cyclic wave from discourse pragmatics to zero (1979: 208f):

discourse → syntax → morphology → morphophonemics → zero

ii) Hopper & Traugott's cline of grammaticality (1993: 7):

content item > grammatical word > clitic > inflectional affix

The fully articulated infinitival marker *to* – see the above options given under (I) – is a grammatical word which operates on the level of syntax: here, *to* indicates that the following infinitive is governed by the matrix verb *want*. When *to* is cliticized (as in options II and III), one might consider it to be a fused morpheme. The reduction given under (III) is a borderline case which can equally be attributed to morphophonemics. In options (IV) and (V), finally, *to* is clearly reduced to zero.

As for the whole construction WANT TO, it seems appropriate to integrate it into another cline of Givón's, which is a specification for the verbal domain of Hopper & Traugott's general cline of grammaticality just cited:

iii) Givón's verbal cline (1979; 220-222):

   lexical verb → auxiliary → affix[43]

It seems uncontroversial that WANT TO is currently in the transition zone between lexical verb and auxiliary status. It is the task of the following sections to determine more precisely its actual position in this blurred area. To begin with, phonological reduction is characteristic of auxiliary verbs in general (compare *is* ~ *'s; will* ~ *'ll*). It is interesting to see, however, that the fusion of *want* and *to* leads to an obscuration of the infinitival marker, so that the above articulations (III)-(V), which I subsume under the spelling *wanna*, appear to be followed by the plain infinitive.[44] As will be recalled, this is a crucial criterion of the central modal auxiliaries.

The sequence *want to* is highly unlikely to be pronounced *wanna* when *want* is a noun. This is in line with the general observation that grammaticalization processes typically occur in very localized contexts (Hopper & Traugott 1993: 2). It may be possible that we are witnessing the very initial stages of a functional split between modal use and nonmodal use, very similar in type to historical changes leading to modalization (cf. Hopper's principle of divergence outlined in section 2.3): roughly at the turn of the 15th century, Middle English CAN (< OE *cunnan*) split into the modal *can* and the nonmodal transitive *con* ('get to know', 'learn', OED 1989). The latter took regular inflections (Warner 1993: 200).[45] Similarly, Old English *agan* split into what are now modal *ought (to)* and nonmodal (di)transitive *owe* (OED 1989: *s.vv. owe; ought*). Section 4.4.3.2 will demonstrate that there are indeed incipient signs of a defective paradigm for modal WANT TO (and especially for the contracted form *wanna*). This contrasts with a regular lexical verb WANT + NP.

Some British speakers believe pronunciations approaching *wanna* to be almost exclusively a feature of American English (cf. Pullum 1997: 97), which is why I adduce the following data from the British National Corpus. These show that one in five British English uses of the sequence *want to* is pronounced *wanna*, i.e. characterized by the absence of residual /t/:[46]

Table 4.8.   Want to vs. *wanna* in the British National Corpus (spoken vs. written)

	SPOKEN (c.10m words)		WRITTEN (c.90m words)	
	Occurrences	% of total	Occurrences	% of total
want to	7,851	69.9%	21,911	85.0%
wants to	1,005	8.9%	3,674	14.3%
wanna	2,381	21.2%	191	0.7%
Total	11,237	100%	25,776	100%

Note that the frequency of *wanna* in speech is around 30 times higher than in writing, where, of course, most instances are quotations (e.g. in journalistic texts) and fictionalized oral utterances. But even in the latter medium, there appears to be a trend towards employing it more often. Compare the last eight years of *The Guardian*, which show an essentially uninterrupted increase in *wanna* spellings:

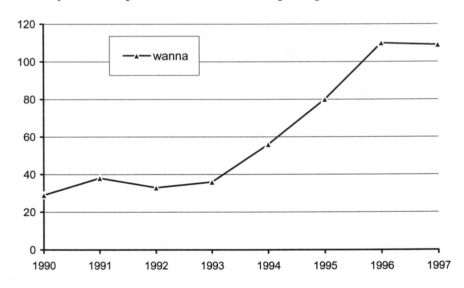

Figure 4.6.   *Wanna* in The Guardian (1990-1997)

By 1997, the total increase on 1990 amounts to some 400 per cent, which can by no means be explained by increased corpus size, despite the inclusion of *The Observer* since 1994. Notice again the almost ideal S-curve pattern of the graph, which has proved to be helpful in describing various graphs in the present study. As for a qualitative observation, while early *wanna* uses in *The Guardian* are commonly employed to characterize (informal) American speech, they have ceased to be used as salient regional markers in more recent years. This suggests that *wanna* no longer functions as some kind of shibboleth,[47] and that it is now more widely perceived to be a feature of British English too (due to more idiolects exhibiting the feature). Chapman (1988: 42) has recently conceded that forms like *gonna* are not restricted to nonstandard English: "Whether we like it or not, 'educated' speakers in relaxed colloquial conversation often say *gonna* ... " Given the high percentage of *wanna* found in the spoken BNC, one can confidently conclude that this holds for *wanna* too. The data also suggest that pronunciations like *wanna* enjoy a higher degree of acceptability in British English today than a generation ago (see also section 4.5).

4.4.2   Abnormal time reference and ellipsis in co-ordination

The historical preterite forms of modals do not commonly have past time reference but typically refer to present time or express such notions as hypotheticality, tentativeness, politeness or counterfactuality (Warner 1993: 9). A recent study by Bybee (1995: 506-508) likens the Modern English behaviour of WANT TO to that of *will* and *shall* in Old English. She demonstrates that the volitional modality in the past tense form "may still be in effect" at coding time (p. 506). This is to say that *wanted* "can be used in present contexts" (p. 507) in sentences like the following (except for the last example taken from Bybee 1995: 506-508):

(48)   I wanted to help you

(49)   If I saw Judy, I wanted to tell her the news

(50)   I wanted to ask you a question

(51)   I just wanted to tell you that ...

It has often been noted that there exists a correlation between past-tense forms and tentativeness or politeness. While this is an option in (50) and (51), it is less likely to explain (48), and it is irrelevant in (49). Further, Bybee (1995) points out that there are indeed a number of verbs that tend to have politeness readings cross-linguistically; significantly, however, "the polite use of the Past tense depends on the presence of the modal verb; it is not possible to get a polite reading of just any verb with the Past tense" (p. 508). Hence, what happened to the preterite present verbs in pre-Old English times (cf. Birkmann 1987) and what happened to the modals since Old English might now be happening to WANT TO. Apparently, then, a cross-linguistic mechanism turning past tense forms of certain mental, stative verbs into non-past meanings is particularly dynamic for English verbs with modal semantics. Obviously, such recurrent paths support an analysis which argues that WANT TO is grammaticalizing into a modal auxiliary.

Another parallel to the central modals is the fact that Aarts & Aarts (1995: 171-73) find *want* to be prominent in elliptical constructions of the following types (examples from *ibid.*):[48]

(52)   *want to* [VP]:   *... if she wants to, she can get in touch with you.*

(53)   *want* [to VP]:   *You can wait outside if you want.*

(54)   *want NP to* [VP]: *... even his eyeballs wouldn't move though he wanted them to.*

In terms of ongoing change it is interesting to see that roughly a generation ago the more drastic type of ellipsis (53) was considered ungrammatical (Stevens 1972: 21). Stevens (*ibid.*) concludes that auxiliaries of the WANT type "seem to divide *want to* I + base; that is, *I want to* I *go now* not *I want* I *to go now*." While his ungrammaticality claim seems dated, his conclusion is probably nonetheless right (see also the discussions on the historical development and on bondedness presented earlier in this chapter). How, then, are the two observations to be reconciled? In Aarts & Aarts' data (1.5m words of post-1985 printed English), the more drastic ellipsis of *to* + VP is less common than ellipsis of the verb only. Compared to Stevens' statement, their data seem to indicate that change is in progress, with the more drastic omission type becoming more acceptable. On the other hand the increasing bondedness between WANT and *to* (see Ch. 4.2.2) makes it more likely that *to* omission is an ephemeral phenomenon so that, except perhaps for some idiomatic expressions like *if you want* or (*do*) *what you want*, the dominant ellipsis strategy (52) is likely to prevail or even oust the more marginal one. In the spoken BNC, both ellipsis strategies (52) and (53) are far more common than tone group-final *wanna*, which is attested, though. Witness a conversation between two male speakers, who unfortunately are not tagged for age, but the context suggests that they are teenagers (like the silent third participant carrying the tape recorder, who is tagged for age):

(55) A   Would you Frenchie her?
      B   Nah.
      A   Why not?
      B   Cos I don't wanna. [Pause] Cos she's got smelly breath.[49]

Regardless of whether *to* is deleted together with the main verb or not, ellipsis of the following verb as such is another feature typical of English auxiliary verbs (Quirk et al. 1985: 137). Many analysts group WANT alongside START, CONTINUE or BEGIN as a catenative. The fact that these more strongly resist ellipsis of the following (*to*) infinitive not only shows clearly that such a classification is inaccurate; it also indicates that WANT has progressed further on its way to auxiliarihood.[50]

4.4.3   Further emerging properties

The present section deals with some ongoing developments. Focusing on WANT TO, it touches two points: (a) the issue of double modals and (b) the possibility of a gradual loss of inflections and nonfinite forms. These topics are interesting in the light of similar historical developments which the central modals underwent. It should be borne in mind, though, that what follows is rather speculative and suggestive, certainly not definitive. Solely on the basis of the data and arguments presented here, it seems daring to even speak of emerging properties. However, the points discussed below, I believe, deserve more thorough consideration and can therefore be understood as suggestions for further research.

4.4.3.1 *Double modals*

There is an enormous literature on the historical development and synchronic analysis of double modals both for the British Isles and the United States of America. A detailed discussion of the issue, however, is neither feasible nor necessary here (see, for instance, the overviews presented in Montgomery & Nagle 1993 or Fennell & Butters 1996). Let us nonetheless briefly consider the figures of Table 4.9 against the double modal discussion. For comparison, the figures of three lexical verbs enjoying similar discourse frequencies as WANT TO (*give, find* and *tell*) are provided too.[51]

Table 4.9.   Modals preceding WANT TO and other verbs in the spoken BNC[52]

	want to	*wanna*	*give*	*tell*	*find*
All instances	7851	2381	8762	6920	5482
might	92	10	25	16	99
may	53	2	8	3	60
will	41	1	223	107	122
'll	53	17	797	667	443
shall	3	0	32	14	5
would	122	4	144	37	70
'd	59	13	96	41	53
should	4	0	54	25	13
could	0	0	99	115	91
can	0	0	278	420	249
must	1	0	29	28	15
Sum all modals + verb	428	47	1785	1473	1220
As % of all instances	5.5%	2.0%	20.4%	21.3%	22.3%
Syntactic double modals (future, subjunctive/irrealis)	282	35	—	—	—
Nonsyntactic double modals	146	12	—	—	—

Four points are worth making. First of all, a comparison of the lexical verbs and WANT TO shows that, at a ratio of roughly 20%, the three lexical verbs are preceded by central modals approximately four times more often than *want to*, and over ten times more often than *wanna*. The data thus confirm Bolinger's (1980b: 296) intuitions, who "sense[s] a certain discomfort with subordinating fully reduced *wanna* to other verbs, including other auxiliaries." And even though a larger-scale study of lexical verbs is required, the homogeneity of the three verbs investigated here suggests that full verbs in general combine far more often with modals than the emerging modal WANT TO, the difference being even more drastic when this occurs in its contracted form. Second, discounting syntactic, i.e. grammatically conditioned infinitival *want to* (future, subjunctive/irrealis), *might* accounts for the vast majority of uses. This trend is also more pronounced for the reduced form *wanna* (where *might* accounts for 83% of nonsyntactic double modals) than for the full form *want to* (where the share is 63%). Again, this sets WANT TO clearly apart from the three lexical verbs, where *might* is one of the less frequent preceding modals.

It is certainly noteworthy that the behaviour of WANT TO is paralleled by the central modals in double modal constructions: *might*, too, figures as the most prominent first item in the double modal debate irrespective of the investigated area (a typical example is *He might could do it*).[53] Third, in Montgomery's (1989) study *may* is the second most frequent matrix verb (or adverb under some analyses), just as in the BNC for WANT TO. And again the lexical verbs behave entirely differently, since *may* (alongside *shall*) is the modal combing least frequently with them. This shows that WANT TO behaves in ways that are very similar to the central modals. Fourth and probably least surprising, a stylistic observation: where full and reduced variants are in competition (*will*, *would*) *want to* shows a greater propensity towards the full forms while *wanna* is almost exclusively preceded by the reduced variants *'ll* and *'d*. Hence phonologically reduced forms tend to co-occur, which seems to create and/or maintain stylistic coherence within utterances.

In sum, Table 4.9 shows that *wanna* is nearer the focal point of the central modals syntactically than the unreduced form since the double modal constraint applies more rigidly.[54] Contra Pullum (1997) and with Bolinger (1980b) we can therefore state that *want to* and *wanna* exhibit different syntactic properties. In this section, differences have largely proved a matter of statistical preference. The next section will introduce some categorical differences in syntactic behaviour, which strengthens the position that the two items are more than just phonological variants.

4.4.3.2 Absence or gradual loss of inflections and nonfinite forms

There are signs which seem to suggest that WANT TO is gradually losing its inflected and nonfinite forms. Aarts & Aarts (1995: 171) find that in their written corpus only 27 per cent of WANT tokens are nonfinite while 73 per cent are finite. In the same corpus, the verb FIND yields approximately the inverse picture. We have seen that in spoken English, too, infinitival *want to* follows less frequently central modals than the infinitives of three lexical verbs (including FIND). But clearly a larger-scale study on English verbs is necessary before any firm conclusions can be drawn that concern the whole area of inflected and nonfinite forms.[55] It may be more illuminating for the moment to look at individual inflected forms, such as occurrences of the progressive. Since WANT is stative, progressive forms should be rare. While this is generally true, some progressive forms can be found in the BNC. Interestingly, however, no unequivocally obligative example is in the spoken material. More significantly, obligative WANT TO has indubitably a defective paradigm: tense shifting of the obligative examples quoted earlier in this chapter is not possible if one wants to use the verb WANT. Recall:

(39)   You've got tooth ache? You wanna see a dentist!

(40)   You want to take the three o'clock bus in order to catch the plane at 5 p.m.

(41)   You definitely wanna talk to Dr. S. from the *Auslandsamt* in order to get that money for the flight.

(42)   You wanna turn right/make a left at the next corner.

(44)   We want to refine those categories. Existing taxonomies don't suffice.

For (39), *Yesterday you *wannaed to see a dentist* is ungrammatical. Equally inappropriate – if obligative semantics is to be retained – is *Yesterday you wanted to see a dentist*. On a similar note, obligative semantics is not expressed in a tense-shifted sentence like

(40)'   Last week you wanted to catch the three o'clock bus in order to catch the plane at 5 p.m.

Related arguments hold for the remaining three examples given above. *Had to* would be the preferred replacement for past environments in all these examples. Furthermore, in the context of a gradual loss of inflections, one could invoke examples (48) to (51), discussed in section 4.4.2. There it was seen that for some uses of *wanted to* the simple past inflection has lost its tense-marking function (e.g. *I just wanted to talk to you*). Finally, even though third person singular *wanna* is extremely rare in British dialects, when it occurs, it naturally does not take third person singular *-s* in the simple present tense. This is yet another property of the central modals. Compare:

(14)   So he wanna [*wannas] be a hero, I suppose, doesn't he? (BNC KE6, Wendy, aged 54, machine minder, central south-west)

Defective paradigms are indicative of decategorialization, one of the five principles of grammaticalization proposed by Paul Hopper (1991: 22):

> Forms undergoing grammaticization tend to lose or neutralize the morphological markers and syntactic privileges characteristic of the full categories Noun and Verb, ...

In sum, it is especially the incoming modal meanings (which cannot be tense-shifted) and, most obviously, pronunciations approaching *wanna* (which is invariable just like the central modals) that exhibit many morphosyntactic signs of modalization.

4.5   Social and stylistic variation in the British National Corpus

Data on social, stylistic and regional variation from the BNC also support the spread of *wanna* along paths that are typical of language innovations in Britain (for a detailed study into variation and its role in language change, see Krug 1998b). Age-related variation, i.e. a study in apparent time as summarized in Table 4.10,[56] indicates that the following generalization holds: the younger the participants, the higher the incidence and the proportions of *wanna*. In fact, there is a perfect continuum, i.e. a steady decrease, in the text frequency of *wanna* (row 2) and contraction ratios (row 3) with increasing age. This, then, is a fascinating example of language change which is still spreading.

Table 4.10.   *Want to* vs. *wanna*: Variation according to age in the BNC

	Speakers aged 1-14	Speakers aged 15-24	Speakers aged 25-34	Speakers aged 35-44	Speakers aged 45-59	Speakers aged 60+
1 Sum *wanna*	521	253	407	294	354	142
2 Per million words	1131	494	365	276	220	90
3 **As % of all forms**	**51.5%**	**44.4%**	**33.6%**	**23.4%**	**20.2%**	**18.1%**
4 Sum *want to*	490	317	804	961	1396	643
5 Per million words	1064	619	722	901	869	407
6 As % of all forms	48.5%	55.6%	66.4%	76.6%	79.8%	81.9%
7 Total of all forms	1011	570	1211	1255	1750	785
8 Per million words	2195	1114	1087	1176	1090	497

The gradual rise in the incidence of *wanna* and in the contraction ratios demonstrate very clearly that this instance of language change is implemented slowly. The data in Table 4.10 make it impossible to argue that there is an abrupt reanalysis of main verb *want to* as modal *wanna* from one generation to the next, even though the difference between the extreme poles (spanning nearly two generations, though) are enormous: contraction ratios rise by a third; the incidence of the construction rises fivefold (but see next paragraph for caveats).

As regards overall incidence of the construction (row 8), all age groups except the youngest and oldest behave rather uniformly. The twofold incidence of the youngest participants compared to the four next-older groups might reflect speech behaviour which is rather unconstrained by social codes. Such factors lie outside the domain of linguistics as conceived here. The fact, however, that the oldest group uses WANT TO less than half as often as the speakers from the remaining age bands can probably be accounted for by a language-internal factor. It may be due to the still unsaturated text frequency of the construction during the formative period of the oldest group's language development.[57] Such a view at least is supported by the British drama data from ARCHER (Figure 4.1, p. 131). These suggest that the rise in the construction ground to a halt approximately in 1950, that is, apparently shortly after the most formative period of the average over-sixty-year-old speaker recorded in the BNC.

As for stylistic and medium-specific variation in the BNC, Table 4.11 shows a clear correlation between coalescence and decreasing degrees of formality. This finding will surprise no-one. Proportionally, spontaneous speech favours the contracted form over four times as much as formal speech, which in its turn is still way ahead (approximately ten times) of the written mode.

Table 4.11.   Want to vs. *wanna*: Stylistic variation in the BNC[58]

	Spontaneous speech (c.4m words)	Formal speech (c.6m words)	Written English (c.90m words)
want to	3554	4297	21911
wanna	1986	395	191
% contracted	35.8%	8.4%	0.86%

4.6   Regional variation in the British National Corpus

Let us conclude the empirical analysis of WANT TO with a brief discussion of regional variation. Map 4.1 (see next page) shows that the south of the United Kingdom, including Wales, is in the lead as regards the use of *wanna* – very nearly approximating the distribution obtained for *gotta*. As was the case for *gotta*, the focal area is England's political and cultural centre, London.[59] This lends full support to contact theories that build on accommodation of idiolects as advanced by Trudgill (1986: Ch. 2). This theory – as well as a refined version in terms of gravity as described in Chambers & Trudgill (1998: Chs. 11.7f) – predicts that in the diffusion of an innovation highly populated areas (such as London) will influence less densely populated areas more strongly than vice versa. Let us quote Trudgill's (1986: 39) illustration of how this mechanism operates on the British Isles:

> For example, a speaker from Norwich ... is 30 to 40 times more likely to meet a Londoner than vice versa ... because the population of London is that much bigger than the population of Norwich.

Obviously, mutual influence correlates inversely with distance between different centres,

> simply because, other things being equal and transport patterns permitting, people on average come into contact most often with people who live closest to them and least often with people who live furthest away. (p. 40)

As Map 4.1 on the next page shows, *wanna* seems to have diffused somewhat further northwards than *gotta* (cf. Map 3.1 in the previous chapter). One might wish to include all regions up to the Midlands among the more progressive areas. Again, chi-squared values for contiguous regions are far higher than for non-adjacent regions, which makes contact and areal spread a likely force in the propagation of this innovation, too.[60]

Map 4.1.   Wanna in the spoken BNC (divergence from mean of all regions)

4.7   Summary

While some results presented in this chapter may have been tentative, the overall conclusion seems uncontroversial: WANT TO is an emerging modal which shows obvious signs of ongoing auxiliarization. Notice, however, that WANT TO will probably not assume *all* criteria of the central modals. One point that was stated for HAVE TO equally holds for WANT TO: it is unlikely that this item will soon (or ever) take NOT negation. The central modals retained this property, which had formerly been available to all verbs. By contrast, the items under investigation undergo auxiliarization at a stage when DO periphrasis for (erstwhile) nonauxiliary verbs is highly grammaticalized. Consequently, according to the Z-scores for WANT, a collocation *don't want (to)* is firmly established (or, in Bybee's terminology, highly entrenched). This indicates a rather high degree of idiomatization, which turns DO negation into a feature that is unlikely to become prone to change.

Most tables and figures in this chapter suggested that American English is in the vanguard as far as the modalization of WANT TO is concerned. Further, it was seen repeatedly that spoken facts exert pressures on the written medium, which tend to follow the developmental paths discovered by the spoken medium. This was interpreted as a reflex of functional influences operating in language change: the auxiliarization of WANT TO is a natural change from below and may be considered an instance of what has been called 'the colloquialization of written norms' (Mair 1997). This finding is in line with most research into the interaction between written and spoken language and, for that matter, between informal and more formal varieties.[61]

The historical discussion revealed that English WANT arose from predominantly impersonal verbal use in Middle English and that it became prominent as both noun and transitive verb in Early Modern English. Both of them had the semantics of 'lack'. From approximately the second half of the 18th century, the modal construction – that is volitional semantics followed by the infinitive – became substantially more common.

As for potentially fruitful future research, what we definitely want to have a look at are the semantic fields of volition, intention and futurity. Now that a general outline of the major developments undergone by WANT has been provided, it makes sense to pursue more fine-grained qualitative and quantitative research such as semantic disambiguation. At the present stage, one can confidently assume that the departure of *will* from volitional semantics towards predominantly futural use has led to an unstable situation and a subsequent major reshuffle in the auxiliary domain which has consequences for the modal system even today. This chapter has clearly underlined that grammatical changes take centuries. Given the fact that the modalization of WANT TO set in only centuries after *will* started to grammaticalize as a future marker in early Middle English, we may quite confidently assume a drag chain, in which WANT TO has apparently been gradually filling the gap in volitive modality.[62] Put differently, WANT has conquered most of the volitional field against a number of rival candidates such as INTEND, WISH or DESIRE, which all are attested with *to* infinitives before WANT. The success of WANT may be partially due to its shortness, but this criterion is not sufficient because it also applies to the much older WISH (which is currently the second most frequent item in the modal [V *to* VP] construction). Chapter 5 will attempt an explanation in terms of iconicity.

Another interesting question that awaits further exploration is whether nonmodal meanings of WANT indeed display incipient signs of obsolescence as has been tentatively suggested here. Such a development would be tantamount to semantic and functional streamlining and reminiscent of the history of the central modals. Evidently, approaches in terms of presence or absence of attributes cannot be expected to answer any question pertaining to the current auxiliarization of WANT TO, since we are dealing with a moving target. That is to say, WANT TO is currently undergoing a phase of relatively rapid changes (considering the fact that it is grammatical in nature). For such a fascinating instance of change in progress frequentative empirical research will remain an indispensable, if not the only appropriate, method by which a more complete picture can emerge.

5 Models and motivations for emerging English modals

5.1 Chapter outline

This chapter is an attempt at generalization and explanation. A note of caution is required from the start: generalizations usually entail simplifications and this is the case here too. Following a synthesis of individual findings of the previous empirical chapters I will discuss related verbs, notably GOING TO, NEED (TO), DARE (TO) and OUGHT (TO). This leads to the conclusion that we are witnessing the rise of a new focal point on the main verb - auxiliary cline which is a much more concisely definable category than that of the quasi-modals and which actually explains some developments within the larger group of quasi-modals.[1] For their recency, for the transformation which they are currently subjected to and for their overall movement towards the central modals, I believe that *emerging modals* is the most appropriate term for the new focal point. Since however the current process of modalization does not – and probably will not – produce items that share all attributes of the central modals, simply because this type of modalization appears to have been replaced by a new kind of modalization (or neomodalization), one might also consider *neomodals* as an appropriate alternative.

Categorization, then, is here conceived as a process in which it is chiefly the more central and frequent members that act as gravitational centres and that influence the more peripheral, less frequent ones. This claim will be supported by simulations of a model which is adapted from classical Newtonian gravitation theory. The gravitation analogy produces intuitively plausible results in the field of emerging modals. It remains to be seen whether it can be extended so as to provide a more general account for productivity in other fields of competing forces.

5.2   Frequency

5.2.1   Early Modern English to present-day English

Discourse frequency has figured prominently throughout the present study and continues to do so in this general round-up. In order to identify recurrent paths, I will plot the longer-term evolution of the three constructions investigated above and integrate the development of BE GOING TO. Since I aim at modelling natural language change, I select the ARCHER drama component (0.23m words), which has repeatedly proven to be the best approximation of spoken discourse. In a first step, I sketch the development on the British side in 50-year intervals. On the one hand, this approach takes us to the highest level of attainable detail, but for the comparatively shallow diachronic depth, it predictably produces somewhat 'untidy' charts. In a second step, I will compare British and American English in periods covering 100-year intervals. This method suggests itself because of the smaller amount of American data and the concomitant limitations for regional comparison (see section 2.7 for a description of the corpora). As a result of this method, minor fluctuations of the 50-year charts are levelled.

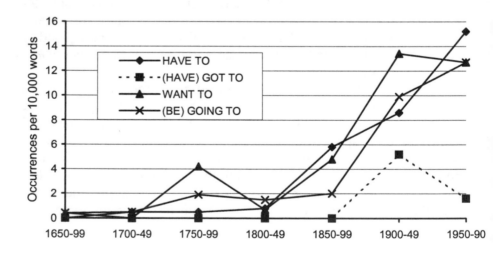

Figure 5.1.   Emerging modals in BrE: Occurrences per 10,000 words in ARCHER drama (50-year intervals)

Most important, Figure 5.1 shows a cluster of rapid changes between 1850 and 1950, thus suggesting that this century is the formative period for all four emerging modals.[2] It would be highly interesting if the observed restructuring in the modal domain coincided with similarly fundamental changes in other domains since this might give rise to typological considerations. To return to a more modest descriptive level, the WANT TO line is a fairly clear case of an S-curve.[3] Perhaps even the increase of GOING TO is currently beginning to slow down, thus entering the saturation phase of an S-curve pattern. GOT TO seems to be decreasing currently, whereas HAVE TO still appears to be on the increase. It will be remembered from the previous chapters that the current drama ratios correspond fairly accurately to contemporary spoken British discourse as recorded in the BNC.

As was noted earlier, the most appropriate method for a long-term regional study is to contrast the parallel British and American subcorpora of ARCHER. Such historical comparison will also permit some tentative statements concerning the issue of divergence or convergence in world Englishes. Figures 5.2 and 5.3 summarize the developments in the speech-based register of British and American English drama. For a register comparison, the text frequencies of the emerging modals are also plotted for fictional language in Figures 5.4 and 5.5.

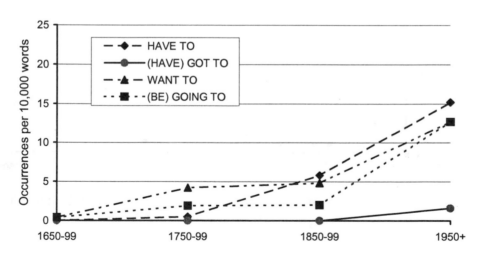

Figure 5.2. Emerging modals across the centuries in British English: Occurrences per 10,000 words in ARCHER drama

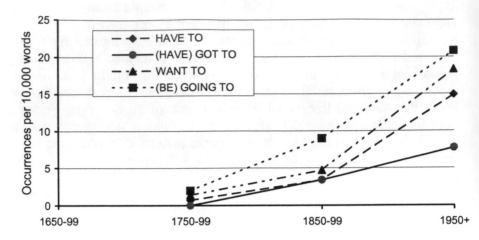

Figure 5.3.   Emerging modals across the centuries in American English: Occurrences per 10,000 words in ARCHER drama

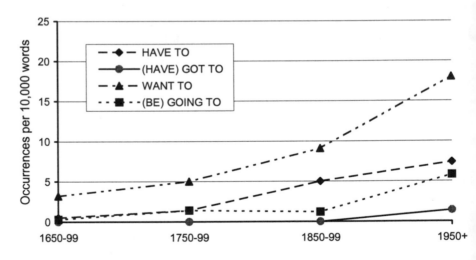

Figure 5.4.   Emerging modals across the centuries in British English: Occurrences per 10,000 words in ARCHER fiction

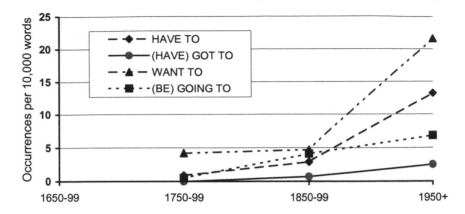

Figure 5.5.   Emerging modals across the centuries in American English: Occurrences per 10,000 words in ARCHER fiction

The comparison of the two registers shows clearly that drama is generally more receptive to natural change than fiction. It is also evident that American English drama is more receptive to change than its British counterpart. First, the gradient of each American curve is significantly steeper than that of its corresponding British curve. Second and connected with the preceding point, the contemporary discourse frequencies (1950+) are substantially higher on the American side (an exception is HAVE TO, to which I return shortly). In the late 18th century, by contrast, the two varieties show nearly identical behaviour with regard to the emerging modals. At the most modest level of generalization, then, we can finally verify Myhill's (1995) assumption for various quasi-modals, which was quoted in Chapter 3. He conjectured rightly that "British and American modal usage differ significantly" (1995: 158). This is certainly true for present-day English.

Historically, the difference is not very striking, though: if we look at the earliest comparable period (1750-1799), American English tends to lag slightly behind British English, more significantly so in fictional than in dramatic writing.[4] At a higher level of abstraction, therefore, the data suggest that two trends found by Kytö (1991a: Chs. 4-6, in particular) for early Modern British and American English (up to 1720) continue into the second half of the 18th century. For one thing, in her data it is also colloquial registers that show the earliest signs of incoming uses and promote their spread. For another, more formal registers in her data too show a higher influence of colonial lag than do speech-based registers.

Let us now proceed to a more general but also slightly more speculative level. If we can generalize from the present data, the two varieties have increasingly diverged over the last two centuries. It is important, however, that divergence can only be determined in terms of degrees since the overall trend on either side of the Atlantic is identical. In other words, allowing for the crude simplification which speaking of national varieties entails, this appears to be a fine example of an episode where American English is currently in the vanguard of change when compared to British English.[5] This may well be a transitional state, though: as the observed differences are not absolute but consist in frequentative preferences, it is not unlikely that the American curves will reach their saturation stages earlier than their British equivalents, so that eventually both varieties might converge again on similar discourse frequencies.

Such data, then, are by no means counterintuitive in so far as they suggest that, at present, (mainstream) American English is ahead of British English. One may in fact assume that American English is leading world English with regard to the investigated set of probably interrelated changes, but this would have to be checked against Australian and New Zealand data. However, at the very least a cross-Atlantic regional trend has been established by comparisons among written genres from 1961 and the 1990s (see Chapters 3 and 4): the developments in press and fictional language from LOB and Brown to their more recent analogues FLOB and Frown suggest strongly that American English is generally leading these particular changes.

As for cross-Atlantic influence, even though it is a commonplace to assume American influence on British English (e.g. Potter 1966: 168f; Foster 1968: Chs. 1f; Crystal 1988: 248; Barber 1993: 262; Trudgill & Hannah 1994: 56; Hundt 1998: 135; Kortmann forthcoming), I believe that it would be mistaken to grant this factor a major role in the specific case of the evolution of new modal verbs. Very recently Trudgill (1998) has sketched the convergence-divergence issues in the areas of phonology, grammar and lexicon. The "homogenisation in the direction of North American usage" at the lexical level (p. 30) contrasts with divergence between the two varieties – and between varieties of English around the world in general – for the level of phonology (p. 31f). Trudgill is rather cautious, however, when it comes to discussing the level of grammar:

At the grammatical level, the picture is not nearly so clear. Grammatical change is much slower than lexical change, and the overall impression much more difficult to determine. There is also the very considerable problem that we cannot be at all sure, just because a grammatical change in American English, say, precedes by some decades an identical change in British English, that the change has been introduced into the latter from the former. This is the well-known historical and anthropological problem of diffusion versus independent development, ... (1998: 31).

Since the ARCHER data suggest that the rise of the emerging modals started in both varieties from very similar levels at approximately the same time, the present study makes a strong case for arguing independent natural change. At the same time, the present study fully confirms Hundt's (1997: 146) observation from short-term developments that American English "is usually more advanced in ongoing morphological and syntactic changes." The above-mentioned exception of HAVE TO, where British English seems to have been leading the change throughout the history of the construction and where the two varieties are currently on the same level, also supports the hypothesis of independent developments.[6]

Drawing grand conclusions from four items is of course somewhat daring, but some facts indicate that generalizations are probably in order. First, we are dealing with trends that have proven to be rather consistent for more than two centuries. Second, the items under investigation enjoy high-frequency status, which reduces the risk of skewed results due to sampling errors. Third, these items come from precisely that area of English grammar where the assumption of an ongoing major restructuring has become commonplace (see the discussion in Ch. 1). Fourth, modality and auxiliary verbs in general are an area where regularity in change is more likely than in others (see, for example, Sweetser 1990; Bybee et al. 1994; Traugott 1996). It is therefore no coincidence that all of Trudgill's examples of grammatical change are related to the auxiliary domain. The fact that ARCHER makes possible long-term observations takes care of the perhaps most important caveat that "grammatical change is much slower than lexical change" (Trudgill 1998:31). Despite several provisos, then, it is not inconceivable that the developments observed in the present study are indicative of general trends in morphosyntax.

5.2.2   String frequency and grammaticalization

Table 5.1 gives the apparent-time distributions for those items whose contracted (i.e. progressive) forms and full (i.e. conservative) forms are transcribed in the BNC: GOING TO, GOT TO, WANT TO. For convenience and comparability, the curves in Figure 5.6 plot the percentages of the innovative forms (i.e. *gonna, gotta, wanna*) for the respective age groups. The figures in Table 5.1 and Figure 5.6 refer to the relevant subcorpus of the BNC, that is, speakers tagged for age (approximately 6m words). Since a discussion in terms of string frequency suggests taking a purely perceptual stance, I here include *all* sequences of the respective constructions (including *got to* or *going to* +NP). If we confine our investigation to modal constructions (as was generally done in previous chapters), the proportions of *gonna* in Figure 5.6 rise considerably (consistently across the age-groups by some 5.5%), those of *gotta* slightly (1.3% on average). Crucially, though, whichever perspective one takes, the overall tendencies remain the same.

Table 5.1.   *Going to, got to, want to* and their contracted counterparts in the spoken BNC

		60+	45 - 59	35 - 44	25 - 34	15 - 24	1 - 14	Total
1	*gonna*	873	1872	1675	1923	1255	1091	8689
2	*going to*	1105	2213	1178	1150	432	420	6498
3	Sum (1+2)	1978	4085	2853	3073	1687	1511	15187
4	*gotta*	245	627	525	621	430	353	2801
5	*got to*	794	1120	831	776	304	218	4043
6	Sum (4+5)	1039	1747	1356	1397	734	571	6844
7	*wanna*	142	354	294	407	253	521	1971
8	*want to*	643	1396	961	804	317	490	4611
9	Sum (7+8)	785	1750	1255	1211	570	1011	6582

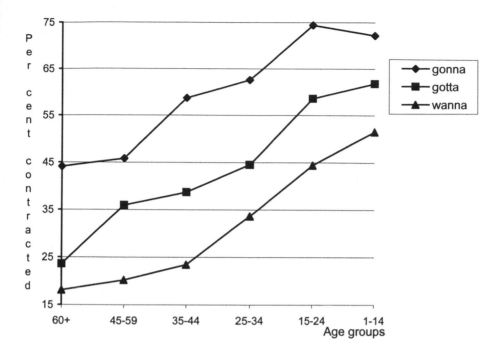

Figure 5.6. A study in apparent time: Full and contracted forms in the spoken
BNC (GOING TO, GOT TO, WANT TO)

All three constructions have strictly increasing curves. The only point
where one curve is falling – the transition from the second youngest to
the youngest group of the *gonna* curve – is not statistically significant
and the standstill can even be accounted for: it is probably motivated by
the fact that the construction with a contraction ratio of around 75% (or
80% if *going to* + NP is excluded) has reached a saturation stage at a
rather high plateau level. The observation of saturation stages leads
naturally to the observation that the *gonna* and *gotta* lines have roughly
the shape of S-curves, with *gotta* having a steeper overall slope than
gonna. Also, *gotta* appears to enter the saturation stage while *gonna* is
near its end. This again makes sense because *gotta* starts out lower than
gonna. *Wanna* starts out even lower than *gotta* and has certainly not yet
reached a saturation phase. It must be stressed, however, that the steep
initial slope of the *gotta* line is rather untypical of S-curves, at least as
we know them from ideal-type curves for the diffusion of innovations
(see e.g. Aitchison 1991: 83-88). These follow the famous 'slow-quick-

quick-slow' pattern, that is: slow start, gaining pace and slowing down towards the final stage.[7]

It should not go unnoticed that there are no intersections in Figure 5.6. The curve that starts out highest (*gonna*) always remains in the pole position, *gotta* is in the middle position throughout, thus leaving the lowest position consistently to *wanna*. Intriguingly this order reflects their discourse string frequencies in the corpus: as Table 5.1 reveals, *going to* and *gonna* together are more frequent than *got to* and *gotta*, which in turn enjoy a greater frequency than *want to* and *wanna*.[8] This finding tallies well with the string frequency factor found for BE and HAVE encliticization (such as *she's, they've*) in Krug (1998a). It states essentially the following:

> *ceteris paribus*, the more often two words occur as a sequence in natural speech, the more likely it becomes that the sequence will undergo univerbation (or coalescence, contraction, fusion).

While the corroboration of the string frequency factor in the above syntactic environments (BE and HAVE cliticization) is little more than proving an intuitively plausible concept, it is more surprising that string frequency captures sequences which at the outset are rather different phonologically. Put differently, *cetera sunt satis paria* ('other things are equal enough') for what will crystallize as the three core emerging modals in section 5.6.2: (BE) GOING TO, (HAVE) GOT TO and WANT TO.[9] More intriguing still, there is a direct correlation not only between string frequencies and contraction ratios but also between these two and degrees of grammaticalization: in view of the data presented in this study and the linguistic literature on BE GOING TO, it would seem that BE GOING TO enjoys the highest, HAVE GOT TO the second-highest and WANT TO the lowest degree of grammaticalization in this set.[10] This claim will receive further support from the prototypicality ranking that is produced by the model proposed in section 5.7.5 (see in particular p. 236).

To sum up the preceding discussion, it seems clear that string frequency is an indicator of increased bondedness between the constituents of constructions; it is likely that it is a fairly robust principle in the grammaticalization of items originally consisting of more than one word;[11] and it is conceivable that it constitutes a factor in language change in general. If any of the preceding assumptions were true, it would seem foolish to exclude performance data from considerations of linguistic theory. In that case, ignoring natural discourse would prevent us from gaining insights into language and language change that cannot otherwise be obtained.

Let me conclude this section with a brief discussion of the relationship between frequency, bonding and phonological erosion. Written attestations of fused (HAVE) GOT TO (i.e. *gotta*), WANT TO (i.e. *wanna*) and BE GOING TO (i.e. *gonna*) do not lag behind the enormous frequency gains. As was seen in 5.2.1, substantial increases in drama were found in the late 19th century (HAVE TO, WANT TO) and the early 20th century (GOING TO, GOT TO). In the OED (1989: *s.vv. gonna, gotta, wanna*) the first attested spellings of contractions date from precisely those periods. This correlation is impressive.[12] It suggests that phonological change actually occurs roughly in sync with drastic increases in frequency, an observation which lends full support to a statement by Bybee & Pagliuca:

> As the meaning generalizes and the range of uses widens, the frequency increases and this leads automatically to phonological reduction and perhaps fusion. (1985: 76)[13]

The contexts of the OED citations show that early contracted forms occur in expressive or nonstandard speech. Moreover, dialectal forms of *gonna* (like *ganna, ginnie, gaunna*) from the 19th century are given in the *English Dialect Dictionary* (1961: *s.v. go*). One should assume, then, that the changes originated in varieties enjoying more covert than overt prestige, which in turn supports the hypothesis that the emerging modals are changes from below.

In summary, as far as (erstwhile) multi-word constructions are concerned, string frequency, fusion and grammaticalization seem to be concomitants of one another. It seems difficult to tell the motivating factors from the consequences within this set, even though received wisdom has it that coalescence is a consequence of frequency (Heine et al. 1991: 15-19; but see Heine 1993: 111 for qualification). As for the relationship between grammaticalization and frequency, it seems next to impossible to determine which of the two is prior – if they can be separated at all.

5.2.3   Autonomous discourse?

The behaviour of emerging modals in interrogatives is a further indicator of the influence which discourse frequency has on syntactic patterns (see Bybee & Scheibman forthcoming for another study showing the impact of usage on constituent structure). Of particular relevance are polar questions. Given the appropriate environments and provided that recoverability of the subject is ensured, the following sentences are acceptable:

(1)   Wanna dance?   <   Do you ...?

(2)   Gonna take a taxi?   <   Are you ...?

(3)   Gotta go home already?   <   Have you ...?

Two equally feasible accounts of (1) to (3) are possible. Both depend on string frequency. One option is to postulate subject deletion from a statement that is transformed into a question by rising intonation (*You wanna dance?* etc.).[14] Another is to assume deletion of both operator and subject (*Do you/ Are you/ Have you ...?*). Regardless of the deletion strategy, such surface constructions are probably not available to all verbs. The constraint does not seem to be exclusively syntactic in nature because such structures are not confined to emerging auxiliaries. While more empirical research into the matter is required, it appears that the constraint is at least partially frequentative because common verbs seem more likely to figure in such patterns than infrequent ones. Compare:

(4)   *Attend faculty meetings?

(5)   ?Drink champagne?

(6)   Like champagne?

(7)   See the difference?

Hendrick (1982) offers an illuminating analysis of auxiliary deletion (HAVE, DO, BE) in interrogatives. Particularly valuable is the part of his analysis that appeals to a combination of markedness and recoverability. The only drawback, I believe, is that his account stays largely within syntactic confines. Generative accounts strive for simplicity and descriptive elegance. For some syntactic contexts, a simpler account than that offered by Hendrick is possible, others are not covered by his account. Functionalists would add that discourse factors also enter into the picture. It seems for instance that due to the high string frequency of *What are you ...?, What do you ...?* and *What have you ...?,* these sequences can result in homophonous realizations. The spoken BNC contains various examples of such constructions. Some are given below. Both complete deletion of the auxiliary – examples (8) to (13) – and occurrences with suggested traces of auxiliary DO (orthographically represented as *d'*) – examples (14) to (17) – can be found:[15]

(8)   What you going to do, you going to do her postcard? (BNC KBN 22)

(9)   What you gonna do? – Sign it. (BNC F7R 66)

(10)   What you want to look at? – I don't know. (BNC KBH 5141)

(11)   What you, what you have to do this? (BNC KBW 15997)

(12)   So what you gotta do tomorrow then? (BNC KE4 1987)

(13)   What you gotta say then father? – Not a lot. (BNC KCT 2288)

(14)   What d'ya wanna know now? (BNC KGU 2210)

(15)   ..., what d'ya wanna know about them? (BNC KGU 1964)

(16)   What d'ya want to do? (BNC KB8 11175)

(17)   What d'ya want to know when someone picks up the phone? (BNC JYM 1230)

In addition, some examples from the written component can be presented, all of which are meant to represent direct speech. It is striking that this type of auxiliary reduction and deletion is particularly prominent when high-frequency verbs (notably *do* and *know*) follow the emerging modals, both in the spoken and written examples. This tallies with Bybee & Scheibman's (forthcoming) data on the reduction of *don't*.[16]

(18)   Whatcha gonna do; convert us or something? (BNC ALH 1550)

(19)   Whatcha gonna tell me? (BNC F9W 1258)

(20)   Wotcha wanna make such a mess for? (BNC CDN 1364)

For convenience, Figure 5.7 shows the possible discourse-based paths to auxiliary omission for the four constructions discussed above.

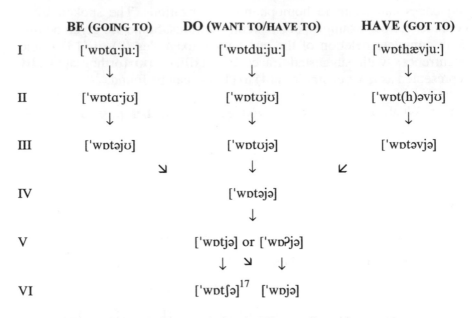

	BE (GOING TO)	DO (WANT TO/HAVE TO)	HAVE (GOT TO)
I	['wɒtɑːjuː]	['wɒtduːjuː]	['wɒthævjuː]
	↓	↓	↓
II	['wɒtɑˑjʊ]	['wɒtʊjʊ]	['wɒt(h)əvjʊ]
	↓	↓	↓
III	['wɒtəjʊ]	['wɒtʊjə]	['wɒtəvjə]
		↓	
IV		['wɒtəjə]	
		↓	
V		['wɒtjə] or ['wɒʔjə]	
		↓ ↓	
VI		['wɒtʃə][17] ['wɒjə]	

Figure 5.7.   Paths to auxiliary omission in *What are/have/do you ...?*

As Figure 5.7 shows, from stage IV onwards, all three sequences converge on one pronunciation. And while BE, HAVE and DO are homophonous at stage IV [ə], they are elided from stage V. It goes without saying that there are further intermediate stages for all three sequences and that other allophones, in particular for the vowels and for /t/, are possible.[18] Reduction of unstressed syllables is a regular process in English, more so within words than across word boundaries. On the grounds of recoverability, auxiliaries and personal pronouns (in this order) are relatively dispensable; the interrogative pronoun is not. Consequently, the auxiliaries are progressively reduced leading to complete elision; the personal pronoun is retained in its weak form; and the one vowel that is likely to remain full is – not surprisingly – that of the interrogative pronoun. The result, stress on the first syllable, is consistent with the predominant Germanic stress pattern for individual disyllabic words (stages V and VI).

It would be interesting to investigate whether such reductions as sketched in Figure 5.7 apply to all verbs at identical rates, or whether frequent verbs like GOING TO, WANT TO, HAVE TO or GOT TO correlate more strongly with drastic reductions of the preceding auxiliaries. This, of course, is my hypothesis. If it were true, we would be seeing the rise of a new interrogative pattern. That is to say, a novel syntactic variant would be motivated by discourse frequency. The same would seem to apply to the interrogative strategies in (1) to (7), which somewhat resemble operator behaviour. Neither issue can be settled at the present stage. In any case, for stylistic homogeneity, the first stages in Figure 5.7 can be assumed to favour fuller pronunciations of the emerging modals, such as [gəʊɳtʊ], [wɒntʊ], [gɒtʊ], whereas the lower stages would also tend towards reduced pronunciations like [gənə] or [wɒnə]. According to the processes sketched in Figure 5.7, the auxiliary omission in *What do/are/have you* (stages V and VI) is best analysed as the result of a gradual reduction process, not as a syntactic operation. This may be one of the reasons why such cases of auxiliary deletion are not discussed in Hendrick (1982).

5.2.4 String frequency and the contraction debate

The previous two sections have argued that bondedness and increased string frequency are central to the grammaticalization of constructions. Fischer (1994), too, comments on the crucial role of adjacency in grammaticalization. She elaborates on Bolinger's (1980b: 297) famous claim that auxiliarization starts as soon as a verb receives an infinitival complement:

> the addition of an infinitive to a verb *may* (it doesn't have to) indeed be the first step on the road to auxiliariness, much more threatening to the independence of this verb, however, is the *juxtaposition* of verb and infinitive. It is this contact which practically seals the fate of the verb in question. (Fischer 1994: 137)

If one looks at the fairly open class of verbs that can take infinitival complements (see e.g. the lists in Quirk et al. 1985: 1187f), it appears that contiguity is a necessary criterion for auxiliarization. However, it is not a *sufficient* criterion. Fischer (1994) probably somewhat overstates the impact of adjacency, even though in a footnote (p. 157f) she concedes that grammaticalization "will perhaps not always affect all verbs followed immediately by a *to*-infinitive (other factors may be involved)." This point must be emphasized. It is certain that contact between verb and *to* infinitive does not inevitably lead to auxiliary status. We therefore need to know more about the 'other factors'. I believe that one of them is string frequency (which will take few readers by surprise). Among other things, it helps to account for some of the phenomena mentioned in various contributions to the famous contraction debate which have remained unexplained (e.g. Chomsky & Lasnik 1977; Postal & Pullum 1982; Pullum 1997; see the discussion in Ch. 2.10). This will be demonstrated in the following paragraphs.

String frequency helps explain why in present-day English some verbs can (and typically do) undergo contraction with a following infinitival *to*, while others can not. The answer is very simple: frequent sequences can, infrequent ones can't. Provided this is correct, however, the latter too may undergo contraction in the future if they increase substantially in discourse frequency. Relevant examples include sequences like *want to, have to, supposed to, mean(t) to, intend to, bound to, care to* or *like to*. These have received a great amount of attention from a variety of syntactic, phonological, morphological and semantic perspectives. It seems that especially syntactic accounts have reached an impasse (see Pullum 1997).

Why not then invoke a simple functionally motivated economy principle which predicts that, other things being equal, the more frequent the sequence of a given verb and following *to* is, the more likely contraction will be. The notion of likelihood indicates that I would not want to set a precise cut-off point. After all, reduction is gradual and so are differences in discourse frequency. But synchronically the overall correlation between frequency and contraction rates is immediately obvious from looking at the most frequent verbs in contemporary spoken discourse (Figure 2.1; Appendix 1; Figure 5.6). A strong point of this principle is that it can accommodate changes in frequency through time: increase will automatically trigger the probability of contraction. This was shown to be the case in section 5.2.2 above.

Furthermore, it is noteworthy that those items which have recently been affected by the most drastic gains in frequency not only exhibit the highest degree of phonological reduction (compare for instance *gonna* and *meant to*), but they also display the largest number of morphosyntactic changes. Not all fates, then, are sealed. In fact, there is no functional feasibility in stating that every verb taking an infinitival complement will become a grammaticalized auxiliary. On functional, cognitive and economical grounds, languages tend to code (i.e.

grammaticalize) modal notions, which are what Haiman (1985: 259) has called 'well-trodden areas'.[19] This coding principle is coherent only so long as the number of grammaticalized items is rather restricted. As many studies – including this one – have shown, there is no living language whose class of auxiliaries is completely closed. Nonetheless the number of items admitted in English is certainly more limited than the class of verbs that can take juxtaposed infinitival *to* complements.

5.3   Mechanisms and pathways of change

5.3.1   Reanalysis

The term *syntactic reanalysis* (or restructuring, rebracketing) can be defined narrowly, that is as change from a biclausal to a monoclausal structure. Understood in this strict sense, it was observed for some, but not all of the constructions investigated in the present study. Understood in a loose sense, that is as recategorialization from main verb to auxiliary status, reanalysis would of course apply to all constructions investigated here. In the narrow sense, it is commonly taken to apply to the development of BE GOING TO (e.g. Hopper & Traugott 1993; Traugott 1994), and was invoked for HAVE TO. WANT TO is an unclear case (see discussion in 4.2), and reanalysis has almost certainly played no role in the development of HAVE GOT TO. This result is broadly consistent with Heine et al.'s (1991: 217) position that "typically, reanalysis accompanies grammaticalization." Most researchers take the view that reanalysis and grammaticalization are closely linked concepts which, however, "must be kept strictly apart" (Heine et al. 1991: 219; in a similar vein, Hopper & Traugott 1993: 60f). Haspelmath (1998) takes a very strong stance against reanalysis in grammaticalization phenomena. He claims that "the large majority of syntactic changes are instances of 'pure' grammaticalization and should be explained ... without reference to reanalysis" (p. 315). The four cases of grammaticalization studied in the present work are not a sufficient number to make quantitative claims as to the proportion of grammaticalization episodes that involve reanalysis. Nonetheless, doubts regarding the ubiquity of reanalysis in grammaticalization seem indeed justified.

5.3.2   Semantic changes

Metaphor may be a relevant force in the very early stages of grammaticalization but it was not observable in the historical corpora used in the present study. It seems almost certain that metaphor plays no more than a marginal role during the period of rapid grammaticalization, that is, when the greatest frequency gains are observed. By contrast, context-induced **inference**, including **subjectification**, was shown to play a central role: first, in the development of a modal meaning from nonmodal semantics (e.g. WANT 'lack' > 'desire'), second, in the generalization of the structure. Significantly, pragmatic inferences continue to be operative in the development of other modalities (e.g. WANT 'desire' > 'intention'). In other words, unlike metaphorical processes, inferences appear to be operative at any point of the grammaticalization path. This language-particular study, then, lends support to the crosslinguistic tendencies found by Bybee et al. (1994: Ch. 8).

Figure 5.8 sketches the major paths of semantic developments identified in previous chapters. The developments of BE GOING TO are added on the basis of the relevant literature (notably Bybee et al. 1994: Chs. 6f; Heine 1993: 97; Hopper & Traugott 1993: Ch. 1). Bold face indicates the core present-day meanings. Notions in brackets are not conventionalized meanings but tend to arise by inferences. Question marks indicate marginal use.

WANT TO   lack ($\rightarrow$ necessity) $\rightarrow$ **volition** $\rightarrow$ intention $\rightarrow$ hypotheticality

                                           $\searrow$ (obligation) $\rightarrow$ (command)

                                            $\searrow$ (?probability)

HAVE GOT TO
   and   possession $\rightarrow$ **obligation/necessity**[20] $\rightarrow$ certainty $\rightarrow$ (prediction)
HAVE TO

GOING TO   physical movement $\rightarrow$ **intention** $\rightarrow$ **prediction** $\rightarrow$(command)[21]

Figure 5.8. Semantic paths of four emerging auxiliaries

It is not necessary to provide a detailed discussion of the semantic paths given in Figure 5.8. This has already been done in the previous chapters. The chart is helpful for identifying recurrent pathways. All four items originate from basic lexical meanings (left-most meanings). The paths tie in with previous cognitive and/or crosslinguistic research (e.g. Heine 1993; Bybee et al. 1994): from left to right we see the much cited development from concrete meanings to more abstract and grammatical (and generally more subjective) notions. Let us now move on from semantic paths to regional paths of development.

5.3.3   Regional diffusion

The present chapter focuses on generalizations. The construction GOING TO is not its central concern and thus the regional distribution of the innovative variant (*gonna*) is presented in Appendix 4 rather than here. Nevertheless, a few remarks on its diffusion are in order. As usual, the darker the area, the higher the incidence of *gonna*. Unlike the distributions of *wanna* and *gotta,* a clear regional pattern does not emerge for this item. Notice that despite a more finegrained distinction (the two extreme poles differ by a mere 2%) than was used in the previous two cases (where the extreme poles differed by 6% and 4.5% for *gotta* and *wanna*, respectively), there is very little regional differentiation. With the grids used for *wanna* and *gotta,* there would have been hardly any differentiation at all. Hence, *gonna* seems to be a rather advanced innovation that is fairly evenly distributed across the UK, i.e. one that has already spread considerably regionally. A further indicator of this fact is that for all regions the contraction ratios of GOING TO exceed those of the previous two items by far (see Appendix 5).

In order to obtain a more complete picture, I integrate the three innovations into a unified map. This is done as follows. Each individual map has five or six groups reflecting certain degrees of progressiveness and conservativeness for one emerging modal (indicated by lighter and darker shadings in the maps). When a region falls into the most progressive group for a particular innovation, it receives a score of six points (when there are six degrees of progressiveness; five points when there are five degrees), the areas falling into the second most progressive group receive five points each (four points, when there are only five degrees), and so on. The three individual scores are then added to produce a cumulative map. An alternative procedure would be to add the percentages by which individual items diverge from the mean (they are given in Appendix 5). This was not done because if a single innovation diverged drastically from the mean, it would have a disproportionate influence on the overall score of the area. By contrast, the method employed should theoretically even out statistical outliers, so that the resulting cumulative map ought to be more reliable than each individual one. Map 5.1 (see next page) presents the result.

In order to test, however, whether it is not the comparative method outlined above that produces spurious results, a second cumulative map is presented. Map 5.1 is based on the divergence of the frequencies of the innovative variants in a given region when compared to the mean for all regions. Map 5.2 (see p. 188), by contrast, provides a comparison of the regions based on the relative proportions of progressive and conservative variants.[22] Crucially, it shows essentially the same pattern as Map 5.1, thus suggesting that the results are rather robust and do not depend heavily on the comparative method employed.

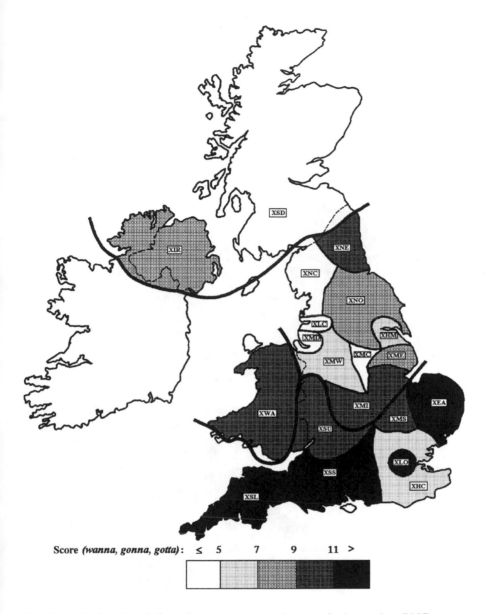

Map 5.1. Regional variation of *gonna, gotta* and *wanna* in the spoken BNC:
Divergence from mean

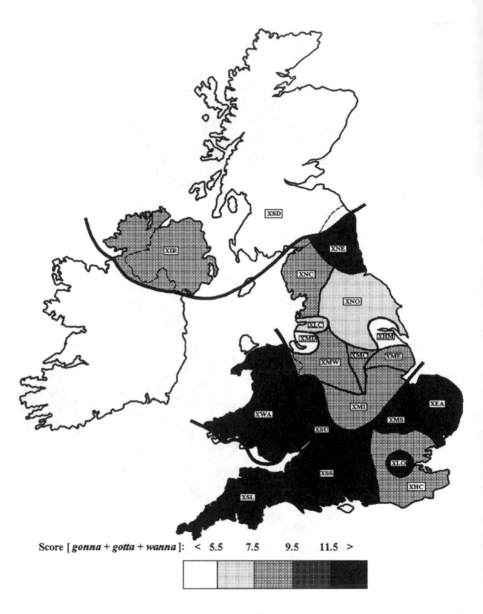

Score [*gonna* + *gotta* + *wanna*]:   <   5.5   7.5   9.5   11.5   >

Map 5.2. Regional variation in the spoken BNC: *Going to, got to, want to* and their
variants *gonna, gotta, wanna*

Here is the place to discuss in more detail some provisos that were raised in the previous chapters on regional distribution. Like previous maps, these ones too have to be taken with a good deal of caution, notably due to the procedure that was adopted for regional tagging in the BNC (see the discussion in Ch. 2.7). Two other potentially distorting factors, however, seem less influential than might be suspected. It was shown repeatedly in this study that age (younger vs. older speakers) and style (formal vs. informal speech) are salient variables in the choice between innovative and conservative variants. One might assume, therefore, that the overrepresentation of younger speakers or informal speech in a given area could skew the results and wrongly suggest certain regional patterns.

To be sure, the BNC is not 100% representative of the British population. Nor are the age groups and informal speech equally distributed across the twenty regions. These are the parameters looked at closely in the present study. It can be assumed that these variables interact further with factors such as socio-economic class, social and regional mobility as well as with education. These parameters could not be investigated in any detail here, and surely such a complex network cannot be disentangled satisfactorily in a single study. Nevertheless, on closer inspection it turns out that at least the distributions according to age and style, which have been investigated here, do not invalidate the regional data, even though some adjustments seem indicated. I will treat both variables in turn.

First, as far as the shares of different age groups are concerned, it seems feasible to divide the six age groups distinguished in the BNC into three larger groups, so that two age-groups each are collapsed: younger speakers (aged under 25), a middle group (aged 25 to 44) and older speakers (45 and over). The average shares of these subclasses across the regions are approximately 20%, 35% and 40% respectively.[23] Of all twenty regions, two diverge drastically from the average distribution: upper and lower south-west England have a dispro-portionately high share of words produced by younger speakers, concomitant with a much lower percentage of words produced by older speakers. Both groups may therefore be assumed to be somewhat less innovative than the maps suggest. Crucially, however, by far the most innovative area is the populous cultural and political centre of Britain, i.e. London (cf. Appendix 5), as would be predicted under the wave model. And London does not differ greatly from the average age distribution, so that one cannot attribute its progressiveness simply to, for instance, the innovative COLT (short for Corpus of London Teenage speech) component that is included within the BNC.

Further, two regions show a disproportionately high share of speech produced by older speakers (60% and over): north-east England, and central northern England. Both regions may thus be assumed to be somewhat more prone to change than the maps suggest. However, only the latter region is at all conservative on the basis of the present study, while north-east England actually belongs to the most innovative regions.[24] To add more puzzles to the current picture, only one out of three further regions exhibiting a noteworthy overrepresentation of older speakers (nearly 60% of the total for the region) is also conservative with respect to the use of emerging modals. This is Merseyside. The remaining two, by contrast, i.e. Wales and the south Midlands, belong to the more innovative regions. Differences in proportions of age groups, therefore, do not seem to affect or even distort the results for regional variation in any consistent way. In particular, unless we resort to contact theories for the propagation of language change, it remains unexplained why rather coherent patterns with similar distributions of innovative variants (reflected in darker or lighter colours in the maps) recur in neighbouring regions despite major differences in the make-up of the regional subcorpora. It seems therefore difficult to dismiss areal factors completely.

The second potentially distorting factor is over- or under-representation of informal speech. There are five regions with strikingly low proportions of informal speech (some 50% or below, comparing with an average proportion of texts from the demographic sample of roughly 80% in the subcorpus of speakers tagged for region). These are Scotland, Merseyside, the Midlands and the Home Counties, and indeed these regions are among those that figure as conservative in the maps. Low proportions of spontaneous speech, therefore, seem to have the effect of portraying a region more conservative in the maps than it probably is in reality. They do not explain away, however, the overall regional patterns that emerge from all the maps presented in this study. Scotland, for instance, lags so far behind the remaining regions in terms of its use of progressive variants that even if a correcting factor were introduced, it would still not be among the progressive regions.

A final illustrative example is Welsh English, which presents a clear case for taking geographical factors into consideration: the statistics show that both older speakers and formal speech samples are over-represented. In other words, both factors identified as reducing the proportions of progressive variants should be operative for this region. Nonetheless, Wales is one of the most progressive areas in both cumulative maps. In sum, since we might be losing interesting information if we simply dismissed the data on regional variation, I suggest accepting them for the time being (but of course also taking them with a grain of salt), until further evidence allows us to judge more confidently on their significance.

Despite the above provisos, then, it seems clear that on aggregate the maps presented in this study lend further support to a hypothesis in terms of northward spread of innovations in Britain. This pathway has been attested, at least for phonological change, since Middle English. It was mentioned earlier that to speak of the spread of certain features across the UK emanating from London is at the same time to revive the old idea of the wave model, according to which language change diffuses from focal areas (Schmidt 1872). It deserves mention that the wave model, the related contact model and functionalism combine well: all emphasize the influence of perceptual, external data and accommodation on speech production. Other researchers have implicitly advocated the wave model for changes in the phonology of England (e.g. Wells 1982; Trudgill 1990; Rosewarne 1994). In their studies, it is largely the pronunciation of London and its adjacent areas whose features spread regionally and make their way into RP. Wells (1982, II: 301) goes further and claims that London proper is the "linguistic centre of gravity ... in England and perhaps in the whole English-speaking world." For Rosewarne (1994: 4) the focal area is somewhat larger, comprising in addition to Greater London the counties surrounding the estuary of the river Thames (hence the term: Estuary English), i.e. Essex and Kent. Trudgill (1990: 75-78), finally, includes the entire region of the Home Counties. On the basis of the present study, the Home Counties would have to be excluded from the focal areas, but this may well be due to the above mentioned make-up of the BNC.

In previous studies the wave model has proved difficult to substantiate except for phonological change.[25] For instance, the dialect boundaries found by Trudgill (1990: 33, 63) for phonological features do not work nearly as neatly for the grammatical or lexical items provided in his study (1990: 84-99, 102-112). It is therefore highly interesting that the diffusion of the emerging modals broadly confirms the south-north movement typical of phonological innovations. It is not altogether surprising, however, that this is the case. As was discussed in section 2.3, grammaticalization includes phonological erosion and has thus an important phonological component to it. The fact that similar distributions were found for *gotta*, *wanna* and *innit* (Krug 1998b) fits in with this scenario. In addition, the present study provides some inverse evidence for the same geographical pattern because almost obsolete grammatical structures (such as *You haven't to go there*, discussed in section 3.4.2 above) and obsolescent structures (such as *I've to go*, discussed in section 5.6.1 below) are today primarily used in what appear to be relic areas in the north. It is tempting, therefore, to speculate on the existence of a regional path of change, which seems to hold today for both phonological and lexicogrammatical innovations, and which is reflected even in the retention of two obsolescent grammatical structures investigated here.

5.3.4　Sex

Sex is the last social parameter we want to look at. Table 5.2 summarizes the distribution of full and contracted variants of WANT TO, GOING TO and GOT TO.[26]

Table 5.2.　Full and contracted variants of emerging modals: Variation according to sex

	wanna	*want to*	*gonna*	*going to*	*gotta*	*got to*
female	956 (27%)	2583 (73%)	4516 (52%)	4146 (48%)	1520 (38%)	2479 (62%)
male	1121 (23%)	3837 (77%)	5299 (50%)	5234 (50%)	1558 (36%)	2711 (64%)

Prima facie, it is surprising that, in relative terms, women consistently use the contracted forms more often than men, given the linguistic commonplace that women "tend to produce more standard speech than men" (McMahon 1994: 231). The differences are not overwhelming, though (2.7% on average). According to chi-squared tests, the differences between the sexes are

- not statistically significant for the use of GOT TO,
- significant at $p < 0.05$ for GOING TO and
- significant at $p < 0.001$ for WANT TO.

The overall differences are of course statistically significant at $p < 0.001$. At five degrees of freedom this seems a very reliable result.

One might suspect, however, that this is an instance where statistical significance is not linguistically significant. The high absolute numbers lead almost automatically to statistically significant results. The fact that all three items display the same tendency reduces the probability of a chance finding considerably, though. When viewed against the backdrop of various other changes and linguistic theory, it is striking that the figures in fact tally with more refined statements on the relationship between sex and innovation (see papers in Coates & Cameron 1988). Witness the following principles identified by Labov (1990: 206-215, my emphasis throughout):

(21)   In the majority of linguistic changes, women use a higher frequency of the incoming forms than men. (p. 206)

More specifically:

(22)   In *change from below*, women are most often the innovators (p. 215).

By contrast:

(23)   For *stable* sociolinguistic variables, men use a higher frequency of nonstandard forms than women (p. 210)

After all, there is some plausibility in the data. Interpreted against the above principles, the data suggest the following:

• If the distribution of progressive and conservative variants is typical (Table 5.2 shows that women use consistently higher proportions of contracted forms), it follows from (21) that the emerging modals are instances of linguistic change. This (like the following two points) is of course only a statistical inference, since Labov's principles are generalizations, not exceptionless rules.

• By negative implication, ongoing change can also be inferred from (23): assuming that the contracted variants are to a lesser extent part of standard English than their uncontracted counterparts, emerging modals will not be cases of stable variation, because women, not men, use them more often.

• Since Table 5.2 suggests that women are indeed the innovators in this specific instance, there is a statistical likelihood – given (22) – that the emerging modals are changes from below.

While the three points mentioned above follow from general tendencies regarding gender-specific behaviour and change, it is striking that the statements derived from such statistical correlations are almost trivially true in the present case. Their main value lies in the fact that they independently underpin the statements made in other parts of this study. One may thus rather confidently predict that *wanna, gonna, gotta* (and also *hafta/hasta*) will become part of standard (spoken) English in all national varieties. In fact, they have already reached this status in some standard varieties (cf. Pullum 1997: 82). This does not mean, of course, that they will soon become the only variants used; probably this will never happen. As the cases of WILL or BE show, competing phonological variants of grammatical items tend to coexist for centuries, and often develop different morphosyntactic properties (cf. **'ll you go there?*). Nor does the hypothesized adoption of *wanna, gonna* and *gotta* into standard varieties imply that genres susceptible to prescriptive influence (i.e. written English generally, in particular formal genres like legalese or academic writing) will make vast use of such advanced contracted forms. It is this need to distinguish various (standard) genres on the one hand, and the spread of innovations across genres of different levels of formality, on the other, that will be discussed in more detail in the next section.

5.4   Towards a model for natural change in spoken and written text types

It has been seen repeatedly that functional-frequentative explanations seem to capture best the diffusion of the innovations investigated here. Informal face-to-face conversation generally initiated the changes. This exerted pressures on more formal spoken varieties. Spoken language was then seen to trigger changes in written English genres, whose susceptibility to change depends primarily on their respective degrees of codification.[27] One of Chafe's (1984) models for the interaction between spoken and written language is a helpful starting point for describing the general direction of change observed for the constructions HAVE TO, (HAVE) GOT TO, WANT TO and (BE) GOING TO:

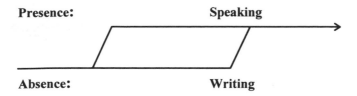

Figure 5.9.   Chafe's (1984: 97) model for the spread of innovations from 'speaking' to 'writing'

Chafe (1984: 96-97) describes his chart as follows:

> This figure should be interpreted as two time lines, one representing spoken language and one written language, moving from left to right. The vertical dimension represents the absence or the significant presence of some feature, as indicated on the left. At some point it emerges in speaking, but remains for a time absent from writing, as shown by the divergence of the two lines in the middle. During the middle period, the feature is one which differentiates speaking from writing. *Eventually, writing begins to catch up, and eventually, the two lines come back together, with writing as well as speaking making significant use of the innovation.* (emphasis added)

As far as the items investigated in the present study are concerned, it is this last stage in Chafe's proposed development (given in italics) which the English language seems to be passing through today. Both spoken and written codes make 'significant use' of both constructions, with the spoken code generally in the lead and the written code 'catching up'. Needless to say, Chafe's diagram is simplistic, as the author himself is aware (1984: 96). The model suggests, for example, a monolithic character for both speaking and writing, i.e. a homogeneity which is highly problematic.[28] Further, from the previous chapters it emerges that one can be far more specific than merely state 'significant use'. Based on the observations for HAVE TO, HAVE GOT TO and WANT TO, a slightly refined model can therefore be suggested. It is still rather simplistic but to some extent this lies in the nature of models. The appeal and clarity of such constructs is necessarily achieved at the expense of adequacy when it comes to accounting for a host of individual developments. Nonetheless, I believe that the model is valuable because it probably captures the majority of natural changes from below.

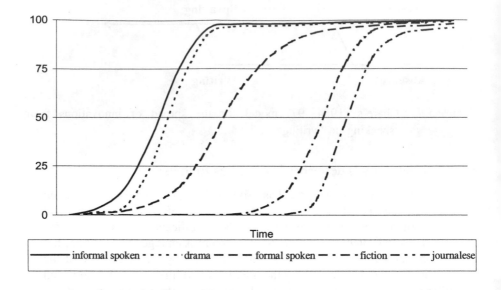

Figure 5.10. Towards an integrated model for change from below in spoken and
written registers

The modified model incorporates a bipolar distinction of speech, which
admittedly is not particularly refined. In principle, however, it can
accommodate any number of written and spoken varieties, including for
instance social and geographical varieties. Of course, I only include the
ones investigated. That is on the written side: drama, press and fictional
language; on the spoken side: formal and informal language. The
modified model is meant to capture the following observations made in
the present study:

- On the most general level, the chart takes into account the overall
  descriptive adequacy of S-curve patterns observed on various
  occasions. Even though graphs established on the basis of actual
  changes in natural language will rarely be neat S-curves, this pattern
  appears to describe individual changes more accurately than the
  straight lines suggested in the original Chafe chart. In defence of
  Chafe's model, however, one might argue that his model makes use
  of rather abstract S-curves too, so that this particular refinement is
  not a dramatic one.

- Still on a general level, changes from below are predicted to start out in informal speech, where, after an initially flat positive slope, they catch on rapidly.

- On the time axis, developments can take longer or less time, so that the slope of individual curves will not always be the same. Overall, the gradient will be steeper for genres that are highly susceptible to change (e.g. informal spoken, drama) and gentler for more rigidly codified genres (i.e. genres that are more susceptible to prescriptive influence, such as academic writing).

- More specifically, while an instance of change in informal speech is still on the rise, the change also starts in other genres. This helps account for why the gap between two genres may be narrowing, as was repeatedly observed for press and fictional language. According to the model, press language was often in the stage of rapid growth, where the slope is still steep, while fictional language, even though it was still more advanced in terms of discourse frequency, had already reached the slowing-down phase.

- It is important to note that frequentative pressures are not only exerted by informal spoken language but by all varieties that are ahead of a given variety in a given change. This seems particularly helpful in accounting for changes in varieties that lean towards the more formal end. Sermons and judicial prose, for instance, are less likely to be influenced directly by informal spoken language but much more so by, say, formal speeches or rather formal press language (such as political reportage), which are more closely related varieties.

- Consequently, mutual influence will correlate inversely with the distance of curves on the time axis. Ultimately, though, most changes will be triggered and mediated by informal spoken language.

- Important for considerations on the value of ARCHER drama data, the model would predict that after an initial time lag the gap between ARCHER drama and informal spoken English consistently narrows. Further, drama will typically be more progressive than formal spoken varieties.

Simplifications and weaknesses include:

- Each genre listed could be broken up into more subgenres, for example press language into political reportage, commentary and sport (from less to more prone to change from below).

- There may be intersections between curves. These were avoided in Figure 5.10 for the sake of clarity. In fact, intersections are likely. As Biber & Finegan (1997) show, text-type conventions may change over time. A genre can, for example, become more formal (roughly 'informational' in their terminology). This is the development which medical prose seems to have undergone. Or a genre can become more informal ('involved'), that is, more prone to change. This apparently is the development undergone by letters, drama and diaries (Biber & Finegan 1997: 260-268).

- The y-axis with its top level of 100 is rather elusive. It is pegged to informal spoken language and can be interpreted in several ways, e.g. as 100% use relative to previous rival constructions (i.e. obligatoriness, which is a rare phenomenon). Or a fictitious value of 100 can be seen as the incidence in informal spoken language at a given point in time. For instance, the functional saturation phase of verbally expressed volition might be a certain discourse frequency of, say, 25% of all modal uses. This is not meant to rule out the possibility, however, that in a different genre the saturation level can be reached at a lower incidence (of, say, 15%). In other words, not all genres will have numerically identical saturation stages. In fact, this will be the typical rather than the exceptional case.

- After the first slow-down the story is not necessarily over. It is not impossible that another S-curve change will follow, which is likely to trigger the same development in other registers in the order described above. This could be accommodated by the model in its present shape if one considered this second increase a new change.

- Finally, the model might be seen to suggest (wrongly) that all changes will eventually spread to all genres. This, of course, is not implied. Some genres, e.g. due to prescriptivism, may never take part in certain changes.

5.5   The marginal modals NEED (TO), OUGHT (TO) and DARE (TO)

Related to the field of emerging modals is the group of marginal modals, which consists of NEED (TO), OUGHT (TO), DARE (TO) and USED TO (Quirk et al. 1985: 138-140). Habitual USED TO qualifies as a member of this class largely on syntactic grounds; semantically it is quite distinct from the remaining marginal modals and also from the core emerging modals discussed above. It is therefore excluded from the discussion here. Partly since Middle English, and partly since Early Modern English, the marginal modals have oscillated between main verb and modal syntax. We will take no more than a cursory look at these items, in particular historical data are only of secondary interest. The main aim of this section is to identify their predominant syntactic strategies in current British speech. Such information is needed in order to integrate NEED (TO), OUGHT (TO) and DARE (TO) into a model which will be presented later in this chapter. It is not necessary to dwell on their diachronic trajectories in great detail, since these are given in the OED (1989), MED (1954ff) and Visser (1963-73). Summaries are provided by Nagle (1989: 99-110), Warner (1993: 201-204), Fischer (1992: 405), Barber (1997: 177-180) and Denison (1998: 168-171). A rough sketch of their most important present-day properties is as follows:

- They take both NOT negation and DO periphrasis.
- In questions, they can be used as operators, but they can also take DO support.
- They can take both bare and *to* infinitives.
- Third person singular inflection for the simple present tense is sometimes present, sometimes absent.

For illustration, some NEED (TO) examples are given below:

(24)   He needn't do it.
(25)   He doesn't need to do it.
(26)   He needs to do it.
(27)   He need only pick up one of the red telephone receivers at his extreme left, ... (Brown G03)
(28)   Our marriage won't hasten his end by so much as a second, for he need not know of it, ... (LOB P17)

Examples (24) to (26) are common in most contemporary dialects of English. A source seems required for the last two sentences, which will not seem natural for some present-day speakers. It is probably no coincidence that these date from the 1960s; no such constructions are attested in the parallel corpora from the 1990s. It has often been stated that the marginal modals currently seem to be moving towards main verb syntax.[29] The obsolescence of structures like (27) and (28) attests to this overall trend towards lexical verb constructions. Note, however, that movement from auxiliary to main verb syntax contradicts the unidirectionality claim of grammaticalization. The discussion of the emergence of a new category (5.7.1) will throw some light on this issue. As will become apparent in the following sections, the three items are by no means a homogeneous set. The properties listed above represent no more than a list of options, and each marginal modal prefers a different set of constructional strategies.

5.5.1   DARE (TO)

Warner (1993: 202) points out that up to the 16th century DARE was a preterite present verb which took bare infinitival complements. In Early Modern English it additionally developed main verb characteristics. These dates are consistent with those given in Visser (1963-73: §§1355-1368) and Fischer (1992: 405). As for trends in present-day English, Barber (1993: 275f) states that "... *dare* and *need* are ceasing to be auxiliaries, and are coming more and more to be used as ordinary lexical verbs." This is in line with Visser's (*ibid.*) more tentative claims (see also Hundt 1998: 61-65). Below I summarize the syntactic behaviour of DARE in the spoken BNC:

- In the vast majority of cases it takes the bare, not the *to* infinitive.[30]
- In the spoken BNC third person singular pronouns are never followed by inflected *dares*.[31]
- The predominant negation strategy is *daren't*.
- Where operator negation occurs, it is typically not in competition with NOT negation. The operators express past tense (*didn't*), counterfactuality, hypotheticality or tentativeness (*wouldn't*). Even after operator negation, the following infinitive is not introduced by infinitival *to* some 90% of the time. This results in hybrid (sometimes called: mixed) structures like *I didn't dare ask* (BNC KC9 1719) or (30) below, which exhibit main verb syntax (DO negation) and auxiliary syntax (bare infinitival complement) at the same time.

- DO negation for present contexts is only used four times in ten million words, and only one instance is followed by infinitival *to*:

(29)   I don't dare! (BNC KD3 44660)

(30)   I don't dare stop for that ... (BNC KDG 874)

(31)   Do not dare! (BNC KDG 2639)

(32)   Over here you know, it's marked up that, and you just don't dare to ...[32] (BNC KPV 3464)

In addition to the examples quoted above, there is one more common type of DO negation combining with DARE: the fixed expression *Don't you dare* + (elided) infinitive, occurring 36 times in the spoken BNC. It is an indirect speech act and expresses a threat or a prohibition. Here, too, DARE is almost always followed by the bare infinitive, as in:

(33)   Yes, don't you dare come over smoking! (BNC KC0 1429)

The infinitive, however, often undergoes ellipsis, as in:

(34)   Don't you dare [*sc.* do that]. (e.g. BNC KP3 1690)

These examples, then, are also hybrid constructions since they portray both main verb syntax (DO support) and auxiliary syntax (bare infinitival complement or ellipsis). There is only one relevant structure in the spoken BNC with unambiguous main verb syntax, i.e. with a following *to* infinitive:

(35)   ..., don't you dare to come near me with those nasty creepy little fingers ... (BNC J9A 776)

Hundt's (1998: 62, 65) investigation of written British data showed roughly equal proportions of auxiliary, main verb and hybrid constructions, but her results yielded no trend towards main verb usage on the diachronic axis. The latter result is compatible with my spoken data, the former is not: BNC data suggest that in British speech the behaviour of DARE (TO) is still very much akin to that of the central modals. On the basis of this clear preference for auxiliary syntax, I will henceforth use DARE rather than DARE (TO). Also, the data give little reason to believe that there is an age-related gradient from auxiliary NOT negation towards main verb DO negation. If change towards main verb syntax were under way in British English with regard to DARE at all, it would confront us with the remarkable situation that it appears to be more advanced in the written mode than in spoken language. A possible explanation would then be that DARE TO is a change from above.[33]

5.5.2   NEED TO

As Warner (1993: 203) informs us, NEED is a regular, i.e. lexical, verb in Old and Middle English. Having been impersonal in Old English (Visser 1969: §1345), it is used in various personal and impersonal constructions in Middle English, and "in the sixteenth century it starts to show modal characteristics" (Warner 1993: 203). This is in line with Barber's analysis (1997: 178), who cites the first clear OED example of auxiliary NEED from 1538. However, Fischer (1992: 405), quoting Visser (1963-73: §1346), maintains that modal characteristics were already present in the late 14th century. I checked the use of NEED (TO) in Shakespeare. It is quite remarkable that in his usage – i.e. at the end of the century which Warner and Barber identify as showing incipient modal behaviour – modal constructions by far outnumber main verb constructions: the ratio of plain to marked infinitives is approximately eight to one. The trend seems to have been reversed since. Various researchers (e.g. Visser 1963-73: §1351) have noted that the main verb construction is more common in present-day English. Witness also Quirk et al. (1985: 138) on present-day English NEED (TO):

> The modal construction is restricted to nonassertive contexts, *ie* mainly negative and interrogative sentences, whereas the main verb construction can almost always be used, and is in fact more common.

As for spoken British English, an apparent-time study based on the BNC suggests a relatively recent shift in negation patterns for NEED from auxiliary NOT negation to main verb DO support:

Table 5.3.   DO support vs. NOT negation of NEED (TO) in the spoken BNC[34]

Age group	1-14	15-24	25-34	35-44	45-59	60+
NOT negation	3	4	9	16	16	36
DO support	12	11	47	38	103	20
DO support of sum	80%	73.3%	83.9%	70.4%	86.6%	35.7%

Table 5.3 shows a striking difference between the over-60-year-olds and the remaining groups. While all speakers under 60 behave rather similarly and predominantly choose DO negation patterns (on average three out of four times), the over-60s opt for NOT negation two out of three times. Since some figures in Table 5.3 are rather small, it seems necessary to provide chi-squared tests. These clearly confirm the tendency suggested by the bottom row of the table: the differences among the five youngest groups are not statistically significant.[35] By contrast, the oldest group differs significantly from each of the remaining age groups.[36] BNC data thus confirm the overall trend towards lexical verb constructions.

Of particular interest are also third person singular pronouns with NEED + *to* or bare infinitive. For convenience, the results are summarized in Table 5.4.

Table 5.4.   3 SG PRES NEED (TO) in the spoken BNC[37]

	need + infinitive		*needs* + infinitive[38]		*need not/ needn't* + infinitive		*does not/ doesn't need* + infinitive	
	bare	*to*	bare	*to*	bare	*to*	bare	*to*
she	0	1	0	14	3	0	0	3
he	2	0	0	34	4	0	0	9
it	0	0	0	75	16	0	0	7
Total	2	1	0	123	23	0	0	19

In spoken British usage a clear preference for main verb syntax emerges from Table 5.4: overall, *to* infinitives outnumber bare infinitives by 143 to 25. Further, uninflected third person singular *need* is rare. When it does occur, it is typically negated (23 out of 25 times). Here it is usually contracted with *not* (*needn't*), which is incompatible with main verb inflection (**needsn't*).

Of all potentially possible interrogative strategies with third person singular pronouns,[39] only four instances of *Does it need to* + infinitive could be found in the spoken BNC.[40] Not much can be concluded from such a low figure, even though the absence of auxiliary question patterns ties in with the general preference for main verb syntax observed above (Table 5.4). Also, the rarity of interrogatives for NEED (TO), which has been noted in previous studies (Hundt 1998: 63), is confirmed by the present data. In sum, NEED TO strongly favours lexical verb properties.

5.5.3   OUGHT TO

The Old English preterite present *agan* had primarily nonmodal semantics (Fischer 1992: 405; see Nordlinger & Traugott 1997 for a detailed account). In Middle English OUGHT occurs both with bare and *to* infinitives. Warner (1993: 203f) notes that for most English verbs such variation "had declined to virtually the modern situation in the sixteenth century." They all tended to favour auxiliary syntax. He calls OUGHT the "puzzling exception ... [because it] went on to generalize the *to*-infinitive" by approximately the end of that century (p. 204). This is supported by my data from Shakespeare, who uses OUGHT with modal semantics fairly consistently with *to* complements. There is one instance of *ought* + bare infinitive under negation, though:

(36)   What know you not,/ Being mechanical, you ought not walk/ Upon a laboring day without the sign/ Of your profession? (*Julius Caesar*, I, i, 2-5)

Two other negated instances are hybrid constructions in that they combine with both *not* and *to*. Hence they are equivocal as to the syntactic status of OUGHT:[41]

(37)   Marry, thou ought'st not to let thy horse wear a cloak, when honester men than thou go in their hose and doublets. (*Second Part of King Henry VI*, IV, vii, 45-47)

(38)   Once, if he do require our voices, we ought not to deny him. (*Coriolanus*, II, iii, 1-2)

In what follows I summarize the main present-day features of OUGHT (TO). As in Shakespeare, a clear preference for *to* infinitives in today's usage can be observed: the overwhelming majority (some 95%) of the 1,277 occurrences in the spoken BNC are immediately adjacent *ought to* (nearly all of which are assertive statements). A rather high degree of bonding between the two elements is therefore in evidence.[42] This also explains why Nordlinger & Traugott's (1997) article is entitled "Scope and the development of epistemic modality: evidence from *ought to*" [my emphasis] and why their article contains hardly any references to plain infinitives (see their Note 13, though). Quirk et al. (1985: 138f) also choose *ought to* as the heading of the relevant chapter (different from *need* and *dare*, where *to* does not figure). In any case, in the spoken BNC *ought* takes almost exclusively *to* complements.[43] Typical examples include:

(39)   He he [*sic*] ought to know about it though. (BNC D98 58)

Negation is rare. Out of a total 29 negative contexts, 22 are hybrid structures like

(40)   I feel I ought not to let it pass without some comment. (BNC HVG 754)

or

(41)   ... they were all standing on the balcony saying that she really oughtn't to wear those shorts cos she's got such thunder thighs. (BNC KP6 691)

As (41) shows, negative contraction, a property of auxiliaries, is possible if rare (four occurrences). True auxiliary syntax and true lexical verb syntax are also rare: *ought not* + bare infinitive occurs twice;[44] DO support occurs four times but not in present contexts (all four examples are *didn't ought to*). In sum, negation exhibits features of both auxiliary and main-verb behaviour.

Interrogatives are equally rare and equally equivocal: two operator constructions compare with two instances of DO support. On grounds of feasibility, only personal pronoun subjects were checked for the operator construction (i.e. *ought I/you etc. (to) ...?*). The two attested examples include the infinitival marker and therefore do not reflect truly modal syntax:

(42)   ..., in the energy business, ought you to be looking longer term? (BNC F8N 113)

(43)   But given that you're using public money, ought you not to have tighter control over this very aspect? (BNC KS4 33)

Example (43) is noteworthy because it combines two auxiliary characteristics (operator position and NOT negation) with one lexical verb property (*to* infinitive). Witness also the two examples of DO support (again only *did* was found, here indicating hypothetical contexts):[45]

(44)   I just wondered did we ought to order anything from [pause] Friends of the Earth catalogue ... (BNC D97 615)

(45)   ..., but what I'm saying is did we ought to look at some sort of action plan brainstorm, call it what you will ... (BNC K6W 110)

As far as questions are concerned, therefore, no decision on the preferred construction is possible either. Let us finally take a look at defective paradigms: unlike *dare*, *ought* has retained its preterite present verb status and is invariable. It thus has neither regular tensed forms (**oughted*) nor does it take third person inflection in the present tense (**oughts*). These are modal characteristics, but as the attested examples of *did(n't) ought to* show, its historical preterite semantics is not necessarily synchronically transparent.

To conclude, it has been seen that OUGHT TO is somewhat equivocal regarding its syntactic behaviour. Overall, however, due to the fact that truly main verb behaviour (*to* infinitives in positive contexts) accounts for some 95% of all uses, while the remaining options (truly modal and hybrid structures) divide the remaining 5 percent among themselves, the affinity with lexical verbs is more striking.

5.6   Motivations

5.6.1   Expressivity, layering, processing constraints

Layering, the existence of younger and older variants to express a grammatical notion, is one of the principles of grammaticalization. Hopper (1991: 22) defines it as follows:

> Within a broad functional domain, new layers are continually emerging. As it happens, the older layers are not necessarily discarded, but may remain to coexist and interact with the newer layers.

Layering seems particularly natural for English. It may be a rather bold prediction, but I believe that due to its rigid word order, no verbal affix (such as the dental preterite suffix from past forms of DO in Germanic) is likely to emerge in the foreseeable future in English. This connection between two apparently unrelated phenomena may not be immediately obvious. The link is to be established as follows: the cliticization of tense-aspect-mood markers on NPs may be yet another consequence of string frequency (or transitional probability, see Bybee forthcoming or Note 9 for an outline of the concept). Due to fixed word order and the preponderance of topicalized personal pronouns in subject position, the bonding between the small, closed paradigm of subject pronouns and the small class of auxiliaries is very tight. In contrast, the bonding between auxiliaries and the verbs following them, which are members of an open class, is much weaker. String frequency, in this case certainly in line with transitional probability, correctly predicts that fusion will occur between pronouns and auxiliaries in English. Hence, unless one regards tense-aspect-mood markers that cliticize onto (pro)nouns – such as *I've (eaten)* or *[*ˈɑ:nə*] < *I wanna*, cf. Ch. 6 below – as an instance of verbal affixation, verbal affixes are unlikely to evolve in English. Of course, confirmation of this hypothesis from a large-scale study of unrelated languages with rigid and loose word order constraints would be necessary. But even in the absence of such evidence, it is interesting that English is not exceptional with regard to cliticization on NPs.[46] The same phenomenon has been observed in other languages: "in many West African languages, the [grammaticalizing] verb appends to [i.e. cliticizes on] the subject pronoun rather than the complement/main verb" (Heine 1993: 55).

At least two factors can be identified as motivating layering: expressivity and processing constraints. In the discussion of HAVE TO and HAVE GOT TO it was seen that the most important difference between the two constructions was the emotive connotation created by *got.* Similar relationships seem to hold for *will* on the one hand and WANT TO or BE GOING TO on the other (see Hopper & Traugott 1993: 65). Increased expressivity thus seems to contribute to the rise of new constructions (recall Frei 1929: 233, quoted in section 3.3 above). The second motivation in the cases at hand is cognitive in nature. Notice that all of the central modals are monosyllabic; most of them have reduced forms such as *can* /k(ə)n/, *must* /m(ə)s(t)/, *shall* /ʃ(ə)l/ (cf. Quirk et al. 1985: 135); and some of them are often reduced to a single consonant phoneme like *will* /l/ or *would* /d/. In information processing such reduced material can be lost. For BE GOING TO, the same point has been made by Hopper & Traugott (1993: 65), who call the developing auxiliary "more substantive (phonologically longer) and thus more accessible to hearers than, e.g., *'ll* or even *will.*" It is significant, though, that this holds for all emerging modals: they contain at least two distinct syllables and typically include a full vowel. Hence their risk of being lost is – at present – considerably smaller. The fact that HAVE TO is almost always disyllabic fits in with this situation, even though in principle the first element could undergo phonological reduction, in which case the quasi-modal would become monosyllabic. While structures such as *I've to go to Brussels* are attested in the BNC (F7C 1150), the evidence suggests that they are obsolescent.[47] Pullum & Postal indeed consider cliticization such as **We've to go* ungrammatical (1979: 699).

As far as field-internal developments are concerned, for the domain of obligation one can rather confidently state a link between the erosion of the old inventory and the emergence of new constructions. Two recent longitudinal studies (Biber et al. 1998: 205-210; Myhill 1995) suggest that the increase in the deontic structures HAVE TO and HAVE GOT TO correlates with a decrease in the central modals. I also conducted a short-term study on the development of items which express obligative semantics. The genre was press language and the period covered the last generation (LOB and FLOB; see Krug 1998c for figures). Here too the older items like *must, should and ought (to)* were in retreat while the use of HAVE TO has increased.

5.6.2   Iconicity and economy: Competing motivations?

This section will argue against the common view that iconicity and economy are always competing forces in language change. I accept the view that economy and ritualization increase grammaticalization (see Haiman 1994a or 1994c). In proposing that economy and ritualization do not necessarily lead to the loss of iconicity, however, I diverge from most previous research. In the field of emerging modals we will see that the reverse can happen: here economy and ritualization actually seem to be *creating* iconicity.

Haiman's iconicity axiom states that *"recurrent similarity of form must reflect similarity in meaning"* (1985: 26; italics original). Proceeding from this assumption, studies in iconicity claim that language structure reflects affinities between concepts.[48] Witness a recent definition of diagrammatic iconicity (Haiman 1994b: 1629):

> Although the component parts of a diagram may not resemble what they stand for, the relationships among those components may approximate the relationships among the ideas they represent.

A well-known example of diagrammatic iconicity is Caesar's *veni, vidi, vici* ('I came, I saw, I conquered'), where the linear order of the clauses reflects the order of events. Compare also a definition of Haiman's 'Iconic Principle of Interpretation' (1994c: 1636): "formal closeness reflects conceptual closeness of elements ..."[49] or, stated negatively, "difference in form iconically reflects their difference in meaning" (*ibid.*). A classic instance of the latter is *kill a chicken* vs. *cause a chicken to die*, where *kill* is taken to imply a more direct method of killing than *cause to die* (1994b: 1630).

Related to the idea of iconicity is the much older concept of analogy, which Bußmann (1996: 215) defines as the "synchronic or diachronic process by which conceptually related linguistic units are made similar (or identical) in form." Much work within the functionalist tradition has been devoted to exploring the roles of economy and iconicity. The history of this line of research is summarized in Haiman (1983: 814) and DuBois (1985: 358). Terminology varies considerably. Below I present an updated overview along the lines of DuBois (1985). Scholars like Saussure (1916), Zipf (1929ff), Malkiel (1968), Givón (1979, 1995), Haiman (1980ff), Horn (1984) and Goldberg (1995) have suggested the following pairs:

(46)   Competing motivations – competing terms:

- iconicity   vs.   economy
- (form-meaning) isomorphism   vs.   least effort
- Q-Principle   vs.   R-Principle
- perceptual separation   vs.   ease of articulation
- transparency (or clarity)   vs.   opacity
- minimal coding   vs.   maximal coding

Terminology and focus may vary but there is wide-spread agreement that these pairs represent opposing forces in language change. Witness for instance Haiman (1985: 18):

> there is an inverse correlation between iconicity and economy ... I believe that the tendencies to maximize iconicity and maximize economy are two of the most important motivations for linguistic forms in general ... (1985: 18)

A consequence of the opposing-forces view is that as grammaticalization proceeds, opacity increases and iconicity is destroyed. This assumption is concisely expressed by Haiman (1985: 259):

the functionalist ... recognizes the existence of competing motivations, in particular, iconic and economic motivations. At any stage of any natural language, there will be areas in the grammar where originally iconically motivated structures have become grammaticalized, and there will be others where they have not.

More recently, Haiman has emphasized the wider notion of ritualization. It is akin to economy since it is taken to include all instances of, *inter alia,* erosion and grammaticalization (1994c: 1633, 1635). The basic assumption regarding the relationship between economy and iconicity (which in his later work is subsumed under the label of motivation), however, has not changed:

> The standard traditional position on language change and motivation ... is that sound change – which is regular – destroys semantic motivation (of which iconicity ... is one major type), while analogical processes – which are irregular – tend to restore it. In fact, both major types of change tend equally to destroy motivation, which may be semantic, pragmatic, phonetic, or syntactic. Insofar as they do, they can be seen as aspects of one fundamental tendency, that of ritualization. (Haiman 1994c: 1633)

Against this backdrop let us consider the evidence of progressive univerbation for the items investigated here:

(47)   *want to*   >   *wanta*   >   *wanna*   /'wɒnə/

(48)   *is/am/are going to* >   *'s/'m/'re going to* >   *gonna*   /'gɒnə/

(49)   *have/has got to*   >   *'ve/'s got to*   >   *gotta*   /'gɒtə/

It was argued earlier that the paths given in (47) to (49) instantiate ongoing grammaticalization and that the variants represent different stages in the evolution of new auxiliaries. This is by no means exceptional but just another instance, from the realm of constructions, of the coexistence of younger and older phonological or syntactic variants (cf. *will* vs. *'ll, is* vs. *'s* on the word level).[50] At the outset there are three rather different structures. WANT is often regarded as a main verb (e.g. Quirk et al. 1985: 146; Radford 1997: 50; Biber et al. 1999: 362); the other two are periphrastic constructions involving an auxiliary (BE GOING TO and HAVE GOT TO). Remarkably, after different reduction processes like assimilation, cliticization and deletion, the results are three instances of univerbation, which are highly similar: first, all have two syllables and a Germanic stress pattern; the vowel of the second, reduced syllable is schwa. We can go into further detail for prototypical pronunciations: each of them has four phonemes whose structure is /CVCə/, where C stands for consonant and V for vowel.

Admittedly, HAVE TO does not fit into this paradigm. As far as phonology is concerned, therefore, it does not conform to the prototype. But many other items do. We may add that *had better* has travelled very much the same path via auxiliary encliticization to auxiliary omission:

(50)   *had better*   >   *'d better* >   *better, betta*   /'betə/[51]

Need to can have the same phonemic structure: /'ni:tə/. Common realizations are ['ni:tə] and ['ni:ɾə].[52] If we allow for complex infinitival complementation patterns (infinitive perfect), contractions like *coulda* /'kʊdə/, *woulda* /'wʊdə/, *shoulda* /'ʃʊdə/ and *mighta* /'maɪtə/ can be included in what appears to be an emerging paradigm.[53] Notice that these constructions are very heterogeneous as regards their etymology. They have in common a semantic affinity with the modal domain. Other items are very similar to the /'CVCə/ pattern but diverge by one phoneme from it, such as *oughta* /'ɔ:tə/, *tryta* /'traɪtə/ and *tryna* /'traɪmə/ (< *trying to*), which due to its more drastic reduction is more interesting (cf. *gonna*).[54] Quantitative or qualitative divergence by one phoneme is also found for items like *hafta* /'hæftə/, *hasta* /'hæstə/ and *usta* /'ju:stə/.[55]

As regards *wanna*, *gonna* and *gotta*, considerations of phonological similarity can be taken two steps further: in British English the full vowel is typically [ɒ] for all three items.[56] Moreover the second consonants – /n/ and /t/ – are alveolar, that is homorganic. The above developments also tally with general phonological concomitants of morphologization. As Hopper & Traugott inform us, these surface on two levels:

a) A quantitative ('syntagmatic') reduction: forms become shorter as the phonemes that comprise them erode.

b) A qualitative ('paradigmatic') reduction: the remaining phonological segments in the form are drawn from a progressively shrinking set. This smaller set of phonemes tends to reflect the universal set of unmarked segments. They tend especially to be apical (tongue tip) consonants such as [n], [t], and [s], the glottal consonants [ʔ] and [h], and common vowels ... The result is that from a synchronic perspective grammatical morphemes tend to be composed of 'unmarked' segments. (1993: 145)

Three out of the four phonemes in the /CVCə/ structure qualify as unmarked: /n/ and /t/ (including the flapped allophone) are apical; vowels are generally unmarked; and schwa is the most unmarked sound in human language. The first phoneme, by contrast, which generally differentiates the items, is often marked (e.g. /g/, /w/, /b/, /k/).

Let us return to the question of whether in the cases investigated here grammaticalization strengthens or weakens iconicity. The answer is that it does both: as grammaticalization proceeds, the items lose in iconicity to the extent that the transparency of the constructions in (47) to (49) decreases from left to right: /ˈgɒnə/ for instance is quite detached from /gəʊ/ both phonologically and semantically.[57] Traces of movement in *gonna* are rather opaque. Similarly, the original possessive semantics of HAVE GOT can be ruled out for modal *gotta*.[58] The data thus underpin Haiman's claim (1994c: 1633) that "ritualization *emancipates* forms from whatever motivation they once may have had." On the other hand, as the discussion of the phonological properties has revealed, grammaticalization has also led to gains in (paradigmatic) iconicity insofar as the rightmost items in (47) to (49) are very much alike formally. Their similarity in form now reflects functional and conceptual closeness, i.e. membership of a new modal category.

Unlike the majority of researchers, who have variously described the pairs in (46) as 'competing motivations', 'clashing forces', 'antinomic principles' or 'rival determinants', Givón appears to subscribe to a more dynamic model of change in which economy is prior to iconicity and should indeed be granted motivational status since it is taken to promote the emergence of iconic forms: "ultimately one may wish to view economy as a major *mechanism* which shape [sic] the rise of iconic representation in language" (1985: 190). In the face of the empirical evidence presented in this study, Givón's dynamic understanding seems more helpful in accounting for developments in the modal domain – and probably also elsewhere (cf. Croft 1990: 256f). The competing-forces view, however, can be saved if the notion of iconicity is understood in a restricted sense, i.e. if it is seen as confined to *syntagmatic* iconicity.

To sum up, I have proposed that the process of grammaticalization need not exclusively lead to de-iconicization. It may in fact increase iconicity or even *create* a new type of (paradigmatic) iconicity. As will become clearer from what follows, the emerging formal resemblance of the items discussed here indicates their affinity with an emerging category.

The type of formal resemblance discussed so far is primarily phonological in nature (converging morphosyntactic developments for emerging modals will be discussed below). Very recently, Andreas Fischer (1999) has discussed the relationship between phonological iconicity and categorization. And even though he is mainly concerned with lexical items, his work on *associative phonological iconicity* (also known as phonaesthesia, secondary onomatopoeia or secondary iconicity) lends strong support to the claim just made, *viz.* that the observed phonological similarity indicates conceptual closeness and thus hints at the development of a new verbal category. To begin with, Fischer (1999: 131) considers associative iconicity to be diagrammatic: "it is motivated not by individual meaning-form relationships, but by relations between forms all expressing a particular meaning." In the present context, this meaning is modal, i.e. an abstract, grammatical notion. Fischer further distinguishes between primary and secondary associative iconicity and describes the relationship that holds between them:

> speakers associate certain sounds or sound combinations with certain meanings (primary association), but they do so partly (primarily?) because they mentally associate these words with others that also contain these sounds or sound combinations (secondary association). ... The latter criterion (secondary association) may well be more important. ... [P]rimary association is supported and strengthened by ... secondary association, i.e. the association of words sharing a certain form (here: sound combination) and certain meanings with other such words. (1999: 129-131)

Notice that he also points to the intimate relationship between associative iconicity, productivity and categorization:

> The existence of ... phonaesthetically associated words ... may cause more such words to be created, and phonaesthetic word clusters thus have a tendency to perpetuate themselves and to grow larger. ... *Association is thus a form of category building,* ... [A]ssociative iconicity manifests explicitly (i.e. iconically) marked linguistic categories (categories of form as well as meaning) ... (1999: 129-132, emphasis added)

Undoubtedly, the productivity of grammatical constructions is much more restricted than that of lexical items, since it takes a lot more usage for the former to come into being. New modal constructions, for instance, cannot be created *ad hoc* – in contrast to lexical phonaesthetic neologisms like *bash, clash, dash, gash, slash, smash* etc. (see Fischer

1998: 129 for further relevant examples). It nonetheless appears that those items that by regular assimilation processes may develop a phonological variant with the 'appropriate' phonemic structure have a better chance of either being adopted into a grammatical category or of surviving in such a category than others. An instance of obsolescence that may be partly due to 'inappropriate' phonological structure is *uton* 'let's'. This was certainly the structurally (and semantically) most idiosyncratic item in the early Middle English inventory of preterite present verbs, from which essentially all PDE central modals are recruited.[59] It is Fischer's claims and my statement of iconicization by grammaticalization that require more refined considerations on categorization. This is the topic of the next section.

5.7   Gravitation and categorization

5.7.1   Why introduce a new category?

In terms of categorization, the simplest account would be to assume that the constructions investigated in the present study (WANT TO and HAVE GOT TO in particular) are currently being co-opted into the category of central modal verbs. While the overall direction of change certainly is towards the central modals, I prefer a slightly different line of argument. I submit that we are seeing the rise of a new category, which I call *emerging auxiliaries* or, more exactly, *emerging modals*. From now on this term is meant to carry more technical, categorial implications and is therefore used in a more specific way than in previous parts of this work, where it was often used essentially as an equivalent to *developing auxiliaries* (or *modals*, for that matter).

On theoretical grounds it is important to note that I do not propose the rise of a major verbal category, but the rise of a subcategory within the higher-level class of modal verbs. I thus embrace a prototype view of modal status, which is similar to Heine's (1993) perspective. Consequently the emerging modals are regarded as proper modal auxiliaries, the unifying criterion being their modal function and semantics. Brinton (1988: 237), Hopper & Traugott (1993) and Traugott (1997) share this view. It would not seem helpful to exclude all verbs taking infinitival *to* complements from auxiliarihood simply because they do not share the syntactic properties of the central modals. On the contrary, adopting a purely morphosyntactic model of categorization would obscure ongoing developments. Few languages seem to have a class of modal verbs that are as rigidly grammaticalized as the English central modals *will, may, should* etc. (Heine 1993: 72f). Items like WANT TO, GOING TO or GOT TO – and in particular their contracted forms – would easily qualify as modal verbs in many languages. Bybee & Dahl (1989: 60) have pointed out that many of the properties of the central modals are due to diachronic coincidence, that is, they are consequences of verbal behaviour that was prevalent in the period when these verbs grammaticalized. (Neo)auxiliarization in Modern English must be different.

Various subcategories have been suggested in the literature on auxiliaries before. Heine (1993: 14f) provides a good summary. Probably most wide-spread is the pretheoretical use of *quasi-auxiliaries* (employed by e.g. Quirk 1965; Bolinger 1980b; Traugott 1997). Others have suggested the terms *semi-modals* (Palmer 1983; Biber et al. 1999), *secondary auxiliaries* (Christie 1991; see Mufwene 1994 for discussion) or a more refined taxonomy which includes such subcategories as *semi-auxiliaries, marginal modals, modal idioms* but also *main verbs* that take *to* complements (Quirk et al. 1985). I do not wish to invalidate such taxonomies because they are usually consistent within the respective frameworks. Still I believe that these classes are either too all-encompassing (such as *quasi-modal*) or too strictly morphosyntactic (hence too narrow) for the present purpose. Indeed such taxonomies prevent us from identifying an evolving, but fairly concisely definable class of verbs. Proceeding from these assumptions I suggest that we are witnessing the genesis of a new focal point on the main verb – auxiliary cline. The core members of the new category are recruited from the classes identified in previous research, which attests to the usefulness of such taxonomies. And, as we shall see below, it is also primarily members from the larger class of quasi-modals which are attracted by the new focal point. It is here that the present study overlaps with Pullum's (1997) strictly synchronic treatment, because by calling the items he investigates 'therapy verbs' he too advocates the existence of a new category.

Occam's razor is a maxim stating that categories must not be needlessly multiplied. I shall therefore present arguments for why the introduction of a new category in the English auxiliary domain is not an unnecessary proliferation. Note first of all that most reductions that lead to the observed phonological similarity are perfectly regular. But some items are more drastically reduced than others (cf. *going to* > *gonna* vs. *want to* > *wanna* or *need to* > *neeta/needa*).[60] And there is no *a priori* reason for the items to converge on a similar phonetic structure. Thus it seems difficult to explain the structural similarity on purely phonological grounds.

One reason for their convergence is probably frequentative in nature. The assimilation processes found between the verb forms *want, going, got* and the following infinitival marker *to* are typical of word-internal sound sequences or of highly frequent word sequences (which presumably themselves are single processing units and thus akin to single words).[61] This, then, at least partially explains why, within the set of emerging modal constructions, the most drastic reductions (*viz.* from *going to* to *gonna*) are found for the most frequent sequence. More speculatively, one might invoke the notion of gravitation at this point: several regular erosive developments affect different items to different extents and thus result in similar phonological forms. Some kind of (gravitational) force appears to slow down the process of erosion at a non-arbitrary point, thus temporarily preventing the items from diverging. This force, then, apparently leads to the emergence of a semi-stable intermediate step on the grammaticalization path of these items from constructions to affixes.

In addition, we can resort to cognitive principles such as Rosch's 'cognitive economy', which predicts that "the task of category systems is to provide maximum information with least effort" (1978: 28). Despite the definitional problems discussed above, crosslinguistic work has demonstrated that the term *modal* is indeed a helpful label (Palmer 1986: Ch. 1; Heine 1993: Chs. 1f; Bybee et al. 1994: *passim*). It is generally understood as a non-affixal grammatical item which has certain semantic properties. Language-internally and crosslinguistically, then, modals tend to be perceived as similar semantically and functionally. Further, language-internally, modals tend to be similar from a morphological and syntactic point of view (take for instance the Germanic inventories of erstwhile preterite-presents).[62] This existence of a grammatical modal category both across and within languages makes it plausible to assume that speakers of a given speech community have at least one mental category for the expression of modality in their language. In English, due primarily to the semantic erosion of the old inventory – probably the ultimate *raison d'être* for the universal principle of layering which leads to the constant renewal of the grammatical inventory of any one language – we are now seeing the emergence of a new modal layer.

Finally, positing the emergence of a new category with formally similar items ties in neatly with Lehmann's theoretical discussion of one of his six parameters of grammaticalization (see Ch. 2.3 for discussion), *viz.* paradigmaticity:

> paradigmaticity is gradually reached in the process of grammaticalization. ...
> The process of paradigmatic integration or **paradigmaticization** leads to a
> levelling out of the differences with which the members were equipped
> originally. (1995 [1982]: 134f; emphasis original)

Lehmann (1995 [1982]: 132f) points to the well-known fact that highly grammaticalized paradigms tend to be smaller than less grammaticalized ones. Significantly, from the relatively open class of verbs that can take *to* infinitives not all can serve as hosts to cliticized *to* (e.g. **attemma* from *attempt to*, see the discussion in 5.2.2 above). The number of members participating in this paradigm, therefore, is rather restricted and hence its members are obviously more grammaticalized than the group of verbs taking *to* infinitives. Granting the emerging modals categorial status, then, is also a taxonomical reflection of precisely this observation.

5.7.2   An 'Iconicity of Grammatical Categories Principle'

It is received wisdom in linguistics that grammaticalization occurs in very localized contexts. Recall for instance Hopper's 'Principle of Divergence' mentioned in section 2.3 above:

> The Principle of Divergence ... refers to the fact that when a lexical form
> undergoes grammaticization, for example to an auxiliary, clitic or affix, the
> original form may remain as an autonomous lexical element ... The Principle
> of Divergence results in pairs or multiples of forms having a common
> etymology, but diverging functionally. (1991: 24)

It is entirely consistent with this principle that in the present study form-meaning isomorphism is being created by grammaticalization (compare also the notion of 'natural grammar' discussed by Heine et al. 1991: 118-122): modal *gonna, gotta,* and *wanna* with a phonemic structure /'CVCə/ typically take infinitives, while NP complements tend to follow the fuller, older forms *going to, got to, got a* and *want a*.[63] The trend towards isomorphism can also be accommodated by two processes described in more recent research (Haiman 1994a; Bybee & Thompson forthcoming): chunking and lexical autonomy. This takes us from a purely phonological level to syntactic reasons for positing a new category. Chunking describes the automatization of frequently recurring sequences as single processing units. It renders them amenable to phonological attrition, as is commonly pointed out in grammaticalization theory (e.g. *going to > gonna*). Lexical autonomy refers to the progressive widening of the semantic and functional gaps between a parent structure (e.g. WANT TO) and its descendant (*wanna*). It was seen in section 4.4 that the two items possess partially different syntactic properties. Or take for instance the fact that *gotta* often occurs with supportive DO in questions and negation, whereas *got to* rarely does (cf. Pullum 1997: 89). This instantiates both chunking and lexical autonomy to the extent that it proves the independent status of the newer, more grammaticalized item.

Phonologically, emerging isomorphism for *gonna* is to some extent supported by data from the BNC. Table 5.5 gives the proportions of modal *going to* (i.e. followed by the infinitive) measured against all instances of *going to* (i.e. followed by a noun phrase or infinitive).

Table 5.5.   Modal *going to* as proportions of all GOING TO sequences: A study in apparent time[64]

		1-14	15-24	25-34	35-44	45-59	60+
1	Sum *going to*	420	432	1150	1178	2213	1105
2	within which are modal	71%	71%	78%	81%	85%	80%
3	within which + NP	29%	29%	22%	19%	15%	20%
4	*gonna* per million words	2369	2452	1727	1570	1166	553

Table 5.5 shows that the two youngest groups have a significantly higher proportion of NP complements after *going to* than the remaining groups. Together with the much higher incidence of contracted *gonna* (row 4), this suggests that the youngest two age groups have further progressed in the functional split towards isomorphism. The emerging distinction is that between modal (or futural) *gonna* + infinitive and lexical *going to* + NP. It is obvious from the data that this is an incipient development. Even for the youngest groups, modal *going to* still accounts for some 70% of all occurrences.

While it is fascinating to spot such ongoing developments, their observation is not entirely surprising. On theoretical grounds, isomorphism is what Givón (1985: 189) would have predicted without even having to look at textual evidence. Witness his 'Iconicity Meta-Principle':

> All other things being equal, a coded experience is easier to *store, retrieve* and *communicate* if the code is maximally isomorphic to the experience.

Hopper & Thompson (1985) have formulated the 'Iconicity of Lexical Categories Principle'. It seems possible to adapt their principle to grammatical domains. Notice first the phrasing of the original principle:

> The more a form refers to a discrete discourse entity or reports a discrete discourse event, the more distinct will be its linguistic form from neighboring forms, both paradigmatically and syntagmatically. (Hopper & Thompson 1985: 151)

Here I propose an 'Iconicity of Grammatical Categories Principle'. Its wording is largely the conversion of Hopper & Thompson's formulation for lexical categories:

(51)   Other things being equal, the more a form refers to what is cross-linguistically realized as a grammatical morpheme, the more distinct its linguistic form will be from neighbouring forms and from its source construction syntagmatically, and the more similar it will be to related forms paradigmatically.

This principle emphasizes a point made above, *viz.* that iconicity – just like grammaticalization (cf. Lehmann 1995[1982]: Ch. 4) – has a syntagmatic and a paradigmatic dimension. The 'Iconicity of Grammatical Categories Principle', then, proposes that grammaticalization typically involves loss of *syntagmatic* iconicity, which is the emancipation from the etymological source of a given item, as well as increased distinctness from its co-text. For the emerging modals, this is to say that while grammaticalizing they are becoming different from their source constructions (e.g. HAVE GOT TO) on the one hand, and from their neighbouring forms in the syntagm (i.e. lexical verbs) on the other. This loss of syntagmatic iconicity, however, tends to be accompanied by gains in *paradigmatic* iconicity, that is to say, the development of formal resemblance with items belonging to the same, potentially emerging, paradigm (here: the class of emerging modals). It is important to note, however, that this principle enjoys greater validity for free grammatical morphemes developing roughly in sync than for layers from very different historical stages. The latter tend to include such heterogeneous items as affixes and free complex constructions, which necessarily differ greatly. Therefore, only when the condition of approximate diachronic coincidence is met will other things be equal enough for the above principle to apply.

That frequently expressed notions tend to grammaticalize is one tenet of functionalism. This is made explicit in, for instance, Bybee's (1999a) new definition of grammatic(al)ization,

> which recognizes the crucial role of repetition ... and characterizes it as the process by which a frequently-used sequence of words or morphemes becomes automated as a single processing unit.

The above 'Grammatical Category Principle' is therefore partly inspired by, very generally, Hopper's notion of emergent grammar or, more specifically, by Givón's 'Principle (27)':

> The notion of Emergent Grammar is meant to suggest that structure, or regularity, comes out of discourse and is shaped by discourse in an ongoing process. ... The notion of emergence ... takes the adjective emergent seriously as a continual movement towards structure ... (Hopper 1998: 156f [1987: 142])

> The more important an item is in the communication, the more *distinct* and *independent* coding expression it receives. (Givón 1985: 206)

Givón goes on to explain that "Principle (27) represents an isomorphism between two levels of *saliency*: The more salient an item is semantically and communicatively, the more saliently it is rendered at the coding level" (*ibid.*). That notions such as futurity, intention or obligation are important in communication seems obvious enough. Therefore, the independent coding of newly developing forms for their expression should not surprise us too much.

The statement of (51) would not deserve the label 'principle' if it were restricted to the few items discussed in the present study. It is therefore important to note that, synchronically, most grammatical categories have several prototypical members which tend to be structurally similar, that is, they share a number of morphological and syntactic, sometimes even phonological properties.[65] The central modals are a case in point: today, the historical preterite forms of three (out of four) central modals, *would, could, should,* have the structure /Cʊd/, where C stands for consonant. Historically, their (stem) vowels were not identical. They are now. On the basis of the OE pronunciations of *cuþe* /'kuːðə/, *wolde* /'woldə/ and *sc(e)olde* /'ʃoldə/, the PDE triplet /kʊd/, /wʊd/, /ʃʊd/ is certainly not predictable, not even with hindsight. If the usual historical phonological developments had applied (i.e. lengthening of the stem-vowel before -*ld*, loss of final schwa, Great Vowel Shift), the three modals would be pronounced something like /kaʊð/, /wuːld/ and /ʃuːld/.[66] Also, discourse frequency apart perhaps, there is no genuinely phonological principle predicting the shortening of each individual stem vowel in these items. Further, as their orthography indicates, *would* and *should* had originally an additional phoneme /l/, unlike the analogical respelling *could*. Phonotactically, the consonant cluster /-ld/ has remained part of English, as words like *pulled, child, mould, howled, fouled* or *fold* show. Simplification of consonant clusters as such is not unusual, but the result that three central modals have become formally nearly identical is certainly noteworthy. It seems that of the variants which were available in Middle English (see e.g. Mossé 1959: §§101-105), precisely those entered into the modern standard which facilitated the emergence of the present iconic system.[67]

Even the remaining central modals, which at a glance look rather different, are not that different on closer inspection: *can, will, shall* and *might* can be seen as forming another subgroup of modals with a /CVC/ structure, where, just like in the cases of *could, would* and *should,* the last phoneme is alveolar. In fact, *mus(t)* too belongs to this group since its final consonant cluster is usually reduced. In other words, only one central modal, *viz. may,* is radically different phonologically from the remaining eight members of its category – if one can speak of 'radical' differences when that difference consists in the absence of one phoneme. In addition, their overall structural coherence can be demonstrated by the fact that all nine central modals share a set of at least twelve morphosyntactic idiosyncrasies not shared by lexical verbs (see Quirk et al. 1985: 137; or section 2.8.2 above).

To consider a different category, prototypical prepositions in English or German consist of two phonemes and share a locative and directional semantics (e.g. E *in, on, at, to;* G *in, an, auf, zu*). English prepositions like *under, over, above, across* follow in terms of core membership, and it seems a comparatively long way to such items as *with regard to.* It is true that the examples invoked above are not representative of the languages in the world. Significantly, however, such tendencies are not restricted to Germanic or Indo-European languages. As Kortmann & König (1992: 682f) note,

> in a wide variety of languages, a core group of highly frequent, monosyllabic, highly versatile primary adpositions can be distinguished from typically disyllabic, less versatile secondary ones and so on, down to one or several layers of marginal and peripheral groups.

A final example can be provided from the domain of adverbial subordinators (or: subordinating conjunctions, e.g. *since, if, while*).[68] Based on a typological study of 50 European languages (Kortmann 1997), this is probably the most weighty piece of evidence invoked so far. For adverbial subordinators, then, the same tendency obtains as for the domain of adpositions just quoted. More interesting still, in the course of time the adverbial subordinators of English have become more similar structurally to the crosslinguistically valid monosyllabic prototype (e.g. OE *þa hwile þe* > ModE *while*).

Generalizations from such research seem possible. First, historically not all members of a category start out from a position of formal resemblance to the prototype. Further, progressive development of shared properties, which is typical in the formation of new categories (e.g. Rosch 1978), is not restricted to the morphosyntactic level: phonology is involved as well. Neither of these observations is new. Hence, the developments in the realm of emerging auxiliaries are by no means exceptional. It is remarkable, though, that the prototype in the case of the emerging modals – a disyllabic item with characteristic morphosyntactic and phonological properties – is not attested in older stages of the language.[69] It is further remarkable that economy and concomitant grammaticalization seem to be triggering the emergence of just such an iconically motivated prototype.

5.7.3   Categorization in grammaticalization and related frameworks

The above considerations are grounded in cognitive principles that appeal to iconicity, isomorphism and prototype theory, all of which are related to grammaticalization theory. I will now discuss the hypothesis of a newly emerging category in the light of some fundamental tenets concerning categorization in grammaticalization theory proper. Hopper

& Traugott (1993: 7) have established a cline of grammaticality which has several focal points where linguistic forms or structures may cluster:

(52) content item > grammatical word > clitic > inflectional affix

They point out that "it is often difficult to establish firm boundaries between the categories represented on clines" (*ibid.*). Indeed, they note that "the study of grammaticalization has emerged in part out of a recognition of the general fluidity of so-called categories" (*ibid.*). Such considerations indicate that the concept of clines is central to categorization in grammaticalization. The term has its origin in Hallidayan functional, that is, synchronic, linguistics and has various near-synonyms such as *gradient, continuum, scale* or *squish*. Such concepts are also useful for diachronic linguistics, because historically "forms do not shift abruptly from one category to another, but go through a series of gradual transitions, transitions that tend to be similar in type across languages" (Hopper & Traugott 1993: 6).[70] In other words, the above cline of grammaticality is valid for both the synchronic categorization and the historical development of words and constructions.

Bybee et al. (1994: 8) note that "it is also typical of grammatical or closed classes to reduce further in size. Individual members are lost, usually by one member generalizing to take over the functions of other members." They cite *will* replacing *shall* in the auxiliary domain. Positing that WANT TO etc. are currently becoming central modals would therefore present a problem to the reduction-of-members hypothesis. This problem too is resolved by stating the evolution of a new category. For this position one can advance various pieces of evidence, both theoretical and empirical. I begin with a discussion of theoretical aspects. Bybee & Dahl (1989: 60) point out what has become a central idea of grammaticalization:

> Since ... lexical morphemes can become grammatical, it would seem to follow that new closed classes items may be added to a language.

Significantly, they note that

> ... it is also the case that new grams are rarely added to existing closed classes, rather, as they grammaticize, they create new closed classes. (*ibid.*)

It is not doubtful that the emerging modals investigated in the present study are moving towards the upper focal point of the main verb – auxiliary verb cline proposed by Quirk et al. (1985: 137; see also section 2.8 above). On the other hand, as was seen in the previous two chapters, it seems equally clear that most of them will not reach this focal point. The notion of *prototype* enters crucially at this point. Developed by the psychologist Eleanor Rosch (e.g. 1975; 1978), this model of categorization has become popular within the domain of cognitive linguistics (see Taylor 1995 for a general introduction; Geeraerts 1997 for diachronic developments). Its value for the typology of auxiliaries has been stressed by, among others, Warner (1993), Heine (1993) and Traugott (1997). For convenience, I quote Heine's (1993: 113) concise summary of the prototype approach to classification:

> Prototypes differ from classical categories in that they cannot be defined by means of necessary and sufficient properties; rather they have the following attributes in particular ...:
>
> - Not every member is equally representative of its category.
> - Prototypical members share a maximum of attributes with other members and a minimum with members of contrasting categories.
> - The structure of categories takes the form of a set of clustered and overlapping attributes.
> - Categories are blurred at the edges; they have fuzzy boundaries.

Compare Traugott (1997: 192) on auxiliaries:

> The positions on this continuum are to be thought of as "cluster points", magnets, as it were, where iron filings (in this instance source verbs) coalesce; or, to use more familiar terminology, they represent clusters of *prototypical properties*. (emphasis added)

While I believe that the magnet metaphor can be helpful, a frequentative approach suggests an alternative model: cluster points do not arise as immaterial magnets *ex nihilo*; rather, the actually existing most frequent source verbs function as magnets and attract other less common constructions. A related analogy to the natural sciences would be one in terms of gravitation theory. This will be discussed in the next sections.

5.7.4   Gravitation theory

This section proposes that gravitation theory can help to account for the changes that are currently affecting the English auxiliary domain. From a theoretical outline I proceed to the formulation of an adapted model for emerging modals. The model will then be put to the test by running two numerical simulations. First of all, however, some common functionalist assumptions need to be recalled in order to bridge the gap between physics and linguistics.

The most fundamental premiss underlying the model to be presented is that language developments, and thus instances of grammaticalization, do not occur in isolation. This premiss pertains to at least two levels: changes of the kind investigated here are assumed not to occur independently of (a) language users, or, more precisely: face-to-face interaction between language users, and of (b) linguistic items from the same conceptual field. This much probably goes unchallenged in the community of grammaticalization scholars and is reminiscent of the well-known, though too simplistic, functionalist position that language (or any of its components, be it syntax or grammar at large) is not an autonomous system (see Croft 1995 for discussion). From this assumption follows another linguistic commonplace, *viz.* that there is an enormous number of factors that bear on a given instance of language change. If this common assumption is correct, as seems likely, the implication is that change is, first, very difficult to model, second, next to impossible to describe accurately and, third, impossible to explain exhaustively or even predict. On the other hand, the assumption also entails that language change is not entirely random but that there are indeed identifiable determinants. Consequently, if we can single out the most salient factors in a specific instance, we can at least attempt to *model* change. This is the aim of the present section.

Two further, more specific, assumptions and observations need to be mentioned. For one thing, the domain of modals in English is organized around prototypes (e.g. Bolinger 1980b or Quirk et al. 1985: 137) in that it comprises central members (such as *can* and *must*) and more peripheral ones (such as NEED (TO) and BE *bound to*).[71] Given the insights of prototype theory (cf. Lakoff 1987, Kleiber 1990, Taylor [2]1995), it seems reasonable to assume that what holds for the horizontal axis of categorization within the entire group of modals also holds for the internal structure of a given subcategory of the modal system. In other words, the group of modal constructions investigated here, too, is likely to have central and marginal members. It is primarily this aspect which the following dynamic approach to categorization tries to test.

The last assumption which needs to be recalled before we can proceed to a discussion of the model proper has received empirical support on various occasions in this book. It is that frequency of occurrence is a major linguistic factor in the diffusion of linguistic change. The starting point for testing the particular usefulness of the gravitation model, therefore, is as follows: larger masses (in our case highly frequent emerging auxiliaries) attract smaller masses (in our case less common constructions) more strongly than vice versa. This is consistent with empirical research carried out by Bybee and her collaborators, who have shown that within paradigms of semantically closely related items, less frequent members are prone to analogical levelling on the model of more frequent members (Hooper 1976; Bybee & Slobin 1982; Bybee 1985: 49-79; cf. also Paul 1975 [1880]: Ch. 5). Let us now consider the classical, Newtonian formula for the force of attraction (F) in physics:

(53)　　$F = \dfrac{G\,m_1 m_2}{d^2}$

where G is a universal gravitational constant; m_1 and m_2 the two masses, and d the distance between them. The gravitation analogy seems superior to the magnet analogy because gravitation stresses that every mass, however tiny, exerts an influence on surrounding masses. This is to say that influence is mutual, but larger masses influence smaller ones far more strongly (via acceleration due to gravitation) than vice versa.[72] Among the immediately appealing properties of the model are the following:

- In principle a potentially infinite number of items can be integrated in a gravitational system.
- While influence in one direction may be the dominant pattern in regularization (e.g. the levelling of irregular past tense forms in English), in certain areas productivity and influence can come in degrees and from opposing directions (e.g. nominalization). Gravitation can capture more than one type of productivity and can in principle integrate a multitude of competing forces.
- The model seems capable of accommodating ongoing developments to the extent that items can become more frequent. This would increase their influence on other, especially functionally and structurally related, items.

I want to stress the word *related* because gravitation is inversely proportional to the square of the distance between masses. It seems an obvious step to equate this spatial measure with linguistic distance – despite the problems that attach to measuring such an entity (see the discussion on p. 229f below). As far as categorization is concerned, verbs appear more likely to impact on verbs, nouns on nouns, and so on. One should in fact be more specific: even though semantic changes can take centuries, it is commonly believed that changes in meaning of one item from a semantic field affect the remaining ones (Williams 1976; Lehrer 1985; Ogura & Wang 1995). As was seen above, the English central modals possess rather uniform and unique morphosyntactic properties due to historical changes. Considering in addition the observed phonological changes in the domain of the emerging auxiliaries (and the central modals too), we can fairly confidently conclude that field-internal changes extend to all basic linguistic levels, i.e.: phonology, morphology, syntax and semantics. This claim is consistent with prototype theory (Rosch 1978), which predicts that the central members of a category will become ever more alike. To sum up, it seems likely that changes in the morphosyntax of semantically related verbs may affect the morphosyntax of other members in that field. It goes without saying that this hypothesis is virtually restricted to semantic notions that serve as source domains for grammatical categories since it is primarily during the process of grammaticalization that one can expect to observe morphosyntactic changes.

The gravitational model has been invoked in linguistics before (Trudgill 1973, partly reprinted in Chambers & Trudgill 1998: Ch. 11). In order to determine the influence of different population sizes in the geographical diffusion of linguistic variables, Trudgill uses an adaptation of the gravity model developed by geographers. He assumes that "the influence of one [centre] on the other will be proportional to their relative population sizes" (1998: 179).[73] For the level of influence from one linguistic item on another, this translates into:

$$(54) \quad I_1 = \frac{C \cdot F_1 \cdot F_2}{d^2} \cdot \frac{F_1}{F_1 + F_2}$$

where I_1 stands for the influence which the first item exerts onto the second; C is a constant; F_1 and F_2 are the frequencies of the two interacting items; and d is the linguistic distance between them. By the same token, the influence of the second item on the first would be:

$$(55) \quad I_2 = \frac{C \cdot F_1 \cdot F_2}{d^2} \cdot \frac{F_2}{F_1 + F_2}$$

As for experimental testability, the problem with gravitation is that it is the weakest known force and hence very difficult to simulate with physical experiments. More feasible are experiments with electric fields.[74] Here a large mass (high frequency) would translate into a high charge; (linguistic) distance would translate into simple metrical distance. Ultimately, one might wish to improve both the (Newtonian) gravitation model and field theory with modern versions of chaos theory, which attempt to account for the slight inaccuracies (subsumed under the notion of 'noise') left by the classical model. I refrain from this task for three reasons. First, the classical Newtonian model is less complex and hence analogies with language are more easily sketched and understood. Second, it would seem pretentious to invoke a refined model targeting the peripheries and subtle inadequacies of the classical gravitation model at a point when not even the classical model itself is applied with a sufficient degree of mathematical rigour. For the time being we probably have to live with some amount of noise. Third, at the present stage, some very basic analogies apart, I do not know how to operationalize chaos theory with any degree of precision and therefore leave this task to future research. Schneider (1997) comments on the over-application of chaos theory, and the mere observation that a new order is emerging from variation seems precisely the kind of weak argument that leads to unfounded parallelisms.

5.7.5   Operationalization of the gravitation model

5.7.5.1   Criteria for determining linguistic distance

This section attempts to operationalize the adaptation of the gravitation model. The formula given in (54) includes four parameters. The gravitational constant G is universal and thus need not concern us.[75] The frequencies of the different items are those identified in section 2.6 for spontaneous speech in the BNC. Absolute occurrences could equally be used, but for transparency and comparability I chose incidence, more precisely, occurrences per 100,000 words. Whether absolute or relative frequencies are chosen does not affect the results.[76] The parameter that is yet unspecified is linguistic distance.

While a certain arbitrariness is unavoidable in the selection of criteria that enter into the calculation of linguistic distance, I chose for inclusion what appear to be the most salient properties. Verbal status and modal semantics are prerequisites here but can be integrated if needed. Most salient to me are four properties, given as (i) to (iv) below. Equal weight is given to the levels of morphosyntax and phonology, a strategy which seems defensible since phonology is indeed a major factor in considerations of similarity (see also the discussion on iconicity and analogy above). The values are assigned according to the relative distance between two items on each cline: when two items fall in the same category their relative distance score is 1 (this is required due to the fact that distance appears in the denominator and thus it must not be zero); neighbouring points receive a rating of 2; adjacent-but-one items of 3, and so on. Similar properties will always be nearer to each other on the clines than less similar properties.[77] For illustration, under each focal point, some relevant examples are given.

(i)   Verbal complementation patterns

only TO infinitive	**bare or TO infinitive**	**only bare infinitive**
HAVE TO, (HAVE) GOT TO, WANT TO, (BE) GOING TO	DARE (TO), NEED (TO), OUGHT (TO)	WILL, CAN, MAY

(ii)   Negation and interrogative strategies

DO support	**DO support or item functions as operator**	**item functions as operator**	**additional auxiliary**
HAVE TO, WANT TO	DARE (TO), NEED (TO), OUGHT (TO)	WILL, CAN	(HAVE) GOT TO, (BE) GOING TO

(iii)   Number of syllables of predominant unmarked (i.e. not negated) phonological realization in spontaneous speech

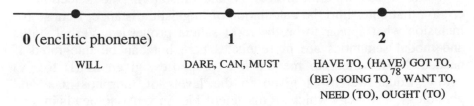

0 (enclitic phoneme)	1	2
WILL	DARE, CAN, MUST	HAVE TO, (HAVE) GOT TO,[78] (BE) GOING TO, WANT TO, NEED (TO), OUGHT (TO)

(iv)   Number of phonemes of predominant unmarked phonological realization in spontaneous British speech[79]

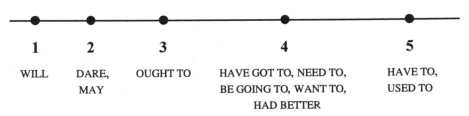

1	2	3	4	5
WILL	DARE, MAY	OUGHT TO	HAVE GOT TO, NEED TO, BE GOING TO, WANT TO, HAD BETTER	HAVE TO, USED TO

On the basis of the dominant properties found for the four most frequent members – HAVE TO, (HAVE) GOT TO, WANT TO, (BE) GOING TO – one can determine the prototype for the class of emerging modals as follows (cf. Taylor 1995: Ch. 11 or Taylor 1998 on the applicability of prototypes to syntactic constructions in general):

(56)   **Prototypical properties of an emerging modal**

    (i)   It takes TO infinitives only.

    (ii)   It takes DO support under negation and in interrogatives.

    (iii)   It consists of two syllables, which consist of

    (iv)   four phonemes. These in turn typically follow the order /CVCə/, where the second consonant is alveolar (cf. p. 211 above).

Two further criteria are implied by positing the fourth criterion: high discourse frequency and commonly realized assimilation processes at the (former) word boundary between the verb and *to*. Modal meanings are understood as well. No item in the class meets all criteria, but this presents no problem to prototypicality and related approaches to categorization. Compare Heine's summary of a categorization model in terms of family resemblance, which he thinks superior to all alternative approaches:

- No attribute is shared by all members of the category.
- No member combines all attributes defining membership within the category. (Heine 1993: 114)

Recall similarly Traugott's (1997: 192) magnet parallel quoted above (see p. 224). Prototypicality considerations also tie in closely with Bybee & Dahl's results:

It should also be remembered that not all members of a closed class are at the same stage in the grammaticization process, rather the individual members may have differing properties, ... (1989: 60)

Significantly, Traugott further claims that

verbs newly entering the domain of a prototype or leaving it will *vary depending on their history* with respect to their match to the prototype. (1997: 192., emphasis added)

The histories of GOING TO and HAVE GOT TO are such that their syntactic behaviour in negation and interrogatives cannot easily be discarded. This will become clearer from the simulation of the model.

An obvious parallel are the lower levels of linguistic categorization. Perhaps the nonexistent prototype of a verbal category can be seen as an analogue of the abstract emic notions known from phonology and morphology (cf. Taylor 1995: 223 on phonemes as prototypes).[80] Accordingly, actually existing verbs would be considered as analogues to phones or morphs. If we allow for such abstract prototypes, as is conventional in current versions of prototype theory, then we can probably also retain Traugott's equation of a prototype and an immaterial magnet. While the hypothesis of an abstract prototype as the gravitational centre within a verbal category is attractive indeed, I do not know how to simulate the forces emanating from such a centre. Therefore I proceed to calculate simulations on the basis of more directly accessible parameters: frequency and linguistic distance.

5.7.5.2   Simulation of gravitation in the field of emerging modals

The first simulation includes seven likely candidates for the class of emerging modals. These are the verbal constructions that were investigated in the present study: HAVE GOT TO, HAVE TO, BE GOING TO, WANT TO, NEED TO, OUGHT TO and DARE. Table 5.6 presents the results. It reads as follows. Essentially, it provides the influences between different constructions which are calculated on the basis of their respective frequencies and the linguistic distances between them. The distances are given as 'similarity index' in each cell. Table 5.6 shows, for instance, that (BE) GOING TO/GONNA and (HAVE) GOT TO/GOTTA are the most similar constructions with the minimum similarity index of 4, scoring the minimum value of 1 on each of the four distance measures. By contrast, (BE) GOING TO/GONNA and DARE (TO) are rather different with an index of 10. The figures above the similarity indices, then, reflect the influence of a given item (that heading the column) on another item (that heading the row).

Table 5.6.   Gravitation in the field of emerging modals

Influence on \ Influence of	329 GOING TO	204 HAVE TO	177 WANT TO	155 GOT TO	28 NEED (TO)	15 OUGHT (TO)	5 DARE (TO)	Total influence on item	Relative influence on item
Frequency per 100,000	329	204	177	155	28	15	5	**Total**	**Relative**
329 GOING TO		401,4	415,7	1020,7	14,7	3,4	0,2	**1856,1**	**5,6**
similarity index		8	7	4	7	8	10		
204 HAVE TO	647,3		671,0	213,3	14,1	3,3	0,2	**1549,2**	**7,6**
similarity index	8		5	8	7	8	10		
177 WANT TO	772,7	773,3		261,4	18,8	4,2	0,3	**1830,8**	**10,3**
similarity index	7	5		7	6	7	9		
155 GOT TO	2166,5	280,7	298,5		13,6	3,2	0,2	**2762,7**	**17,8**
similarity index	4	8	7		7	8	10		
28 NEED (TO)	173,3	102,5	118,9	75,0		5,9	0,4	**475,9**	**17,0**
similarity index	7	7	6	7		5	7		
15 OUGHT (TO)	73,7	44,5	50,0	33,1	9,5		0,5	**211,4**	**14,1**
similarity index	8	8	7	8	5		6		
5 DARE (TO)	16,2	10,0	10,6	7,5	2,4	1,6		**48,3**	**9,7**
similarity index	10	10	9	10	7	6			
Total influence of item	**3849,7**	**1612,5**	**1564,6**	**1611,1**	**73,1**	**21,5**	**2,0**	**8734,4**	
Relative influence of item	**11,7**	**7,9**	**8,8**	**10,4**	**2,6**	**1,4**	**0,4**		

Let me illustrate a calculation of the mutual influence between two items, GOING TO and HAVE TO. Here the values for the different variables are as follows (cf. equations (54) and (55) above):[81]

F_1 (Frequency of GOING TO) = 329 (occurrences per 100,000 words)
F_2 (Frequency of HAVE TO) = 204 (occurrences per 100,000 words)
d (linguistic distance between the two constructions) = $1_i + 4_{ii} + 1_{iii} + 2_{iv} = 8$
   where the individual scores for linguistic difference result from the following facts:

     (i)   both constructions fall into the same group for verbal complementation patterns, because they only take TO infinitives,
     (ii) HAVE TO takes DO support, whereas GOING TO requires an additional auxiliary (BE) under negation and in questions,
     (iii) both constructions typically consist of two syllables in spontaneous speech, but
     (iv) GOING TO typically consists of four, HAVE TO of five phonemes.

The total force between GOING TO and HAVE TO is computed by the first of the two fractions of the formula, while the second fraction simply gives the frequency of each construction relative to the sum of the two interacting constructions:

Influence$_1$ (GOING TO on HAVE TO; cf. equation (54)):

$$I_1 = \frac{329 \cdot 204}{8^2} \cdot \frac{329}{329 + 204} = 1048.7 \cdot 61.7\% = 647.3$$

In other words, the influence of GOING TO on HAVE TO is, relative to its proportion, roughly 62% of the total force acting between the two constructions. Consequently, the influence of HAVE TO on GOING TO consists in the remaining 38% of the total:

Influence$_2$ (HAVE TO on GOING TO; cf. equation (55)):

$$I_2 = \frac{329 \cdot 204}{8^2} \cdot \frac{204}{329 + 204} = 1048.7 \cdot 38.3\% = 401.4$$

Since this part of the simulation is straightforward, we need not concern ourselves with individual cells any more.[82] It is in particular two summary measures produced by the model which are of linguistic significance. Both are headed 'Total influence' in the table. The *column* totals indicate the influence which the item heading the column exerts on the remaining items in the field; the *row* totals, then, indicate the influence which the system exerts on the item heading the row. We shall look at these two measures in turn. A ranking on the basis of the column totals is as follows:

(57)   Total influence exerted by items

GOING TO > HAVE TO > GOT TO > WANT TO > NEED TO > OUGHT TO > DARE

The order produced by gravitation in (57) is almost identical to a frequency ranking, which can be seen in the first column of Table 5.6.[83] The similarity between hierarchies in terms of frequency and hierarchies in terms of overall influence is not surprising, though. It can be inferred from the parameters of the formula given in (54): in the first fraction, frequency enters as a factor in the numerator and, in the second fraction, the relative proportions of the total force acting between two items (masses) correlate directly with their respective frequencies.

The second summary measure (line totals) indicates the total force produced by the remaining items in the system on each item. Again, it produces an order that is similar to a ranking in terms of frequency:

(58)   Total influence exerted on items

GOT TO > GOING TO > WANT TO > HAVE TO > NEED TO > OUGHT TO > DARE

It seems obvious enough that a certain force acting upon two items of different frequencies (or, by analogy, masses of different sizes) will have a greater impact on the less frequent item (i.e. the smaller mass). Therefore it appears necessary to provide a measure which gives the influence (force) relative to the prominence of the item (mass) it acts upon. This is what the last column indicates. It is calculated as follows: 'Total influence on items' (second last column) divided by 'Frequency of items' (first column). It produces the following order (from higher to lower values), which seems to have no resemblance to a frequency ranking:

(59)   Relative influence exerted on items

GOT TO > NEED TO > OUGHT TO > WANT TO > DARE > HAVE TO > GOING TO

Synchronically, this measure is purely descriptive and indicates the relative pressure exerted on an item. Perhaps it also has predictive potential diachronically, since it appears to be a good indicator of the relative stability for each item in the field. If this is true, the order in

(59) can be read as a cline indicating susceptibility to change. It is striking that the two most frequent constructions, GOING TO and HAVE TO, score lowest on this measure. If anything, therefore, (59) has a slight resemblance to an inverse frequency ranking. In fact, this is not entirely surprising. If one follows Bybee's (1985) model on representation in the mental lexicon, which assumes that strong entrenchment is created by repetition (for details see 3.4.1.2), one would not expect the most frequent (i.e. most strongly entrenched) item to change drastically. The ranking in (59) therefore probably predicts correctly that GOING TO is the item least prone to change. Notice that this statement holds for the *present* state of the system. No doubt, GOING TO has undergone fundamental changes in the past. Most obvious today are perhaps its high contraction rates (see Figure 5.6). It is entirely consistent with intuitions that an item which has reached the end of the saturation stage (in terms of contraction ratios) should change less substantially than items which have not reached this stage (like WANT TO and HAVE GOT TO; see Figure 5.6).

To sum up, if (59) is read as a hierarchy indicating susceptibility to change, the model would suggest: first that GOING TO and HAVE TO are not very prone to change; second that DARE and WANT TO are in an intermediate position; and third that OUGHT TO is nearer the pole that is prone to change, which is represented by NEED TO and GOT TO. Most of this seems plausible. Perhaps surprisingly, the rather infrequent DARE leans rather towards the more stable pole of the cline. It was seen in section 5.5.1, however, that DARE indeed appears relatively immune to the general trend towards DO support and *to* infinitive by which the other two marginal modals, NEED (TO) and OUGHT TO, are affected.

A second relative measure can be calculated. By analogy with the relative influence *on* the individual items just discussed, one can provide a formula for the relative influence *exerted by* a given item within a field. It is a measure indicating 'influence exerted by a given amount of mass (frequency)'. This yields the following hierarchy:

(60)   Relative influence exerted by items

    GOING TO > GOT TO > WANT TO > HAVE TO > NEED TO > OUGHT TO > DARE

In the present simulation, the ranking of the items in terms of relative influence is very nearly that of their total influence, but this does not render the measure vacuous. The next simulation (see rankings (62) to (65) below) includes the central modal WILL. There it will be seen that the difference between total and relative influence depends heavily on how many attributes a given item shares with the remaining items in the field. It is only due to the overall homogeneity of the items in the previous simulation (i.e. due to the small linguistic distances between them) that relative and total influence rankings are almost identical.

There is another more interesting and more speculative reading of (60). If we compare its ranking to the prototypical properties of emerging auxiliaries listed in (56), it appears that the values for the individual items (the bottom row in Table 5.6) correspond rather well to their match to the prototype. For convenience, the ranking in terms of category-internal centrality and relative differences between the items are projected on the following cline (from left to right in an order of descending centrality):

(61)   **Prototypicality ranking in the field of emerging modals**

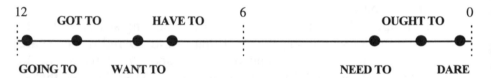

This order indeed seems to bear some resemblance to a cline of centrality: the higher the value (the more an item is to the left), the more central a member of the category it appears to be. Accordingly, GOING TO and GOT TO are the most prototypical members of the class of emerging modals, closely followed by WANT TO and HAVE TO. This ranking is convincing in so far as it is the top three items that have progressed most towards formal similarity (see the discussion on iconicity above). NEED TO, OUGHT TO and DARE (in that order) lag far behind in terms of central membership to the class. Parallels between the emerging modals and the early stages of category formation in the case of the central modals are evident: Warner (1993: 238) has argued that the rise of the class of central English modals, too, started with a "small group of items (perhaps only *mot, sceal, uton*)." We know that, even though *uton* went out of use, the class of central modals comprises three times as many members today.

In the adaptation of the gravitation formula (see p. 227) similarity with frequent members has more momentum than similarity with less frequent members. If we accept that the values of the bottom row in

Table 5.6 indicate degrees of centrality, then prototypes would be established by a combination of frequency and properties shared among the members of a given category. Shared syntactic, morphological and phonological criteria seem uncontroversial in determining prototypes. Adopting frequency as a criterion for prototypicality might seem more controversial. In fact, however, it tallies with the general tendency in prototype theory to adopt a position that grants frequency a major role in determining prototypes for basic level categories (Taylor 1995). In sum, despite all simplifications and attendant caveats, the model appears to have some plausibility.

5.7.5.3 *Simulation of gravitation in the field of emerging modals including the central modal* WILL

Some researchers could suspect that the gravitation model is tautological because it might seem to prove the impact of frequency by attributing too much weight to this parameter. To begin with, this argument is weakened by the fact that the prototypicality ranking in (60) diverges significantly from a simple frequency order. To counter related potential criticisms, the model is put to another test. In the next simulation, the most frequent modal verb, WILL (including *'ll* and *won't*), is included in the system, but no other modifications to the model are made. Appendix 6 presents the results. Detailed discussion of the second simulation is not necessary since the overall result is rather similar. Only the major deviations from the previous simulation will be outlined. Below the hierarchies for the four summary measures are given:

(62)   Total influence exerted by items

GOING TO > WILL > HAVE TO > GOT TO > WANT TO > NEED TO > OUGHT TO > DARE

(63)   Relative influence exerted by items

GOING TO > GOT TO > WANT TO > HAVE TO > WILL > NEED TO > OUGHT TO > DARE

(64)   Total influence exerted on items

GOT TO > GOING TO > WANT TO > HAVE TO > WILL > NEED TO > OUGHT TO > DARE

(65)   Relative influence exerted on items

NEED TO > GOT TO > OUGHT TO > DARE > WANT TO > HAVE TO > GOING TO > WILL

Being more than twice as common as the second most frequent item (GOING TO), WILL easily leads the field in terms of discourse frequency. However, the positions of WILL regarding influence as reflected in the gravitation model are very different. It falls well behind GOING TO in overall influence on the system. More significantly, it comes only fifth as regards relative influence, ahead only of the three relatively in-frequent marginal modals. Thus, for instance, the factor 28, by which WILL outnumbers NEED (TO) in terms of discourse frequency, is reduced to 1.6 in terms of relative influence on the system. This is due to the average linguistic distance from the remaining items in the field, which for WILL is far greater than for all others.[84] Some analysts might believe that the position of WILL in (63) still grants it too much influence in the field. But then the overall movement of the four core items towards more modal behaviour (e.g. the obscuration of the infinitive marker) seems to justify its middle position. In conclusion, given the generally satisfactory degree of plausibility of the two simulations, it seems rather improbable that the gravitation model is entirely vacuous. For illustrative purposes a simplified gravitational field is depicted in Figure 5.11. It is a synthesis of the results of the above simulations. In particular, it highlights the following aspects:

- The field of emerging modals has a prototypical structure. Figure 5.11 tries to unify the ranking given in (61) and the linguistic distances between the items in the field.[85]

- The prototype proper does not exist, but the four items GOING TO, GOT TO, WANT TO and HAVE TO show the closest match to the prototype, thus forming the core emerging modals.[86]

- WILL is one representative of the group of central modals. DARE, NEED TO and OUGHT TO are oscillating between central modal and emerging modal behaviour.

- While from a diachronic perspective the general direction of change for all three items seems to be towards the emerging modals, DARE is synchronically the item still nearest to the central modals. NEED (TO) and OUGHT (TO), by contrast, are syntactically and phonologically closer to the newly developing class of emerging modals.

- Historically, HAVE TO was nearer the central modals too, but by largely discarding NOT negation (such as *I haven't to tell you*) and monosyllabic realizations (such as *I've to go*), it has continuously moved towards emerging modal morphosyntax and phonology.

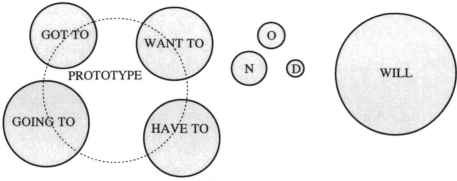

N = NEED (TO); O = OUGHT TO; D = DARE (TO)

Figure 5.11. The system of emerging modals (including the central modal WILL)

By way of conclusion, it must be emphasized that if the gravitation model is seen to suggest a tight class of verbs, it is misunderstood. The reverse is true, it is meant to model precisely the dynamics in the domain of emerging auxiliaries. That this class cannot be tight should be clear from the formula and, in particular, from the discussion of related auxiliary constructions in 5.6.2. In the present study it was possible to discuss in detail only the core members of the emerging modals, and briefly their interaction with three more marginal members of the class. New members are conceivable, indeed expected. As was indicated in the discussion of iconicity and economy, promising candidates – if not already peripheral emerging auxiliaries – are, *inter alia*, conative TRY TO (*tryta* or *tryna)* and another desiderative modal construction: WISH TO (*wishta*).

5.8   Some implications of the gravitation model

The gravitation model has two kinds of implications. One of its advantages over other models is its capacity to account for syntactic oddities which in formal grammars have to be explained away as performance errors. Furthermore, it has more theoretical implications for the framework of grammaticalization. I begin by outlining the former.

5.8.1   DO support for BE GOING TO and HAVE GOT TO

In standard English two out of the four core emerging modals take DO support in questions and negative contexts, while the strategies of BE GOING TO and HAVE GOT TO are unique within the current system. DO support was consequently identified as one attribute of the prototype. Assuming a framework in terms of gravitation, it will not be altogether surprising that the prototypical negation strategy occasionally surfaces also with the two exceptions – primarily with the contracted forms:

(66)   You see, I must admit [name] you see not I don't [name] gonna do as good a job as [name] ... (BNC JN6 493)

(67)   What do you gonna call it? (BNC KPV 2831)

(68)   ... say you don't gonna gallop five fur- you didn't gallop five furlongs, ... (BNC HDH 414)

(69)   No, you don't got to negotiate, you've got to [pause] be able to speak to people on a [pause] regular basis. (BNC KD7 2004)

It should be pointed out that all the above examples are uttered by native speakers.[87] Some researchers might object that in particular (68) is an anacoluthon and that (69) is a slip of the tongue as the standard construction in the following clause seems to suggest. Granted; they are interesting nevertheless. And at least example (67) is a clear case. Also, Peter Trudgill (personal communication) has pointed out that DO support for *gotta* is rather frequent with dialect speakers. Pullum (1997: 89) informs us that the same is true for colloquial American English. As is well known (e.g. Schneider 1997; Anderwald & Kortmann forthcoming), dialects are much less, if at all, affected by codification than the standard and can thus often be seen as foreshadowing a natural development – here towards prototypical emerging modal behaviour.[88] Let me add a remark on (69), which is especially interesting because the context seems to betray the motivation for the use of DO periphrasis: the preceding utterance is the question *Ho, you gotta negotiate about cars and prices?* Notice that this 13-year-old speaker omits the auxiliary, which doubtless facilitates the reanalysis of *gotta* as a (modal) verb in its own right by the second speaker. Only then does he return to what is probably his usual pattern for HAVE GOT TO, which is to include HAVE. While I do not believe that GOING TO will take DO support in the foreseeable future (recall its low score for susceptibility in both simulations above), it seems conceivable that GOT TO will at some point. Such syntactic oddities can simply be regarded as indicating pressures from the prototype and, at least in the case of GOT TO, as incipient signs of movement towards the prototype. They would be rather difficult to explain within most existing theories of syntax.

By the same token, auxiliary omission, which is very common with (HAVE) GOT TO, would not only be seen as an economy-driven phenomenon. While economy is certainly a factor, HAVE deletion additionally seems to reflect movement towards the prototype. In the standard British dialect, auxiliary omission with (BE) GOING TO would be considered ungrammatical by most grammarians, while cliticization of BE is standard usage. It should be pointed out, however, that in allegro speech the distinction between encliticization and deletion will not always be straightforward on purely phonetic grounds. The most elusive sequences are cases where BE is usually reduced to a schwa (< *are*) and follows a vowel, such as in *you are* and *they are*. The worst-case scenario for the phonetician who wants to trace BE is when *you* and *they* occur as weak forms (which is common), so that schwa meets schwa at the word boundary. Given the strong tendency for English towards liaison, it seems next to impossible to distinguish *you're gonna go* from *you gonna go.*[89] In rapid speech both are likely to be realized as /jəgənəˈgəʊ/. A rather broad ('enhanced') orthographic transcription scheme was adopted for the BNC. In such cases many transcribers can be expected to have inserted the auxiliary in its clitic form in order to produce grammatical sentences. Nonetheless, some instances of auxiliary deletion are attested, for example, the following two produced by a female teacher, aged 40:

(70)   I said you gonna call it Where's Wally? [book title] ... the children had been saying to John [pause] you gonna have a picture of yourself in Where's the Wally thing? (BNC KD0 465)

The fact that this example has two instances of BE deletion reduces the probability that this could be a typing error. What further adds to the credibility of these examples is that the whole passage is rather narrowly transcribed, including for instance the marking of pauses and items like *erm*.

5.8.2 Why WANT?

The development of WANT from nonmodal semantics in Middle English to a central member of the emerging modals is something of a mystery. There was certainly no way of predicting this development in Middle English. The rise of WANT would seem to contradict an observation made by Bybee & Pagliuca (1985: 72), that the morphs generally serving as sources for grammatical morphemes are characterized by "very frequent and general use." WISH had a much better starting position for a variety of reasons. For one thing, it was initially more frequent than WANT because it is older. For another, WISH already had volitional semantics in Old English, which WANT fully developed only in the 18th century. It is important to note, therefore, that frequency is not the only criterion which determines whether an item enters into grammaticalization. Bybee et al. (1994: 10) state that there is additionally "the reference plane of basic, irreducible notions – whether they concern existence or movement in space or psychological or social states, perspectives, and events – which serves as the basis for grammatical meaning in human languages." It remains a problem in the domain of volitional semantics, however, that an entirely new construction developed and spread at the expense of others that existed prior to it.

Phonological form, and therefore ultimately iconicity, might possibly be a motivating force again. WANT TO is structurally more similar to GOT TO and GOING TO than the older WISH or other rival candidates like DESIRE or INTEND.[90] Perhaps this helps to account for why WANT TO became the prime volitional modal after *will* had been grammaticalized as a future marker. But this is rather speculative and the motivations for the rise of WANT will have to await further investigation such as inquiries into field-internal developments.

5.8.3 Implications for grammaticalization theory

5.8.3.1 *A frequentative cut-off point in grammaticalization?*

Previous chapters have shown that auxiliary status in the English verbal domain correlates with a certain text frequency (approximately five occurrences per 10,000 words). This was apparently a threshold both synchronically for spontaneous speech and in diachronic change, where the steepest increase occurred precisely at those periods when this measure was exceeded. I considered whether this text frequency might actually constitute a cut-off point for grammatical status in the case of English verbs. The gravitation model helps to reconcile such a claim – which would certainly be too strong – with the numerous existing low-frequency counterexamples that enjoy grammatical status (here e.g. *ought to, shall*). In general, cut-off points are nonsensical. Nonetheless, it is noteworthy that highly productive items are capable of exerting noticeable influences on low-frequency items, while the reverse effect is much less likely (cf. Hooper 1976). The best solution, then, is not to regard high discourse frequency as criterial for grammatical status, but to see high frequency as a necessary criterion for achieving 'magnet' status or, more precisely, the status of a gravitational centre within a category. This at least is what the adapted gravitation formula used in the above simulations predicts. Items that exceed the frequency of semantically and structurally similar items by far (such as in the present case GOING TO, HAVE TO, WANT TO, HAVE GOT TO) will be the driving forces in their system, both in the formation of the category and in the attraction of new members.

5.8.3.2 *Apparent anti-unidirectionality in grammaticalization*

Tabor & Traugott (1998) hold the widely spread view that lexical verbs can gradually assume auxiliary status (which the present study seeks to underpin). Consonant with the unidirectionality claim in grammaticalization, which they call "a tantalizing idea," they rule out the reverse process: "We predict that there will be no such gradual development which changes an auxiliary verb into a main verb."

It was seen above that in British English the marginal modals NEED TO, OUGHT TO and DARE (TO) are currently acquiring ever more features of lexical verbs such as DO support and TO infinitives (see also Quirk et al. 1985: 140). This tendency is probably even more pronounced in American English. *Prima facie*, this observation presents a formidable challenge to the unidirectionality claim, because it affects three nonperipheral items. Additionally they belong to one class and the apparent drift towards lexical verb has been going on since Early Modern English, so that their development cannot be considered unique or sporadic. The same holds for the highly frequent deontic construction

HAVE TO, which has also assumed DO support at the expense of NOT negation.

Notice further that the developments of DARE, NEED, OUGHT and HAVE TO present counterevidence to Zipf's Principle of Economic Abbreviation: adding infinitival *to* or an operator DO to a construction makes it evidently longer. Moreover, the fact that today disyllabic pronunciations of deontic HAVE TO are preferred over cliticized, obsolescent HAVE TO (e.g. *I've to go*) is equally 'uneconomic'. While it seems clear that this economy principle simply does not enjoy universal applicability, unidirectionality can probably be saved.[91]

If we accept a claim made earlier (5.7.1), *viz.* that the English emerging auxiliaries should be considered proper auxiliaries, then the problem disappears altogether. On this view, the marginal modals would be changing from one auxiliary subdomain to another. That is to say, rather than move down or to the periphery from the focal point of central modals on the main verb – auxiliary cline, they move to the side. In other words, the marginal modals do not move towards main verb behaviour but towards the new focal point which is part of, not below or outside of, the auxiliary domain. Most other quasi-modals, however, that are attracted towards the class of emerging modals, become more grammaticalized. Perhaps it is more adequate to conceive of the main verb – auxiliary continuum not as a linear cline but as sets in a plane.

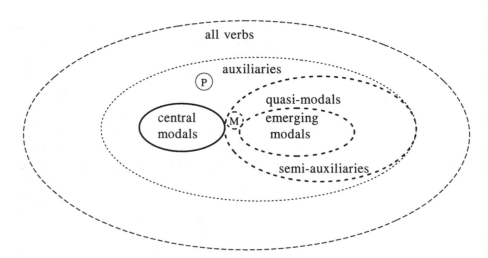

M stands for 'marginal modals'; P for 'primary verbs'.

Figure 5.12. Grammaticalization and assimilation among verb classes

On the most general level, Figure 5.12 tries to accommodate Heine's observation (1993: 129) that "any explanatory model that does not take the dynamics of linguistic evolution into consideration is likely to miss important insights into the nature of auxiliaries." Broken lines of an ellipsis indicate that a class is not completely closed, thus allowing for changes in categoriality. More specifically, Figure 5.12 is meant to capture the following aspects: first, the class of central modals was formed by a historical process of grammaticalization and is closed. Its members can reduce in number but new members are not admitted. Second, the class of emerging modals is a relatively closed class. Its grammaticalization is of limited productivity and it draws new members from the larger class of quasi-modals (including semi-auxiliaries), which in turn recruits new members from the open class of verbs. Auxiliarization of verbs, therefore, seems better described as *movement towards the centre* than as upward movement on a scale.[92] This representation leaves the unidirectionality hypothesis intact, since movement in the reverse direction should not occur.

Regardless of the representation of the cline, the problem remains *why* the marginal modals have changed and continue to do so. Linguistic distance as operationalized in the gravitation model seems to play a role. At least for OUGHT and NEED, one factor may be that they never were fully-fledged modal verbs. Throughout their history they have vacillated between full verb and auxiliary verb uses. DARE is different, it was a true modal. As for another potential factor, it is striking that, unlike the majority of central modals, DARE, NEED and OUGHT have no weak or even clitic forms. Perhaps this makes them similar to the emerging modals during the very early stages of category formation. Such a factor would again point to iconicity as a motivating force. But the existence of reduced forms is not a sufficient criterion since the same would apply to *may* and *might*, so that this problem cannot be solved at the present stage. What seems certain, however, is that we need not give up the 'tantalizing idea' of unidirectionality.

5.8.4 Inadequacies of the model, possible refinements and wider applications

The fit of the gravitation model could be increased by including further criteria. A possible candidate is the absence versus presence of phonemic structure /'CVCə/. On the syntactic side, refinements are possible too. For the marginal modals the existence of auxiliary constructions alongside lexical verb strategies was subsumed under a single criterion. More fine-grained syntactic distinctions (e.g. preferences in questions, negations or 3SG PRES) would obviously yield a more complete picture. For the phonological criteria only the dominant realization in spontaneous face-to-face interaction was taken into account. Including other variants would be more adequate. Furthermore, only integer values were assigned to the properties, with adjacent points on the clines consistently differing by one. Weightings might improve the results since some properties seem more important for category membership than others. For instance, the absence of *to* infinitives makes the central modals appear rather distant categorially from items that take only *to* complements. One might wish to rate such salient properties higher, but this has not been done in the present work because such a procedure might have suggested that an otherwise useless model was tuned to fit. I leave fine-tuning to future studies.

One might also wish to include a dynamic element in the model. It seems that items which are increasing rapidly are driving forces in the creation of a new focal point and they also appear to affect neighbouring items more strongly than relatively stable, or even decreasing older items. The gravitational constant could be assigned values that take into account diachronic increase (positive or higher values) or decrease (negative or lower values) of a given item.

One major problem remains for the model in the present state even if a greater number of distinctions and more fine-grained ones are made. Theoretically, an infinite number of items can be included in gravitational systems. However, the model will work best in a homogeneous environment. For instance, if we included all central modals in a simulation alongside the emerging modals, the items of each subgroup among themselves would create high influence scores, thus yielding a skewed overall picture. Forces pulling towards modal behaviour and forces pulling towards emerging-modal behaviour must clearly be kept apart. A possible solution would be to allow for positive and negative forces, which can neutralize or outweigh each other.

As was seen, using gravitation appears to be a promising way to model ongoing change in the domain of English auxiliaries. The gravitation model may have much wider applications in linguistics, though. Quite conceivably, it might prove useful in modelling analogical processes in general. Indeed, in principle any area of language where several forces compete seems to be a fruitful ground for gravitation theory. A strong point is that it can incorporate different degrees of productivity by assigning different values to the mass analogues in the original formula (p. 226). These will usually in one way or another correlate with frequency. Take for instance the German perfect or passive inflection. Some neologisms take only the dental formative, others additionally take the dental formative plus the prefix *ge-*. Hence *habe gefightet* 'have fought/worked hard', *habe ge-emailt* 'have written emails' or the particularly interesting *habe upgedatet* 'have updated' and *habe (ab)geloost (sic)* 'have lost' contrast with *habe computert* 'have worked on the computer' and *ist grammatikalisiert* 'is grammaticalized'. Evidently, donor language, phonemic structure and number of syllables play an important role in speakers' decision in favour of one or the other pattern. Such criteria would enter the formula as measures indicating distance. Other areas are nominalization or pluralization in languages where competing affixes are available. In other words, gravitation could be helpful for the investigation of extremely limited productivity, as in the present study. But it may also improve our understanding of highly productive grammatical processes (like pluralization or perfect and passive formation), and of processes in derivational morphology (like nominalization).

6   Conclusion

In this study I have focused on recent developments in the domain of English auxiliary verbs. Rather than rely on reinterpretations of previous research and rather than rely primarily on intuitions or theory-dependent premises, I chose a relatively theory-neutral, if broadly functional, approach with a strong emphasis on empirical research. Inductive and deductive methods were employed interactively: hypotheses were checked against independent corpus data, and often hypotheses actually emerged from inspection of the data. This approach was chosen to some extent out of sheer necessity (lack of adequate data), but also out of the conviction that new insights can be gained more readily from new data. An empirical approach seemed necessary because a survey of the literature on English auxiliary expressions reveals that conflict is often grounded in camp affiliations rather than in genuine efforts to make descriptive and explanatory progress (a prime example is the contraction debate discussed in Chapter 2). Moreover, where there is consensus, it is unfortunately not always well-founded. Sometimes it may simply arise from continuing assent to a once-made claim that seemed uncontroversial at the time it was made; or it may go back to a venerable researcher (like, for instance, Jespersen or Visser) whose outstanding authority few dare to question.

Needless to say, I do not claim to have offered an exhaustive account of recent developments in the English auxiliary domain. However, I have included what in my opinion ought to be integrated in future work. As a detailed study of auxiliarization, this work is also meant to contribute to the synchronic understanding of the auxiliary category, and of grammaticalization in general. Such matters are outlined in what follows. Generalizations and explanations were sought in the previous chapter already, and areas for potentially fruitful future research were identified along the way. A comprehensive summary is therefore not required here. If one sentence were to capture the results of this study, it would probably be that ample evidence has been presented for "the primary hypothesis of functionalist or usage-based linguistics," *viz.* "that language use shapes grammar" (Bybee & Scheibman forth-coming). A similarly general result is that a linguistic commonplace is fully confirmed: grammatical change indeed spreads gradually and takes centuries (e.g. Aitchison 1991: Ch. 7; Trudgill 1998). Somewhat more exciting is the finding that change is not always slow, but that there are stages of rapid development. As in previous research, the famous S-curve with its rumba pattern 'slow-quick-quick-slow' has been helpful in describing the spread of the changes throughout this investigation.

More specific claims have been made, too. I have proposed that a new category of modal expressions is currently emerging. Stating the evolution of new categories is by no means a new idea in grammaticalization research either. In fact, it can be traced in the earliest proponents of the theory:

> La 'grammaticalisation' de certains mots crée des formes neuves, **introduit des catégories** qui n'avaient pas d'expression linguistique, **transforme l'ensemble du système**. Meillet (1912: 387; my emphasis)

> (The 'grammaticalization' of certain words creates new forms and **introduces categories** which had no linguistic expression; **it changes the organization of the system**.)

It appears, however, that Meillet's view is too narrow. As was seen, grammaticalization can create (sub)categories which *did* have a linguistic expression before: modal categories as such are not new to English, but the category of emerging modals is. This coexistence of newer and older expressions in a functional domain is also what more recent work, in particular Hopper's (1991) principle of layering, would lead one to expect.

Meillet's statement also brings us full circle to the initially quoted (Ch. 1) received wisdom in linguistics, according to which a 'wholesale reorganization' (Bolinger 1980a) is currently affecting the English auxiliary system. This, at least, is now empirically well-founded. I hope that the present work can be seen as a modest step towards a better understanding of this process. Let us now turn to a brief summary of the major points which were made in the previous chapters.

This study stresses the pervasive influence of **text frequency** in the development of language and the usefulness of this measure in linguistic descriptions and explanations. This in turn brings us full circle to another point mentioned in Chapter 1, *viz.* Hopper & Traugott's observation of "an urgent need for additional reliable statistical studies" (1993: 112). They (*ibid.*) have pointed out that "more work is necessary to diagnose grammaticalization in its early stages and to develop the kinds of statistical parameters which will reveal it." While this remains true, it is hoped that the present study can contribute to overcoming this gap in our knowledge.

On the basis of the previous chapters, four particular points are worth making as far as frequency is concerned. First, on the diachronic dimension, textual frequency proves helpful in spotting important stages of individual changes. The changes that led to the modalization and spread of HAVE GOT TO, WANT TO and BE GOING TO have occurred essentially since Early Modern English. HAVE TO is much older, BE GOING TO is slightly older. Generally, after several centuries of rather marginal occurrence, leaps in discourse frequency in both British and American English can be observed. One can be more specific for fictional writing and drama (the latter was generally seen to be a good approximation of spoken language): regardless of the age of the individual constructions, clusters of rapid changes are found in the 19th century and the early 20th century.

A second frequency-related point is that statistical studies in apparent time prove helpful for charting when the spread of a given modal construction (i.e. a whole paradigm such as WANT TO, including all variants) comes to a halt. Apparent-time studies also show whether specific innovative variants (e.g. *wanna, gonna, gotta*) are still spreading or have reached saturation stages in a given speech community.

Third and perhaps most important, frequency seems to be a fundamental parameter in the genesis of the new category. It not only helps to determine scores of mutual influence between several items in the field of emerging modals; it also helps to isolate degrees of prototypicality and to identify an abstract prototype within that field.

The fourth point regarding text frequency, finally, is that this parameter enters crucially into discerning the motivation behind the changes which are currently affecting NEED (TO), DARE (TO) and OUGHT TO. It ties in with the above observations that Warner (1993), building on Rosch's work, assumes an intricate relationship between category formation and frequency gains:

> More speculatively, in some circumstances an increase in frequency and salience of items or attributes may make a category more coherent and distinct. (Warner 1993: 238)

The present work lends full support to Warner's assumption. Furthermore, it has somewhat specified the relevant circumstances: semantic and structural similarity of prospective new members, for instance, appear to be prerequisites for the process. Furthermore, it is argued that frequency is a chief motivating force in the creation of phonological similarity. Considering the history of the central modals, it would not be altogether surprising if in the future the tendency towards maximization of shared attributes extended from the level of phonology to syntactic properties for the emerging modals, too. Let us integrate Warner's observations and my empirical results into Heine's discussion of frequency, erosion and iconicity. Heine (1993: 111f) maintains that "it is the pragmatic factor of frequency of use that appears to be most immediately responsible for erosion." He suggests the following chronological order:

(1)   Desemanticization > High frequency > Loss of information value > Erosion

Heine (*ibid.*) rightly suspects that this sequence "has to be taken with care, and it may require reconsideration in the light of a more adequate empirical basis than is now available." While it is not fully clear to me where to draw the line between 'Desemanticization' and 'Loss of information value', I fully agree with him when he points out that this sequence "does not take care of the fact that, rather than succeeding each other, the four processes overlap or may even be ongoing simultaneously" (*ibid.*). If the present study provides 'a more adequate empirical basis' than was available in 1993, then drastic frequency gains and phonological erosion indeed occur in sync. Another issue Heine raises may have become somewhat clearer now:

> The sequence [given in (1)] does not account for all the forces that can be held responsible for erosion; the question as to how this sequence relates to the parameter of **iconic coding**, for example, remains entirely open to further research. (1993: 111f; emphasis added)

I have suggested that iconic coding and erosion need not necessarily be counterforces. For the items under investigation, different reduction processes are leading to very similar products of univerbation. Similarity of their phonological structure is patent but, to some extent, similarity of their morphosyntactic properties can be observed, too. *Wanna, gonna* and *gotta* have assumed various features that are typical of modal verbs in general, and of the category of emerging modals in particular. Hence, the result of different processes of modalization is a fairly homogeneous set of items. On this basis and on the basis of Fischer's (1999) considerations on associative iconicity, it was argued that erosion may give rise to a new, more abstract type of iconicity: rather than betray the etymological origin of an item (i.e. syntagmatic transparency or iconicity), the newly developed type of **paradigmatic iconicity** indicates category membership. The question whether this is a general principle of grammaticalization certainly deserves more attention and calls for further research based on crosslinguistic comparison.

Even though the items investigated here are developing certain modal features also found with the central modals (*will, would, may, might, can, could, shall, should, must*), according to the dynamic model of categorization proposed above, the emerging modals will not assume all characteristics of the central modals. They are more likely to keep streamlining on the model of the prototype of their own category. Thus, seemingly unmotivated digressions from the standard grammar in informal British and American varieties – such as DO support with GOT TO – receive a systematic explanation. Further, just as it is possible to show that grammaticalization in the field of emerging modals leads to increased paradigmatic iconicity, so it is possible to demonstrate that grammaticalization is responsible for incipient isomorphism, because early signs of a functional split can be identified (e.g. modal *gonna, gotta* + infinitive vs. nonmodal *going to, got to* + NP).

In the early phase after the revival of grammaticalization research in the 1980s, work focused on syntactic aspects. Since the late 1980s, attention has shifted to semantic and pragmatic aspects (e.g. Brinton 1988; Traugott 1988ff; Sweetser 1988, 1990; Bybee et al. 1991, 1994; Heine et al. 1991). While this study recognizes the importance of both formal and semantic domains, it also stresses the role of phonology in grammaticalization (cf. Bybee & Thompson forthcoming). If the present data are significant for the framework of grammaticalization more generally, then phonetic variation and phonological developments must not be seen as epiphenomenal. Indeed, they can be a major force in the early stages of category formation. Taken together with the observed importance of frequency, it seems an obvious step to assume that discourse factors (i.e. speech production and perception) play a fundamental role in grammaticalization.

Grammaticalization research focusing on the interaction between phonology, morphosyntax and semantics, but paying particular attention to phonetic detail, is therefore likely to yield interesting results.[1] One possible project would be to investigate the layers for 'intention' in English. One might suspect that a new layer is emerging in that domain. Bybee and Thompson (forthcoming) observe that *I'm gonna* is often reduced to /ˈaɪmənə/. In common propositions, reduction is often more drastic. Consider:

(2)   ['ɑnə'goʊrə'taʊn] for *I'm gonna/wanna go to town.*

In (2) the history of clitic /nə/ is ambiguous since it can be regularly derived from either *wanna* or *gonna*.[2] Crucially, etymology does not make a difference, since for 'intention' there is referential identity between the two items. More detailed investigations into historical developments within such semantic fields as volition/intention/future or obligation/necessity are bound to yield interesting results, too.

To resume the summary of the main points: it emerges very clearly from the analysis that the rise of the three most prototypical new modals – HAVE GOT TO, BE GOING TO and WANT TO – are **natural changes from below**. It is further likely that in the long run their contracted variants will become the new spoken standard in all varieties of English. Already, this appears to be the situation in American English (Pullum 1998: 82). And for British English, too, there is at least a statistical likelihood for this to happen given (a) the results of the apparent-time studies and (b) the fact that women consistently lead these particular changes in Britain (cf. Labov 1990).

As far as **regional variation** is concerned, present-day American English was usually seen to be in the vanguard of change, regardless of whether a change originated in the United States or in Britain. This fact tallies with the hypothesis that we are dealing with changes from below that will become standard. After all, new norms in world English typically converge on American usage (Marckwardt & Quirk 1965; Greenbaum 1990: 18; Hundt 1996: 134f; Mair 1998; Trudgill 1998). However, it is not considered important where the constructions and subsequent changes were first attested, since we can safely assume that we are dealing with independent developments. Cross-Atlantic influence need not and should not be invoked for natural grammatical changes which spread by face-to-face interaction – and not through the media, as is sometimes believed (cf. Trudgill 1998). It is much more appropriate, then, to say that American English appears to be leading world English in this area of grammar.[3]

Still on the diatopic dimension, regional spread within Britain from the South to the North seems to be a recurrent path. Different from the cross-Atlantic dimension, however, this path strongly supports contact theories (more exactly: the wave model) for the geographical diffusion of the observed changes. Changing patterns of preference along a regional cline with neighbouring areas behaving similarly and the political and cultural centre representing the centre of gravity are probably best explained as changes that spread through the encounter of idiolects.

Similar **semantic developments** can be observed for all items under investigation. Traugott (1996) has identified three major forces in semantic change: subjectification, metonymy-driven inferencing and metaphor. In the present study the first two in particular proved helpful in accounting for the observed changes. It was suggested that subjectification and other types of pragmatic inferences are not only crucial in the development of epistemic from deontic senses, a point which is commonly stated in the literature on modality; they also seem to be operating in the rise of modal from nonmodal semantics (e.g. 'lack' > 'volition'; 'possession' > 'obligation'). Consistent with established theory (Kronasser's law, 1952), the source domains for modality in the present study were concrete lexical notions. Progressively, extension to more abstract meanings occurred. Thus, in the present study, the prime mechanism of change in both the rise of modal meanings and extensions within the modal domain is not metaphor but the conventionalization of pragmatic inferences.

Further, we saw similar **motivations** for the emergence of the individual modal constructions and for the new layer of emerging modals in general. Two prime factors can be isolated. The first is the well-known creative force of expressivity, which is already mentioned in Meillet's (1912) work. It is semantic-pragmatic in nature and intimately connected with the tendency for older layers to erode semantically. The second factor is information processing, and closely connected with phonological erosion. As far as the relationship between the two is concerned, it seems reasonable to assume that the creation of new layers is triggered primarily by the semantic erosion of older items. And while semantic erosion continues to be operative at later stages, it is the phonological erosion of the old inventory (e.g. *'ll, 'd*) which additionally promotes the spread of the disyllabic new-layer items investigated here (e.g. *gonna, hafta*).

Two models were suggested, one rather general for the spread of change within a language, the other more specific for change in the field of emerging English modals. The former is meant to capture the **interaction between several varieties** in the diffusion of natural change from below. It tries to account for the fact that different spoken and written varieties are affected by change at different rates. It was seen repeatedly that less prestigious varieties are ahead in individual changes, thus further attesting to the fact that we were dealing with changes from below.[4] It is argued that informal spoken language ultimately triggers most such changes. But change is mediated in more complex ways by interaction between written and spoken registers. The respective speeds of change in turn seem to depend largely on the degree of codification of a given register, where codification is conventionalized by use. Once representative samples for given varieties (e.g. regional) are available, this will allow one to determine degrees of progressiveness for any one feature. If, say, regional (national or intranational) patterns were recurrent, one might rank varieties in terms of progressiveness more confidently than is possible at the present stage.[5]

The second model is an attempt at a dynamic approach to categorization. It is an analogy to **gravitational fields**, and is meant to capture the interaction between several items in a given functional domain. If the model is correct, mutual influence correlates with textual frequency as well as with formal and phonological similarity. The rudimentary nature of the two models leads me to some concluding remarks on potentially fruitful future research. It is patent that both models could be considerably refined by adding (a) criteria to the gravitation model or (b) registers to the interaction of genres model. It also remains to be seen whether the gravitation model is helpful in accounting for developments in other domains like nominalization, as was tentatively suggested.

The modal domain itself is still a highly promising research area. Much closer investigation of American English and its relation to British English is required than was possible here. The completion of the Santa Barbara Corpus of Spoken English (see Chafe et al. 1991 for an outline) will make such work more feasible. Other national varieties, including creole-based languages need to be compared to the present data. Closer examination of the historical changes which affected the marginal modals NEED (TO), OUGHT TO and DARE is needed too. The jury on their relation to the unidirectionality claim in grammaticalization is probably still out. Moreover, despite a vast number of studies on the central modals, we still have too little frequentative information about their history (Kytö 1991 is a valuable starting point). According to the literature, some central modals (in particular *shall, must* and *may*) have been dying for centuries. We want to know how dead they really are, how their decline has come about and how lively other modals are. Biber et al.'s work (1998: Ch. 8.2; 1999: Ch. 6.6) is a first step in this direction.

Many other items seem worth investigating which were excluded from the present study primarily because they are less frequent than the emerging modals. Additionally, this helped to avoid a semantic and syntactic heterogeneity of items that would have been difficult to handle within a single study. There is a group of relatively common verbs serving auxiliary functions which certainly merits a study in its own right. Its members conventionalize such *Aktionsarten* as frequentative, iterative or continuative (KEEP, GO *on*); inceptive or ingressive like START, BEGIN or TAKE *to*; terminative (STOP); or conative like TRY.[6] Other items related to the modal domain which seem to be undergoing interesting developments are HAD BETTER and adhortative *let's*.[7] The latter is interesting because a synonymous invariant marker (*uton*) once existed but dropped out of use in early Middle English (Warner 1993: 186). This fact makes the emergence of a new adhortative marker look like a functionally motivated therapeutical change.

Of particular interest to the study of grammaticalization are those items which permit a variety of complementation strategies. For instance, the following patterns found with constructions that are related to the auxiliary domain are worth investigating:

- bare infinitive (e.g. HELP)
- *and* plus bare infinitive (e.g. TRY, GO, COME)
- *to* infinitive (e.g. BEGIN, START, HELP, COME, PLAN, BE *trying*)
- gerundial complements (e.g. KEEP, START, TRY)
- preposition followed by gerundial complement (KEEP *on*, BE *planning on*)

Investigation into the histories of newer and older variants can be expected to shed new light on the phenomenon of layering. Also, the whole area of complex complementation like *want/help sb. to do sthg.* was excluded from the present study. And even for the constructions looked at in some detail here, semantic nuances could hardly be tackled within the scope of a single study, so that much work still remains to be done.

Moreover, a whole group of quasi-auxiliaries ought to be investigated within a single study because they seem to constitute a subclass. The members of this class contain three elements: one is adjectival, participial or prepositional and invariant; their verbal element which inflects for tense etc. is BE; like the emerging modals they take *to* infinitives. Relevant items are BE *(un)able to*, BE *about to*, BE *allowed to*, BE *bound to*, BE *due to*, BE *expected to*, BE *likely to*, BE *meant to*, BE *obliged to*, BE *supposed to*, BE *(un)willing to*. Related is BE *to*. It is not inconceivable that gravitation models hold potential for this group of items. From the above considerations it is evident that verbal complementation in the tense-aspect-mood-modality complex remains a fascinating area which is full of riddles still awaiting further exploration.

Although this study is restricted to English, it provides some hypotheses which can be tested in crosslinguistic work on verbal grammaticalization. The discussion of unidirectionality has yielded the result that traditional one-dimensional verbal clines (or continua, scales) between lexical verbs and central modals are less than ideal. I have suggested that verbal grammaticalization is better seen as movement in space towards certain centres. Due to the restrictions imposed by having to plot models on paper, a two-dimensional grammaticalization diagram was proposed. It goes without saying that a three-dimensional model would be more appropriate. The same is true for the gravitation model. The models yielded plausible results for emerging English modals. It remains to be seen whether similar approaches lead to descriptive progress for auxiliarization processes in other languages or for the investigation of productivity in different grammatical domains. It seems clear, however, that only a dynamic approach to categorization which adopts discourse frequency as an important parameter will lead to a more complete understanding of verbal grammaticalization in any living language.

Notes

Chapter 1

1. The scarcity of frequentative grammaticalization research has been noted by Hopper & Traugott (1993: 112): "There is an urgent need for additional reliable statistical studies of a variety of phenomena in which early grammaticalization appears to be involved."
2. The term *auxiliation* was originally coined by Benveniste (1968). In the present work I will follow the tradition of most European-based studies in grammatic(al)ization, which use the longer terms. For the sake of simplicity, groups of phonological variants are given above as orthographic variants. That this is a crude simplification needs no comment. More phonetic detail will be provided in the empirical chapters.
3. See Croft (1995) for a clarification of autonomy and functionalist claims. Perhaps in recognition of this, in Hopper's revised version the omnipresence of flux is stressed to a lesser extent. Notice in particular the following revision: "The notion of Emergent Grammar is meant to suggest that structure, or regularity, comes out of discourse and is shaped by discourse *as much as it shapes discourse* in an on-going process." (1987: 142, italics added; the italicized words are omitted in 1998: 156).

    It must be conceded, however, that the diminished role of flux in this passage is nearly outweighed by rather strong claims made in another place, where the difference between *emergent* and *emerging* is discussed (1998: 157): "The term *emerging* might be applied to a subsystem that is becoming part of an already existing grammar, for example, one might speak of an 'emerging definite article', ..." While such a use of *emerging* is indeed intended in the present study, none of the following possible implications is:

    > The form might then be thought of as an incomplete definite article, ... However, this perspective still presupposes that there is a fixed code, and understands a form to be on the way to occupying its rightful place in the synchronic grammatical system. It sees the incompleteness of the category to be in some sense a deficiency that the language is working teleologically to correct. (1998: 157)

Chapter 2

1. On the recent reassessment of the dichotomy between internally and externally motivated language change, see Romaine (1995), Newmeyer (1998: Ch. 3) or Mufwene (forthcoming).
2. In a recent article, however, Croft (1995) demonstrates that not all functionalist approaches are inconsonant with structuralist-generativist autonomy claims. He argues that "the structuralist-functionalist dichotomy is a continuum" (1995: 491) and that the two different camps are not quite as fundamentally different as much of the – partly rather polemical – literature suggests.
3. For a discussion of approaches that are commonly associated with functionalism and their links with related theories such as cognitive grammar, functional typology and grammaticalization, see Harris & Campbell (1995: Ch. 2) or Croft (1990; 1995).
4. Compare Hopper & Traugott's (1993: 7) cline of grammaticality (*content item > grammatical word > clitic > inflectional affix*). This not only provides a grid for the synchronic categorization of different linguistic items, but it also outlines the typical historical grammaticalization path for any given item.
5. Compare also Hopper's (1987, 1998) related concept of emergent grammar.
6. More detailed reviews of the history of grammaticalization research are given in Lehmann (1995 [1982]: 1-9) or Heine et al. (1991: 5-26).
7. They are not fully congruent, of course. For an excellent summary and comparison of the two approaches, see Croft (1990: 230-239).
8. For reasons that will become evident below, I refrain from labelling this line of research *dialectology*.
9. EUROTYP stands for the international research programme "Typology of European Languages" of the European Science Foundation. GRAMCATS is short for the research programme and the database compiled for "A Cross-Linguistic Study of Grammatical Categories" at the University of New Mexico at Albuquerque (see Bybee et al. 1994: xv-xix).
10. Mufwene (1996a) for instance takes contact not only to be the critical factor in the genesis of African-American English (AAE) but also in the development of nonstandard white American varieties of English (WAVEs).
11. See Chambers & Trudgill (1998) for a thorough exposition of both approaches.
12. My emphasis. This is certainly the most concise summary of recent trends. Schneider says essentially the same in his introduction to the book proper (1996: 1-12), but the crisp version quoted above appears only in semipublished form (*Varieties of English Around the World: New Titles and Complete Series List,* 1995).
13. Much of this neglect is due to lack of adequate sources. While relatively small databases suffice for phonological studies, much larger ones are required for the study of syntax. With the availability of the BNC, syntax studies have become somewhat more feasible (but see the notes of caution in 2.7.3).

14. The reverse trend seems to hold for American dialects (cf. Mufwene 1996a).

15. For a more comprehensive survey and brief descriptions of English corpus projects, see Taylor et al. (1991: 319-54); McEnery & Wilson (1996: 181-87). For a more detailed description of English diachronic corpora, see papers in Kytö et al. (1994). The sources used in the present study are described in more detail in Chapter 2.7 below.

16. Harris (1987) adopts a similarly wide view of the auxiliary (AUX) category.

17. All of these notions themselves have given rise to much debate, but that need not concern us here.

18. See Bybee et al. (1994: *passim*) or Bybee 1999a. Compare also the discussions in the chapters on grammaticalization and economy.

19. The nearest approximation to that speech variety in the BNC is provided by the SARA search option DIV, which opens a data base approximately equivalent to the demographic sample (Aston & Burnard 1998: 113). According to Tony Dodd (BNC discussion list, 29 Feb. 2000), the 100 DIV-marked texts contain 3,949,806 words.

20. Biber et al. (1999: Ch. 5) provide a helpful inventory of the 112 most common lexical verbs in four registers of British English (conversation, fiction, news, academic writing). For the present study fresh corpus research seemed necessary since Biber et al. limit their searches to lexemes. That is, they do not distinguish between, for instance, *want* + NP and *want to* + base form of the verb. For obvious reasons, I list separately high-frequency verbs related to the modal realm that take infinitival *to* complements (e.g. GOING TO, NEED TO, SUPPOSED TO, USED TO, TRY TO, LIKE TO).

21. Notice that Figure 2.1 does not list phrasal or prepositional verbs. This is not needed for the present purposes since they do not commonly take infinitival complements.

22. A decision on whether a given verb ought to be granted grammatical status is necessarily arbitrary to some extent since grammaticalization is a gradient concept (Hopper & Traugott 1993: 7). Quirk et al.'s (1985) work suggests itself as a reference point as it is the most comprehensive descriptive English grammar currently available.

23. The enclitic forms *'ll* and modal *'d* are treated as items in their own right since they are, if debatably, potentially ambiguous. The figures for BE, GO, HAVE, GET, WANT and LIKE do not include forms of BE GOING TO, HAVE TO, HAVE GOT TO, WANT TO and LIKE TO. The chart is generally based on phrase searches in the BNC, which is a sufficient estimator for most items at this stage. However, frequent word forms that are ambiguous between verbal and nominal, adjectival or prepositional status (such as *being, thought, like(s), use(s), considering, might*) were disambiguated with the help of the part-of-speech option.

24. For a synchronic description see, for instance, Quirk et al. (1985: 120-35). On their diachronic developments see the relevant chapters in Denison (1993).

25. Consider in particular cases like *you see, I see, you know, I know* or *I mean*. For MEAN clearly adjectival and nominal uses were of course not considered.

26. This is particularly true for ongoing changes: "What we *are* short of are detailed records of language changes actually in progress" (Aitchison 1991: 31). As far as grammaticalization is concerned, unfortunately even some of the fundamental claims (e.g. unidirectionality) and criteria (e.g. decrease in scope, increase in bonding) are not unanimously agreed.

27. Predictions based on synchronic variation patterns will of course be enhanced by exploiting grammaticalization theory. This makes very explicit claims about which synchronic variants are etymologically younger, i.e. less grammaticalized, and which older, i.e. more grammaticalized (see, for instance, Heine et al. 1991: 156-61).

28. Denison might have added Mitchell's (1985) more recent two-volume grammar on Old English, which I shall consult too, of course.

29. When the statistical analyses for the present study were conducted, only the prefinal versions of FLOB and Frown were available. Cross-checking with the published corpora, however, showed that the versions are virtually identical. Corpora for further varieties (Indian, Australian, New Zealand English) modelled on Brown are available. Their investigation, however, lies outside the confines of the present study. For detailed information on the four corpora used here see the respective manuals (Francis & Kučera 1989; Johansson et al. 1978; Hundt et al.1998; 1999).

30. For more elaborate distinctions between spoken and written varieties see, for instance, Koch & Oesterreicher (1985). Particularly helpful seems their distinction between conceptually and medially spoken or written texts (1985: 17-23). In essence, they posit a categorical dividing line for the medium only: 'graphic' versus 'phonic' 'code' (or 'medium'). For their second parameter, 'conception', they propose a continuum between the poles 'spoken' and 'written'. This is to say that, conceptually, there is a gradient between two ideal modes: one typically spoken communicative strategy and one typically written communicative strategy with various intermediate stages (cf. Hymes 1967 and Biber 1988 for related frameworks).

31. More detailed descriptions of the BNC sampling process and text types covered are provided in Aston & Burnard (1998: 28-32) and Burnard (ed., 1995: 19-24).

32. Judging from the spelling mistakes in the BNC, the tone of his article seems slightly too optimistic, though. Cf. e.g.: "Each transcriber was trained over a period of several weeks during which time transcripts were carefully monitored. For particularly strong regional accents we recruited transcribers who were familiar with the accents" (1995: 227).

33. I do not conduct investigations into socioeconomic class because this parameter is tagged rather unreliably in the BNC.

34. Many competing terms and more fine-grained differentiations exist, including *alethic, dynamic, facultative, evidential* or *existential* types of modality. These need not concern us here; for detailed discussion see the aforementioned works. *Root modality* is used by many researchers synonymously with *deontic modality*. This is partially motivated by the fact that deontic modality often serves as the source domain for the development of epistemic meanings (see especially Sweetser 1990; Coates 1995).

35. Witness, for instance, Coates (1983: 169): "insofar as futurity always involves an element of doubt or uncertainty, it inevitably overlaps with modality." In a related fashion, Bybee et al. (1994: 280) state: "We have argued here and earlier ... that the central functions in future grams [short for *grammatical morphemes*] are intention and prediction. It follows from this that future is less a temporal category and more a category resembling agent-oriented and epistemic modality, with important temporal implications."

36. Cf. the adaptations in Westney (1995: 17) or Traugott (1997: 192).

37. Important contributions to the debate not mentioned above include Andrews (1978); Aoun & Lightfoot (1984); Bouchard (1986); Browning (1991); Chomsky & Lasnik (1977; 1978); Goodall (1991); Jaeggly (1980); Lightfoot (1976; 1986); Postal & Pullum (1978; 1986); Pullum & Postal (1979); Pullum & Zwicky (1988). Many of the papers were published in *Linguistic Inquiry*, three of them in the moratorium edition alone.

38. Pullum's British acquaintances, for instance, "do not really find *wanna* a natural item in their speech" (1997: 97). As will be borne out by the empirical chapters, this is possibly attributable either to the age of his contacts or to the fact that British English has changed since he left the British Isles.

39. From Pullum's wording it is unfortunately not clear whether he refers to marginal acceptability or marginal discourse frequency. Both seem correct.

40. Not surprisingly, in 100m words of contemporary spoken and written British English (BNC) not a single occurrence of *I want to/wanna be precise* can be found. Against the backdrop of such examples, Chomsky's (1986: 151) statement that externalized language "has no status in linguistic theory" gives rise to inferences that are probably not intended by the author. Occasionally natural language as such seems to have no status in some strands of linguistic theory.

Chapter 3

1. In addition to Fleischman, compare also Price's (1971: 200) analysis for some Romance analogues of HAVE TO. As for English, Mitchell (1985, I: 401-402) dismisses a host of examples presented in the relevant literature as proof of obligative semantics for HAVE TO in late Old English. But even though Mitchell does not agree with van der Gaaf's and Visser's interpretations of individual examples, he does not invalidate the general path of development outlined by the former. His conclusion (1985, I: 402), in fact, seems almost irrelevant to the argument: "As always, *we* [today] can see the writing on the wall [i.e. the rise of obligative semantics for HAVE TO]. I do not think that it was visible to the Anglo-Saxons in this particular instance." Probably changes in progress such as this one are typically not 'visible' to the contemporary language users.

2. It remains a fact, though, that Fischer's (1994) interesting word order-driven account is the only analysis that diverges in major ways from the traditional account. Much in her analysis hinges on the exceptionally wide view she takes of 'possession', which rules out 'obligation' readings for all HAVE TO examples prior to Early Modern English – despite openly admitting to the contrary (1994: 142). This, of course, somewhat weakens the force of her argument.

3. On the grammaticalization of 'possession' see Heine (1998).

4. Notations for understood elements are of course highly theory-dependent, but the use of different notations would not affect the general argument presented here. Even assigning clause boundaries is to some extent model-dependent, but potentially controversial issues like verbless clauses (sometimes referred to as 'small clauses') play no role in the present case.

5. Cf. Fleischman (1982); Hopper & Traugott (1993: 2-4, 42-44, 61); Heine (1993: 42, 118) on BE GOING TO, HAVE TO and the Romance inflectional future.

6. Similar statements in later work include Fleischman (1982: 59) and Bolinger (1980b: 293). Interestingly, Francis (1958: 258) considers /gontə/ the typical pronunciation for *going to*. Present-day work (e.g. Bybee & Thompson forthcoming), by contrast, assumes no residual /t/, which perhaps partly explains the recent spread of the spelling *gonna*. It must be added, though, that Francis' transcription does not rule out lenition or deletion of /t/ (cf. common pronunciations of *winter* in American English).

   As far as assimilation in *have to* is concerned, the first recorded spelling of *hafta* in the *OED* (*s.v. hafta*) is from 1941. This may be a reflection of Kenyon & Knott's observation (1944: *s.v. have*) that "*the pron*[*unciation*] 'hæftə, 'hæftʊ *is universal in unaffected familiar speech in US and England*" (italics and bold original). In Palmer & Blandford ([3]1969: 125, 135), by contrast, *have* in *have to* is consistently transcribed as having final /v/. But this does not necessarily rule assimilation out since the work does not focus on word-boundary assimilation processes. In general, however, unlike *gonna* and *wanna*, *hafta* is rarely recorded in pronunciation dictionaries (even in the late 20th century, cf. Windsor-Lewis 1972; Wells 1990; Jones 1997).

7. In addition, semantic or textual factors come into play, but they do not affect the general argument presented. While *really* in Tables 3.2 and 3.3 is best classified as an 'intensifier', *actually* generally serves as an 'assumption correcting' device.

8. *Prima facie* it might appear that there is little if any bonding between subject and HAVE, and that it would be more adequate not to include this last group in the cline of bondedness. While it is true that the subject position can be occupied by members of the open class of nouns, this group is nevertheless included here since in actual spoken discourse subjects are typically pronouns.

9. On the relationship between reanalysis, actualization and grammaticalization see Harris & Campbell (1995: 77-89) or Haspelmath (1998).

10. An apokoinou analysis might also be profitably applied to a previous problematic case. Recall the discussion of stage (III) in Heine's account of the development of modal HAVE TO (p. 55):

    (III)   I have a letter to write,

where the high degree of clause fusion seemed to undermine all previous attempts at analysis. Notice, however, that if HAVE is analysed as apokoinou here, this use is no longer covered by Bußmann's narrow definition of the term, because HAVE in (III) very clearly stands in the first clause – always assuming that there are indeed two clauses. However, other authorities of English grammar subscribe to a much wider notion of the term which would cover the above case, e.g. Mitchell (1985, II: 905), who quotes Meritt's (1938: 3-7) definition: "In general the term applies to that feature of language wherein it seems necessary to understand a word twice although it is expressed but once. ... It is a kind of verbal economy: a word or closely related group of words, expressed but a single time, serves at once a twofold grammatical construction." Meritt's definition is wide in two respects: firstly, he does not limit the term *apokoinou* to words but includes larger units (which is consistent with Bußmann). Secondly, and more significantly, Meritt – unlike Bußmann – does not restrict the possible reference of an apokoinou to two neighbouring sentences, but uses the term 'portions of discourse' (p. 16). This can relate to both smaller units (e.g. words) and larger units (e.g. longer stretches of discourse) than Bußmann's definition. In any case, then, and irrespective of definitional issues, what this discussion demonstrates is that a biclausal analysis is debatable as early as stage (III).

11. For an outline of the notion of subjectification, see Traugott (1988, 1989, 1995 or 1996). Notice that her concept of subjectification does not merely describe the process that leads to one traditionally observed semantic property of modals, *viz.* subjectivity. On the one hand, Traugott's term is more specific in that it gives the details of the process while allowing for degrees of subjectivity. On the other hand, however, it is more general since it is shown to apply to many areas of language change.

More specifically, Traugott's use of *subjective* is closely related to Lyon's (1977: 792) concept of *subjectivity* observed for epistemic modality. However, it is necessary to keep Traugott's use of *subjective* apart from the common use of *subjective deontic modality* which contrasts with *objective deonticity* (cf. Lyons 1977: 792f, 833; Palmer 1989: 7, 10f, 131; Warner 1993: 15). The latter dichotomy refers to the fact that the source of an obligation or permission can be either the speaker's authority (giving subjective modality); or it can lie outside the speaker, which is then considered a case of objective (or nonsubjective) deontic modality.

12. Some analysts might take issue with the fact that Traugott's HAVE TO examples are past. Since, however, HAVE TO expresses a strong (usually external) obligation, the inference from present-tense *You have to go* to *You probably will go* is typically invited, too. After all, futures are commonly derived from constructions like HAVE TO (e.g. Romance futures).

13. That HAVE GOT TO existed also in American English at this early stage can be derived from its mention (as being incorrect) in a grammar from 1829 (Webster 1996: *s.v. have got*).

14. In the spoken component of the British National Corpus, approximately 9,000 occurrences of modal *got to* and *gotta* compare with some 6,000 instances of *must*.

15. The alternative scenario is sketched in Krug (1998c).

16. In the example from Oscar Wilde (13), however, neither *have* is rendered in its reduced form. But then, clitic forms of HAVE rarely occur in Wilde's comedies, a fact that seems attributable more to the (spelling) conventions applying to the contemporary comedy of manners and to Wilde's literary aspirations than to actual speech behaviour of the upper classes at the time. It is difficult to believe, for instance, that auxiliary HAVE was very rarely reduced in upper crust speech of Wilde's times, when contractions like *I've* can at least be traced back to Shakespearean times. The matter is of course more complex: English seems to have changed track from eliding the final phonemes of HAVE – resulting in forms like *ha*, particularly common in auxiliary function in Middle and Early Modern English – to the now current elision of the stem vowel resulting in encliticization.

17. As this book goes to press, I learn that the same point is made independently by Gronemeyer (1999; I am grateful to Marianne Hundt for bringing this article to my notice. Gronemeyer (1999: 34) bases her claim not so much on historical data but on a principle referred to by Croft as 'intraference':

> the development of obligation *got to* ... is the result of an analogy with *have to*. This very fast development is aided by the fact that the stative use of *got* is already well established at this time [i.e. 19th late century]. The use of *got to* in the same sense as *have to* is a clear case of what Croft ... has called 'intraference' – a language-internal analog of interlingual interference ... Intraference occurs when two linguistic units are similar enough (especially in meaning) to be used interchangeably to express the same content.

18. According to Haiman (1994a, c), grammaticalization is a type of ritualization, which is essentially comes into being by repetition. The following aspect of ritualization is relevant here: automatization of a frequently occurring *sequence* of units leads to the reanalysis of the sequence as a *single* processing unit or chunk (in storage and production). Hence the term *chunking* (psychological and historical evidence for this process is given in Boyland 1996).

19. Prosodic reasons may play a role, too.

20. This structure is obsolescent (see the discussion in section 5.6.1)

21. For taking part in the elicitation test I wish to thank all the British and American lecturers of the Freiburg English Department and the American students of my seminar on contrastive linguistics.

22. Of course it is not a priori clear whether HAVE is deleted here or in row 5, but since no other verb form occurs in row 2, row 5 seems far more likely. By the same token, HAVE deletion in row 6 is preferred to row 2. The same applies to Table 3.5.

23. In the spoken BNC, *I've/have* alone is more frequent than *have/'ve got*. A further factor might be that present-day English tends towards enclitic rather than proclitic forms, although even this in itself might be a consequence of string frequency rather than an independent factor. In fact, it would be interesting to speculate on the motivations of the apparent trend for English towards enclitic forms (in Shakespeare, *'tis* still by far outnumbers *it's*, and the ratio of 44:1 is difficult to explain on metrical grounds alone; cf. also Note 16 on the development of enclitic *'ve*).

24. It must be stressed, though, that fuzzy boundaries between categories indeed pose a problem for most formal approaches. Grammaticalization highlights them and often enough it is the underlying cause of fuzziness – as in the case of *gotta*.

25. Goodall (1991) is one of the few formal accounts that explicitly argue for restructuring and one which is bold enough to present a phrase structure diagram. However, he fails to account for the apparently unmotivated fact that after restructuring I(NFL) follows the contracted V(erb), in that case *wanna* (1991: 244).

26. A further discourse factor plays a role in the deletion of HAVE. Deletion is facilitated by the fact that the string *I got* by itself is grammatical and frequent. This contrasts for instance with *I going*, which is not grammatical in unmarked and frequent statements but only attested in rare interrogatives or even rarer inversions after semi-negatives like *hardly*. This may help account for the fact that BE GOING TO/*gonna* is seldom found with auxiliary omission.

27. I hesitate to invoke the factor for the umpteenth time, but it seems obvious enough that string frequency triggers the automatic production of reduced auxiliaries after personal pronouns.

28. As the discussion in Hopper & Traugott (1993: Chs. 4.5, 5.2) makes clear, 'loss of meaning', in the present instance refers to concrete meaning aspects.

This process is accompanied, however, by the acquisition of modal, that is, grammatical meaning.

29. A prototype – and common-sensical – approach to distinguishing between *got to* and *gotta* would focus on two criteria: absence of two /t/ phonemes plus the reduction of the vowel in *to* (glottal stop followed by released [t] should count as two phonemes). When both criteria are met, this is a prototypical example of *gotta*. A pronunciation ['gɒɾə] with a flapped /t/, similar to American English realizations ['gɑːɾə] or ['gaɾə], would be covered by this definition. In a limited set of verbal complements, that is, verbs beginning in a vowel, British English sandhi rules could help distinguish between *gotta* and *got to*. While the former (ending in schwa) can be followed by intrusive /r/, the latter (ending in /ʊ/) is more likely to have either linking /w/ or no liaison at all (I thank Petur Knutsson for a stimulating discussion on the issue). Regrettably, such narrow transcriptions are not available for large amounts of data.

30. Notice, however, that this simple correlation applies only so long as other things are equal. Information processing constraints, semantic weight and prosody may act as counterforces (cf. the discussion on p. 65 above).

31. On the role of constructions in grammaticalization in general, see Traugott (forthcoming).

32. That a comparative study for the two varieties is needed is suggested by Myhill's (1995: 158) remark: "British and American modal usage differ significantly." While his remarkable intuitions will indeed prove correct, it remains Myhill's secret how intuition alone can positively ascertain statistical differences in preference.

33. His post-World-War II data (comics) hardly allow a comparison with the earlier plays.

34. For feasibility I restrict my searches of HAVE TO to contiguous structures. For HAVE GOT TO adjacent *got to* is criterial.

35. Compare similarly McCrum et al. (1992: 386): "It is important to note that, historically, ... influential changes have always occurred at the centre, not the periphery, in Britain, not the United States – or anywhere else for that matter." Notice, however, that while this statement is true historically, it seems far less obvious what 'the centre' is today. English now is clearly a pluricentric language, and if any national variety had to be isolated as 'the centre of gravity', most linguists would presumably agree on US English (cf. the discussion in Hundt 1998: Chs. 2, 7).

36. As late as 1800, HAVE TO compares in productivity to verbs like FIT or JOIN in present-day English. This fact, then, to some extent justifies Mitchell's (1985) rejection of modal status for Old English, which was quoted in note 1 of this chapter.

37. The slightly earlier rise of HAVE TO in fictional writing is largely due to the idiomatic expression HAVE TO SAY, whose crucial role in the development of truly modal HAVE TO will be dealt with in section 3.4.

38. Notice that the scale on the y-axis of drama is twice that of fiction so that the gradients differ in fact more than the graphs suggest.

39. Related in perspective to Lightfoot are the accounts by Roberts (1985; 1993: Ch. 3.3) and van Kemenade (1992). In fact, however, both take an intermediate position. Roberts, for instance, argues that syntactic restructuring occurred rather abruptly (in the first part of the 16th century), while "the lexico-semantic changes are gradual, and have been going on throughout the recorded history of English" (1993: 310). In a similar vein, van Kemenade (1992: 287) argues for a "gradual and lexical nature of the change", but he emphasizes in particular the role of word-order change in the rise of the modals.

40. See, however, Barber (1997: 178f) for the position that at the beginning of Early Modern English a present-past distinction was still intact for forms like *shall* and *should*. And, of course, in present-day English there are still some uses of *could, would, might* and even *must* which have past time reference (cf. Jacobsson 1994).

41. A similar observation was made by Douglas Biber (personal communication). Notice also that to dramatists, an actual standstill in spoken language can seem like a reversal of a trend. Hence in drama, which has proven highly susceptible to change, zero growth can figure as a decline (cf. Labov 1969).

It may seem regrettable that not the complete British material is used for Figures 3.1 and 3.2 since consulting twice the amount of material spanning the whole century (and not only the second half) might seem superior. While this is doubtless true for the investigation of a full century of British English looked at in isolation, it would skew the results of the comparative study with American English at hand. American English would then generally appear (even) more innovative because it contains data only from the second half of each century. Moreover, the differences between consulting full centuries and the second halves are not very striking for British English, which is why I refrain from presenting more charts here and in the following chapters. The data are not lost in any case, since they are always presented in the charts for the 50-year spans.

42. While this is obvious for American English even from the raw figures in Table 3.8, it is surprising in the case of British fictional writing. But the critical value of $p < 0.05$ is exceeded here, too, if only by a small margin.

43. Evidently, it is primarily string frequency alongside increased bonding (see p. 58) that is responsible for this assimilation process.

44. In tracing the history of modal HAVE TO, all contiguous examples followed by the infinitive were taken into the count. Different from the approach generally adopted for present-day English (where clear nonmodal uses were excluded), the alternative method was adopted here for the diachronic investigation because it is the main goal of this investigation to elucidate the nature and history of the verbal complements that follow HAVE TO. Consequently, for early uses, deontic modality is often debatable.

45. *Had to* can express both notions: past (as in *I had to go*) and irrealis in conditional clauses (as in *If I had to go*).

46. Of course, animate subjects can occur in epistemic environments too. To take a notorious example from pragmatic textbooks: *There's a yellow Buick in front of the house; he (therefore) must be at home.* Nevertheless, inanimate subjects are particularly prone to a probability reading. A way around epistemic modality is for inanimate subjects to occur in equative structures, where the grammatical subject is not the agent: *For most of us, traditional Italian pastas are sufficiently healthy without imposing extra-healthy ingredients on them. The conclusion has to be cook, eat, enjoy - and profit* (BNC A0C 1063). Notice, however, that in this example the underlying agent (the one who concludes, generic or not) is animate, too.

47. Traugott (1997: 199f) treats the origin of epistemic *must* within her framework of subjectification. She too considers epistemic modality as arising from deontic/root modality via ambiguous contexts.

48. Compare another national stereotype which is often invoked in the literature on inferences: *He is an Englishman; he is, therefore, brave* (e.g. Grice 1989 [1975]: 25; Horn 1992: 262).

49. Obviously, main verb *be* in the same sentence is conducive to the use of *innit*. For the general development of the invariant tag *innit* in British English, see Krug (1998b).

50. The situation for the past tense is slightly more complex. *Must* is originally a preterite form, but this is opaque for speakers of present-day English (cf. Jacobsson 1994).

51. In dating the developments below I follow Warner (1993: 186).

52. This is of course a very rough long-term trend, and since in many individual cells the figures are rather small, some caution is required. Övergaard (1995) is a detailed study of the mandative subjunctive in the 20th century. She finds that in (written) American English the periphrastic subjunctive has been losing ground again since approximately the 1920s, a trend which (written) British English seems to have followed after the Second World War.

53. The high proportion of WILL + *have to* is nevertheless somewhat surprising since HAVE TO by itself invites future readings by implicature – probably the main reason for why HAVE is a source for future morphemes crosslinguistically. The only feasible explanation is that new meanings tend to originate "in heavily redundant contexts" (Traugott 1996: 5). Kytö (1991a: Ch. 3) makes a similar observation for the emergence of the epistemic meaning of CAN. Such redundancy is probably due to the fact that the new meaning is still part of pragmatic negotiation and not yet an integral part of the semantics of the construction.

54. Notice, however, that this is consistent with Ellegård (1953: 201): "It is in fact not unlikely that each verb has its own history."

55. Cf. Heine's stages in the evolution of HAVE TO discussed at the beginning of this chapter. Intriguingly, an analogous situation applies in the domain of related infinitival constructions. 'Raising' constructions with verbs of saying (or thinking), e.g. *They considered her to be clever*, are attested earlier under extraction (Warner 1982: 142-146), and they are still more frequent and considered more acceptable in such environments in present-day English (Mair 1990: 191-196). Compare for instance: ??*I thought this structure to be unacceptable* vs. *We discussed a structure which I thought to be unacceptable*.

56. It is obvious that this construction is in no way modal. I list it because it appears several times in Shakespeare and because I set out to investigate all early contiguous HAVE TO constructions that are followed by an infinitive (cf. Note 44, p. 269).

57. Notice that the older meaning of *get* 'receive' here is traceable too. This holds in particular for times when messengers played a more important role, since these had received messages which to pass on to the addressee.

58. Compare also Brinton (1991: 33): "Another possible route of development is an analogical extension from instances of the infinitive *to do with.*" She also notes in passing (p. 28) that verbs of communication are rather frequent with HAVE TO in Old English.

59. The absolute figures for the earliest period may appear unimpressive. Notice, however, that (a) ARCHER is a carefully sampled representative corpus, (b) and related with the preceding point, the examples do not stem from one single source text, (c) the same tendency is found in the fictional component and (d) in Shakespeare's dramas, too.

60. The often stated modern English division of tasks between HAVE TO (obligation by external force, giving objective deontic modality) and *must* (often internal force, giving subjective deontic modality; cf. Palmer 1989: 131) does not appear to apply rigidly to *say* complements, at least not to the early examples quoted in this section.

61. Bybee (1999a) sketches a somewhat similar scenario for the extension of verbal complements for *can*, which has generalized from mental ability via general ability to root possibility.

62. On mechanisms of semantic change in general see Bybee et al. (1994: Ch. 8).

63. This is paralleled, for instance, by the Greek perfective form κεκτῆσθαι 'to possess' from 'to have acquired' or by Latin *accepi* 'I have received', hence often 'I know'. Compare similarly *cognovi* ('I have got/come to know', 'I have understood'; hence 'I know'), which from classical Latin onwards is attested only in perfective form with present semantics (Georges 1913: *s.v. cognosco*).

64. Notice that this example can also be interpreted as elliptical: *..., if you have the courage to send such a message, I have not* [sc. the courage] *to deliver it.* Under this interpretation, it is an instance of possessive, not modal, HAVE (TO).

65. It may be relevant that O'Casey is an Irish writer, since a regional factor seems to play a role here. Richard Matthews (p.c.) has pointed out to me that this use of HAVE NOT TO was quite common in the 19th century and was, until recently, occasionally heard in Scottish and northern English. As the discussion of examples (83) to (90) will reveal, spoken BNC data strongly support this assumption.

66. I omit participial constructions (progressive and gerundial *not having to*). These are rare and, more importantly, here DO and NOT negation are not in competition.

67. In addition to the 6 instances quoted in the text, there is one example *I hadn't to tell anyone* (BNC KNS 255), whose speaker is not tagged for age.

68. Cf. Hooper (1976) on a related finding for the analogical levelling of Old English strong verbs. Of course, the semantic difference between HAVE NOT TO and DO NOT *have to* noted above is significant, too.

69. Notice for instance that the failure of HAVE GOT TO to co-occur with auxiliaries compares with some 6,000 occurrences of infinitival *have to* in the spoken BNC (i.e. c.75% of all its uses). These divide neatly into approximately 3,000 instances each for preceding DO (negation, interrogatives) and modal verbs.

70. This is not a *hapax legomenon*. There are seven clear cases of modal *gotta to* in the BNC.

71. The slightly higher figures for negation of HAVE TO when compared to Table 3.12 result from the inclusion of participial constructions in the present table.

72. I thank Peter Trudgill for bringing this to my notice.

73. Here, in 3.3.2.2 and in Appendix 3, the data for *got to* were disambiguated: *got to* + NP (e.g. *They got the stage ...*) was excluded. The figures for modal *got to* were extrapolated from two random samples of 100 examples each by the following formula: arithmetic means of modal *got to* in two samples [%] multiplied by overall occurrences of *got to*.

74. Due to cases of adverb interpolation (e.g. *I've really got to/gotta ...*) and inversion (e.g. *Have you got to/gotta ...?; Not only have I got to ...*), instances of ellipsis for *gotta* and *got to* are slightly rarer than the figures in the table suggest, as four random samples of 100 examples showed. However, the fact that *gotta* favours *have* ellipsis more than *got to* becomes even more patent when this is taken into account.

75. For a recent refinement see Rohdenburg (1998).

76. Two random samples of twenty adjacent and twenty nonadjacent regions were compared.

77. I thank Lieselotte Anderwald for supplying me with the relevant percentages. The figures are based on a database of speaker profiles in the BNC which was compiled by Sebastian Hoffmann at Zurich.

Chapter 4

1. Note for instance that a crying infant essentially communicates 'I want/lack something'.
2. On terminology and definitional issues, see the discussion in section 2.8 above.
3. Bouma's (1973) data is not natural spontaneous speech but 20th century literary prose, drama and radio drama. Ranging from 18.8% to 24.6%, the share of 'volition' is rather similar in four different authors.
4. Take, for instance, Romanian *a vrea* + infinitive; the English *will* future; Old Georgian *unda* 'want' > Modern Georgian 'obligation' or 'epistemic necessity' (Harris & Campbell 1995: 174). Bybee et al. (1994: 254) cite seven languages with desire futures: Inuit, Buli, Danish, Nimboran, Bongu, Dakota, Tok Pisin.
5. Spelling variants such as *wonted, wont(i)* when meaning 'lack' are taken into the count. See Hogg (1982) on the dialectal distribution of the variants.
6. Notice, though, that Allen (1995: 224) and Bradley & Stratmann (1891) cite some early examples with stem vowel <a>. In all quotations from the Helsinki Corpus, orthography and form of citation remain unchanged, except that I add 'H' for Helsinki. HCM is short for Helsinki (sub)Corpus of Middle English, HCE and HCO stand for Early Modern English and Old English, respectively.
7. As is obvious from the data cited in this section, negative concord, which later became stigmatized, was the rule rather than the exception in the Middle English standard.
8. Another verb which features prominently in the debate, BEHOFIAN, apparently did not become used in impersonal constructions until the 12th century (Allen 1997).
9. It must be conceded, though, that in the case of the modern central modals the impersonal structures were different in that it was their dependent infinitival verb forms which lacked a nominative subject. This foreshadows modal syntax more directly. Parallel to the development of WANT (TO), of course, is the case of NEED (TO), which, having been impersonal in Old English, occurs in both impersonal and personal constructions in Middle English, and in personal constructions in Modern English.
10. Of course, the dating of Middle English texts is notoriously subject to debate (many researchers, for instance, ascribe the *Cursor Mundi* to the early 14th century). I cite the dates given in the manual to the Helsinki Corpus (Kytö 1991b).
11. Allen (1995: 224), for instance, still regards oblique Experiencers of WANT as dative case in the early 13th century.
12. Various analysts posit SOV constituent order for Old English (rather than concentrate on the position of the verb as does Traugott). Some assume SVO from as early as c.900 (e.g. West 1973). While a decision between SVO and SOV has important theoretical and typological implications, this aspect need not concern us here, where the central point is that the subject occupies the first slot. During the Middle English period this tendency was ever more strengthened (from 1200 SVO is uncontroversial), and at the end of the Middle English period SVO figures as an almost exceptionless rule.

13. See, for instance, Lambrecht (1994) for a recent monograph on information structure in discourse. For a discussion of further principles see Croft (1990: 194ff). Theme-rheme considerations are by no means new in the discussion of English impersonals and can in fact be traced back to van der Gaaf (1904) and Jespersen (1909ff). Compare for example Elmer's (1981: 8) notion of 'pseudo-subject' for the dative Experiencer in Old English or Krzyszpien's (1984) discussion of thematic roles.

14. The only potential counterexample (16) is in fact not controversial either, since ME (*no*) *man* is generally treated as a pronoun too (e.g. Mossé 1952: §73). Even those analysts who do not include it within the pronominal system proper acknowledge its affinity with indefinite pronouns (e.g. Brunner 1962: 71).

15. Notice that this ties in with an observation made by, among others, DuBois (1985; 1987) and Haiman (1985), who note that natural discourse rarely allows more than one nominal (more exactly, non-pronominal) argument. Accordingly the 'natural' state of events for WANT would be [pronominal topic (here human Experiencer) – VERB – nominal argument (here Stimulus)]. It is surprising that this 'natural state' for discourse is dominant even in written Middle English.

16. Allen (1995: Ch. 4) provides higher totals for other verbs displaying the same tendency, so that the behaviour of WANT is by no means idiosyncratic.

17. Theoretically, *werkys* could be analysed as genitive singular, too, and this example is particularly elusive because the preceding clause contains plural *werkys*, whereas the following clause has anaphorically the unequivocal singular *þat werk*. The more appropriate analysis, however, is transitive WANT (hence plural) because such constructions are common with other verbs and because the late date makes it next to impossible that we have to do with a genitive Stimulus (which would be an Old English remnant construction type for a verb that did not then exist).

18. Compare also Allen's (1995: 347) scepticism regarding the role of case syncretisms in the replacement of object Experiencers by subject Experiencers. Allen (1995) provides convincing evidence for gradual loss of impersonal verbs. She argues for a gradual, lexically implemented reassignment of grammatical relations for the personal Experiencer. This is interpreted as counterevidence to reanalysis. It is important to note, however, that her lexical changes result in a "change to parameter settings" (p. 446) so characteristic of reanalysis. This makes the two positions 'change by reanalysis' and 'gradual lexically implemented change' seem less diametrically opposed.

19. Borderline cases are mostly -*ing* forms that are ambiguous between verbal (progressive) and adjectival use.

20. This figure does not include the 18 instances of *for want of*.

21. Raw frequencies between the two periods can be compared because of very similar corpus sizes.

22. The nominal status of *want* in *for want of* is debatable even in Early Modern English. Today it is obviously best analysed as a complex preposition (Quirk et al. 1985: 671).

23. The Z-score is a statistical test which allows judgements as to the degree of bonding between collocates. The higher the Z-score, the greater the collocability of the two items.
24. The apparent decrease in the early 19th century is partly attributable to a sampling problem because one text from the preceding period alone accounts for more than half of all instances of WANT TO found in that period.
25. The modest increase in British fictional language seems to contrast with the more substantial increases in the relevant ARCHER material. This may well be a consequence of the different designs of the corpora. While the one-million-word corpora are true synchronic cuts (all texts are from the same year), ARCHER subcorpora contain texts spanning fifty years.
26. I avoid the more common expression *changes from below* because not all such changes go unnoticed, unless the term is employed in a very narrow sense, i.e. as change occurring below the level of consciousness. This is what the term *covert innovations* is meant to imply. It should be added that Hundt & Mair (forthcoming) explicitly mention the existence of the two types of innovation. However, they do not seem to cover all those innovations narrowing the gap between spoken and written norms under the heading of colloquializations but only those that are "conscious rhetorical devices to create an involved ... style".
27. While there is also no *want of* in the fictional component of FLOB, one single instance of *want* (NP) followed by *of* in Frown-fiction can be found. One such example in all four British and American subcorpora (totalling some 0.9m words) is of course a negligible quantity. Not surprisingly, it results in a negative Z-Score for the sequence of two highly frequent individual items, which indicates an exceedingly low collocability.
28. The figures in this table (produced by the tagging programme) have to be taken with a grain of salt. They are overall (>90%) reliable but, for instance, many of the 79 allegedly nominal uses of *want* are in fact verbs.
29. Further support can be obtained from Aarts & Aarts (1995: 174), who arrive at very similar proportions on the basis of their corpus of written English.
30. Due to clause fusion some analysts might prefer a biclausal analysis. But this need not concern us here. Central is the uncontroversial clause boundary between *want* and *to*.
31. There are some notable exceptions, though. A few common matrix clauses take indirect questions of the type [*I/you (don't) know* – interrog. pron. – personal pron. – *wanna...*]: *You know where you wanna go?* (BNC KDV 1317); *Oh I don't know what I wanna do tonight* (BNC KP4 1390).
32. Compare Fischer & van der Leek (1987) on a somewhat related line of argument for the rise of transitive LIKE.
33. See Croft (1998: 90f) for a more radical position: "distributional patterns do not establish grammatical categories in the strict sense. What matters is the semantic interpretation of a word in a particular grammatical construction. ... In fact, this interplay between grammatical constructions and the words that

speakers fit into them is the source of the richness and flexibility of language as a means of communicating experience."

34. Recall the sampling problem (Note 24) which is largely responsible for the apparent decrease in the early 19th century.
35. This rather bold claim will be couched in more cautious terms in Chapter 5.
36. It appears odd that this point needs mention at all since it seems obvious enough that multifactorial analyses should lead to a more comprehensive picture of any change.
37. This type of reanalysis has of course nothing to do with the conversion of a biclausal into a monoclausal structure.
38. E.g. *Collins Cobuild English Dictionary* [2]1995: *s.v. want*, no.6. As far as I can see, this meaning was first mentioned, as being recent, in the linguistic literature by Kirchner (1940). It had occasionally been mentioned earlier in style books and dictionaries, though (e.g. *English Dialect Dictionary*, Wright, ed., [1]1905; cf. references in Kirchner 1940). Mossé, who also makes an early modalization claim for WANT, provides a good summary (1947: 209-211):

> Un autre verbe tend, depuis peu, à prendre la valeur d'un auxiliaire de mode; c'est *to want*. On dit maintenant *one wants* [= ought] *to be careful in handling poisons; you want to* [= must] *have your teeth seen to; you don't want to* [= must not] *overdo it for a bit; you don't want to* [= need not] *be rude.*
> ['Another verb, in recent times, has tended to take on the value of a modal auxiliary. This is *to want*. One says now *one wants* [= ought] etc.' (transl. MK)]

39. Example (44) has an additional necessity reading.
40. This is not without consequences for the investigation of languages for which we have only synchronic data (cf. Sweetser 1990: 22).
41. Meanings in brackets are currently rare (and not fully conventionalized) or were rare in the periods when the changes occurred. '?' indicates marginality. Section 4.4.2 will identify a further (hypothetical) reading.
42. The last pronunciation is proposed by Bolinger (1980b: 296) and represents American English. Of course, however, a nasalized /ɒ/ is conceivable in British English, too. In what follows I shall take the simplified view that the spelling *want to* covers all pronunciations that have residual /t/, while the spelling *wanna* is used to indicate /t/-less realizations.
43. Related models with more fine-grained differentiations have been offered by Lehmann (1995 [1982]: 37), Ramat (1987: 8-12) and Heine (1993: 58-66), who provides a detailed account of the changes generally involved in the passage from one stage to the next, more grammaticalized one.
44. Particularly at stages (IV) and (V) WANT appears to govern a plain infinitive. Nevertheless, in present-day British English disyllabic pronunciations seem to prevail, which vindicates adopting the spelling <wanna>. Notice also that in general phonological reduction of *to* is more common when it functions as infinitival marker than in its prepositional use (Ingram 1989: 34).
45. Compare also the related *ken* 'know' which has survived in Scottish English (OED 1989: *svv. ken, can*).

46. Notice that Pullum himself has lived in the US for a considerable time. The British acquaintances he quotes who "do not really find *wanna* a natural item in their speech" (1997: 97) possibly fall into one of the three older age groups of Table 4.10, for which this statement is arguably true. Notice further that there may well be a difference between the perception or introspection of native speakers on the one hand and actual usage on the other.

47. To present some textual evidence, let us have a closer look at 1992. Of a total of 33 instances, ten occur in headlines or fictionalized oral utterances, 23 in quotations. 14 of these are utterances by US-citizens, one each by an Italian and a Mexican in the USA and one by a drug addict in Denmark. This leaves only 6 *wannas* to British speakers. Their utterances, in turn, occur in situations which one would expect to be on lower stylistic levels and/or social strata (football, London working class district, army, drug scene). This is slightly different from more recent coverage. Admittedly, *wanna* still always indicates informal language, the majority of examples still appear in quotations from popular culture or fictionalized oral utterances, and it is still sometimes used for portraying American speakers. Nevertheless, there are at least some less marked examples such as that from 1997, attributed to the then party leader Paddy Ashdown in a political commercial on television:

> Narrowing his eyes and furrowing his brow as if looking at something a long way away – like, perhaps, a Liberal Democrat government – Paddy says: "I'll tell ya what I wanna see ..." He explains the improvements in education which will be made possible by the party's now-legendary 1p rise in income tax. (*Guardian* 12 April 1997; article entitled "The Election Mediawatch").

I take it, though, that the former shibboleth-like status was largely restricted to written representations of spoken language. Spoken British English has for some time been exhibiting the feature too, only to a lesser extent than American English. While this statement is probably still valid today, the gap between the two dialects has apparently narrowed, certainly among younger speakers. Phonetically, the difference in vowel quality of the stressed vowel is therefore a much better discriminator than the presence or absence of residual /t/.

48. In their search in the TOSCA corpus (1.5m tokens written PDE), out of a total 868 verbal uses of WANT, 40 are cases of ellipsis (Aarts & Aarts 1995: 171-3).

49. The fact that the phonologically reduced variant *wanna* is dispreferred under VP ellipsis is to some extent paralleled by the central modals, which are highly unlikely to figure as reduced forms in such contexts, too. Cf.: *I can* [k(ə)n] *go if you can* [kæn] (??[kən], *[kn̩]); *I will come, since you will* (*'ll).

50. Other verbs (notably TRY and WISH) behave very much like WANT with regard to VP ellipsis, and thus display an affinity with modal verbs and modal constructions too.

51. GIVE and TELL are chosen because they are the two verbs most similar to WANT TO in terms of discourse frequencies in informal speech (cf. Figure 2.1). That the three verbs differ considerably in terms of frequency in Table 4.9 is due to two facts. For one thing, Figure 2.1 presents the frequencies of entire

paradigms (including all word-forms such as *gives, told*), whereas here only uninflected forms qualify. For another, the present table is based on the entire spoken component of the BNC, whereas Figure 2.1 is based on the spontaneous speech component. The fourth verb chosen is FIND because with Aarts & Aarts (1995, to be discussed in the next section) a comparative study of WANT and FIND based on a written corpus already exists which calls for a comparison with spoken data.

52. Discontinuous structures of modal + Verb such as *might not want to* or *might I want to* are not included in the count.

53. See Fennell & Butters (1996) for lists of attested forms in African American Vernacular English, Caribbean English creoles and Southern US English; Brown (1991) for Hawick Scots.

54. Of course, the central modals in their turn also developed the double modal constraint progressively (Nagle 1993; 1995).

55. Notice that in the previous section only infinitives preceded by central modals were taken into consideration (but not, for instance, infinitival purposive clauses) and that various finite and nonfinite verb-forms (e.g. inflected forms, participles) were not investigated either.

56. On the methodology of apparent time studies, see McMahon (1994: 239-43).

57. It is highly implausible that people over 60 are desireless.

58. For obvious reasons, this table includes only contiguous forms of *want* and *to*.

59. The overrepresentation of *wanna* in London (+8.2% when compared to the mean of all regions) is more than twice that of the second-most innovative area, north-east England. The latter area actually somewhat spoils an otherwise neat diagram, at least if seen from a perspective arguing contact-induced spread. For the arguments presented in the section on regional variation of the previous chapter (3.5), I here refrain from a detailed discussion of the correlation between the variable 'region' and possible distorting factors such as the over-representation of informal speech or younger speakers. The reader is referred to section 5.3.3 below.

60. As in the previous chapter, two random samples of twenty adjacent and twenty non-adjacent regions were compared. Figures could be provided but are not necessary here, since it is obvious that there are some very homogeneous areas such as that south of what Trudgill (1990) has identified as the most important modern dialect boundary (including south-west England, the South Midlands, London, the Home Counties and East Anglia), to which on the present map the neighbouring areas of Wales and the Midlands (XMI) can be added. Or take the conservative north-western area stretching from the central and north-west Midlands to Scotland. East of it lies another rather conservative region including northern England (XNO), Humberside and the north-east Midlands.

61. Cf. Chafe (1984: 96f) and the discussion on the colloquialization of written norms in section 4.2.3.1 above.

62. The need for filling this gap is clear from the fact that many speakers feel few if any traces of volition or intention when using *will*.

Chapter 5

1. On terminology and taxonomies used in the verbal domain, see Chapter 2 above or the extensive discussion provided in Heine (1993: Ch. 1).
2. This does of course not mean that the constructions were not used before. See Chapters 3 and 4 above on the history of HAVE (GOT) TO and WANT TO. See Mossé (1938: §290); Mustanoja (1960: 592f.); or Danchev & Kytö (1994) on early uses of BE GOING TO.
3. The deviation from an ideal S-curve in the late 18th century can largely be accounted for by a sampling problem, see the discussion in section 4.2.2.2.
4. In fact, except for WANT TO (which is favoured three times more often in British than in American English), the figures for the earliest comparable drama data are virtually identical. In fiction, by contrast, British English is consistently (if only slightly) more innovative than American English. The exception, of course, is HAVE GOT TO, which is not attested in either variety at that early stage.
5. In fact, the term *variety* suggests a homogeneity that does not exist. Ultimately, then, all 'varieties' are to some extent fictions, as Algeo (1989) points out.
6. The idea that the preference of HAVE TO in British English is related to the neglect of (HAVE) GOT TO suggests itself but it is difficult to prove.
7. Compare for instance a recent study by Los (1998: 27) for similarly imperfect S-curves obtained from real data.
8. It must be conceded that the overall text frequency of (*got to* + *gotta*) exceeds that of (*want to* + *wanna*) by a smaller proportion than an adherent of string frequency might have wished. Monitoring of speech seems to be a factor that somewhat blurs an otherwise clear tendency (cf. the comfortable 100-odd-point lead GOING TO has over the remaining two constructions). As was seen in section 3.5, formal speech does not favour the use of HAVE GOT TO. If we look at spontaneous speech only, the difference in the totals between the two strings GOT TO and WANT TO becomes more striking.
9. In recent usage-based accounts (e.g. Bush 1999; Bybee forthcoming) the notion of transitional probability (TP) has figured prominently alongside string frequency (SF). This issue requires a brief excursion. For the sequence of two words X and Y, TP is defined statistically as the raw frequency of the sequence XY (which is string frequency) divided by the raw frequency of X. In other words, transitional probability gives the percentage of a word sequence (e.g. GOT TO) relative to all occurrences of the first word in that sequence (here: *got*). While the more sophisticated notion of TP is intuitively a more appealing concept than the rather crude notion of SF, I am not aware of any set of data where TP has proved a superior predictor for the fusion of adjacent items. Also in the present case, TP would falsely predict contraction ratios in the order *gonna* > *wanna* > *gotta* (the TP values based on the spoken BNC are

0.68, 0.50 and 0.19, respectively). Somewhat ironically, the very study arguing for the superiority of transitional probability (Bush 1999) shows that it is string frequency which better predicts the rate of word-boundary palatalization processes (e.g. *don't you*).

I do not wish to invalidate the concept of transitional probability as a whole, though. Indeed it seems that it applies to different environments than string frequency. Bybee (forthcoming), for instance, who applies both notions profitably, studies French liaison, i.e. the *addition* (or rather retention) of sounds in certain phonological environments. The data presented as evidence for string frequency, by contrast, typically involve the omission and weakening of sounds, i.e. *erosion*. More research is needed on the matter. Ultimately, one might in fact want to combine the two measures, so that the weaknesses of either concept could be mitigated. However, in the absence of such studies I suggest sticking to the simpler concept, certainly for fusion involving phonological erosion as investigated here.

10. There are further indicators suggesting that the cline found for univerbation (GOING TO > GOT TO > WANT TO) indeed reflects the order of their respective degrees of grammaticalization. For example, subject independence is not fully realized with WANT TO (cf. the criteria of modality discussed in Chapter 2.8). Compare: *It's going to/ got to rain.* But **It wants to rain.* Or: *This paper is going to/ ?has got to/ ??wants to show...* Behaviour regarding voice neutrality points in the same direction: *Someone's going to/ got to do it ~ It's going to/ got to be done.* But *Someone wants to do it ~ ??It wants to be done.*

11. On a different level, however, string frequency also has a bearing on the grammaticalization of single-word items. If we look at the English central modals, it seems evident that at least two of their syntactic constraints – NOT negation and inversion in interrogatives – are due to string frequency (cf. Bybee & Thompson forthcoming): highly entrenched sequences of auxiliary + NOT and auxiliary + personal pronoun in Old and Middle English probably made these strings immune to the changes that affected the less frequent lexical verbs, which now regularly take operator DO (NOT).

12. Only *hafta* is recorded 50 years after the observed leap in text frequency. This may be due to the fact that the assimilation processes in the sequence *have to* are generally not felt to be extraordinary enough to merit a distinct spelling.

13. As for later reduction, Bybee et al. (1994: 6) point out that "phonological reduction continues to take place throughout the life of a gram."

14. For *gonna*, one would in addition have to assume auxiliary deletion: *[You're] gonna take a taxi?* This seems plausible since when BE follows pronouns in statements, it usually occurs in its enclitic form. This cannot stand sentence-initially and thus is naturally deleted together with its host.

15. It should be clear, however, that in the examples with suggested traces of auxiliary DO, the adjacent phonemes /t/ (in *what*) and /d/ (from DO) will not necessarily be realized separately.

16. It is further striking that lexical verbs which commonly figure after auxiliary deletion or reduction are high-frequency verbs. These often occur in fixed expressions like *What d'ya mean?* (e.g. BNC KPK 859) or *Whatcha/ What d'ya think?* (e.g. BNC JJR 54; KP9 185).
17. With ['wɒdʒə] another option exists. It is particularly common for *What do you ...?* and can be explained in terms of a further erosive process, i.e. as lenition of the affricate /tʃ/. Or it can be seen as deriving from what is sometimes presented orthographically as *what d'ya* (but probably not as *w(h)atcha* or *wotcha*). This would accommodate the fact that assimilation processes at the former word boundary between *do* and *you* can be prior to the deletion or lenition of word-final /t/ in *what*.
18. Notably /t/ would often be flapped at stage IV. I included just one variant, the glottal stop at stage V. As is indicated in the chart, a glottal stop would prevent the assimilation process giving rise to the first option listed under stage VI.
19. English tends to code modalities verbally, the exception being epistemic modality, which is also often expressed by adverbs such as *probably, perhaps* etc.
20. The two meanings are not further distinguished here. Palmer (1989: 113-116, see there for semantic detail) has pointed to the problem of indeterminacy. Referring to the distinction between 'discourse-oriented deontic modality' and 'dynamic necessity' for *must* and HAVE (GOT) TO, he notes that "there is no clear dividing line between the two meanings" (p. 113).
21. An example of a command by implicature is "You're gonna take off your shoes before you come in here." (Bybee et al. 1994: 211).
22. In other words, Map 5.2 is based on the contraction ratios. This is to say that it compares the proportions of the contracted forms relative to all contractible sequences (i.e. *gonna + going to; gotta + got to; wanna + want to*). The method for establishing the cumulative map is very much the same as for Map 5.1: for each emerging modal five degrees of progressiveness are calculated on the basis of Appendix 5, using contraction ratios (CRs). The scale for *wanna* and *gotta* ranges from CRs < 20% to CRs > 50%; that for *gonna* from CRs < 40% to CRs > 70%. Each band is ten percentage points, i.e. the cut-off points distinguishing between degrees of progressiveness are 20%, 30%, 40%, 50%, 60% and 70%. For the cumulative map, a region scores 5 points, if it is in the most progressive group for one emerging modal; 4 points if it is in the second most progressive group, and so on. The scores for all three emerging modals are then added to produce the overall score.
23. The remaining 5% of the speakers tagged for region are not tagged for age. I thank Lieselotte Anderwald for transforming the Zurich database of BNC speaker information into an Access database, thus enabling me to calculate the relevant figures.
24. Notice that this quantitative result stands in sharp contrast to Beal's (1993) qualitative treatment of the grammar of Tyneside and Northumbrian English. She finds that the "proximity to Scotland is reflected in the linguistic

characteristics of the area" (p. 187). However, she also stresses the provisional nature of her characterization and the need for quantitative research: "It must be said at the outset, however, that the reader is unlikely to encounter anybody who will use all of these features all of the time ... A vast amount of research would be needed in order to quantify the amount and type of variation for each feature, so for the time being I have presented these features as if they were invariable. It is important to remember that this is an idealization" (p. 191f).

25. Quantitative verification of the wave model is virtually nonexistent.

26. The table presents raw figures from the BNC (percentages of the respective variants are given in brackets). Random samples confirmed that there are no significant differences between the sexes in the use of *got to* or *going to* + NP. Further disambiguation was therefore considered unnecessary.

27. As should be clear from the context, *codification* is used here (and in what follows) to characterize individual registers and roughly means 'conventionalization by use' (cf. Greenbaum 1990: 18). I do not refer to the use of *codification* which implies the existence of dictionaries, grammars etc. for a language at large, even though my use of the term does not preclude the existence of style books for a certain register, for instance.

28. It will be remembered from the discussion in section 2.7.2 that a categorical distinction between 'writing' and 'speaking' is justifiable for the medium (or code) only, while, conceptionally, there is a gradient between the poles of an ideal-type spoken conception and an ideal-type written conception.

29. Hundt (1998: 61-68) provides a convenient synopsis of relevant research as well as a regional comparison of British, American and New Zealand usage. The references in Denison (1998: 168-171) complement those given by Hundt.

30. Only 26 out of 341 instances (or 7.6%) of DARE in the spoken BNC are *to* infinitives or *to* constructions with an understood infinitive. These 26 examples include two doubtful instances of *daring to*, which may be interpreted as either verbal and/or participial or adjectival.

31. For feasibility I only checked the pronouns *he, she, it*. They are generally rare with DARE (perhaps avoided?). There are 2 instances of *he dare*, 5 of *he daren't*, 2 of *she daren't*. There is no instance of (*he/she/it*) *doesn't dare* (*to*) in the 10m words of the spoken BNC.

32. Unfortunately, the speaker is interrupted by his interlocutor, so we cannot know whether he would have actually added an infinitive. But this is of minor importance.

33. Corpus data are ambiguous. While a comparison of spontaneous and formal speech in the BNC does not corroborate the hypothesis of a change from above towards main verb syntax (partly due to low raw frequencies of individual constructions), lexical constructions, i.e. *to* infinitives and DO support indeed enjoy higher text frequencies in the written component of the corpus (concomitant with lower text frequencies of NOT negation). More research is needed therefore to elucidate the matter.

34. Only competing contiguous constructions were investigated, i.e.: *need not, do(es) not need to* and their contracted counterparts *needn't* and *do(es)n't need to.*
35. The chi-squared value is 7.35 (p = 0.12). At four degrees of freedom, the alternative hypothesis ('The five youngest groups exhibit differential behaviour with regard to the investigated negation strategies') is fairly confidently rejected – despite the fact that two cells have expected frequencies of less than five.
36. The difference is in three cases significant at the 0.1% level and twice (with the two youngest groups) at the 1% level. The expected frequency is never less than five in these individual tests comparing the over-60s with the remaining age groups. Of course, the differences across all age groups are significant at the 0.1% level, too.
37. Only contiguous examples were investigated. Elided infinitives are included in the count.
38. There is no occurrence of *needs not* in the spoken BNC.
39. These include *need/s it/she/he* and *needn't it/she/he* followed by *to* or bare infinitives.
40. Again, I include only present tense examples. Additionally, one instance each of *did it need to ...?* and *would it need to ...?* was found.
41. The second person singular inflection in (37) is regular for Early Modern English modals (Barber 1997: 177).
42. I found nine instances of adverb interpolation of the type [NP *ought really/perhaps to* + infinitive].
43. Very occasionally bare infinitives can be found. Unfortunately the BNC search options do not allow a systematic search of OUGHT + plain infinitive, but while scanning the material I came across the example *We're hoping to get a mini bus, I don't think we ought take a bus because we were very badly treated when we did that* (BNC D95 114). It is, however, conceivable that in a sequence [ɔːtʰətʰeɪk], which ought properly to be transcribed as *ought to take*, a weakly pronounced schwa is overheard by the transcriber, in particular when the preceding /t/ is heavily aspirated. If this example is not a transcription error, however, it is probably no coincidence that it was uttered in a pensioner's meeting; the obsolescence of such constructions seems certain. Quirk et al. (1985: 140), for instance, consider the *to*-less form ungrammatical in assertive contexts.
44. E.g. ... *telling them there ought not be electrical equipment over night* (BNC FLS 321). There is one additional anacoluthic example of NOT negation.
45. For feasibility, the maximum number of intervening words between DO and *ought* was restricted to five.
46. Not every noun (or even complex NP) is equally likely to become the host of clitic tense-aspect-mood markers. For frequentative reasons that are spelt out in some detail in Krug (1998a), pronouns are the prototypical hosts.

47. A phrase search *'ve to* in the 10m words of the spoken BNC yields a mere 73 hits, of which 68 are actually instances of deontic HAVE TO (cf. the fact that there are approximately 11,000 sequences *have to* in the same corpus; auxiliary *have* as in *I've eaten*, by contrast, is cliticized more often than not in spoken English). Interestingly, with *'ve to* a clear preponderance of older speakers can be observed: out of 50 occurrences whose speakers are tagged for age, only six are attributed to speakers under 30. This compares with 21 occurrences which are attributed to speakers aged 60 and over. Such a distribution clearly points to an obsolescent structure, although this one is not as obsolete as the type *You haven't to* ('must not') *go there* discussed in section 3.4.

There is another interesting parallel: both structures seem to be pre-dominantly northern features. Deontic *'ve to* is overwhelmingly used in the north of England and in Scotland: even though Scotland accounts for only 7 to 8 percent (depending on whether sentences or words are taken as a basis) of the material tagged for region, 17 occurrences (or 34 percent) out of a total of 50 areally tagged *'ve to* examples are uttered by Scottish speakers. Another third (16 occurrences, or 32 percent) of the total is attributed to northern English speakers (tagged for central northern England, northern England or Lancashire). Ten occurrences are uttered by speakers from the Midlands (excluding the south Midlands); 3 by speakers tagged for Ireland, two by speakers tagged for Wales. Only two occurrences (or 4 percent) are attributed to truly southern speakers – i.e. speakers coming from areas south of the most important modern dialect boundary identified by Trudgill 1990; these include south-west England, the Home Counties, London, the south Midlands and East Anglia; see Map 3.1 – even though London alone accounts for some 15 percent of the material tagged for region. Southern speakers are thus clearly underrepresented as far as this obsolescent construction is concerned. Again, therefore, the correlation between conservative linguistic behaviour and northern speech on the one hand, and that between progressive linguistic features and southern speech on the other, is strengthened.

48. Iconicity is one of the most prominent functionalist arguments against the autonomy of syntax (or grammar, for that matter). See Newmeyer (1998: Ch. 3) for a discussion from a formalist perspective.

49. Haiman here refers only to causatives and co-ordinate constructions. I will try to show that this principle enjoys wider currency.

50. Hopper (1991: 22, 28-30; quoted in section 2.3) has identified semantic *persistence*, i.e. the retention of (traces of) an earlier meaning, as a principle of grammaticalization. The coexistence of older and newer variants such as *want to ~ wanna* or *will ~ 'll* can perhaps be seen as an analogue of this principle on the phonological and syntactic levels (cf. also p. 194 above).

51. It would be interesting to investigate whether the word-final /r/ in modal *better* is always pronounced in generally rhotic accents. Common /r/ deletion would

strengthen the case for advocating iconicization and auxiliarization. Denison (1993: 422) notes that BETTER is sometimes used with NOT negation in tags (his example is *We better hurry up, bettn't we?*). While such structures showing central modal behaviour are not attested in the spoken BNC and thus seem to be rare, they demonstrate that *better* indeed shows strong signs of modalization.

52. The latter pronunciation is typical of American speech, but also occurs in British English. Here, pronunciations like ['niːd̥də] and ['niːd̥tə] are common, too.

53. Notice, though, that unlike the remaining items these do not take infinitival complements. Still they are related on semantic grounds and also syntactically: both take nonfinite verbal complements. I count diphthongs as one phoneme.

54. Of course, less reduced pronunciations such as /'traɪŋtə/ coexist.

55. The last three examples are not empty respellings; the devoicing of the verb-final consonants are assimilation processes typical of word-internal sound sequences.

56. I use British transcription conventions. American English is slightly different: the quality of the full vowel is rather [ɑ], its length varies, and it is usually more nasalized in *gonna* and *wanna*; /t/ is generally flapped. Bybee et al. (1994: 6) and Bybee & Thompson (forthcoming) use schwa for the stressed vowel in *gonna*, which might indicate that *gonna* in this variety is more advanced on its way to morphologization (even though this is a common pronunciation in British English, too). Ambiguous statements in pronunciation dictionaries, however, demonstrate that more detailed phonological studies are necessary (cf. Windsor-Lewis 1972; Wells 1990; Jones [15]1997: *s.v. gonna*).

57. Cf. also Bybee (forthcoming) on the relationship between frequency and opacity, exemplified by the case of *gonna*:

> the connections between the words and morphemes of such [high frequency] phrases and other instances of the same words or morphemes in other constructions become weaker. The potential loss of association is heightened by phonetic and semantic or functional change. The extreme outcome of this process is seen in grammaticization, where parts of grammaticized constructions are no longer associated with their lexical sources, e.g. the difficulty English-speaking children have when they begin to read of identifying the *from* they know as *gonna* with the three morphemes *go, ing* and *to*.

58. For *wanna* the argument is more complex. While no trace of the original 'lack' meaning is present, it still expresses volition, like its full verb relative that takes NPs.

59. Cf. also Campbell (1959: 343-346) on the Old English inventory of preterite present verbs. Birkmann (1987) is a study of preterite presents in (primarily) older stages of the Germanic languages.

60. Spellings like *needa* or *neeta* are rare but attested (even outside the linguistic literature, for which see references in Pullum 1997: 82). Usually, they occur in fictionalized (American English) utterances. Compare, for instance, one

fictional example imitating impaired speech and one informal webpage reporting on scientific work:

> Chaz swallowed. "you *needa* get stoned, manny, thats, thasz, um....... thats what you *needa* do, ok?   come on..." (emphasis added; website entitled "Mergeform (published in Berkeley Fiction Review 9/97);" http://www-inst.eecs.berkeley.edu/~trevor/fiction/mergeform.html)

> Should be done soon, then all I *needa* do is replace the models. (emphasis added; website entitled: "Defiant in development!"; Aug 08, 1999; http://feedback.interplay.com/sfcommand/msg1/13621.html)

61. It seems certain, for instance, that mainstream American speakers more commonly flap their /t/s in *want to* than in *winter* or even *rent to*.

62. It needs to be borne in mind, though, that the modals in the Germanic languages have not developed in step, not even in individual languages. Nevertheless, the overall direction of their changes, best documented for English (e.g. Warner 1993), seems to be towards more coherent classes.

63. It must be conceded, though, that due to a different source construction *want a* and particularly *got a* seem less likely to diverge as drastically from the modal usage.

64. Percentages were extrapolated from two random samples of 100 instances each. The standard deviation was always below 2.1.

65. Ultimately, one would need to corroborate this claim by more typological work. A starting point is a crosslinguistic study by Bybee (1986) on bound grammatical morphemes (verbal inflections). She has shown that semantically coherent verbal affixes (expressing tense, aspect or mood) are not structurally similar, at least not as far as their position relative to the verb is concerned. In other words, she finds that there is no correlation between the structural criterion 'affix position' (post- or pre-verbal) and semantic class (e.g. tense or mood). In order to obtain a fuller picture of the presence or absence of structural similarity for bound and/or free grammatical morphemes, however, we would require comparative studies of further formal properties, i.e. of phonological, morphological and syntactic properties.

66. The fact that the loss of /l/ occurred very early (it probably went hand in hand with the lengthening of the stem vowel) does not invalidate this argument. The general assumption that low-stress words like *and, under* (including perhaps *wolde* and *sc(e)olde*), did not undergo vowel lengthening might be augmented by considering that the commonly invoked items are of high frequency (cf. Zipf 1929ff). See Labov (1994: esp. Chs. 15-18) for a reconciliation of sound change with lexical diffusion theories.

67. It must be added, however, that postvocalic /lC/ is prone to change generally. Take, for instance, the loss of /l/ in words like *palm* or *calm*. Or consider the loss of /l/ in other (usually frequent) words like *walk* and *talk; or alright, already, almost* (in the last three words, where /l/ deletion is optional, the two phonemes are not part of the same syllable, though). Consider, finally, the trend for [ɫ] to become vocalized in Estuary English (e.g. *milk, help*).

To return briefly to the stem vowels, it must be conceded that their development in at least *would* and *should* is not exceptional. The stem vowel in all three items was shortened and centralized from /u:/ to /ʊ/, a development which not all relevant items underwent, though. It is not inconceivable that a frequency factor plays a role here, too. While the principle covering the majority of erstwhile /o:/ pronunciations seems to be that the vowel in the eME sequence /o:k/ <-ook> underwent both raising and laxation, while other sequences were only raised, there are a good many exceptions to this pattern. But certainly only few high-frequency words exist which did not take part in the laxation of the vowel (cf. *foot, good, should, could, would*, with *food, mood, goose, lose, shoe, fool*). And the few high-frequency words like *you* that still retain a long /u:/ have developed weak-form variants like /jʊ, jə/. This fact, and other ambivalent cases like *room* or *roof*, actually seem to indicate that this change is still in progress.

68. See Krug (forthcoming) for further evidence from the domain of Romance personal pronouns.

69. For details on the prototypical emerging modal, see sections 5.2.3, 5.7.5 (in particular p. 230) and 5.8.1.

70. This is widely agreed upon. A notable exception is Lightfoot (1979, 1991), who argues for cataclysmic change in the development of the central English auxiliaries.

71. Indicative of this prototypical structure is also the abundance of labels that are used in the literature for verbs of intermediate status between main and auxiliary verb discussed above (cf. central modals, quasi-modals, secondary modals, semi-auxiliary etc.).

72. For instance a body that is dropped from two meters above the surface of the Earth will be accelerated towards the centre of the Earth, while the position of the Earth will be affected only to a negligible extent.

73. While this assumption is a simplification of the physical facts, it is a good approximation in Trudgill's model. For simplicity it will be adopted here too. A more sophisticated model might incorporate the acceleration force due to gravitation instead of calculating proportions of influence according to relative weight (frequency). In a field of two masses (items of different frequencies) the acceleration acting on the smaller mass (infrequent item) is more pronounced. This is exactly what the modified gravitation formula predicts too.

74. After all, I can profit from a previous profession. This seemed far from likely when I changed the métier. I thank the physicist Dirk Rudolph for stimulating discussions on the matter.

75. That Trudgill assigns varying values to it is strictly speaking not compatible with gravitation theory, but in his application it improves the fit of the model.

76. Absolute values in Table 5.6 are not required since I do not provide units of measurement. What is important in the present model are values relative to the remaining ones. The relationships among the items remain the same, in-

dependently of whether absolute frequency or incidence is chosen as the basis for the calculation.

77. For an earlier model which measures phonological and morphological differences numerically see Bybee et al. (1994: Ch. 4).

78. The choice of two syllables for BE GOING TO and HAVE GOT TO may appear arbitrary since both can consist of more syllables. This, however, is not true for the large majority of occurrences: the operator HAVE is almost always reduced to a single consonant phoneme (like BE) or even omitted; and the potentially trisyllabic *going to* is contracted to *gonna* over 50 percent of the time (cf. Figure 5.6).

79. Due to bondedness, I here consider only the sequences /'gɒnə/ and /'gɒtə/. The usually cliticized or omitted auxiliaries BE and HAVE are regarded as meaningless constituents of the preceding subject (see the discussion in section 3.2.2). This is not a mathematical trick. The overall result is hardly affected if we add for BE GOING TO and HAVE GOT TO one phoneme each. Diphthongs count as a single phoneme.

80. Ad-hoc formations for the abstract prototype that spring to mind are *verbeme* or *modaleme*. In principle, this idea is by no means new. Compare the wider notions suggested in work following the Bloomfieldian tradition such as *grameme, tagmeme* and *syntagmeme* (e.g. Pike 1962); or Bybee's (1985) term *gram* (for grammatical morpheme). Furthermore, the notion of *allo-construction* (or *allosyntagm*; Pike 1962: 236) seems particularly helpful in describing the coexistence of variants of a construction (e.g. WANT TO /'wɒntʊ, 'wɒntə, 'wɒnə/) – a phenomenon which is typical of highly frequent linguistic items (Bybee forthcoming).

81. The value for the constant C is left unspecified. Mathematically, its value in the present calculation is therefore $C = 1$.

82. It should have become clear from the illustration that it is only linguistic variables which enter into the present calculation of gravitation – assuming, of course, that *frequency* is granted the status of a linguistic variable.

83. This order appears to contradict that obtained in 5.2.2. But this is simply a consequence of the fact that for string frequency, only contractible sequences are relevant, while in this section the frequency of the entire constructions is relevant. That WANT TO outnumbers GOT TO is due to the fact that the latter is highly defective. Notably the virtual absence of GOT TO in past environments contrasts with a high currency of *wanted to*.

84. While the sum of the similarity indices for WILL is 80, those for the remaining items in the field rank between 52 and 60 (the lower the score, the less the average distance).

85. Since this is a reduction to two dimensions, (linguistic) distances between items and sizes of items (as indicators of frequency) are not to scale. As four criteria were identified, only a polydimensional model can lead to a fuller

statement (cf. Pike 1962 or Quirk 1965: 208f on dimensions of grammatical constructions).

86. Notice that this result is by no means tautological. The prototypical properties of an emerging modal given in (56), p. 230, are identified solely on the basis of the dominant properties of the four most frequent members. This involves no arbitrary definition of what is and what is not a prototypical property. The result obtained from the gravitation model, reflected in Figure 5.11, however, emerges solely from the calculation and thus is a mathematical corroboration of a previously made qualitative observation. The consonance of the results in fact demonstrates that the model does not produce erratic figures but that the figures indeed have linguistic correlates.

87. The speakers are a male sales executive, a female student aged 22, a retired man and a male financial adviser (35 years old), respectively.

88. Obviously, dialects also often retain conservative features.

89. Note that these are not marginally productive examples. Overall, some two thirds of GOING TO sequences are contracted in the spontaneous speech component of the BNC.

90. Of course, these items are far from synonymous today, even though they are broadly related to the domain of volition and even though they overlap in meaning and implicatures. Matthews (1991: 155-172) provides a detailed semantic-pragmatic treatment. He demonstrates, for instance, that WANT TO and WISH TO differ with regard to the presence (in the case of WANT) or absence (WISH) of presupposed realizability.

    Field-internally, it is important that WANT TO is probably the most neutral volitional verb and (now) covers roughly the ground previously occupied by *will*. Also, it is multiply polysemous and can evoke various types of implicature (see Ch. 4 and the summary given in Figure 5.8), whereas related items such as INTEND TO, PLAN TO, DESIRE TO and WISH TO are more specific in meaning. This is of course the prime reason for the high frequency of WANT TO in present-day English (cf. also Bybee et al.'s notion of generalization; 1994: 289-293). Nevertheless, it does not explain why the construction spread in the first place, since its original meaning 'lack' too is rather specific semantically, and this notion is certainly further away from the core volitional current meaning of WANT (TO) than the semantics of WISH (TO) in Middle English.

91. In these instances, iconicity and economy actually *are* competing forces: by taking on the new properties the marginal modals are becoming more similar to the emerging modals. HAVE TO, of course, has already become one of the core members of the class.

92. In fact, a three-dimensional model would be more adequate since the marginal modals are less central than their position in a two-dimensional system suggests.

Chapter 6

1. On a more general level, Bybee (1998: 237) argues that "the study of phonetic variation and detail, especially as they interact with lexicon and grammar, is likely to yield new and fascinating insights into a very subtle and complex pattern of human behavior."
2. I thank Douglas Lightfoot (personal communication) for not being able to tell me whether he meant *I'm gonna* or *I wanna go to town*. Notice that like the prototypical clitic, /nə/ consists exclusively of unmarked sounds.
3. One reason for the progressiveness of American English is again phonological in nature. In American English /t/-flapping is much more common in the relevant environments (/'Vntə/, /'VtV/) than in British English. This facilitates the assimilation processes leading to the contracted forms. Compare, for instance, *winter, better, water* with *want to, got to,* and also *goin(g) to.*
4. For the sake of clarity, one might add that the term *prestigious* here refers to overt prestige, even though this ought to be evident from the context.
5. Notice that a cline of progressiveness does not contradict what is said above on the relationship between British and American English. 'Origin of a construction', 'influence between national and intranational varieties' and 'degrees of progressiveness at a certain point in time' are three different aspects that need to be kept apart. Varieties can in principle be more and less progressive without influencing each other.
6. Some largely synchronic studies dealing with these items are Biber et al. (1998: 95-105), Mair (1995; 1998: 149-152; forthcoming) or Kjellmer (forthcoming). Brinton (1988: Ch. 3) offers much valuable information on the history of English aspectualizers.
7. Hopper & Traugott (1993: 10-14) provide an outline; Krug (1994: 118-129) is a corpus-based treatment including a discussion of differences between British and American usage.

Appendices

Appendix 1. 100 high-frequency verbs in spontaneous speech (except the top 30, cf. Figure 2.1): Occurrences per million words*

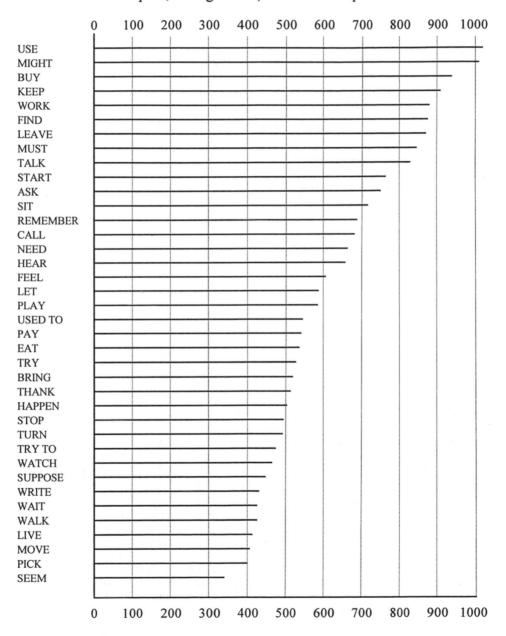

Appendix 1 (ctd.). 100 high-frequency verbs in spontaneous speech

(occurrences per million words)

* For the Appendix the same method was employed as for Figure 2.1. The figures for USE, SUPPOSE and TRY do not include forms of (BE) USED/SUPPOSED TO and TRY TO (which are given separately). However, the more marginal *to* complements of START, HELP, HATE and HOPE are not listed individually.

Appendix 2. Constructions yielding adjacent contraction verbs and *to* (table adapted from Postal & Pullum 1982: 131)

	Construction Type	Representative Example(s)
1	Null subject of *to*-clause controlled by subject of trigger verb	I wanna look at the chickens. Which chickens do you wanna look at?
2	*Wh* Movement from subject position of *to*-clause.	*Who do you wanna look at the chickens?
3	NP Movement from subject of *to*-clause to subject position of trigger verb	There hasta be a catch to this. There usta be an old castle round here someplace. [British English] There wanna be a few changes made round here.
4	Parenthetical phrase with initial *to* inserted after trigger verb.	*I wanna, be precise, a yellow, four-door De Ville convertible.
5	Subject of *to*-clause moved rightward by ('stylistic'?) rule of Heavy NP Shift.	*I wanna present themselves in my office all those students whose grade for Grammar 103 was lower than A+.
6	The *to*-clause has a subjectless infinitive as its subject.	*I don't wanna flagellate oneself in public to become standard practice in this monastery.
7	Infinitival clause extraposed to a position immediately following contraction trigger.	*It seems like to wanna regret that one does not have.
8	Restrictive relative clause ending in a contraction trigger precedes the infinitival *to* of the complement of *want*.	*I don't want anyone who continues to wanna stop wanting.
9	Purpose clause with initial *to* follows a contraction trigger.	*One must wanna become an effective overconsumer. [Ungrammatical if structure with the meaning 'in order to' is assumed.]
10	The infinitival *to* following a contraction trigger is part of a coordinate constituent.	*I wanna dance and to sing.
11	The form *to* follows a trigger verb that is part of a coordinate constituent.	*I don't need or wanna hear about it.

Appendix 3. Modal *got to* and *gotta* (variation according to style, excluding HAVE ellipsis)

	Private speech (c. 4m words)	Public speech (c. 6m words)
1 *have got to*	73	144
2 *'ve got to*	1810	1447
3 *has got to*	44	98
4 *'s got to*	373	286
5 *had got to*	4	15
6 *'d got to*	28	85
7 *-n't got to*	57	19
8 *not got to*	7	3
9 *have/'ve/has/'s/had/'d got* sthg. *to* infinitive*	485	341
10 *have gotta*	24	15
11 *'ve gotta*	1165	406
12 *has gotta*	17	13
13 *'s gotta*	383	119
14 *had gotta*	2	0
15 *'d gotta*	10	12
16 *not gotta*	5	1
17 *-n't gotta*	45	5
18 Total of rows 1 - 8 and 10 - 17	4047	2668

*Figures in row 9 are arrived at through extrapolation from four samples of 200 examples each.

Appendix 4.   Regional variation of *gonna* in the spoken BNC:
Divergence from mean of all regions

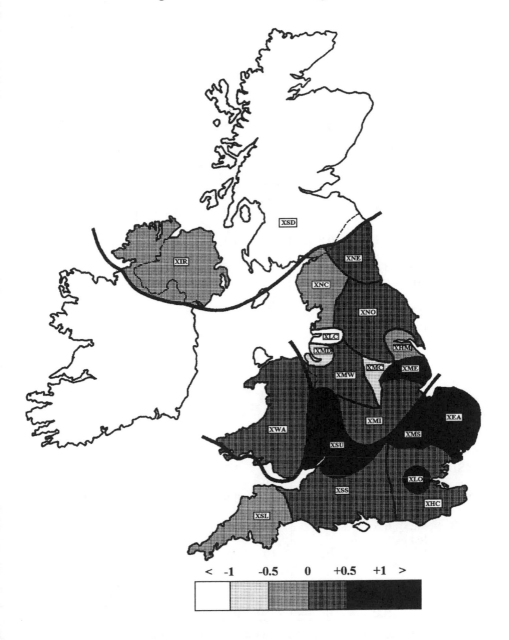

Appendix 5. Gonna, gotta and *wanna* and their full forms in spoken BNC

Area	gonna			gotta			wanna		
	Occur-rences	% of sum	% divergence from mean	Occur-rences	% of sum	% divergence from mean	Occur-rences	% of sum	% divergence from mean
XEA	428	6.4	+1.3	231	10.3	+5.2	102	7.1	+2.0
	129			161			136		
XHC	827	12.3	+0.3	194	8.6	-3.4	156	10.9	-1.1
	705			360			568		
XHM	46	0.7	-0.5	3	0.1	-1.1	5	0.3	-0.9
	77			20			68		
XIR	98	1.5	-0.2	11	0.5	-1.2	26	1.8	+0.1
	69			20			41		
XLC	190	2.8	-1.4	31	1.4	-2.8	22	1.5	-2.7
	145			120			102		
XLO	1244	18.6	+2.7	460	20.4	+4.5	345	24.1	+8.2
	624			512			392		
XMC	342	5.1	-1.0	119	5.3	-0.8	58	4.1	-2.0
	342			246			234		
XMD	141	2.1	-0.8	24	1.1	-1.8	20	1.4	-1.5
	252			81			122		
XME	324	4.8	+0.7	47	2.1	-2.0	41	2.9	-1.2
	170			73			139		
XMI	200	3.0	+0.4	58	2.6	0	38	2.7	+0.1
	164			132			118		
XMS	163	2.4	+0.5	48	2.1	+0.2	39	2.7	+0.8
	47			94			53		
XMW	545	8.1	+0.1	124	5.5	-2.5	73	5.1	-2.9
	342			242			278		
XNC	325	4.8	-0.3	70	3.1	-2.0	45	3.1	-2.0
	206			134			112		
XNE	240	3.6	+0.2	68	3.0	-0.4	97	6.8	+3.4
	96			73			113		
XNO	118	1.8	+0.1	30	1.3	-0.4	18	1.3	-0.4
	133			67			87		
XSD	277	4.1	-2.8	74	3.3	-3.6	43	3.0	-3.9
	312			201			190		
XSL	213	3.2	-0.4	199	8.8	+5.2	72	5.0	+1.4
	83			94			55		
XSS	442	6.6	0	268	11.9	+5.3	100	7.0	+0.4
	164			310			153		
XSU	105	1.6	+0.6	19	0.8	-0.2	35	2.4	+1.4
	36			23			21		
XWA	437	6.5	+0.4	172	7.6	+1.5	97	6.8	+0.7
	186			129			111		
Sum	6705	100	0	2250	100	0	1432	100	0

For each area, top figures give the contracted variants, bottom figures the uncontract
variants. For each item, the third column gives the divergence from the mean of all regio
See Map 3.1 (p. 112) for the regions and codes.

Appendix 6. Gravitation in the field of emerging modals (including the central modal WILL)

Influence on \ Influence of		GOING TO	HAVE TO	WANT TO	GOT TO	NEED (TO)	OUGHT (TO)	DARE (TO)	WILL	Total influence	Influence on unit
Frequency per 100,000		329	204	177	155	28	15	5	780		
329 GOING TO			401,4	415,7	1020,7	14,7	3,4	0,2	1253,4	3109,5	9,5
	similarity index		8	7	4	7	8	10	12		
204 HAVE TO		647,3		671,0	213,3	14,1	3,3	0,2	643,5	2192,7	10,7
	similarity index	8		5	8	7	8	10	14		
177 WANT TO		772,7	773,3		261,4	18,8	4,2	0,3	665,8	2496,6	14,1
	similarity index	7	5		7	6	7	9	13		
155 GOT TO		2166,5	280,7	298,5		13,6	3,2	0,2	700,4	3463,1	22,3
	similarity index	4	8	7		7	8	10	12		
28 NEED (TO)		173,3	102,5	118,9	75,0		5,9	0,4	174,2	650,2	23,2
	similarity index	7	7	6	7		5	7	11		
15 OUGHT (TO)		73,7	44,5	50,0	33,1	9,5		0,5	115,1	326,4	21,8
	similarity index	8	8	7	8	5		6	10		
5 DARE (TO)		16,2	10,0	10,6	7,5	2,4	1,6		59,8	108,1	21,6
	similarity index	10	10	9	10	7	6		8		
780 WILL		528,7	168,3	151,1	139,2	6,3	2,2	0,4		996,1	1,3
	similarity index	12	14	13	12	11	10	8			
Total influence		4378,4	1780,8	1715,7	1750,2	79,3	23,7	2,4	3612,3	12346,7	
Influence per unit		13,3	8,7	9,7	11,3	2,8	1,6	0,5	4,6		

References

Aarts, Jan – Flor Aarts
  1995   *Find* and *want*: A corpus-based case study in verb complementation. In: Bas Aarts & C. Meyer (eds.), *The verb in contemporary English: Theory and description.* Cambridge: Cambridge University Press, 159-182.

Aitchison, Jean
  1980   Review of Lightfoot 1979. *Linguistics* 18, 137-146.
  1991   *Language change: Progress or decay?* Cambridge: Cambridge University Press.
  ^{2}1994 [^{1}1987] *Words in the mind: An introduction to the mental lexicon.* Oxford: Blackwell.

Algeo, John
  1989   Americanisms, Briticisms, and the standard: An essay at definition. In: Joseph. Trahern (ed.), *Standardizing English: Essays in the history of language change.* Knoxville: University of Tennessee Press, 139-157.

Allen, Cynthia L.
  1986   Reconsidering the history of *like*. *Journal of Linguistics* 22, 375-409.
  1995   *Case marking and reanalysis: Grammatical relations from Old to Early Modern English.* Oxford: Clarendon.
  1997   The development of an 'impersonal' verb in Middle English: The case of *behoove*. In: J. Fisiak (ed.), *Studies in Middle English linguistics.* Berlin: Mouton de Gruyter, 1-21.

Anderwald, Lieselotte - Bernd Kortmann
  Forthcoming Typology and dialectology: A programmatic sketch. In: J. van Marle – J. Berns (eds.), *Present Day Dialectology: Problems and discussions.* Berlin; New York: Mouton de Gruyter.

Andrews, Avery
  1978   Remarks on *to* adjunction. *Linguistic Inquiry* 9, 261-268.

Anglo-Saxon Dictionary (Dictionary and supplement)
  1898   Joseph Bosworth et al. (eds.), Oxford: Oxford University Press.

Aoun, Joseph – David W. Lightfoot
  1984   Government and contraction. *Linguistic Inquiry* 15, 456-472.

Asher, R. E. (ed.)
  1994   *The encyclopedia of language and linguistics* (10 vols.). Oxford: Pergamon.

Aston, Guy – Lou Burnard
  1998   *The BNC handbook: Exploring the British National Corpus with SARA* (Edinburgh Textbooks in Empirical Linguistics). Edinburgh: Edinburgh University Press.

Austen, Jane
1813   *Pride and prejudice.* London: Penguin [ed. by T. Tanner, 1985].
Auwera, Johan van der
1998   Conclusion. In: J. van der Auwera (ed.), 813-836.
Auwera, Johan van der (ed., in collaboration with Dónall P.Ó Baoill)
1998   *Adverbial constructions in the languages of Europe* (Empirical
              Approaches to Language Typology: EUROTYP 20-3). Berlin:
              Mouton de Gruyter.
Auwera, Johan van der – Vladimir A. Plungian
1998   Modality's semantic map. *Linguistic Typology* 2:1, 79-124.
Baltin, Mark R
1995   Floating quantifiers, PRO, and predication. *Linguistic Inquiry*
              26:2, 199-248.
Barber, Charles
1993   *The English language: A historical introduction.* Cambridge:
              Cambridge University Press.
1997   *Early Modern English.* Edinburgh: Edinburgh University Press.
Barcelona, Antonio (ed.)
2000   *Metaphor and metonymy at the crossroads: A cognitive
              perspective.* Berlin: Mouton de Gruyter.
Barnbrook, Geoff
1996   *Language and computers: A practical introduction to the
              computer analysis of language.* Edinburgh: Edinburgh University
              Press.
Barss, Andrew
1995   Extraction and contraction. *Linguistic Inquiry* 26:2, 681-694.
Bauer, Laurie
1989   The verb *have* in New Zealand English. *English World-Wide* 10,
              69-83.
1994   *Watching English change: An introduction to the study of
              linguistic change in standard Englishes in the twentieth century.*
              London: Longman.
Beal, Joan
1993   The grammar of Tyneside and Northumbrian English. In: J.
              Milroy & L. Milroy (eds.), *Real English: The grammar of
              English dialects in the British Isles.* London: Longman, 187-213.
Benveniste, Émile
1968   Mutations of linguistic categories. In: W. Lehmann & Y. Malkiel
              (eds.), *Directions for historical linguistics: A symposium.* Austin:
              University of Texas Press, 85-94.
Berglund, Ylva
1999   Exploiting a large spoken corpus: An end-user's way to the BNC.
              International Journal of Corpus Linguistics 4:1, 29-52.

Biber, Douglas
1988   *Variation across speech and writing.* Cambridge: Cambridge
            University Press.
1995   *Dimensions of register variation: A cross-linguistic comparison.*
            Cambridge: Cambridge University Press.
1998   Dimensions of variation among 18th century speech-based and
            written registers. Paper presented at ICAME, Newcastle,
            Northern Ireland .
Biber, Douglas – Susan Conrad – Randi Reppen
1998   *Corpus linguistics: Investigating language structure and use.*
            Cambridge: Cambridge University Press.
Biber, Douglas – Edward Finegan
1997   Diachronic relations among speech-based and written registers in
            English. In: T. Nevalainen & L. Kahlas-Tarkka (eds.), *To explain
            the present: Studies in the changing English language in honour
            of Matti Rissanen.* Helsinki: Société Néophilologique.
Biber, Douglas – Edward Finegan – Dwight Atkinson
1994a   ARCHER and its challenges: Compiling and exploring a
            representative corpus of historical English registers. In: U. Fries;
            G. Tottie & P. Schneider (eds.), *Creating and using English
            language corpora: Papers from the Fourteenth International
            Conference on English Language Research on Computerized
            Corpora, Zürich 1993.* Amsterdam; Atlanta, GA: Rodopi, 1-13.
Biber, Douglas – Edward Finegan – Dwight Atkinson – Ann Beck – Dennis Burges
            – Jean Burges
1994b   The design and analysis of the ARCHER Corpus: A progress
            report. In: Kytö et al. (eds.), 3-6.
Biber, Douglas – Stig Johansson – Geoffrey Leech – Susan Conrad – Edward
            Finegan
1999   *The Longman grammar of spoken and written English.* London:
            Longman.
Birkmann, Thomas
1987   *Präteritopräsentia: Morphologische Entwicklungen einer
            Sonderklasse in den altgermanischen Sprachen* (Linguistische
            Arbeiten, 188). Tübingen: Niemeyer.
Bisang, Walter
1998   Grammaticalization and language contact, constructions and
            positions. In: A. G. Ramat & P. Hopper (eds.), 13-58.
Bolinger, Dwight
1980a   *Language. The loaded weapon.* London: Longman.
1980b   *Wanna* and the gradience of auxiliaries. In: G. Brettschneider &
            C. Lehmann (eds.), *Wege zur Universalienforschung:
            Sprachwissenschaftliche Beiträge zum 60. Geburtstag von
            Hansjakob Seiler.* Tübingen: Narr, 292-299.

1981   Consonance, dissonance and grammaticality: The case of *wanna*. *Language and Communication* 1, 189-206.

Bouchard, Denis
1986   Empty categories and the contraction debate. *Linguistic Inquiry* 17, 95-104.

Bouma, Lowell
1973   *The semantics of the modal auxiliaries in contemporary German.* The Hague: Mouton.

Boyland, Joyce Tang
1996   *Morphosyntactic change in progress: A psycholinguistic treatment.* Doctoral dissertation Berkeley, CA.

Bradley, Henry – Francis H. Stratmann
²1891 [¹1878] *A Middle-English dictionary: Containing words used by English writers from the twelfth to the fifteenth century.* Oxford: Oxford University Press.

Brinton, Laurel J.
1988   *The development of English aspectual systems: Aspectualizers and post-verbal particles.* Cambridge: Cambridge University Press.
1991   The origin and development of quasimodal *have to* in English. Paper presented at the 10ᵗʰ International Conference on Historical Linguistics, Amsterdam, ms. 59pp.

Brinton, Laurel J. – Dieter Stein
1993   Functional renewal. In: H. Andersen (ed.), *Historical linguistics 1993: Selected papers from the 11ᵗʰ International Conference on Historical Linguistics.* Amsterdam: Benjamins, 33-47.

Brown, Penelope – Stephen C. Levinson
²1987   *Politeness: Some universals of language usage.* Cambridge: Cambridge University Press.

Brown, Keith
1991   Double modals in Hawick Scots. In: P. Trudgill & J. K. Chambers (eds.), *Dialects of English: Studies in grammatical variation.* London: Longman, 74-103.

Browning, M. A.
1991   Bounding conditions on representation. *Linguistic Inquiry* 22, 541-562.

Brunner, Karl
⁵1962   *Abriss der mittelenglischen Grammatik.* Tübingen: Niemeyer.

Burchfield, Robert W. (ed.)
³1996 [¹1926]   *The new Fowler's modern English usage.* Oxford: Clarendon.

Burnard, Lou (ed.)
1995   *User reference guide for the British National Corpus.* Oxford: Oxford University Computing Services.

Bush, Nathan
1999   *The predictive value of transitional probability for word-boundary palatization in English.* MA thesis Albuquerque, NM.
Bußmann, Hadumod
1996   *Routledge dictionary of language and linguistics.* Translated and edited by G. Trauth & K. Kazzazi. (German original: *Lexikon der Sprachwissenschaft,* 1990.) London – New York: Routledge.
Bybee, Joan L.
1985   *Morphology: A study of the relation between meaning and form.* Amsterdam: Benjamins.
1986   On the nature of grammatical categories: A diachronic perspective. *Eastern States Conference on Linguistics* 2: 17-34.
1988   The diachronic dimension in explanation. In: John Hawkins (ed.), *Explaining language universals.* Oxford: Blackwell, 350-379.
1995   The semantic development of past tense modals in English. In: J. Bybee & S. Fleischman (eds.), *Modality in grammar and discourse.* Amsterdam: Benjamins, 503-517.
1997   Semantic aspects of morphological typology. In: J. Bybee; J. Haiman & S. Thompson (eds.), *Essays on language function and language type. Dedicated to T. Givón.* Amsterdam: Benjamins, 25-37.
1998   Usage-based phonology. In: M. Darnell; E. Moravcsik; F. Newmeyer; M. Noonan & K. Wheatley (eds.), *Functionalism and formalism in linguistics: General papers* (2 vols.). Amsterdam: Benjamins, I, 211-242.
1999a   Mechanisms of change in grammaticization: The role of frequency. In B. Joseph & R. Janda (eds.), *Handbook of historical linguistics.* Oxford: Oxford University Press, ms. 26pp.
1999b   Fusion in grammaticization: Automatization and the suffixing preference". Paper given at the conference *New reflections on grammaticalization,* Potsdam, June 1999.
Forthcoming Frequency effects on French liaison. In: Bybee & Hopper (eds.).
Bybee, Joan L. – Östen Dahl
1989   The creation of tense and aspect systems in the languages of the world. *Studies in Language* 13:1, 51-103.
Bybee, Joan L. – Paul Hopper (eds.)
Forthcoming *Frequency and the emergence of linguistic structure: Proceedings from the Symposium on Frequency Effects & Emergent Grammar at Carnegie-Mellon University, May 28-30, 1999* (Typological Studies in Language). Amsterdam: Benjamins.
Bybee, Joan L. – William Pagliuca
1985   Cross-linguistic comparison and the development of grammatical meaning. In: J. Fisiak (ed.), 59-83.

Bybee, Joan L. – William Pagliuca – Revere D. Perkins
1991   Back to the future. In: E. Traugott & B. Heine (eds.), 17-58.
Bybee, Joan L. – William Pagliuca – Revere D. Perkins
1994   *The evolution of grammar: Tense, aspect, and modality in the languages of the world.* Chicago: University of Chicago Press.
Bybee, Joan L. – Joanne Scheibman
Forthcoming The effect of usage on degrees of constituency: The reduction of *don't* in English. Paper given at the *Workshop on Constituency and Discourse.* University of California, Santa Barbara. May 1997, ms. 19pp. To appear in *Linguistics.*
Bybee, Joan L. – Dan Slobin
1982   Rules and schemas in the development and use of the English past tense. *Language* 58:2, 265-289.
Bybee, Joan L. – Sandra A. Thompson
Forthcoming Three frequency effects in syntax. *Proceedings of the Berkeley Linguistics Society 1997*, ms. 11pp.
Campbell, Alistair
1959   *Old English grammar.* Oxford: Clarendon.
Chafe, Wallace
1984   Speaking, writing, and prescriptivism. In: D. Schiffrin (ed.), 95-103.
1998   Language and the flow of thought. In: M. Tomasello (ed.), *The psychology of language: Cognitive and functional approaches to language structure.* Mahwah, NJ: Erlbaum, 93-111.
Chafe, Wallace L. – John W. Du Bois – Sandra A. Thompson
1991   Towards a new corpus of spoken American English. In: K. Aijmer & B. Altenberg (eds.), *English corpus linguistics: Studies in honour of Jan Svartvik.* London; New York: Longman, 64-82.
Chambers, Jack K.
1993   Sociolinguistic dialectology. In: D. Preston (ed.), *American dialect research.* Amsterdam: Benjamins, 133-164.
Chambers, Jack K. – Peter Trudgill
²1998 [¹1980] *Dialectology.* Cambridge: Cambridge University Press.
Chapman, Raymond
1988   We Gonna Rite Wot We Wanna: The Appeal of Misspelling. *English Today* 14, 39-42.
Chomsky, Noam
1981   *Lectures on government and binding.* Dordrecht: Foris.
1986   *Knowledge of language: Its nature, origin, and use.* New York: Praeger.
1995   *The minimalist program.* Cambridge, Mass.: MIT Press.

Chomsky, Noam – Howard Lasnik
1977   Filters and control. *Linguistic Inquiry* 8, 425-504.
1978   A remark on contraction. *Linguistic Inquiry* 9, 268-274.
Christie, Pauline
1991   Modality in Jamaican Creole. In: W. Edwards & D. Winford (eds.), *Verb phrase patterns in Black English and Creole.* Detroit: Wayne State University Press, 217-233.
Chung, Sandra – Alan Timberlake
1985   Tense, aspect and mood. In: T. Shopen (ed.), *Language typology and syntactic description.* Cambridge: Cambridge University Press, III, 202-258.
Clear, Jeremy
1993   The British National Corpus. In: G. Landow & P. Delany (eds.), *The digital word: Text-based computing in the humanities.* Cambridge, Mass.: MIT Press, 163-187.
Coates, Jennifer
1983   *The semantics of the modal auxiliaries.* London: Croom Helm.
1995   The expression of root and epistemic possibility in English. In: J. Bybee & S. Fleischman (eds.), *Modality in grammar and discourse.* Amsterdam: Benjamins, 55-66.
Coates, Jennifer – Deborah Cameron (eds.)
1988   *Women in their speech communities: new perspectives on language and sex.* London: Longman.
Collins Cobuild English Dictionary
[2]1995 [[1]1987]   John Sinclair et al. (eds.). London: Harper Collins.
Croft, William
1990   *Typology and universals.* Cambridge: Cambridge University Press.
1995   Autonomy and functional linguistics. *Language* 71:3, 490-532.
1998   The structure of events and the structure of language. In: M. Tomasello (ed.), *The psychology of language: Cognitive and functional approaches to language structure.* Mahwah, NJ: Erlbaum, 67-92.
Crowdy, Steve
1995   The BNC spoken corpus. In: G. Leech et al. (eds.), *Spoken English on computer: Transcription, mark-up and application.* London: Longman, 224-234.
Crystal, David
1988   *The English language.* London: Penguin.
[4]1997 [[1]1980] *A dictionary of linguistics and phonetics.* Oxford: Blackwell.

Danchev, Andrei – Merja Kytö
1994   The construction *be going to* + infinitive in Early Modern
              English. In: D. Kastovsky (ed.), *Studies in Early Modern English*
              (Topics in English Linguistics, 13). Berlin: Mouton de Gruyter,
              59-77.
Darnell, Michael – Edith Moravcsik – Frederick Newmeyer – Michael Noonan –
              Kathleen Wheatley (eds.)
1998   *Functionalism and formalism in linguistics* (2 vols.): *General
              papers*. Amsterdam: Benjamins.
Defoe, Daniel
1719/20   *The farther adventures of Robinson Crusoe*. London: Dent [ed. by
              G. Pocock, 1966].
Denison, David
1986   On word order in Old English. *Dutch Quarterly Review* 16, 277-
              295.
1990   The Old English impersonals revisited. In: S. Adamson et al.
              (eds.), *Papers from the 5th International Conference on English
              Historical Linguistics* (Current Issues in Linguistic Theory, 65).
              Amsterdam: Benjamins, 111- 140.
1993   *English historical syntax: Verbal constructions*. London: Longman.
1998   Syntax. In S. Romaine (ed.), *The Cambridge History of the
              English Language: 1776-1997* (5 vols.). Cambridge: Cambridge
              University Press, IV, 92-329.
Dickens, Charles
1837/38   *Oliver Twist*. London: Penguin [ed. by P. Fairclough, 1985].
Diewald, Gabriele
1997   *Grammatikalisierung: Eine Einführung in Sein und Werden
              grammatischer Formen*. Tübingen: Niemeyer.
Dik, Simon C.
³1981 [¹1978] *Functional Grammar* (Publications in Language Sciences, 7).
              Dordrecht: Foris.
1989   *The theory of Functional Grammar*. Dordrecht: Foris.
Dixon, Robert M. W.
1997   *The rise and fall of languages*. Cambridge: Cambridge University
              Press.
DuBois, John W.
1985   Competing motivations. In: J. Haiman (ed.), 343-365.
1987   The discourse basis of ergativity. *Language* 64, 104-113.

Eliot, George [Mary Ann Evans]
1860   *The mill on the floss*. New York; London: Norton [ed. by C. Christ, 1994].

Ellegård, Alvar
1953   *The auxiliary* DO: *The establishment and regulation of its use in English* (Gothenburg Studies in English, 2). Stockholm: Almqvist & Wiksell.

Elmer, Willy
1981   *Diachronic grammar: The history of Old and Middle English subjectless constructions*. Tübingen: Niemeyer.

English Dialect Dictionary
1961   Joseph Wright (ed.), Oxford: Oxford University Press.

Fennell, Barbara A. – Ronald R. Butters
1996   Historical and contemporary distribution of double modals in English. In: E. Schneider (ed.), 265-288.

Fischer, Andreas
1999   What, if anything, is phonological iconicity? In: M. Nänny & O. Fischer (eds.), *Form miming meaning: Iconicity in language and literature*. Amsterdam: Benjamins, 123-134.

Fischer, Olga
1992   Syntax. In: N. Blake (ed.), *The Cambridge History of the English Language: 1066-1476* (5 vols.). Cambridge: Cambridge University Press, II, 207-408.

1994   The development of quasi-auxiliaries in English and changes in word order. *Neophilologus* 78, 137-164.

Fischer, Olga – Frederike van der Leek
1983   The demise of the Old English impersonal construction. *Journal of Linguistics* 19, 337-368.

1987   A 'case' for the Old English impersonals. In: W. Koopman et al. (eds.), *Explanation and linguistic change* (Current Issues in Linguistic Theory, 45). Amsterdam: Benjamins, 79-120.

Fischer, Olga – Anette Rosenbach – Dieter Stein (eds.)
In press   *Pathways of change: Grammaticalization in English*. Amsterdam: Benjamins.

Fisiak, Jacek (ed.)
1985   *Historical semantics, historical word-formation* (Trends in Linguistics: Studies and Monographs, 29). Berlin: Mouton de Gruyter.

Fleischman, Suzanne
1982   *The future in thought and language: Diachronic evidence from Romance*. Cambridge: Cambridge University Press.

Foley, William A. – Robert D. VanValin
1984   *Functional syntax and universal grammar* (Cambridge Studies in Linguistics, 38). Cambridge: Cambridge University Press.

Foster, Brian
1968   *The changing English language.* Harmondsworth: Penguin.
Francis, W. Nelson
1958   *The structure of American English.* New York: Ronald.
Francis, Winthrop Nelson – Kučera, Henry
⁴1989 [¹1964]   *Manual of information to accompany a standard corpus of present-day edited American English, for use with digital computers.* Providence, RI: Department of Linguistics, Brown University.
Frei, Henri
1929   *La grammaire des fautes.* Paris: Geuthner.
Gaaf, W. van der
1904   *The transition from the impersonal to the personal construction in Middle English* (Anglistische Forschungen, 14). Heidelberg: Carl Winter.
1931   *Beon* and *habban* connected with an inflected infinitive. *English Studies* 13, 176-188.
Gabelentz, Georg van der
1891   *Die Sprachwissenschaft: Ihre Aufgaben, Methoden und bisherigen Ergebnisse.* Leipzig: Weigel.
Garrett, Andrew
1998   The origin of auxiliary *do. English Language and Linguistics* 2:2, 283-330.
Geeraerts, Dirk
1997   *Diachronic prototype semantics: A contribution to historical lexicology.* Oxford: Clarendon Press.
Georges, Karl Ernst
1913   *Ausführliches lateinisch-deutsches Handwörterbuch* (2 vols.). Darmstadt: Wissenschaftliche Buchgesellschaft.
Givón, Talmy
1979   *On understanding grammar.* New York: Academic Press.
1984   *Syntax: A functional-typological introduction* (Vol. I). Amsterdam: Benjamins.
1985   Iconicity, isomorphism and nonarbitrary coding in syntax: Iconicity in syntax. In: J. Haiman (ed.), 187-220.
1993   *English grammar: A function-based introduction* (2 vols.). Amsterdam: Benjamins.
1995   *Functionalism and grammar.* Amsterdam: Benjamins.
1998   The functional approach to grammar. In: M. Tomasello (ed.), *The psychology of language: Cognitive and functional approaches to language structure.* Mahwah, NJ: Erlbaum, 41-66.
Gleason, Henry Allan
1965   *Linguistics and English grammar.* New York: Holt, Rinehart and Winston.

Goldberg, Adele E.
1995   *Constructions: A construction grammar approach to argument structure.* Chicago: University of Chicago Press.

Goodall, Grant
1991   *Wanna*-contraction as restructuring. In: C. Georgopoulos & R. Ishihara (eds.) *Interdisciplinary approaches to language: Essays in honor of S.-Y. Kuroda.* Dordrecht; Boston: Kluwer Academic, 239-254.

Goossens, Louis
1987   The auxiliarization of the English modals: A Functional Grammar view. In: M. Harris & P. Ramat (eds.), 111-143.

Greenbaum, Sidney
1990   Whose English? In: C. Ricks & L. Michaels (eds.), *The state of language.* London: Faber & Faber, 15-23.

Grice, Herbert Paul
1989 [1975] Logic and conversation. In: H. P. Grice, *Studies in the way of words.* Cambridge, Mass.: Harvard University Press, 22-40.

Gronemeyer, Claire
1999   On deriving complex polysemy: The grammaticalization of *get. English Language and Linguistics* 3:1, 1-39.

Haiman, John
1980   The iconicity of grammar: Isomorphism and motivation. *Language* 56:3, 515-540.
1983   Iconic and economic motivation. *Language* 59:4, 781-819.
1985   *Natural syntax: Iconicity and erosion.* Cambridge: Cambridge University Press.
1994a   Ritualization and the development of language. In: W. Pagliuca (ed.), 3-28.
1994b   Iconicity. In: R. E. Asher (ed.), 1629-1633.
1994c   Iconicity and syntactic change. In: R. E. Asher (ed.), 1633-1637.

Haiman, John (ed.)
1985   *Iconicity in syntax.* Amsterdam: Benjamins.

Halliday, Michael A.K.
²1994 [¹1985] *An introduction to functional grammar.* London: Arnold.

Harley, Trevor A.
1995   *The psychology of language: From data to theory.* Erlbaum: Taylor & Francis.

Harris, Alice C. – Lyle Campbell
1995   *Historical syntax in cross-linguistic perspective.* Cambridge: Cambridge University Press.

Harris, Martin – Paolo Ramat (eds.)
1987   *Historical development of auxiliaries* (Trends in Linguistics: Studies and Monographs, 35). Berlin: Mouton de Gruyter.

Haspelmath, Martin
1998   Does grammaticalization need reanalysis? *Studies in Language*
              22:2, 315-351.
Hawkins, John
1986   *A comparative typology of English and German. Unifying the
              contrasts.* London: Croom Helm.
Haynes, Charles S.
1967   *A grammar of modal and catenative auxiliaries in contemporary
              informal spoken American English.* Doctoral dissertation New
              York.
Heine, Bernd
1993   *Auxiliaries: Cognitive forces and grammaticalization.* Oxford:
              Oxford University Press.
1998   On explaining grammar: The grammaticalization of *have*-
              constructions. *Theoretical Linguistics* 24:1, 29-41.
1999   On the role of context in grammaticalization. Paper given at the
              conference *New reflections on grammaticalization*, Potsdam,
              June 1999.
Heine, Bernd – Ulrike Claudi – Friederike Hünnemeyer
1991   *Grammaticalization: A conceptual framework.* Chicago:
              University of Chicago Press.
Heine, Bernd – Mechthild Reh
1984   *Grammaticalization and reanalysis in African languages.*
              Hamburg: Buske.
Hendrick, Randall
1982   Reduced questions and their theoretical implications. *Language*
              58:4, 800-819.
Hengeveld, Kees
Forthcoming   Mood and modality. In: G. Booij; C. Lehmann & J. Mugdan
              (eds.), *Morphology: A handbook on inflection and word
              formation.* Berlin; New York: Mouton de Gruyter, ms. 30pp.
Hofland, Knut – Stig Johansson
1982   *Word frequencies in British and American English.* Bergen:
              Norwegian Computing Centre for the Humanities.
Hogg, Richard M.
1982   Was there ever an /ɔ/-phoneme in Old English? *Neuphilologische
              Mitteilungen* 83, 225-229.
Hooper, Joan L.
1976   Word frequency in lexical diffusion and the source of
              morphophonological change. In: W. M. Christie (ed.), *Current
              progress in historical linguistics* (North-Holland Linguistic
              Series, 31). Amsterdam: North Holland, 95-105.
Hopper, Paul J.
1987   Emergent Grammar. *Berkeley Linguistics Society* 13, 139-157.

1991   On some principles of grammaticization. In: E. Traugott & B. Heine (eds.), I, 17-35.

1998   Emergent Grammar (revised version of Hopper 1987). In: M. Tomasello (ed.), *The psychology of language: Cognitive and functional approaches to language structure.* Mahwah: Erlbaum, NJ, 155-175.

Hopper, Paul J. – Sandra A. Thompson

1985   The iconicity of the universal categories 'noun' and 'verb'. In: J. Haiman (ed.), 151-183.

Hopper, Paul J. – Elizabeth C. Traugott

1993   *Grammaticalization.* Cambridge: Cambridge University Press.

Horn, Laurence R.

1984   Toward a new taxonomy for pragmatic inference: Q-based and R-based implicature. In: D. Schiffrin (ed.), 11-42.

1992   Pragmatics, implicature, and presupposition. In: W. Bright (ed.), *International encyclopaedia of linguistics* (4 vols.). Oxford: Oxford University Press, III, 260-266.

Hübler, Axel

1998   *The expressivity of grammar: Grammatical devices expressing emotion across time* (Topics in English Linguistics, 25). Berlin; New York: Mouton de Gruyter.

Hüllen, Werner – Rainer Schulze (eds.)

1988   *Understanding the lexicon: Meaning, sense and world knowledge in lexical semantics.* Tübingen: Niemeyer.

Humboldt, Wilhelm von

1825   Über das Entstehen der grammatikalischen Formen und ihren Einfluß auf die Ideenentwicklung. *Abhandlungen der Königlichen Akademie der Wissenschaften zu Berlin,* 401-430.

Hundt, Marianne

1997   Has BrE been catching up with AmE over the past thirty years? In: M. Ljung (ed.), *Corpus-based studies in English: Papers from the 17th International Conference on English Language Research on Computerized Corpora (ICAME 17) 1996, Stockholm.* Amsterdam: Rodopi, 135-151.

1998   *New Zealand English grammar - fact or fiction? A corpus-based study in morphosyntactic variation* (Varieties of English Around the World, 23). Amsterdam: Benjamins.

Forthcoming What corpora have to say about the grammaticalisation of voice in *get*-constructions. *Studies in Language,* ms., 31pp.

Hundt, Marianne – Christian Mair

1999   'Agile' and 'uptight' genres: The corpus-based approach to language change in progress. *International Journal of Corpus Linguistics.*

Hundt, Marianne – Andrea Sand – Rainer Siemund
1998   *Manual of information to accompany the Freiburg-LOB Corpus of British English*. English Department: University of Freiburg.
Hundt, Marianne – Andrea Sand – Paul Skandera
1999   *Manual of Information to accompany the Freiburg-Brown Corpus of American English*. English Department: University of Freiburg.
Hymes, Dell
1967   Models of the interaction of language and social setting. *Journal of Social Issues* 23, 8-28.
Ingram, John C. L.
1989   Connected speech processes in Australian English. *Australian Journal of Linguistics* 9, 21-49.
Inkelas, Sharon – Draga Zec
1993   Auxiliary reduction without empty categories: A prosodic account. *Working Papers of the Cornell Phonetics Laboratory* 8, 205-253.
Jacobsson, Bengt
1979   Modality and the modals of necessity *must* and *have to*. *English Studies* 60, 296-312.
1994   Recessive and emergent uses of modal auxiliaries in English. *English Studies* 75, 166-182.
Jaeggli, Osvaldo A.
1980   Remarks on *to* contraction. *Linguistic Inquiry* 11, 239-245.
Jespersen, Otto
1909-1949 *A modern English grammar on historical principles* (7 vols.). Heidelberg: Carl Winter.
1924   *The philosophy of grammar*. London: Allen & Unwin.
Johansson, Stig
1979   American and British English grammar: An elicitation experiment. *English Studies* 60: 195-215.
Johansson, Stig – Geoffrey N. Leech – Helen Goodluck
1978   *Manual of information to accompany the Lancaster-Oslo/Bergen Corpus of British English, for use with digital computers*. Oslo: Department of English, University of Oslo.
Johansson, Stig – Signe Oksefjell
1996   Towards a unified account of the syntax and semantics of GET. In: J. Thomas & M. Short (eds.), *Using corpora for language research: Studies in the honour of Geoffrey Leech*. London; New York: Longman, 57-75.
Jones, Daniel
[15]1997 [[1]1917] *English pronouncing dictionary*. Cambridge: Cambridge University Press.

Käding, Friedrich Wilhelm
1897   *Häufigkeitswörterbuch der deutschen Sprache.* Steglitz: Privately
            published.
Kemenade, Ans van
1989   *Syntactic change and the history of English modals* (Dutch
            Working Papers in English Language and Linguistics, 16).
            Leiden: Vakgroep Engels, Rijksuniversiteit.
1992   Structural factors in the history of English modals. In: M.
            Rissanen et al. (eds.), *History of Englishes: New methods and
            interpretations in historical linguistics: A selection of papers
            presented at the Sixth International Conference on English
            Historical Linguistics at Helsinki 1990* (Topics in English
            Linguistics, 10). Berlin; New York: Mouton de Gruyter, 287-309.
Kemenade, Ans van (ed.)
Forthcoming *Functional properties of morphosyntactic change* (Special issue
            of *Linguistics*). New York: Walter de Gruyter.
Kennedy, Graeme D.
1998   *An introduction to corpus linguistics.* London: Longman.
Kenyon, John S. – Thomas A. Knott
1944   *A pronouncing dictionary of American English.* Springfield,
            Mass.: Merriam.
Kirchner, G.
1940   'To want' as an auxiliary of modality. *English Studies* 22: 129-
            136.
Kjellmer, Göran
forthcoming Auxiliary marginalities. Paper presented at ICAME, Newcastle,
            Northern Ireland.
Koch, Peter – Wulf Oesterreicher
1985   Sprache der Nähe - Sprache der Distanz: Mündlichkeit und
            Schriftlichkeit im Spannungsfeld von Sprachtheorie und
            Sprachgeschichte. *Romanistisches Jahrbuch* 36, 15-43.
Kortmann, Bernd
1997   *Adverbial subordination: A typology and history of adverbial
            subordinators based on European languages.* Berlin: Mouton de
            Gruyter.
Forthcoming Reflections on the future shape of English. In: O. Blumenfeld
            (ed.), *Linguistic and Literary Studies.* Iasi: Department of
            English, ms. 25pp.
Kortmann, Bernd – Ekkehard König
1992   Categorial reanalysis: The case of deverbal prepositions.
            Linguistics 30, 671-697.

Kortmann, Bernd – Paul Georg Meyer
1992   Is English grammar more explicit than German grammar, after all? In: C. Mair & M. Markus (eds.), *New Departures in Contrastive Linguistics* (2 vols.). Innsbruck: Institut für Anglistik, I, 155-166.
Kretzschmar, William A., Jr.
1996   Foundations of American English. In: E. Schneider (ed.), 25-50.
Kroch, Anthony S.
1989   Function and grammar in the history of English: Periphrastic DO. In: R. Fasold & D. Schiffrin (eds.), *Language change and variation.* Amsterdam: Benjamins, 133-172.
Kronasser, Heinz
1952   *Handbuch der Semasiologie: Kurze Einführung in die Geschichte, Problematik und Terminologie der Bedeutungslehre.* Heidelberg: Winter.
Krug, Manfred
1994   *Contractions in spoken and written English: A corpus-based study of short-term developments since 1960.* MA thesis Exeter, England.
1996   Language change in progress: Contractions in journalese in 1961 and 1991/92. In: S. McGill (ed.), *Proceedings of the 1995 Graduate Research Conference on Language and Linguistics.* Exeter: School of English & American Studies, 17-28.
1997   Book notice on Lehmann 1995. *Language* 73, 670-671.
1998a   String frequency: A cognitive motivating factor in coalescence, language processing and linguistic change. *Journal of English Linguistics* 26:4, 286-320.
1998b   British English is developing a new discourse marker, *innit*? *Arbeiten aus Anglistik und Amerikanistik* 23:2, 145-197.
1998c   *Gotta* - the tenth central modal in English? Social, stylistic and regional variation in the British National Corpus as evidence of ongoing grammaticalization. In: H. Lindquist et al. (eds.), 177-191.
1998d   Recurrent paths in the evolution of new English auxiliaries. Paper presented at the Berkeley Germanic Linguistics Roundtable.
1998e   Progressive and conservative British English dialects: Evidence from the BNC. Paper presented at ICAME, Newcastle, Northern Ireland.
In press   The auxiliarization of *want* and *wanna*. In: O. Blumenfeld (ed.), *Proceedings of the International Conference From Margin to Centre 1996, Iasi.* Iasi: Department of English.
Forthcoming   Frequency - Iconicity - Categorization: Evidence from Emerging Modals. In: J. Bybee & P. Hopper (eds.), *Frequency and the emergence of linguistic structure.* Amsterdam: Benjamins, 24pp.

Krzyszpien, Jerzy
1984   On the impersonal-to-personal transition in English. *Studia Anglica Posnaniensia* 17, 63-69.

Kuryłowicz, Jerzy
1975 [1965]   The evolution of grammatical categories. *Esquisses Linguistiques* 2, 38-54.

Kytö, Merja
1991a   *Variation and diachrony, with early American English in focus.* Frankfurt/Main: Lang.
1991b   *Manual to the diachronic part of the Helsinki Corpus of English Texts: Coding conventions and lists of source texts.* Helsinki: Department of English.

Kytö, Merja – Matti Rissanen – Susan Wright (eds.)
1994   *Corpora across the centuries: Proceedings of the First International Colloquium on English Diachronic Corpora, Cambridge, 25-27 March 1993.* Amsterdam; Atlanta, GA: Rodopi.

Labov, William
1969   *A study of non-standard English.* Washington D.C.: Center for Applied Linguistics.
1970   The study of language in its social context. *Studium Generale* 23, 30-87.
1990   The intersection of sex and social class in the course of linguistic change. *Language Variation and Change* 2, 205-254.
1994   *Principles of linguistic change I: Internal factors* (Language in Society, 20). Oxford: Blackwell.

Lakoff, George
1970   Global rules. *Language* 46:3, 627-639.

Lambrecht, Knud
1994   *Information structure and sentence form: Topic, focus and the mental representations of discourse referents.* Cambridge: Cambridge University Press.

Langacker, Ronald W.
1987   *Foundations of cognitive grammar: Theoretical prerequisites* (Vol. I). Stanford, Cal.: Stanford University Press.
1990   Subjectification. *Cognitive Linguistics* 1, 5-38.
1991   *Foundations of cognitive grammar: Descriptive application* (Vol. II). Stanford, Cal.: Stanford University Press.

Lass, Roger
1997   *Historical linguistics and language change* (Cambridge Studies in Linguistics, 81). Cambridge: Cambridge University Press.

Leech, Geoffrey N.
1971 [²1987]   *Meaning and the English verb.* London: Longman.

Lehmann, Christian
1985   Grammaticalization: Synchronic variation and diachronic change. *Lingua e Stile* 20, 303-318.
1991   Grammaticalization and related changes in contemporary German. In: E. Traugott & B. Heine (eds.), II, 493-535.
1995 [1982]   *Thoughts on grammaticalization* (Lincom Studies in Theoretical Linguistics, 1). Munich: Lincom Europa.
1999   New reflections on grammaticalization and lexicalization. Paper given at the conference *New reflections on grammaticalization*, Potsdam, June 1999.

Lehrer, Adrienne
1985   The influence of semantic fields on semantic change. In: J. Fisiak (ed.), 283-296.

Lessau, Donald A.
1994   *A dictionary of grammaticalization* (Bochum-Essener Beiträge zur Sprachwandelforschung, 21). Bochum: Brockmeyer.

Li, Charles N. (ed.)
1977   *Mechanisms of syntactic change*. Austin: University of Texas Press.

Lightfoot, David W.
1976   Trace theory and twice-moved NPs. *Linguistic Inquiry* 4, 559-582.
1979   *Principles of diachronic syntax*. Cambridge: Cambridge University Press.
1986   A brief response [*sc.* to Postal & Pullum 1986]. *Linguistic Inquiry* 17, 111-113.
1991   *How to set parameters: Arguments from language change*. Cambridge, Mass.: MIT Press.

Lindquist, Hans – Staffan Klintborg – Magnus Levin – Maria Estling (eds.)
1998   *The major varieties of English: Papers from MAVEN 97*. Växjö: Acta Wexionensia.

Lockwood, David – Peter Fries – James Copeland (eds.)
Forthcoming   *Functional approaches to language, culture and cognition* (Amsterdam studies in the theory and history of linguistic science: Series IV, Current issues in linguistic theory, 163). Philadelphia: Benjamins.

Los, Bettelou
1998   The rise of the *to*-infinitive as verb complement. *English language and Linguistics* 2:1, 1-36.

Lyons, John
1977   *Semantics* (2 vols.). Cambridge: Cambridge University Press.

McCawley, Noriko
    1976   From OE/ME 'impersonal' to 'personal' constructions: What is a 'subjectless' S? In: S. B. Stever et al. (eds.), *Papers from the Parasession on diachronic syntax*. Chicago: Chicago Linguistic Society, 192-204.

McCloskey, James
    1988   Syntactic theory. In: F. Newmeyer (ed.), *Linguistics: The Cambridge Survey* (4 vols.). Cambridge: Cambridge University Press, IV, 18-59.

McCrum, Robert – William Cran – Robert MacNeil
    ²1992 [¹1986]   *The story of English*. London: Faber & Faber.

McEnery, Tony – Andrew Wilson
    1996   *Corpus linguistics*. Edinburgh: Edinburgh University Press.

McMahon, April M. S.
    1994   *Understanding language change*. Cambridge: Cambridge University Press.

Mair, Christian
    1990   *Infinitival complement clauses in English*. Cambridge: Cambridge University Press.
    1995   Changing patterns of complementation, and concomitant grammaticalisation, of the verb *help* in present-day British English. In: B. Aarts & C. Meyer (eds.), *The verb in contemporary English: Theory and description*. Cambridge: Cambridge University Press, 258-272.
    1997   The spread of the *going-to*-future in written English: A corpus-based investigation into language change in progress. In: R. Hickey & S. Ruppel (eds.), *Language history and linguistic modelling: A festschrift for Jacek Fisiak on his 60 birthday*. Berlin; New York: Mouton de Gruyter, 1537-43.
    1998   Corpora and the study of the major varieties of English: Issues and results. In: H. Lindquist et al. (eds.), 139-157.
    Forthcoming   Arrested Americanisation? Standard British English in the Nineteen Nineties. Paper presented at ICAME 1998, Newcastle, Northern Ireland.

Malkiel, Yakov
    1968   The inflectional paradigm as an occasional determinant of sound change. In: W. Lehmann & Y. Malkiel (eds.), *Directions for historical linguistics*. Austin: University of Texas Press, 21-64.

Matthews, Richard
    1991   *Words and worlds: On the linguistic analysis of modality*. Frankfurt/Main: Lang.
    1993   *Papers on semantics and grammar*. Frankfurt/Main: Lang.

Meillet, Antoine
1912   L'évolution des formes grammaticales. *Scientia* (*Rivista di Scienza*) 12:6, 384-400.
Middle English Dictionary (MED)
1954ff   Hans Kurath et al. (eds.), Ann Arbor: University of Michigan Press.
Milroy, James – Leslie Milroy
1978   Belfast: Change and variation in an urban vernacular. In: P. Trudgill (ed.), *Sociolinguistic patterns in British English*. London: Arnold, 19-36.
²1991 [¹1985] *Authority in language: Investigating language prescription and standardisation.* London; New York: Routledge & Kegan Paul.
Mindt, Dieter
1995   *An empirical grammar of the English verb: Modal verbs.* Berlin: Cornelsen.
Mitchell, Bruce
1985   *Old English syntax* (2 vols.). Oxford: Clarendon.
Montgomery, Michael B.
1989   Exploring the roots of Appalachian English. *English World-Wide* 10, 227-278.
Montgomery, Michael B. – Stephen J. Nagle
1993   Double modals in Scotland and the southern United States: Trans-atlantic inheritance or independent development? *Folia Linguistica Historica* 14, 91-107.
Mossé, Fernand
1938   *Histoire de la forme périphrastique* être + participe présent *en Germanique.* Paris: Klincksieck.
1947   *Esquisse d'une histoire de la langue anglaise.* Lyon: IAC.
1959   *A handbook of Middle English* (translated from French by James A. Walker). Baltimore; London: Johns Hopkins University Press.
Mufwene, Salikoko S.
1994   On the status of auxiliary verbs in Gullah. *American Speech* 69:1, 58-70.
1996a   The development of American Englishes: Some questions from a creole genesis perspective. In: E. Schneider (ed.), 231-264.
1996b   Creolization and grammaticization: What creolists could contribute to research on grammaticization. In: P. Baker & A. Syea (eds.), *Changing meanings, changing functions: Papers relating to grammaticalization in contact languages* (Westminster Creolistics Series, 2). London: University of Westminster Press, 5-28.
Forthcoming   Language contact, evolution, and death: How ecology rolls the dice. *Proceedings of the International Language Assessment Conference, Summer Institute of Linguistics 1998*, ms. 39pp.

Mustanoja, Tauno F.
1960   *A Middle English syntax: Part I* (Mémoires de la Société
             Néophilologique de Helsinki, 23). Helsinki: Société
             Néophilologique.

Myhill, John
1995   Change and continuity in the functions of the American English
             modals. *Linguistics* 33, 157-211.

Nagle, Stephen J.
1989   *Inferential change and syntactic modality in English.* Frankfurt/
             Main: Lang.
1990   Modes of inference and the gradual/rapid issue: Suggestions from
             the English modal. In: H. Andersen & K. Korner (eds.),
             *Historical Linguistics 1987: Papers from the eighth International
             Conference on Historical Linguistics* (Current Issues in
             Linguistic Theory, 66). Amsterdam: Benjamins, 353-362.
1993   Double modals in early English. In: H. Aertsen & Robert J.
             Jeffers (eds.), *Historical linguistics 1989: Papers from the 9ᵗʰ
             International Conference on Historical Linguistics.* Amsterdam:
             Benjamins, 363-370.
1995   The English double modals: Internal or external change? In: J.
             Fisiak (ed.), *Linguistic change under contact conditions.* Berlin;
             New York: Mouton de Gruyter, 207-215.

Newmeyer, Frederick J.
1998   *Language form and language function.* Cambridge, Mass.: MIT
             Press.

Nicolle, Steve
1998   *Be going to* and *will*: A monosemous account. *English Language
             and Linguistics* 2:2, 223-243.

Nolan, Francis – Paul E. Kerswill
1990   The description of connected speech processes. In: S. Ramsaran
             (ed.), *Studies in the pronunciation of English: A commemorative
             volume in honour of A. C. Gimson.* London: Routledge, 295-316.

Nordlinger, Rachel – Elizabeth Traugott
1997   Scope and the development of epistemic modality: Evidence from
             ought to. English Language and Linguistics 1:2, 295-317.

Nübling, Damaris
2000   *Prinzipien der Irregularisierung: Eine kontrastive Analyse von
             zehn Verben in zehn germanischen Sprachen* (Linguistische
             Arbeiten, 415). Tübingen: Niemeyer.

Övergaard, Gerd
1995   *The mandative subjunctive in American and British English in
             the 20ᵗʰ century.* Stockholm: Almqvist & Wiksell.

Ogura, Mieko – William Wang
1995   Lexical diffusion in semantic change: With special reference to universal changes. *Folia Linguistica Historica* 16, 29-73.
Oxford English Dictionary (OED)
²1989 [¹1933ff] James Murray et al. (eds.), Oxford: Oxford University Press.
Pagliuca, William (ed.)
1994   *Perspectives on grammaticalization.* Amsterdam: Benjamins.
Palmer, Frank R.
1983   Semantic explanations for the syntax of the English modals. In: F. Heny & B. Richards (eds.), *Linguistic categories: Auxiliaries and related puzzles.* Dordrecht: Reidel, II, 205-217.
1986   *Mood and modality.* Cambridge: Cambridge University Press.
²1989 [¹1979] *Modality and the English modals.* London: Longman.
1994.   Mood and modality. In: R. E. Asher (ed.), 2535-2540.
Palmer, Harold E. – F. G. Blandford
³1969 [¹1924] *A grammar of spoken English* (Revised and rewritten by Roger Kingdon). Cambridge: Heffer.
Paul, Hermann
⁹1975 [¹1880] *Prinzipien der Sprachgeschichte.* Tübingen: Niemeyer.
Pike, Kenneth L.
1962   Dimensions of grammatical constructions. *Language* 38, 221-244.
Plank, Frans
1984   The modals story retold. *Studies in Language* 8, 305-366.
Pocheptsov, George
1997   Quasi-impersonal verbs in Old and Middle English. In: J. Fisiak (ed.), *Studies in Middle English linguistics.* Berlin: Mouton de Gruyter, 469-488.
Poplack, Shana – Sali Tagliamonte
Forthcoming   The grammaticization of *going to* in (African American) English. *Language Variation and Change.*
Postal, Paul M.
1974   On raising: One rule of English grammar and its theoretical implications. Cambridge, Mass.: MIT Press.
Postal, Paul M. – Geoffrey K. Pullum
1978   Traces and the description of English complementizer contraction. *Linguistic Inquiry* 9, 1-29.
1982   The contraction debate. *Linguistic Inquiry* 13, 122-138.
1986   Misgovernment. *Linguistic Inquiry* 17, 104-110.
Potter, Simeon
1966   *Our language.* Harmondsworth: Penguin.
Price, Glanville
1971   *The French language: Present and past.* London: Arnold.

Pullum, Geoffrey
1982   Syncategoremacity and English infinitival *to*. *Glossa* 16, 181-215.
1997   The morpholexical nature of *to*-contraction. *Language* 73, 79-102.
Pullum, Geoffrey K. – Paul M. Postal
1979   On an inadequate defense of 'Trace Theory'. *Linguistic Inquiry* 10, 689-706.
Pullum, Geoffrey K. – Arnold M. Zwicky
1988   The syntax-phonology interface. In: F. Newmeyer (ed.), *Linguistics: The Cambridge survey* (4 vols.). Cambridge: Cambridge University Press, IV, 255-280.
Quinn, Heidi
1995   *Variation in NZE syntax and morphology: A study of the acceptance and use of grammatical variants among Canterbury and West Coast teenagers*. MA thesis Canterbury, NZ.
Quirk, Randolph
1965   Descriptive statement and serial relationship. *Language* 41, 205-217.
1972   *The English language and images of matter*. London: Oxford University Press.
Quirk, Randolph – Sidney Greenbaum – Geoffrey Leech – Jan Svartvik
1985   *A comprehensive grammar of the English language*. London: Longman.
Radford, Andrew
1997   *Syntactic theory and the structure of English: A minimalist approach*. Cambridge: Cambridge University Press.
Ramat, Anna Giacalone – Paul Hopper
1998   Introduction. In: A. G. Ramat & P. Hopper (eds.), 1-11.
Ramat, Anna Giacalone – Paul Hopper (eds.)
1998   *The limits of grammaticalization*. Amsterdam: Benjamins.
Ramat, Paolo
1987   Introductory paper. In: J. Harris & P. Ramat (eds.), 3-19.
Roberts, Ian G.
1985   Agreement parameters and the development of English modal auxiliaries. *Natural Language and Linguistic Theory* 3: 21-58.
1985   *Verbs and diachronic syntax: A comparative history of English and French*. Dordrecht: Kluwer Academic.
Rohdenburg, Günter
1996   Cognitive complexity and increased grammatical explicitness in English. *Cognitive Linguistics* 7, 149-182.
1998   Syntactic complexity and the variable use of *to be* in 16th and 18th century English. *Arbeiten aus Anglistik und Amerikanistik* 23:2, 199-228.

Romaine, Suzanne
1995   Internal vs. external factors in socio-historical explanations of change: A fruitless dichotomy? *Berkeley Linguistics Society* 21, 478-490.

Rosch, Eleanor
1975   Cognitive representations of semantic categories. *Journal of Experimental Psychology: General* 104:3, 192-233.
1978   Principles of categorization. In: E. Rosch & B. Lloyd (eds.), *Cognition and categorization.* Hillsdale: Erlbaum, 27-48.

Rosewarne, David
1994   Estuary English: Tomorrow's RP? *English Today* 37, 3-8.

Saffran, J. R. – R. N. Aslin – E.L. Newport
1996   Word segmentation: The role of distributional cues. *Journal of Memory and Language* 35: 606-621

Saussure, Ferdinand de
1916   *Cours de linguistique générale.* Paris: Payet.

Schiffrin, Deborah (ed.)
1984   *Meaning, form, and use in context: Linguistic applications.* Washington D.C.: Georgetown University Press.

Schlegel, August Wilhelm von
1818   *Observations sur la langue et la littérature provençales.* Paris: Librairie grecque-latine-allemande.

Schmidt, Johannes
1872   *Die Verwandtschaftsverhältnisse der indogermanischen Sprachen.* Weimar: Böhlau.

Schneider, Edgar
1996   Introduction. In: E. Schneider (ed.), 1-12.
1997   Chaos theory as a model for dialect variability and change? In: A. Thomas (ed.), *Issues and methods in dialectology.* Bangor: Department of Linguistics, 22-36.

Schneider, Edgar (ed.)
1996   *Focus on the USA* (Varieties of English around the World). Amsterdam: Benjamins.

Seefranz-Montag, Ariane von
1983   *Syntaktische Funktionen und Wortstellungsveränderung: Die Entwicklung 'subjektloser' Konstruktionen in einigen Sprachen* (Studien zur theoretischen Linguistik, 3). Munich: Fink.

Shakespeare, William
1591ff   *Complete works of William Shakespeare.* London: HarperCollins [ed. by P. Alexander London, 1994].

Sigley, Robert
1997   Text categories and where you can stick them: A crude formality index. *International Journal of Corpus Linguistics* 2: 199-237.

Stein, Dieter
1990   *The semantics of syntactic change: Aspects of the evolution of* DO
            in English. Berlin: Mouton de Gruyter.
Stephany, Ursula
1993   Modality in first language acquisition: The state of the art. In: N.
            Dittmar & A. Reich (eds.), *Modality in language acquisition.*
            Berlin: Walther de Gruyter, 133-144.
Stevens, William J.
1972   The catenative auxiliaries in English. *Language Sciences* 23, 21-
            25.
Strang, Barbara M. H.
1982   Some aspects of the history of the *be + ing* construction. In: J.
            Andersen (ed.), *Language form and linguistic variation: Papers
            dedicated to Angus McIntosh.* (Current Issues in Linguistic
            Theory, 15). Amsterdam: Benjamins, 427-474.
Stubbs, Michael
1996   *Text and corpus analysis: Computer-assisted studies of language
            and culture.* Oxford: Blackwell.
Sweetser, Eve E.
1988   Grammaticalization and semantic bleaching. *Berkeley Linguistics
            Society* 14, 389-405.
1990   *From etymology to pragmatics: Metaphorical and cultural
            aspects of semantic structure* (Cambridge Studies in Linguistics).
            Cambridge: Cambridge University Press.
Tabor, Whitney – Elizabeth C. Traugott
1998   Structural scope expansion and grammaticalization. In: A. Ramat
            & P. Hopper (eds.), 229-272.
Taylor, Lita – Geoffrey Leech – Steven Fligelstone
1991   A survey of English machine-readable corpora. In: S. Johansson
            & A. Stenström (eds.), *English computer corpora: selected
            papers and research guide.* Berlin: Mouton de Gruyter, 319-354
Taylor, John R.
[2]1995 [[1]1989] *Linguistic categorization: Prototypes in linguistic theory.*
            Oxford: Clarendon.
1998   Syntactic constructions as prototype categories. In: M. Tomasello
            (ed.), *The psychology of language: Cognitive and functional
            approaches to language structure.* Mahwah, NJ: Erlbaum, 177-
            202.
Thieroff, Rolf
1999   On the areal distribution of tense-aspect categories in Europe. In:
            Ö. Dahl (ed.), *Tense and aspect in the languages of Europe*
            (EUROTYP, 6). Berlin; New York: Mouton de Gruyter, ms. 40pp.

Torres Cacoullos, Rena
1999   Construction frequency and reductive change: Diachronic and
            register variation in Spanish clitic climbing. *Language Variation
            and Change* 11, 143-170.
Trask, Robert L.
1996   *Historical linguistics*. London: Arnold.
Traugott, Elizabeth C.
1972   *The history of English syntax*. New York: Holt, Rinehart &
            Winston.
1982   From propositional to textual and expressive meanings: Some
            semantic-pragmatic aspects of grammaticalization. In: W.
            Lehmann & Y. Malkiel (eds.), *Perspectives on historical
            linguistics*. Amsterdam: Benjamins.
1988   Pragmatic strengthening and grammaticalization. *Berkeley
            Linguistics Society* 14, 406-416.
1989   On the rise of epistemic meanings in English: An example of
            subjectification in semantic change. *Language* 65:1, 31-55.
1992   Syntax. In: R. M. Hogg (ed.), *The Cambridge History of the
            English Language: The beginnings to 1066* (5 vols.). Cambridge:
            Cambridge University Press, I 168-289.
1994   Grammaticalisation and lexicalisation. In: R. E. Asher (ed.),
            1481-1486.
1995   Subjectification in grammaticalisation. In: D. Stein & S. Wright
            (eds.), *Subjectivity and subjectivisation: Linguistic perspectives*.
            Cambridge: Cambridge University Press, 31-54.
1996   Semantic change: An overview. *Glot International* 2, 3-7.
1997   Subjectification and the development of epistemic meaning: The
            case of *promise* and *threaten*. In: T. Swan & O. Westvik (eds.),
            *Modality in Germanic languages: Historical and comparative
            perspectives*. Berlin: Mouton de Gruyter, 185-210.
1999   Constructions in grammaticalization. In: B. Joseph & R. Janda
            (eds.), *Handbook of historical linguistics*. Oxford: Oxford
            University Press.
Traugott, Elizabeth C. – Bernd Heine (eds.)
1991   *Approaches to grammaticalization*. (2 vols.). Amsterdam:
            Benjamins.
Traugott, Elizabeth C. – Ekkehard König
1991   The semantics-pragmatics of grammticalization revisited. In: E.
            Traugott & B. Heine (eds.), I, 189-218.
Trudgill, Peter
1973   Linguistic change and diffusion: Description and explanation in
            sociolinguistic dialect geography. *Language in Society* 2: 215-246.
1986   *Dialects in contact*. Oxford: Blackwell.
1990   *The Dialects of England*. Oxford: Blackwell.

1998   World Englishes: Convergence or divergence? In: H. Lindquist et al. (eds.), 29-34.

Trudgill, Peter – Jean Hannah
³1994 [¹1982] *International English: A guide to varieties of standard English.* London: Arnold.

Visser, Frederikus Th.
1963-73   *An historical syntax of the English language* (3 vols.). Leiden: Brill.

Warner, Anthony R.
1982   *Complementation in Middle English and the methodology of historical syntax: A study of the Wiclifite sermons.* London: Croom Helm.
1993   *English auxiliaries: Structure and history* (Cambridge Studies in Linguistics, 66). Cambridge: Cambridge University Press.

Webster's dictionary of English usage
1996   E. Ward Gilman (ed.), Springfield, Mass.: Merriam-Webster.

Wells, John C.
1982   *Accents of English* (3 vols.). Cambridge: Cambridge University Press.
1990   *Longman pronunciation dictionary.* London: Longman.
1997   Our changing pronunciation. *Transactions of the Yorkshire Dialect Society* 19: 42-48.

West, Fred
1973   Some notes on word order in Old and Middle English. *Modern Philology* 71, 48-53.

Westney, Paul
1995   *Modals and periphrastics in English: An investigation into the semantic correspondence between certain English modal verbs and their periphrastic equivalents.* Tübingen: Niemeyer.

Wierzbicka, Anna
1987   The semantics of modality. *Folia Linguistica* 21, 25-43.

Wikle, Tom
1997   Quantitative mapping techniques for displaying language variation and change. In: C. Bernstein; T. Nunnally & R. Sabino (eds.), *Language variety in the South revisited.* Tuscaloosa: University of Alabama Press, 417-433.

Wilde, Oscar
1880ff   *Complete works of Oscar Wilde: With an introduction by Vyvyan Holland.* London; Glasgow: Collins [ed. by J.B. Foreman, 1966].

Williams, Joseph M.
1976   Synaesthetic adjectives: A possible law of semantic change. *Language* 52:2, 461-478.

326   *References*

Windsor-Lewis, John
    1972   *A concise pronouncing dictionary of British and American
                  English.* London: Oxford University Press.
Wischer, Ilse & Gabriele Diewald (eds.)
    Forthcoming   *New reflections on grammaticalization: Proceedings of the
                  International Symposium on Grammaticalization at Potsdam
                  University, 17-19 June 1999.* Amsterdam: Benjamins.
Woods, Anthony – Paul Fletcher – Arthur Hughes
    1986   *Statistics in language studies.* Cambridge: Cambridge University
                  Press.
Wright, Georg H. von
    1951   *An essay in modal logic.* Amsterdam: North Holland.
Zipf, George K.
    1929   Relative frequency as a determinant of phonetic change. *Harvard
                  Studies in Classical Philology* 15, 1-95.
    1935   *The psycho-biology of language: An introduction to dynamic
                  philology.* Cambridge, Mass.: MIT Press.
    1949   *Human behavior and the Principle of Least Effort: An
                  introduction to human ecology.* New York: Hafner.

Index